1989

W9-DFF-385

ARGUING
PERSUASIVELY

Ronald Emery Lee
Karen King Lee
Indiana University–Bloomington

Longman
New York & London

Arguing Persuasively

Longman Inc., 95 Church Street, White Plains, N.Y. 10601

Associated companies:
Longman Group Ltd., London
Longman Cheshire Pty., Melbourne
Longman Paul Pty., Auckland
Copp Clark Pitman, Toronto
Pitman Publishing Inc., New York

Developed under the
advisory editorship of
Beverly Long, School of Speech Communication
University of North Carolina at Chapel Hill

Executive editor: Gordon T. R. Anderson
Production editor: Camilla T. K. Palmer
Text design: Jill Wood
Cover design: Jill Francis Wood
Production supervisor: Eduardo Castillo

Library of Congress Cataloging in Publication Data

Lee, Ronald Emery.
    Arguing persuasively/Ronald Emery Lee and Karen King Lee.
        p.   cm.
    Bibliography: p.
    ISBN 0-582-28670-0
    1. Debates and debating.   2. Reasoning.   I. Lee, Karen King.
    II. Title.
    PN4181.L44 1988   88-9439
    808.53 — dc19   CIP

ISBN 0-582-28670-0

94 93 92 91 90 89 9 8 7 6 5 4 3 2 1

CONTENTS

Preface   vii

SECTION ONE: CONTEXTS OF ARGUMENT   1

1. **Defining the Argumentative Situation**   3
   Basic Terms   3
   Elements of the Argumentative Situation   6
   Conclusions   12

2. **Ethical Limits of Argument**   15
   Pluralism   15
   Argument Fields   17
   Fields of Argument and Ethical Standards of Discourse   19
   Sample Cases   19
   Ethics of Argument and Persuasion   24
   Conclusions   25

3. **Burdens of Argument**   28
   Responsibility and Argument   29
   Presumption and the Burden of Proof   29.
   Burden of Rebuttal   33
   Burden of Validity   34
   Conclusions   42

SECTION TWO: RESOURCES FOR ARGUMENT   45

4. **Types of Propositions**   47
   The Functions of Propositions   47
   Kinds of Propositions   48
   Interpreting the Proposition   55
   Conclusions   56

5. **Discovery of Issues**   58
   Approach to Rhetorical Discovery   58
   Issues   60
   Stock Issues   *133,314*   61
   Conclusions   69

6. Discovery of Data   71
    Kinds of Data   73
    Locating Data   75
    Recording and Organizing Data   81
    Rhetorical Selection of Data   83
    Conclusions   87

7. Forms of Argument   89
    Argument$_1$ and Argument$_2$ 90
    Warrant and Backing   91
    Definitional, Material, and Psychological Backing   93
    Arguments Backed by Definition   94
    Arguments with Material Backing   94
    Arguments with Psychological Backing   100
    A Cautionary Note   103
    Conclusions   103

SECTION THREE: TESTS OF ARGUMENT   107

8. Evaluation of Supporting Material   109
    General Tests of Proof   109
    Specific Tests of Proof   112
    Rhetorically Effective Use of Proof   120
    Conclusions   122

9. Evaluation of Argument   124
    Legitimizing a Wider Variety of Arguments   125
    Reasonability and the Norms for Good Argument   128
    Conclusions   143

SECTION FOUR: PRESENTATION OF ARGUMENT   147

10. The Affirmative Case   149
    Designating the Affirmative   150
    Constructing the Affirmative Case: Propositions of Fact   150
    Constructing the Affirmative Case: Propositions of Value   155
    Constructing the Affirmative Case: Propositions of Policy 161
    Conclusions   168

11. The Negative Case   170
    Designating the Negative   170
    Constructing the Negative Case: Propositions of Fact   171
    Constructing the Negative Case: Propositions of Value   178
    Constructing the Negative Case: Propositions of Policy 183
    Conclusions   189

12. Strategies of Refutation   191
    The Nature of Refutation   192

Approaches to Refutation   195
Conclusions   209

13. Strategies of Questioning   212
Rhetorical Functions of Questioning   213
Preparing for Questioning   218
The Practice of Questioning   219
Conclusions   221

SECTION FIVE: PERFORMANCE OF ARGUMENT   223

14. Debate Formats and Speaker Duties   225
Formats   225
Speaker Duties   229

15. An Intercollegiate Debate   234
First Affirmative Constructive   235
Cross-Examination   238
First Negative Constructive   240
Cross-Examination   245
Second Affirmative Constructive   247
Cross-Examination   251
Second Negative Constructive   253
Cross-Examination   257
First Negative Rebuttal   259
First Affirmative Rebuttal   262
Second Negative Rebuttal   264
Second Affirmative Rebuttal   267

16. A Public Debate   275
Negative Statement   276
Affirmative Statement   283
Rebuttal   295
Rebuttal   298
Head-to-Head   304

Glossary of Terms in Argumentation   319

Select Bibliography   325

Index   334

For Eleanor, Florence, Calvin and
In memory of James King and Leonard
and Dorothy Tatchell

PREFACE

Arguing Persuasively is designed to meet the needs of students enrolled in undergraduate courses in argumentation. Because the text stresses the relationship between theories of argument and dimensions of persuasion, the book may also be appropriate for certain offerings in public communication.

The conception of argumentation we have adopted creates certain imperatives. These principles shaped the writing of the book. Three specific perspectives were central to the enterprise.

1. The study of argument ought to be featured in the foreground, but its relationship to the general principles of persuasion should serve as the background context. For instance, the psychological drive for consistency, rather than the logical law of noncontradiction, is the key to understanding effective argument.

2. Argumentation is inherently social. In other words, the standards of argument are relative to the communities addressed. Science, law, fine arts, religion, and politics all differ in their criteria for acceptable argument. One field is not more reasonable than another but each is different.

3. The teaching of argumentation ought to center on the world of practical affairs and not work off assumed analogies with formal debate. Such an analogy focuses on rigid rules rather than standards relative to the pertinent domain of discourse.

The adoption of these principles provides *Arguing Persuasively* with some unique features. Far from being idiosyncratic, we believe these commitments bring undergraduate instruction in argumentation into harmony with contemporary theories of argument.

1. Discussion of the discovery and management of data begins with the demands of the situation and not from the nature of the proposition. From the perspective we adopt, the advocate asks what evidence is required to satisfy the relevant field rather than inquiring into what can be said in favor of or against the proposition. Because many textbooks work from models that mirror classical theories of invention, they emphasize subject matter rather than the audience as a starting point.

2. The ethical tension between the effectiveness and worthiness of argument is a central issue in the book. *Arguing Persuasively* adopts an ethical and theoretical commitment to pluralism that is viewed as inherent to standards of the reasonable. This section comes early in the book and pervades all that comes later.

3. The traditional burdens of argument—presumption, burden of proof, burden of rebuttal, validity—are treated as relative concepts. Conventional textbooks usually adopt, implicitly or explicitly, a single paradigm of decision making and define the various burdens accordingly. As a result, these books are forced to justify the application of presumption in academic debate to the province of science; or the use of formal validity when dealing with political controversies in the contingent world of everyday argument. This book separates the universal features of argument from those dependent on context.

4. The range of acceptable argument is expanded. Arguments from authority, motive, and consequence, for example, have been labeled fallacious in other treatments. This blanket rejection is at odds with the behavior of ordinary advocates. For instance, we are confident that most people would find arguments from motive relevant in disputes over ethical issues. Similarly, few would find fault with the reasonableness of deciding technical questions by relying on arguments from authority.

5. Questioning is treated in a persuasive context. Many textbooks discuss cross-examination in mechanical terms. They provide a list of do's and don't's gleaned from observations of academic debate. Consequently, the suggestions are centered on winning strategies rather than on an audience-centered notion of influence. Our perspective places questioning back in its rhetorical context and does not separate it out as a contest stratagem.

6. The treatment of proof requirements as field-dependent demands a more detailed discussion of research methods than conventional textbooks provide. If the standards of reasonability emanate from the field addressed, the advocate must become familiar with what counts as proof in various domains of discourse.

7. Course offerings in argumentation are concerned traditionally with both the theory of argumentation and the skills of advocacy. Argumentation is both a domain of knowledge and a realm of practice. The book's final section provides material for instructors who use debate as a classroom experience in public argument. This final section includes a description of debate formats, a discussion of speaker duties, and annotated transcripts of intercollegiate and public debates.

This book is a product of a variety of influences over the past dozen years. But our experience as students of the late Douglas Ehninger has most profoundly shaped this manuscript. He certainly would not have agreed with all that is presented here, but we hope he would have approved of the passion with which we advocate argumentation as a standpoint.

We would also like to thank friends and colleagues who generously spent time reading and commenting on the manuscript. Our gratitude goes especially to Dale Hample, Jack Kay, Stephen DePoe, Jack Rhodes, Warren Decker, and Thomas Hollihan.

Finally, we would like to thank the staff at Longman for their professionalism and hard work. We are especially grateful to our editor, Gordon Anderson, for his enthusiasm and for his friendly and tactful advice.

Bloomington, Indiana　　　　　　　　　　　　　　　　　　　　　　*R. E. L.*
February 1988　　　　　　　　　　　　　　　　　　　　　　　　　*K. K. L.*

CONTEXTS OF ARGUMENT

"You *cannot* lift up the front end of a Buick."

"In this state, you *cannot* drink until you are twenty-one."

"A woman *cannot* be elected President."

"You *cannot* talk about married bachelors."

What would each speaker answer to the question, "Why do you say 'cannot'?" The first would reply, "The limits of human strength prevent any lone individual from lifting a full-sized car." The second would say, "The law prohibits minors from drinking." The third would remark, "The current disposition of the electorate would deny any woman a majority of the vote." The fourth would explain, "The meaning of the words preclude the sensible use of the phrase 'married bachelors.'"

Even the simple word "cannot" is only understandable when accompanied by the surrounding words of a sentence. When we move beyond a single word, misunderstandings rapidly multiply. It seems one can barely remember a day when the familiar cry, "You took my remarks out of context," didn't appear in the morning paper.

Trying to grapple with the complex talk of argument without considering context is foolhardy. Context is what distinguishes argumentation from logic; marks off ethical advocacy from deception, manipulation, and coercion; and discriminates between effective and ineffective argument. The first three chapters of *Arguing Persuasively* provide the reader with an approach to understanding the role of context in the study of argumentation.

1

1

DEFINING THE ARGUMENTATIVE SITUATION

Shortly after taking office in 1981, Ronald Reagan spoke to the American public about the dire state of the economy. He described the problems of inflation, high interest rates, and slumping productivity. He argued that cutting taxes and decreasing federal regulation would create the atmosphere necessary for economic recovery. The presentation was in many ways an overly simple explanation of a complex problem. The President backed his claims with anecdotal evidence, appealed to the people's faith in the American Dream, and discussed his proposal in very broad strokes.[1]

A few years earlier, another president addressed the nation about a problem of urgent national concern. He went so far as to label the energy crisis the "moral equivalent of war." In contrast with Reagan, this speaker's presentation was tightly argued, provided detailed evidence, and outlined specific proposals for the alleviation of the nation's ills.

Surprisingly, Reagan persuasively argued for the Economic Recovery Act and the other President, Jimmy Carter, was greeted with a collective yawn. Carter was so distressed by this reaction that he isolated himself at Camp David and dishearteningly announced the onset of a "national malaise."[2]

What are we to make of this result? For some, the effect of these two contrasting speeches serves as evidence of the power of "mere rhetoric" to manipulate a gullible citizenry. For others, it suggests the failure of formal rules of reasoning, learned in logicians' classrooms, to provide an appropriate method for analyzing public argument.

The tension between the logical and the persuasive is the essential problem for those who study public argument. In part, this quandary stems from a common misunderstanding of the basic terms of argumentation.

BASIC TERMS

We frequently use the terms "logical" and "persuasive" in the course of everyday conversation. But we often use them so loosely that the real grounds for evaluating disputes are confused. For the purpose of illustration, consider the following conversation:

> "Susan, how can you possibly say that Woody Allen is a better director than Steven Spielberg? Sometimes you really are exasperating when you make such *illogical* assertions."
>
> "Tom," Susan replied angrily, "you are a sexist. You are unwilling to listen to my arguments, no matter how *persuasive*, because I am a woman. It just violates your image of yourself to find anything your girlfriend says of any value."
>
> "This just proves my point. When you know I'm right you revert to name calling. Does every argument have to disintegrate into a silly power struggle about the superiority of one gender over another?"

We came to this conversation in the middle. We are not privy to the support Susan offered for her contention that Woody Allen is a better movie director than Steven Spielberg. But we do know that Tom has labeled the relationship between the supporting reasons and the conclusion "illogical." In addition, Susan has implied that her position was "persuasive" but Tom's sexist attitudes prevented him from judging her arguments on their merits.

Regardless of the reasons Susan might have offered in defense of her choice of Woody Allen, Tom's use of the term "illogical" seems *technically* inappropriate. *Logic is the study of the formal principles of reasoning. Logicians do not examine how people do in fact argue, for logic is a theoretical rather than an empirical science.*[3] The "theoretical"/ "empirical"distinction undermines Tom's reference to logic.

A comparison with mathematics is helpful. If you put three pairs of socks in the washing machine and when you take them out you count only five socks, this would never be grounds for concluding that $3 \times 2 = 5$. Rather, you would immediately think that you had counted wrong, dropped one of the socks on the way from the laundry room, or had only placed five socks in the washing machine at the start. The point is that factual evidence, in this case the actual socks, would never be sufficient to make you doubt the validity of the equation $3 \times 2 = 6$. This is precisely the feature of logic we wish to emphasize. Like mathematics, logic is a theoretical rather than an empirical science.

Logic is the discipline that establishes rules for the valid inference from a set of premises to a conclusion. These rules, like the laws of mathematics, operate independently of context.[4] In other words, $2 + 2 = 4$ no matter who says it or under what conditions. Similarly, the claim that

> All men are mortal;
> *Socrates is a man;*
> Therefore, Socrates is mortal.

is valid regardless of the circumstances under which it is presented. Arguments are logical, just as arithmetic equations are rational, because they adhere to a particular form. In the Socrates example, we could substitute any noun in the proper pattern for "men" and "man" or for "Socrates" and the argument would still be formally correct.

> All geese are mortal;
> *Jim is a goose;*
> Therefore, Jim is mortal.

and

> All houses are white;
> *Mount Vernon is a house;*
> Therefore, Mount Vernon is white.

These are perfectly fine logical arguments.

We seriously doubt that this is what Tom had in mind when he accused Susan of speaking "illogically." Tom probably objected to the content of Susan's explanation more than its form. Perhaps he gauges directors by the average gross receipts of their films and Susan, on the other hand, uses standards that he would label "esoteric" and "artsy." Given Tom and Susan's differing approaches to evaluating filmmakers, logic seems an inappropriate method for resolving their dispute.

Recall that in Susan's reply to Tom, she did not use the term "logic" but instead described her position as "persuasive." Tom might have meant that he found her presentation not "illogical" but "unpersuasive."

Persuasion is the process or act of influencing the attitudes, beliefs, or behavior of others. Persuasion entails the achievement of a desired end. It would be odd indeed to hear someone say that "Susan persuaded Tom but still failed to win his agreement." This strikes us as contradictory because the transitive verb "to persuade" ought to be completed in an effect.[5]

Persuasive presentations are often logical, but not necessarily so. It would not be unusual to judge an argument "persuasive" but "illogical" or "logical" but "unpersuasive." If by labeling the argument "illogical" Tom really meant "unpersuasive," then he was saying that Susan's efforts at influencing his attitudes were unsuccessful. But it is quite clear that he was conveying something more than a general report of failure. Tom was indicating that Susan failed on some specific ground.

Tom told Susan that he found the grounds for her judgment of film directors unreasonable. Or, to use another word, Tom found Susan's choice of Woody Allen *unjustified.*

Justification is an ordinary word that we encounter frequently in everyday conversation. "To justify" is "to prove or show to be just, right, or reasonable."[6] College students often see the term in their professors' test questions. Consider the following examination item:

> In the course of your reading, you have encountered three different accounts of the American revolution. Sketch each view briefly. Which view do you find most compelling? Justify your answer.

Given sufficient familiarity with the histories of the American Revolution, students should be able to justify their answers. Justification would involve offering supporting reasons for the superiority of one explanation over another. Which theory best accounted for the facts? Which historical school had most effectively countered the objections of its critics? Which account was most compatible with general theories of historical development?

In another familiar context, jurors are asked to judge the merits of the prosecution's case. Each juror determines whether the state has adequately supported a guilty verdict. The legal system has set out a standard of proof—guilty beyond a reasonable doubt—and criteria that must be fulfilled in any given case—evidence that a crime was committed and that the defendant committed that crime.

In yet another context, food critics are charged with justifying their choice of recommended restaurants. The critic's task is to persuade the public that the food is satisfying, that the service is polite and efficient, and that patrons receive good value for their dollar. Matching the individual dining experience with the relevant criteria is the critic's art.

In these three illustrations—the history test, the jury trial, the restaurant review—the context is an indispensable variable in the process of justification. The student, the prosecutor, and the food critic each applied criteria relevant to their subject. Unlike the theoretical rules of logic, the business of justification draws on immediate circumstances.

Argumentation is the theory and practice of justification based on conceptions of the reasonable. Argumentation specialists understand that the standards of reasonability differ from the battlefield to the courtroom, the laboratory to the legislature, and the classroom to the boardroom. Each field establishes criteria for argument based on the constraints of the situation. A course in argumentation ought to help students discover the grounds of the reasonable in any given situation and master the employment of worthy appeals to effect a desired end.

ELEMENTS OF THE ARGUMENTATIVE SITUATION

Argumentation, whether public or private, involves *communication*. To justify a case, the advocate must explain the supporting reasons. The explanation may address the reader of the history exam, the members of a jury, or the readership of the food critic's newspaper column. We even communicate with ourselves to resolve troublesome choices and bolster sagging convictions.

Argumentative situations are defined by audiences, topics, advocates, and occasions. These elements constrain choices and shape the appropriate grounds of justification. Each situational element requires elaboration.

AUDIENCES

An audience is made up of "those whom the speaker wishes to influence by his argumentation."[7] Speakers think more or less consciously about those people they wish to persuade. Obviously, effective advocates picture an audience that closely resembles the one they actually address. The history student and prosecuting attorney have a very good opportunity to investigate first hand what lines of argument are acceptable to the professor and the jury. The food critic's task is more difficult. Like most authors, the columnist has only the most general picture of the newspaper's readers. The advertising department may have done surveys and compiled general demographic profiles. Or perhaps our critic has created an image of the audience from hints in reader mail.

For the cynic, audience adaptation may suggest the presentation of arguments shaped by the whims of current opinion. Such a view calls up images of unscrupulous politicians discovering firmly held "principles" and moral "conscience" in the latest poll results. Or, it evokes pictures of advertising executives determining product qualities by scanning image research. The more pleasant phrase for this approach is "selling out"; the forceful word that better conveys moral disdain is "prostitution." As James Andrews wrote, "To sell oneself or one's ideas for any price, including audience acceptance is prostitution."[8] Nancy Legge, in her study of ethical stances in argument, observed that "ghostwriters serve as prostitutes when they write speeches for a person or idea which they do not support."[9] But argumentation is concerned with *both the effective and the worthy*. Public opinion may serve as a starting point for argument, but it is not a substitute for the advocate's convictions. Analyzing reader and listener dispositions can facilitate understanding, premise building, and cooperation. To find common ground upon which to begin an argument should not entail, in Plato's words, a concern for audience pleasure without regard for what is right.[10]

Audiences are shaped by more than individual whims of fancy. In the process of growing up in a society, we come to have certain expectations about the appropriate manner of justification. These are expectations that are shared by communities of people and cut against individual idiosyncrasies. As college students, you have been sitting in classrooms since you were five years old. Even before you went to school, your parents, television, and older brothers and sisters provided a picture of what classroom instruction was supposed to be like. Of course, there is some individual disagreement among students about how they feel about Ms. Smith or Mr. Jones as an instructor. However, the evaluation of teachers by students is remarkably uniform. We have grown up with common notions of the teacher's function and within limits we react in remarkably similar ways. Likewise, reading the answer to an examination question, listening to the prosecutor, or digesting the advice of the local restaurant critic is done with learned standards of justification. Consumers of argument expect reasons and evidence appropriate to the situation. These shared expectations shape the choices we make in supporting claims.

TOPICS

The subject matter and the form of the question one is asking about the subject matter shape the argumentative situation. For the purpose of illustration, consider the following two examples:

PORNOGRAPHY

> FACT: Is there a relationship between exposure to pornography and sex crimes?
> VALUE: Is a commitment to freedom of expression a moral defense of pornography?
> POLICY: Should restrictive zoning laws be enacted to control the spread of pornography?

ABORTION

> FACT: At what point is the fetus viable outside the mother's womb?
> VALUE: What constituents define humanness?
> POLICY: Should a Right-to-Life Amendment be enacted to protect the unborn?

Pornography and abortion represent two discrete subject matters. Fact, value, and policy represent three question forms one might use in exploring pornography and abortion.

On the surface, the topics of pornography and abortion are a great deal alike. Both are emotionally charged public issues; both separate people politically; both are religious as well as political issues. In fact, to a great extent people find themselves on the same side of these issues. Those who favor legalized abortion often defend liberal pornography laws; and those who oppose legalized abortion often call for stricter controls on pornography. So one might well conclude that there is little difference in the two argumentative situations. In many ways, this is a correct assessment.

Let's focus on some subtler distinctions. Compare the two questions of fact. What kind of proof would be demanded in each case to support an answer to the question? The factual inquiry about pornography calls for the citation of studies in criminology, sociology, and psychology that establish the presence or absence of a pornography-sex crime link. The factual question in the abortion case is different. Fetal viability is not a question for the *social sciences* but for the *biological sciences*. Critical listeners would demand medical testimony from experts in obstetrics and pediatrics before assenting to an answer. The topic shapes the situation by directing the advocate to appropriate domains of proof.

Not only are there differences between subject matters (pornography and abortion) but also between question forms. In Chapter Four, the lines of development appropriate to each topic form are taken up in detail. Here we are only interested in demonstrating that the argumentative situation is transformed as the topic moves from fact to value to policy.

Upon reflection, it seems intuitively clear that issues of fact and value are different. Facts may influence our judgments of value, but they can never be the entire justification. The question of value in the abortion case is instructive in this regard. We may ask a biologist to determine when life begins. Is a cell alive? We may ask obstetricians to give the current prospects for fetal survival after only a six-month gestation period. But we would never determine on scientific or technical grounds the issue of humanness. If the abortion controversy turned only on demonstrable factual considerations, the question would be easily resolved. Pro-choice and pro-life advocates are not *essentially* disagreeing over issues of fact, but rather over the fundamental philosophical question of what it means to be human. Is the fetus human? There are no litmus tests to gauge the presence of the defining constituents of humanness. The fact that the abortion controversy rages primarily within political and religious institutions rather than in academies of science and technology demonstrates the influence of the topic form on the shape of the argumentative situation.

Similarly, these differences are present in the contrast between value and policy. The sample value question in pornography asks the advocate to justify ranking the protection of free expression above the value of controlling obscenity. The policy question probes the wisdom of using local zoning laws to control pornography. The value question is essentially philosophical and the policy question essentially practical. The person reflecting on the competing values of free speech and the control of obscenity will think about cultural tradition, inquire into personal feelings, and consider the consequences of restrictions on free speech and the unrestrained spread of pornography. The town council will ask if the policy will work, if there are disadvantages to using zoning in this way, and whether other alternatives are more attractive. The agenda of relevant criteria for decision making changes as one moves from value to policy.

When we enter a controversy, our expectations are shaped by subject matter and question form. As advocates, we draw up mental lists of appropriate lines of argument and persuasive souces of proof based on an understanding of the topic's demands.

ADVOCATES

The people involved in a dispute obviously shape the lines of argument that will be pursued. They do this in a variety of subtle ways, but three main influences are worth elaboration. Participant attitudes, credibility, and mutual relationship define the argumentative situation.

Consider the following cases:

CASE ONE

Eight-year-old Christopher is making a case to his mother for a more liberal bedtime. He claims that his bedtime is out of line with the bedtimes of his elementary school classmates.

CASE TWO

Professor Emery disagrees with her Department's latest curriculum decision. She feels that a course in rhetorical criticism ought to be required for all majors. She is determined to argue this point at the next faculty meeting.

In both instances, the advocates' initial attitudes toward the topic are likely to create an adversarial atmosphere. But the intensity of the attitudes and the reasons they are held will shape the direction of the dispute. If Christopher's mother is not impressed by arguments about what other parents are doing, Christopher is going to have to come up with another line of argument. If Professor Emery's justification for disagreement is pedagogical the argument will run in a particular direction, if it is administrative it will go in another direction. The attitudes of the key players in any dispute will determine lines of argument.

Credibility, oftentimes called *ethos*, refers to audience perception of an advocate's character and expertise. In the two sample cases, the bedtime dispute is likely to turn on questions of character and the faculty dispute on issues of expertise. Few parents consider eight-year-olds authorities; and only the most unpleasant university departments resolve disputes by questioning the character of faculty members.

Christopher's mother may well decide the bedtime issue by asking herself whether her son deserves this reward. If he has been acting responsibly of late, she may well feel that she ought to let him stay up later. This is essentially a judgment that turns on his character references.

Professor Emery's colleagues will ask themselves whether she is an expert in this particular curricular issue. If Professor Emery is trained in organizational communication, then her view may hold less sway than the opinion of the rhetorical scholars on the faculty.

In each case, the advocates, in order to be successful, must adjust their case to fit audience perceptions of credibility. Perhaps Christopher could remind his mother of his exemplary behavior when relatives visited, talk about his good grades in school, or enlist his father as a character witness. Professor Emery might remind her colleagues that she used to teach criticism before joining this faculty. Or she might make sure that her arguments are consistent with positions taken by specialists in rhetorical criticism in the published literature.

Finally, the history of the participants' relationship shapes the situation. In our two illustrations, the relationship among the participants is markedly different. The mother is the child's superior; Professor Emery is her colleagues' peer. The mother and the child have a highly personal relationship; Professor Emery and her colleagues have a professional relationship. Christopher's argument will have to be delivered respectfully; Professor Emery's argument will not involve pleading for permission but asking for careful consideration. Christopher can call on the emotional ties between him and his mother in making his case; Professor Emery cannot reduce this discussion to a matter of personal favor but can argue only on the basis of professional judgment. But beyond these expected relational norms, there might be special personal histories that influence communicative behavior. Christopher's relationship with his mother may well be affected by her philosophy of child rearing; the fact that they are both part of a step family; and the trauma they have experienced with Christopher's extended illness. Each one of these factors may influence the claims that are advanced and the way those claims are received. In Professor Emery's case a special circumstance is created because her husband is also a member of the faculty. Because the two Emerys are so concerned about perceptions of an alliance built on personal rather than professional grounds, they compensate by wearing a mask of critical impartiality toward each other. Consequently, Professor Emery cannot count on sympathetic support from what ordinarily would be a natural professional ally. Various idiosyncratic histories of relationships can upset conventional expectations.

Advocates bring baggage to the argumentative situation that includes the attitudes they have about the subject, their reputation with the audience, and the nature of the relationship they enjoy with those involved. Each of these variables will determine the manner in which claims can be supported and refuted.

OCCASIONS

In the *Rhetoric*, Aristotle constructs a theory around three speaking occasions. He describes speaking before the court, the legislative assembly, and on ceremonial occasions. Arguments occur in a wider variety of contexts than those outlined by Aristotle, but the notion that the *occasion* shapes communication remains important.

Certain occasions sanction particular kinds of argumentative strategies. The infamous Friday afternoon after work discussion permits a wider range of rhetorical choices than the interscholastic debating contest. In the first case, questioning of participant motives, introduction of irrelevant but amusing anecdotes, undermining speaker credibility by dredging up embarrassing past escapades, ridicule, and so forth are not only permitted but encouraged. The resolution of argument is sublimated to the greater cause of celebrating the end of the work week and the beginning of the weekend.

The interscholastic contest, on the other hand, places a more stringent code of decorum on the debaters. Judges and audiences have come to expect carefully prepared lines of attack and defense. The issues rather than the individual personalities must remain the focus.

The occasion structures the expectations of the audience and confines the latitude the speakers may take in presenting their case. Just as it's inappropriate to wear a loud plaid jacket to a funeral, it is inappropriate to use lines of argument unsuited for the occasion.

CONCLUSIONS

In this chapter, we have maintained that argumentation is the theory and practice of reasonable justification. Argumentation is distinguished from logic because it deals with those issues that grow out of the context of concrete situations. Most disputes are not resolved by appeal to formal procedures, but must be tested against communal conceptions of reasonableness. These standards spring from the particulars of audience, topic, advocate, and occasion.

At the beginning of the chapter, two presidential pleas for public support were described. The results of Reagan's appeal for the Economic Recovery Act and Jimmy Carter's call for support of measures to ease the energy crunch seem paradoxical. Reagan's efforts were rewarded by passage of a tax cut package by a hostile Congress, and Carter's efforts were frustrated by the unenthusiastic response of the American public. Surprisingly, a textual analysis of the speeches reveals a more tightly argued presentation for energy legislation than for tax cuts.

This is not at all paradoxical if the speakers' efforts are viewed in terms of the argumentative situation. What are the public's expectations for presidential addresses? Do listeners expect a technical account of the energy situation including the number of cubic feet of natural gas in reserves, the geometric expansion of demand, and the technical aspects of legislative proposals? Does such an explanation even make sense as a goal of public argument in this situation?

Ronald Reagan understood very well that the average citizen knew little about the technical controversies raging between supporters of supply-side economics and more traditional Keynesian conceptions. He understood the public forum as a place to make a general presentation of our economic difficulties. The problem was described in very human terms—thus the heavy reliance on anecdotal evidence—with little stress placed on abstract economics. The general principles, not the technical details, supporting the Economic Recovery Act were explained. And perhaps most importantly, cherished American values of progress, hard work, and optimism were closely linked to the Administration's approach to a sagging economy.

Given this scenario, which spokesman provided the more reasonable case? If justification springs from the nature of the situation, which argument was more compelling? This perspective, we believe, reconciles effectiveness with worthiness and dispels the sense of paradox.

NOTES

1. See Richard L. Johannesen, "An Ethical Assessment of the Reagan Rhetoric: 1981–1982," in *Political Communication Yearbook 1984,* eds. Keith R. Sanders, Lynda Lee Kaid, and Dan Nimmo (Carbondale: Southern Illinois Univ. Press, 1985), pp. 226–241.
2. David S. Broder, "Carter Seeking Oratory to Move an Entire Nation," *Washington Post,* 14 July 1979, p. A1.
3. "Logic," *A Dictionary of Philosophy,* ed. Antony Flew (New York: St. Martin's Press, 1979).
4. See Chaim Perelman and L. Olbrechts-Tyteca, *The New Rhetoric: A Treatise on Argumentation,* trans. John Wilkinson and Purcell Weaver (Notre Dame: University of Notre Dame Press, 1969), pp. 2–3.
5. See Douglas Ehninger, "Toward a Taxonomy of Prescriptive Discourse," in *Rhetoric in Transition,* ed. Eugene E. White (University Park: Pennsylvania State Univ. Press, 1980), pp. 94–95.
6. "Justify, " *Webster's Seventh New Collegiate Dictionary* (1969).
7. Perelman and Olbrechts-Tyteca, p. 19.
8. James R. Andrews, *Public Speaking: Principles into Practice* (New York: Macmillan, 1987), p. 60.

9. Nancy J. Legge, "Ethical Standards for Argumentation: An Extension of the Sexual Metaphor," Master's thesis, Indiana University, 1984, p. 55.

10. See Plato, *Gorgias*, trans. W. C. Helmbold (Indianapolis: Bobbs-Merrill, 1952), pp. 22–26.

2

ETHICAL LIMITS
OF ARGUMENT

The line separating strategy from deception, audience adaptation from manipulation, and the hard sell from coercive persuasion is often difficult to recognize. The moral challenge for the advocate is to argue both persuasively and responsibly.

Worthiness and effectiveness are old foes; their continuing struggle has generated an entire pejorative vocabulary. Those preoccupied with the ethical, and contemptuous of the practical, are ridiculed as "romantics" and "idealists." Just as vehemently, those obsessed by results to the exclusion of principle are accused of "selling out" and practicing "sophistry."[1]

In this chapter, we explore an argumentation perspective on the tension between effective and responsible advocacy. First, we begin by exploring argumentation's commitment to pluralism. Second, we define the concept of "argument fields." Finally, ethically troublesome cases of argument are analyzed.

PLURALISM

The term "pluralism" crops up in high school civics classes, in the Latin phrase on our currency—"E Pluribus Unum"—and in the caustic name calling sessions between moderates and a host of "arch" and "ultra" this or that political advocates.[2] When we contemplate the meaning of pluralism, we may visualize the celebratory rhetoric of Fourth of July orations, President Reagan's array of national heroes introduced during the State of the Union Address, or the mix of races and nationalities composing the American team at the Los Angeles Olympics. We give thanks for our peaceful religious diversity when we see pictures of warfare between Moslem and Jew, Protestant and Catholic, and sect against sect, on the evening news. In more sentimental moments, we can almost picture church, temple, and mosque respectfully coexisting on opposite sides of the American town square.

Whether or not the tolerant ideal of American politics falls short in practice, the cherished value of pluralism defines the national character. It acts as a benchmark for judging public conduct. Racists, sexists, and anti-Semites have all been bludgeoned with pluralism's rhetorical club.

The ethical dimensions of pluralism become clearer when we contemplate its opposites. To be an ethical *absolutist* is to maintain that there are universal standards of good and bad, right and wrong. Conversely, to be an ethical *relativist* is to maintain that there are *no* universal standards of good and bad, right and wrong.[3] To hold that only a single ethical perspective can be tolerated is to exclude from the conversation all those who refuse to bow to your view. To maintain that each ethical pronouncement has only the force of individual opinion is to argue that right and wrong have as little moral force as last year's clothing fad. Neither absolutism nor relativism represents public life as portrayed in our founding manifestoes.

The term "public" requires emphasis. Of course, we have personal standards of conscience that are absolute or relative. But here we are concerned with standards of persuasive argument in the public arena. For some people, a religious tradition sets out standards of conduct that have absolute authority in their lives. For others, they conduct their lives on an ad hoc basis making decisions based on feelings and circumstances as they present themselves. But there is a major difference between adopting private systems of morality and *imposing* those systems on others. We can coexist in a society made up of people from various traditions because public life respects private choice.

Pluralism is committed to the proposition that ethical decisions concerning the public are subject to reasonable justification. This is not to say that at certain times we do not hold particular principles above debate, but we do so because their justifications have proven so persuasive that they are no longer contested. Yet, should the occasion arise advocates of these principles would again be forced to render justification through reasoned argument.[4] To the relativist, the pluralist answers that there are standards of ethical judgment that are better than others. Some justifications are more compelling than others. Through public argument we form standards of conduct that are applied to the community.

Consider some examples. We hold the preservation of human life as a nearly unquestioned value. Yet, human life is sacrificed in war for causes taken to supersede life itself. Criminals are executed to balance the scales of justice. These conflicts of value are continually disputed as each case of armed conflict and capital punishment must be justified again to the public's satisfaction.

Three avenues of action are open to us: we may shrug, walk off and adopt a posture of indifference; we may look for methods to force compliance; or we may make a case for our position through argument. In this sense, the pluralist ethic and the techniques of argument are inextricably bound together.

ARGUMENT FIELDS

It is one thing to talk idealistically about pluralism and another to develop a practical view of argument that can operationalize this commitment. The notion of "argument fields" has been developed in the last thirty years to cut between absolutism and relativism.[5]

FIELD DEFINED

What do we mean by a "field"? A field can roughly be thought of as an area of study. Biology, chemistry, psychology, and sociology are separate disciplines. Each area of study is defined by principles that govern the conduct of those operating in the discipline. For example, the tradition of the social sciences shapes psychology and sociology. The rules of natural science govern biology and chemistry. But even under the umbrellas of social and natural science, additional distinctions are made. Psychology and sociology are distinguished by their respective areas of study and guiding theories. Each field has different ends and procedures for attaining those ends.[6]

Obviously, not all fields are as straightforwardly conventional as the academic disciplines. Society has had to establish sets of rules to adjudicate a whole series of disagreements. But can these less well-defined fields, quasi-fields, appeal to ends and procedures that will satisfy the disputants?

THE LAW AS A MODEL FIELD

Because of this difficulty argumentation theorists looked for a field where a variety of diverse topics were disputed. The law was an obvious candidate.

First, the law deals with far less than certain knowledge. The process of adjudicating competing claims, sentencing defendants, figuring monetary awards, and so forth, cannot be decided by the formal procedures of the logician or the mathematician. The law deals with the problems of the real world.

Second, the law rules on difficult questions of value. For example, the Supreme Court's 1972 landmark obscenity decision in *Miller v. California* illustrates this point. "[Obscenity]," the Court said, "must be limited to works which, taken as a whole, appeal to the prurient interest in sex, which portray sexual conduct in a patently offensive way, and which, taken as a whole, do not have serious literary, artistic, political, or scientific value."[7] The determination of "patently offensive" and "serious literary, artistic, political, or scientific value" requires an evaluation that goes beyond the mere facts of the case.

Third, the law deals with problems in a wide range of different fields. Patent law deals with engineering; rape trials turn on medical testimony of sexual contact; insanity pleas are decided on the weight of psychiatric testimony; and security cases involve complex issues of finance. The courts also take up less clearly defined areas of social interaction in hearing divorces, determining custody, litigating civil disputes, and so on.

Notice that *justice* is a form of the word *justification*. Judges have to provide *worthy* and *effective* justifications for their decisions. Decisions are worthy if they are reasonable given the nature of the law and the specific circumstances. Decisions are effective if the community is convinced justice was done. Stable societies convince the citizenry that the legal system dispenses justice.

INFORMAL FIELDS

Still you may say, "It is all well and good to adjudicate disputes in a legal setting where the rules are laid down and enforced, but what about the arguments that occur between friends, in families, and among colleagues at work? How can a notion of fields address these disputes?" The answer is that ends and procedures for argument still exist in these situations. Obviously, in a mature academic discipline everyone in the enterprise agrees on given ends and rules of procedure to accomplish those ends. But participants in the culture learn the ends and rules of behavior in a wide variety of social settings. For example, we understand the purpose of families and the ways in which members of a family are supposed to treat each other. Our culture has taught us to have a particular view of friendship and we have absorbed the various rules of friendship. The subject matter, the relationship between the people involved, and the setting are all features that direct us to the established rules of argument. Bruce Gronbeck, taking much the same approach as we have articulated here, defined fields as "collections of communicative rules which specify what may be disputed by whom, when, how, where, and to what end."[8] Because communicative interaction contains so many elements, "no single approach to field analysis will suffice."[9]

Return for a moment to law as a model field. You can see that the law has set up its myriad procedures based on all these elements. The very same subject matter may be disputed in a civil and in a criminal dispute, but the standards of proof, the rules of evidence, and the court procedures will be significantly different. The differences are explained by the separate purposes of the trials. In other instances, the same crime may be the subject of two different trials, because the two defendants are of different ages. The state views its relationship to juveniles differently than its relationship with adults. The government holds that there is a protective presumption in its dealing with citizens under the age of majority. In certain judicial procedures, the judge acts not as referee in a battle between two separate sides but as an arbiter looking to foster cooperation toward a common purpose. Yet, in each of these various legal settings the ends and rules of procedure are understood. Argumentation is deemed reasonable because it adheres to the criteria appropriate for the field. Similarly, informal fields form appropriate standards of reasonableness out of the mix of elements in the situation. These standards are recognized by us because they pull on established social traditions.

FIELDS OF ARGUMENT AND ETHICAL STANDARDS OF DISCOURSE

In judging the ethics of any persuasive effort, two separate questions are raised. First, *were the advocate's actions consistent with current standards of practice?* Second, *are current standards of practice ethical?*

The first question is related to accepted standards in a given field. Inhabitants of a society learn the code of acceptable practice. This is as true of ethical practice in argument as it is of the community's traffic code. Without too much trouble most of us separate acceptable and unacceptable uses of deception, manipulation, and coercion. For example, it is perfectly acceptable for the police to deceive criminals through sting operations. It is unacceptable for law enforcement officials to deceive criminals in order to trick them into confessing.

Of course, some calls are close and require reflection, but the vast majority do not. Those issues that are controversial and require close examination demand that we ask the second question; *are current standards of practice ethical?* "In justifying the action concerned," Stephen Toulmin wrote, "one no longer refers to the current practice: it is the injustice of the accepted code, or the greater justice of some alternative proposal, which is now important."[10] Regular viewing of the Oprah Winfrey or Phil Donahue program provides a feel for the issues that are challenging our ethical code of conduct. A list of issues may include: treatment of women, sexual conduct, abortion, pornography, capital punishment, treatment of the elderly, and so forth. In all of these areas, serious arguments are going on over society's ethical responsibility. Likewise, these controversies extend to ethical standards for argument and persuasion. In the following section, we present six troublesome cases for examination. In the analysis of these cases, we illuminate the manner in which we approach conflicted ethical issues.

SAMPLE CASES

Because ethical decisions entail an appropriate application of a general principle to specific circumstances, the burden of responsible advocacy is best understood through an examination of troublesome cases. Illustrations of deceptive, manipulative, and coercive argument are discussed.

DECEPTION

Popular judgment of the foreign policy of John Kennedy and Lyndon Johnson has been strikingly different. Kennedy is remembered for his decisive action during the Cuban Missile Crisis; Johnson's legacy is forever tarnished by the agony of Vietnam. Two events, one small and historically inconsequential and the other a serious moral indictment, say a great deal about how we feel about these men.

EVENT ONE

In October 1962, President Kennedy was scheduled to speak in Chicago. Just before his address, the White House announced that the President had come down with a slight illness and would have to cancel his speech. In fact, John Kennedy was not ill. He returned to Washington to discuss what should be done in the face of incontrovertible evidence that the Soviets were planning to base atomic weapons in Cuba.

EVENT TWO

The Johnson Administration frequently told the public that the resolution to the Vietnam conflict was right around the corner. It could now see the "light at the end of the tunnel" because the Viet Cong and North Vietnamese could not hold out much longer against the superior military might of the United States. Subsequently, with the exposure of the Pentagon Papers, testimony by principals in the Administration, and granting of public access to other important defense documents, it has become clear that defense strategists never in fact believed that there would be any quick resolution to the war. Johnson felt compelled to defend his policy through politically expedient reassurances of military progress.[11]

Each of these cases is an example of justification. The White House press secretary offered a false justification for Kennedy's speech cancellation. In the second case, the Johnson Administration, over a number of years, offered an equally false defense for escalating military involvement in Southeast Asia.

Lying occurred in both cases. Kennedy's deception in the Cuban Missile Crisis has been forgotten. We dare say that most of us would look on it as a harmless smoke screen used to protect important national security interests.

Johnson's deception is more serious. The pollster George Gallup evaluated the country's mood in February 1968: "I think the mood of America is one of rather great confusion and disillusionment. All the time we've been operating, 32 years now, I've never known a time like this—when people were so disillusioned and cynical. I think this goes back pretty much to their feeling of the inadequacy of leadership in our country."[12] The President's loss of moral authority was even given a name, the "credibility gap."

How can we reconcile our different feelings about these two incidents? An ethical absolutist would argue that lying is wrong, always wrong, and that both Kennedy and Johnson deserve equal condemnation. But even casual reflection would make us uncomfortable with such a pronouncement. In our lives, we know that the occasional innocent deception can spare hurt feelings. Is it more important to make Aunt Eleanor feel appreciated or to express our uncensored opinion about the quality of her tuna casserole? Only the most naive student of politics would suggest that a completely deceptionless government could exist. Security agencies must infiltrate hostile groups, police must use undercover operations to catch criminals, and Presidents must balance honesty against national security.

On the other hand, the thoroughgoing relativist might not be bothered by either of these cases. Kennedy had to lie to prevent panic and harmful media speculation. Johnson understood the importance of containing communism in Asia. He also understood that in a democratic society popular support for foreign policy initiatives is essential. As the father of the containment doctrine George Kennan has pointed out, "it is clear that the main element of any United States policy toward the Soviet Union must be that of a long-term, *patient but firm* and vigilant containment of Russian expansive tendencies." But it is easier for the USSR to press for the long term because public opinion is a less important variable of Soviet foreign policy.[13] The relativist might challenge critics to explain what other course was open to Johnson if he truly believed holding firm in Vietnam was in the vital national interest of the United States.

Those who press unbending principle argue for condemnation and those who celebrate pragmatic action defend Kennedy and Johnson. We feel a need for moderation; society has clearly been more favorable to Kennedy than Johnson, but on what ground can our feelings be supported? Consider these two situations carefully and we will return to them later.

MANIPULATION

To *manipulate* is "to control or play upon by artful, unfair, insidious means especially to one's own advantage."[14] The manipulative advocate views the listeners as objects. The genuine arguer seeks to engage the audience in a sincere and open discussion of the issues.

Again, the principle seems clear enough in the abstract, but when confronted with troublesome cases the line between appropriate and inappropriate argument becomes clouded. Consider two common examples of public argument.

EXAMPLE ONE

In a familiar television commercial for a name brand toothpaste, the following scene serves as an audiovisual argument for the product. Two attractive young women are shopping in the clothing section of a ski shop. One says to the other, "I'm sure if I buy this sweater Jim will pay attention to me." The second girl replies, "it isn't the sweater Lisa, it's your teeth. They just aren't white enough." "Well what should I do?" Lisa is counseled to buy the advertiser's brand of toothpaste. In the closing scene, we see Jim and Lisa go off smiling for a romantically charged ski weekend. But before they drive off for the mountains, the two women congratulate themselves on their accurate diagnosis of the problem—Lisa's use of the wrong toothpaste.

EXAMPLE TWO

Experts on child development have become increasingly concerned with Saturday morning advertising directed at the preschool market. Do children really understand the difference between programming and commercials? Are they able to erect the normal defenses of older children against the allure of manufacturers' sophisticated appeals? Now the situation has become even more clouded with the introduction of cartoon shows that have commercial products as the stars. The difference between a G. I. Joe ad and the cartoon character G. I. Joe is blurred.

Each of these cases requires a decision about what counts as manipulation. The obviously misleading suggestion that a change in toothpaste will provide romantic satisfaction is typical of many commercials. The gorgeous model curls up on top of the automobile manufacturer's newest model. The seductive voice suggests you wear a particular men's cologne or "nothing at all."

Perhaps example two is more troublesome. After all, the toothpaste is pitched to an audience that understands the tricks of Madison Avenue. But can a two- or three-year-old child effectively fend off tactics honed through sophisticated test marketing?

Think about these two cases. Do both examples represent acceptable practice? Either or neither? We will return to the issue of manipulation later.

COERCION

Justifications for argument are frequently based not on the free assent to reason, but on the promise of reward or the fear of reprisal. Rather than press for understanding and acceptance, the advocates wish only to force their will on the audience.

"Some communicators," Brockriede explains, "are not primarily interested in gaining assent to warrantable claims. Instead, they function through power, through an ability to apply psychic and physical sanctions, through rewards and especially punishments, through commands and threats."[15]

It seems difficult to imagine any defense for coercive rhetoric. But there are cases that will not immediately strike us as ethically out of bounds. Consider two controversial uses of coercive argument.

CASE ONE

> Sheila's mother was at her wits' end. Her seven-year-old daughter had walked to the corner and crossed the highway. Sheila knew very well that this was forbidden. This was the second time this had happened and attempts at reason had failed. This time Sheila's mother was clearer. She told her daughter if she ever crossed the road again by herself she would not be allowed to play outside for two weeks.

CASE TWO

> The antiapartheid group on campus had met with the University's trustees on three occasions. The outcome of these meetings had been unsatisfactory. The Board had decided to maintain their portfolio of stocks in American companies that did business with South Africa. The protestors, having exhausted all other options, decided to exercise their one remaining alternative. The next day students took over the University President's office and refused to leave until their demands were met.

Some readers might respond that these cases are really red herrings because coercion is not argument. Perhaps they fail to meet the criteria of *genuine* argument, but they at least masquerade in the form of argument. Each begins with a premise and draws a conclusion. If Sheila crosses the highway again, then she will not be allowed to play outside for two weeks. If the University does not agree to a plan of South African divestment, then the protestors will not relinquish the President's office. Threats fit the form of argument (this example is a hypothetical if-then structure) even if the substance of the appeal violates our ethical sensibilities.

The scenarios in both sample cases have on occasion been sanctioned by society. Despite the move to more humane and less authoritarian parenting styles, all parents threaten their children with reprisals for misbehavior. The civil rights and antiwar protests of the 1960s and 1970s are frequently, perhaps even most often, viewed as morally defensible. Politics, even in thoroughly democratic societies, functions at base on a threat of coercion. Run a red light and get a traffic ticket. Drive while under the influence of alcohol and go to jail. File your taxes late and pay a penalty plus interest.

Coercion is everywhere, usually cloaked in civil language, but no less threatening. We permit some forms of coercive speech and sanction others. What is the ground upon which we draw these distinctions? Consider the two cases and we will return to coercive communication later.

ETHICS OF ARGUMENT AND PERSUASION

Of the six sample cases, two require careful consideration and the rest are easily decided by applying current codes of conduct. This is not to say that specific individuals will not disagree with even the decisions in the easy cases, but that society is not currently conflicted about these matters.

In the examples of deception, current codes of political conduct permit incidental lying for a greater cause but disallow practiced deception for political gain. The forced resignation of Richard Nixon emphatically demonstrated this principle. In the manipulation cases, both forms of advertising are presently allowed. Finally, current practice permits reasonable threats of punishment to control a child but denies protestors the right to occupy a campus building.

In exploring these six cases, we found two that were difficult. Advertisers' use of commercials directed at preschool children and the student protestors' demand for university divestment are problematic. They are troublesome because social critics are challenging current standards of ethical practice in these two areas.

These moralists argue that present standards in these two areas are *inconsistent* and promote unacceptable *consequences*. Directing commercials at children is inconsistent with other laws that treat children as special citizens that require unique protections. The law of the marketplace expressed in *caveat emptor* ("buyer beware") cannot apply to children. Second, such a practice has unacceptable consequences. Children are bombarded with commercial spots for candy, sugared cereal, war toys, etc. These products begin a negative pattern of behavior that the child may never break. In addition, these commercials prompt children to work on their parents to buy them these products.

This may well create unnecessary family strife as the parents must fight the television.

Likewise, political activists argue for the moral high ground in the debate over apartheid. Our society has come to revere the efforts of the civil rights workers in the 1950s and 1960s, so how can we condemn peaceful efforts to free millions of people of color living in South Africa? The consequences of inaction have repeatedly been chronicled in the press. But there are important competing values present in this situation. First, the right to the use of property is violated by the students' actions. After all, the university president's right to conduct business is severely disrupted by this action. Second, a commitment to nonnegotiable demands may circumvent the process of argumentation. Refusal to discuss and justify positions escalates into violence. The bombing of the Mathematics Research Center at the University of Wisconsin as protest against campus defense research is a classic example.

Changes in the code of conduct do not come quickly. Arguments are put forward, refuted, and defended until a consensus emerges. But in each case reasoned justification is at the heart of the process. Public standards of moral conduct are the product of argument, not of forced imposition.

CONCLUSIONS

A review of major points in the chapter should help clarify the conception of ethics we have adopted. Remember, this is a view of ethics in public discourse and is not meant to discredit anyone's personal code of conduct.

First, there is an obvious conflict between argumentation's twin foci on *worthiness* and *effectiveness*. After all, the marketing expert must boost sales; the attorney must successfully litigate; and the academic department must attract students. But each must do so within established guidelines of conduct.

Second, democratic societies are founded on a pluralistic ethic. Democratic commitments assume a free marketplace of ideas. The right to vigorously participate in the civil life of society assumes that discussion and debate will lead to justified decisions rather than deceptive, coercive, or manipulative imposition by some group. The failure of pluralism leads to the authoritarianism of ethical absolutism or the moral anarchy of ethical relativism. In democratic societies, we found our ethical code on reasoned justification. We hold nothing beyond argument.

Third, this pluralistic ideal is realized through appeal to the reasonability of "argument fields." Different areas of life require different

133,314

standards of ethical judgment. What is viewed as deceptive in one area may be perfectly acceptable in another. We appeal to the rules that have come to define these separate fields. The variety of disputes adjudicated by the courts attest to the reasonability of such a procedure. Divorce, murder, trespassing, probate, bankruptcy, etc. are all addressed by the court using different standards of judgment in each case. Yet, we accept each verdict as reasonable. We make similar judgments about the ethics of our communicative behavior.

Fourth, sample cases of troublesome ethical issues in argument demonstrated the utility of the field approach. Judgments about cases of deception, manipulation, and coercion are ordinarily easily made. Controversial cases are more difficult. The code of conduct for deciding ethical behavior in a given field may be changing. Consideration of the *consequences* of maintaining the present code and its *consistency* with other important values are the determinants of the appropriateness of the existing standards.

NOTES

1. The term "Sophist" originally referred to teachers of eloquence in ancient Greece. Plato's criticism of the Sophists in the *Gorgias* created the negative connotation.
2. See, for example, Patricia Robert Harris, "Religion and Politics: A Commitment to a Pluralistic Society," reprinted in *Contemporary American Speeches*, 5th ed. (Dubuque, IA: Kendall/Hunt, 1982), pp. 278–287.
3. Antony Flew, *Dictionary of Philosophy* (1982).
4. See, Chaim Perelman, "Value Judgments, Justifications and Argumentation," *Philosophy Today* 6 (1962): 45–50.
5. The term "argument field" was first used by the British philosopher Stephen Toulmin in *The Uses of Argument* (London: Cambridge Univ. Press, 1958).
6. For a more technical discussion of intellectual disciplines, see Stephen Toulmin, *Human Understanding* (Princeton, NJ: Princeton Univ. Press, 1972), pp. 145–155.
7. The opinion of the Court was written by Chief Justice Warren Burger. See *Miller v. California* 413 US 15 (1972).
8. Bruce E. Gronbeck, "Sociocultural Notions of Argument Fields: A Primer," in *Dimensions of Argument*, eds. George Ziegelmueller and Jack Rhodes (Annandale, VA: Speech Communication Association, 1981), p. 15.
9. Ibid.
10. Stephen Toulmin, *An Examination of the Place of Reason in Ethics* (London: Cambridge Univ. Press, 1950), p. 151.
11. For a discussion of the ethical implications of selling the Vietnam War, see Hannah Arendt, "Home to Roost: A Bicentennial Address," *New York Review of Books*, 26 June 1975, pp. 3–6.

12. "Gallup Calls Public Disillusioned and Cynical," *The New York Times*, 10 February 1968, p. 12.
13. X [pseudonym for George F. Kennan], "The Sources of Soviet Conduct," *Foreign Affairs* 25 (1947): 566–582.
14. "Manipulate," *Webster's Seventh New Collegiate Dictionary* (1969).
15. Wayne Brockriede, "Arguers as Lovers," *Philosophy and Rhetoric* 5 (1972): p. 2.

3

BURDENS OF ARGUMENT

A quick scan of the *Oxford English Dictionary* finds a synonym list for "burden" sure to dampen the most festive mood. "Burden" is "a load," "a load of labour, duty, responsibility, blame, sin, sorrow, etc.," and "an obligatory expense . . . often with the additional notion of pressing heavily upon industry and restraining freedom of action."[1]

In common use, we associate "burden" with unpleasantness. Certain animals are called "beasts of burden." Reflecting whimsically on the single life, settled couples talk of a time when they were not "burdened with family responsibilities." Often in a voice tinged with defensiveness, parents speak of their children as "joys, not burdens." Reaganomics has peppered political speech with phrases describing the federal deficit as a "burden on economic expansion."

This semantic baggage makes our charge to embrace the "burdens of argument" seem odd. Why should anyone want to embrace such a dour concept?

Our reply is built on two synonyms that approximate the argumentation sense of "burden"—"duty" and "responsibility." Accepting duty and responsibility is always a double-edged sword because it provides the reward of order by limiting the range of freedom. We gain a sense of fulfillment when we faithfully discharge our responsibilities and, yet, those responsibilities constrict our freedom of action.

Duty and responsibility are so essential to civilized life that they are the defining qualities of human community. For example, if we saw two adults and two children in close proximity to one another, but upon extended observation failed to detect any evidence that these four people had a sense of duty toward or responsibility for each other, we would never label them a family. Think of any defined group—corporation, church, school, nation, club—and each has a collective identity because duties and responsibilities are understood. In Stephen Toulmin's influential work *Reason in Ethics*, he argued that "the only context in which the concept of 'duty' is straightforwardly intelligible is one of communal life . . . [here] we learn to renounce our claims and alter our aims where they conflict with those of our fellows."[2]

RESPONSIBILITY AND ARGUMENT

The burdens of argument regulate communicative freedom by pre-
scribing the duties of arguers. Just as failure to fulfill family responsibilities brings social sanction, violation of the burdens of argument is
punished by the community of reasonable people. Those we deem
violators are ignored and ineffective; in extreme cases, they are scorned
with harsh labels. Those who claim to have discovered a miracle
medical cure without adequate scientific support we call "quacks."
Lawyers who practice before the bar using methods that short-circuit
judicial procedure we call "shysters." Politicians who prey on our
basest emotions in order to circumvent reasonable discussion of public
affairs we label "demagogues." In each case, the judgment of reasonable people censures those who fail to responsibly accept the burdens
of argument.

These burdens stem from the public character of argumentation.
The burdens are grounded in consideration for the audience. Our
regard for the audience, much like our regard for members of our
family, determines the duties and responsibilities of argument. Because
these burdens are audience-centered, they are dynamic in character.
What is expected of us changes as we move from one set of circumstances to another; just as communal duties change as we move from
family to club to business.

Even though the specific standards change from one situation to
another, the kinds of burdens are constant. In other words, there are
general duties we have for all audiences but these duties must be
fulfilled in different ways as the circumstances change.[3]

PRESUMPTION AND THE BURDEN OF PROOF

During the writing of this book, we had occasion to hear one of our
friends use the word "presume." The United States Senate had just
passed a sweeping tax reform bill. This bill established two tax rates of
15 and 27 percent for individuals, increased the tax burden on corpora-
tions, and removed millions of the working poor from the tax rolls. In
order to raise the revenue for these lower individual rates, many of the
special preferences that had historically filled the tax code were re-
pealed. This bill drastically reduced government's role as arbiter of
individual and corporate spending decisions. In the future, people
would donate to charity or invest capital for reasons other than reaping
potential tax benefits.

During a discussion of the tax bill, our friend said she "*presumed*
that the Senate had acted wisely.*" What should we take this word
"presume" to mean in this context?

If you look up "presume" in a dictionary, you are likely to find a definition similar to this: "To assume or take for granted; to presuppose; to anticipate, count upon, expect. Specifically in Law: To take as proved until evidence to the contrary is forthcoming."[4]

Contrast the phrase "I *presume* the Senate acted wisely" with "I am *sure* the Senate acted wisely" and "I am *unsure* the Senate acted wisely." The three terms—presume, sure, and unsure—differ in the strength of their commitment. To say "I am *sure*" is to express a definitively positive attitude toward the Senate action. To say "I am *unsure*" is to refrain from expressing either a positive or negative attitude toward the legislative action. To say "I *presume*" is to express an *initial approval* of the act's wisdom.[5]

Keep this ordinary sense of "presume" in mind as we turn to a more technical definition of "presumption" and "burden of proof." The best place to start is with the father of these concepts. The English logician and rhetorician Richard Whately first introduced presumption and burden of proof in his popular nineteenth-century textbook, *Elements of Rhetoric*. In the final edition of the book, he explained these concepts in the following manner: "The most correct use of . . . 'Presumption' . . . [is] a *pre-occupation* of the ground, as implies that it must stand good till some sufficient reason is adduced against it; in short, that the *Burden of proof* lies on the side of him who would dispute it."[6]

The difference between our ordinary sense of "presume" and Whately's more technical definition of "presumption" turns more on linguistic differences than differences in fundamental meaning. "Presumption" is a noun; "presume" is a verb. "Presumption" is; "presume" does. "Presumption" is "pre-occupied ground"; "presume" expresses "initial approval." To put it together in one phrase, *presumption is expressed as an initial approval of pre-occupied ground*.

This phrase "pre-occupied" ground is understandable when "burden of proof" is defined. Before we are willing to accept a new position, we require sufficient reason to abandon the old position. Before we are willing to abandon the ground we now occupy, we must be given a sufficient reason. *Burden of proof is the flip side of presumption. The advocate of change upholds the burden of proof by providing sufficient reason to overcome presumption.*

At this point, you are probably thinking that this is all well and good in the abstract, but in what sense was our friend "initially approving of pre-occupied ground" in saying that she "presumed the Senate had acted wisely"? This is the very question that makes presumption and burden of proof troublesome concepts. Before we can address this question directly, you need to understand two additional concepts.

FIELD-INVARIANT SENSE OF PRESUMPTION AND BURDEN OF PROOF

In the last chapter, we discussed *argument fields*. Different fields of argument employ different standards. Standards for ethical behavior in advertising are different from standards of ethical behavior in politics. Our expectations of appropriateness change as circumstances vary. But yet, in every situation we found an ethical code covering communicative conduct. We had little trouble figuring out what was acceptable in each area. In other words, the presence of an ethical code was *field-invariant*, but the specific ethical standards were *field-dependent*.

So the phrase "field-invariant sense of presumption and burden of proof" means that every argument situation assigns presumption and burden of proof to the participants. Those advocating change must accept the burden of proof and those arguing for maintenance of current arrangements enjoy presumption. In every circumstance presumption "expresses an initial approval of pre-occupied ground."

Why is this? Why would every possible circumstance for argument assign presumption and burden of proof? Is it because everyone has read a text on argumentation theory, or is there some more basic reason? Presumption and burden of proof are not rules imposed by authors of argumentation texts; they are facts of social life. Try to imagine a world in which there was no concept of presumption and burden of proof. Without such concepts, we could not define ourselves as reasonable beings. People are reasonable because they adopt standards of proof. Only people behaving irrationally change without sufficient justification. Presumption and burden of proof define what is minimally sufficient to adhere to a proposition.

For example, assume that the Food and Drug Administration did not place any burden of proof on developers of new drugs. The medical community would be unable to distinguish drugs with therapeutic value from sham cures. The process of drug development is rational because those who argue for a change in drug regimes must provide sufficient reason for the alterations.

FIELD-DEPENDENT SENSE OF PRESUMPTION AND BURDEN OF PROOF

"As a stance fields take," Charles Willard observed, "presumption plays no favorites. It is nothing but an abstract claim that every advocate must have good reasons, leaving up to the fields what good reasons are."[7] As we have seen, every argumentative situation assigns presumption and burden of proof, but the standards for fulfilling the burdens vary from one situation to the next. If the variation in standards were wild and unpredictable, arguers would be unable to act reasonably. Just as the ethical standards discussed in Chapter Two were easy to identify, so too are the characteristics of presumption and burden of proof. Two specific patterns of adjustment can be located through analysis of the audience.

First, our definition of presumption employed the phrase "pre-occupied ground." The constituents of pre-occupied ground change between fields of argument. For instance, an investigator conducting a scientific experiment assumes that the null hypothesis is pre-occupied ground. Unless the experimental hypothesis is confirmed at the .05 level of confidence, the null hypothesis will remain operative.

In another case, Ron and Karen argued over where to spend their five-day vacation. Ron maintained that they should go to Traverse City, Michigan, and Karen suggested that they take a cruise in a paddle wheel steamer down the Mississippi. This case involves a field less sharply defined than the field of experimental science. This field is a product of the history of Ron and Karen's relationship and the traditional expectations we all have about vacation travel. Analyzing such a loosely defined field requires careful analysis of the audience. In this case, Ron and Karen are both the arguers and the audience. The task is to come to a mutual agreement about a vacation destination. In order to complete the task, both parties must become convinced that the vacation destination is satisfactory. The "pre-occupied ground" is not going to Traverse City and not going on a Mississippi cruise. What standards of proof must each advocate meet to overcome this presumption?

We might begin by asking what the purpose of a vacation is.[8] We assume that there is a general understanding of what the term "vacation" means and what purposes it ought to fulfill. A vacation is a time for fun and relaxation. We typically look for vacation spots that are tailored to fit our particular requirements for fun and relaxation. So, in this case, Ron would want to present arguments that explain why Traverse City would meet Karen's vacation requirements. Karen, of course, would want to follow a similar procedure in fulfilling her burden of proof in advocating the Mississippi cruise. Notice in this kind of loosely defined field that the personal idiosyncrasies of the particular audience play a greater role than they do in the tightly defined field of experimental science.

Presumption and the burden of proof say very little about the ultimate disposition of the argument. To carry the burden of proof is to overcome only the *initial* approval for pre-occupied ground. As the argument progresses, additional reasons might be offered for rejecting the change. This situation addresses a new burden that we take up in the following section.

BURDEN OF REBUTTAL

The phrase "burden of rebuttal" is nearly self-explanatory. The advocate assumes a burden to *address legitimate opposing arguments*. Typically, disputes involve several extended lines of argument. An initial case is presented; the opposition provides reasons to reject the case; the original advocates counter the opposing arguments, and so forth.

Arguers cannot expect to carry the day unless they are willing to engage the opposition. Without the burden of rebuttal, the audience is not given a satisfactory opportunity to weigh the merits of competing positions.

The burden of rebuttal is fixed in our society through a whole series of laws and traditions. The First Amendment is based on John Stuart Mill's belief in the "marketplace of ideas."[9] Mill's contention that decisions are best made when there is unfettered freedom to express ideas animates our whole democratic tradition.

The fair time provisions, which enforce equal time for opposing candidates, are a legislative expression of this principle. Not fixed in law, but increasingly demanded by the public, is the tradition of presidential press conferences and candidate debates. Citizens expect to see their leaders answer arguments from the press and opposition. In other words, the public demands that office holders fulfill the burden of rebuttal.

The courts guarantee the defendant the right to confront his accusers. This principle assures the defendant the right of rebuttal and demands that the prosecution answer the charges of the defense.

In the course of our everyday affairs, we uphold the tradition of fair play. It would strike us as unfair to criticize someone without giving them a chance to respond. We would hardly call an interaction where the parties did not address each other's points an argument. In fact, we would more likely label it a tirade or shouting match. The very meaning of engaging in an argument requires that the parties uphold the burden of rebuttal.

You may have noticed that our definition of the burden of rebuttal is qualified by the term *legitimate*. The advocate must address all *legitimate* opposing arguments. The existence of the burden of rebuttal is field-invariant. Every situation that can be defined as argumentative imposes this burden. However, the standards for what counts as a legitimate opposing argument is field-dependent.

Return to our earlier examples of the investigator conducting an experiment. Let's assume that our scientist is testing the relationship between the incidence of child abuse and the probability that the victim will commit a violent criminal act. Our investigator gathers data, analyzes it, and concludes that an abused child has a significantly greater chance of committing a violent crime when an adult than a nonabused child. Responding to the findings, two critics argue that the conclusions are unfounded. The first critic maintains that the findings are incorrect because he knows of a victim of child abuse who has never committed a violent criminal act. The second critic argues that the findings are unsubstantiated because the investigator did not use an adequate control group. The experimental group was made up of abused males of low socioeconomic status. The control group was made up of nonabused females from upper-middle-class families.

The first critic presented an illegitimate argument. No one in the scientific community would take such anecdotal evidence seriously. Of course, there will be examples of abused children who do not become criminals. The investigator was only claiming that there is a statistically significant increase in the probability of violent criminal activity among victims of child abuse. We doubt that any sociologist would expect the investigator to answer such a charge. The second critic, however, leveled a very damaging charge. If this charge remains unchallenged, the study results will be dismissed. The scientific community demands adequate methodological defense of sociological findings.

In other fields, different criteria confer legitimacy. For example, mainstream politicians are not expected to answer the charges of fringe candidates. During the Reagan–Mondale campaign, Reagan was obligated to answer the charges leveled by the Democratic challenger but not those made by Gus Hall and the American Communist Party. Gus Hall was not deemed a sufficiently serious contender to demand the attention of the President.

In summary, every field of argument (invariant) demands that the advocate answer legitimate opposing arguments. The determination of legitimacy, however, varies from one field to the next (dependent).

BURDEN OF VALIDITY

We frequently use and hear the word "valid." The radio talk show host tells callers that they "make a valid point." You are supposed to meet a friend for lunch at 12:30 and the friend shows up twenty minutes late. Upon arrival she explains that just before leaving the office she got a long distance telephone call. You judge your friend's explanation a "valid excuse." You go to your instructor's office to discuss your grade on the midterm examination. You explain that although your response to question five was different than expected it is still "a valid answer."

FIELD-INVARIANT SENSE OF VALIDITY

What does this ordinary sense of "valid"mean? Notice in all of these cases valid is an adjective. "Valid" modifies "point," "excuse," and "answer." It seems to mean something akin to "good," "acceptable," "adequate," or, perhaps, "true." Certainly to label an object "valid" is to say something positive about it.

But does the meaning of "valid" change when it modifies "argument"? "Valid argument" seems quite close to the meaning of "good argument," "acceptable argument," "adequate argument," or "true argument." Certainly the speaker is saying that a "valid" argument is worthy of the audience's approval.

Let's stop and examine this definition of validity more closely: a valid argument is one worthy of audience approval. First, this sense of validity rules out arguments that are merely effective. Arguments must be *worthy* of approval and not merely capable of engendering approval. In fact, we would not find it odd to hear someone say that they presented a "valid though unpopular" argument. The philosopher Charles Stevenson observed that "people often use invalid methods, and these sometimes help them to win arguments. Common acceptance does not imply validity."[10]

Second, we chose the word "approval" rather than "acceptance." Frequently, we approve of arguments we do not accept. For example, an argument may be carefully structured, adequately supported by evidence, and competently presented but not have sufficient force to persuade us to abandon our position. The pornography debate often uses arguments that are approved yet not accepted. For instance, feminist groups have carefully structured, adequately supported, and competently presented the argument that pornography degrades women. But some people, even though approving of the argument, find other reasons to reject regulation of pornography. They often contend that freedom of speech is a more important value. Audiences may approve of the degradation argument but not accept it as justification for regulation of the press.

Third, the *audience* is the group that arbitrates approval. Some arguments are worthy of some audiences' approval and not others. Notice that the definition does not say the audience will approve, an effectiveness standard, but that the argument is *worthy of audience approval.*

These facets of validity apply to all genuine argumentative situations. Argumentation is a method of decision making only because we can recognize valid arguments. Any reasonable enterprise must have a notion of validity.

FIELD-DEPENDENT SENSE OF VALIDITY

If the presence and force of validity are field-invariant, the standards for judging any given argument valid are field-dependent. Because the audience arbitrates the approval of arguments, validity standards vary as circumstances change.

For those who have taken a course in logic, the discussion of field-dependent standards of validity will sound strange. Recall from Chapter One that *logic is the study of the formal principles of reasoning* and that *argumentation is the study of justification.* The formal principles of logic apply universally regardless of context. Consequently, logical validity is defined in formal, abstract, contextless terms. An argument is logically valid when "its conclusion necessarily follows from the premises; *if* the premises of the argument are true, then its conclusion cannot be false; the conclusion too must be true."[11] It is the form of the argument, not the relationship of the argument to a context, that confers validity. Return to an illustration from Chapter One:

> All houses are white;
> *Mount Vernon is a house;*
> Therefore, Mount Vernon is white.

This argument meets the standards of logical validity. First, if you accept "all houses are white" and "Mount Vernon is a house," it must follow that "Mount Vernon is white." Second, the first premise is false, but "if it were true" the conclusion would also be true. Therefore, our illustration is formally valid.

But real people do not talk in syllogisms nor do they typically make arguments that are dependent on the formal transposition of terms. We argue with teachers about answers to test questions, with friends over the merits of the basketball team's newest recruiting class, with intimate others over where to spend the weekend, etc. None of these arguments can ever hope to meet the criteria of formal logical validity. The relationship between reason and conclusion is only probable. The criteria for the adequacy of a reason to support a conclusion will change as we argue about tests, basketball, and weekend plans.

Where do we look for validity criteria? We look to the audience's expectations of a good argument for the particular circumstances. Or more technically put, *validity standards inhere in relevant argument fields.*

These validity standards are discovered in any given situation by asking these questions:

1. Given the circumstances of this dispute, is this argument relevant?
2. Given the circumstances of this dispute, can this argument be adequately supported with evidence?
3. Given the circumstances of this dispute, can the argument's conclusion be reasonably inferred from the argument's premises? Put less technically, does the conclusion follow reasonably from the supporting reasons?

Compare these criteria with the ordinary sense of "valid," at the beginning of this section, and with the logicians' formal notion of "validity." These three criteria make up what any member of an audience would demand of an argument before approving of it. Only the third criterion approximates the logicians' conception of validity.

The similarity comes from the emphasis on the relationship between premises and conclusion, but after that the similarity ends. The premises, in our formulation, "reasonably infer" the conclusion; in the logicians' formulation, the conclusion "necessarily follows" from the premises. The "reasonable inference" is a judgment made in particular circumstances.

EVALUATING ARGUMENTS

Adolf Hitler's Mein Kampf

Validity is a concept used to evaluate arguments. We ought to be able to use the concepts outlined here and distinguish good from bad arguments. Perhaps the easiest way to proceed is by examining an argumentative composition that has been universally condemned. If our concept of validity cannot explain the errors in this view, then grounds would exist for rejecting this field-based notion of validity.

Book One of Adolf Hitler's *Mein Kampf* (1925) represents an essential part of the creed of National Socialism. Several excerpts from the work provide the skeleton of the argument and the flavor of the Hitler prose.

"There are some truths," Hitler wrote, "which are so obvious that for this very reason they are not seen or at least not recognized by ordinary people. They sometimes pass by such truisms as though blind and are most astonished when someone suddenly discovers what everyone really ought to know."

With this appeal to the supposedly self-evident, the argument for Aryan racial superiority was launched. "Even the most superficial observation shows that Nature's restricted form of propagation and increase is an almost rigid law of all innumerable forms of expression of her vital urge. Every animal mates only with a member of the same species. The titmouse seeks the titmouse, the finch the finch, the stork the stork, the field mouse the field mouse, the dormouse the dormouse, the wolf the she-wolf, etc."

The consequences of breaking this so-called law of nature was explained in the following paragraph: "Any crossing of two beings not at exactly the same level produces a medium between the level of the two parents. This means: the offspring will probably stand higher than the racially lower parent, but not as high as the higher one." Interracial propagation is described in *Mein Kampf* as "contrary to the will of Nature for a higher breeding of all life.... The stronger must dominate and not blend with the weaker, thus sacrificing his own greatness."[12]

What standards of validity are suggested by this text? Notice that Hitler appealed to the laws of nature and the science of genetics. Consequently, the text demands that the reader bring the standards of scientific assessment to the argument.

Given scientific standards, did Hitler's evidence support the argument and did the reasons he offered support a reasonable inference to the conclusion? To both queries, the answer is an emphatic "No!"

First, the section of *Mein Kampf* quoted here confused the notion of "species" and "race." The law of nature described as the premise for his argument discussed breeding between species, but when this is later applied to humans this premise is transformed into an argument about breeding between races. Obviously, different breeds or races of dogs, for example, breed all the time in nature. Propagation between a wolf and a tiger is not analogous to breeding between an Aryan and a non-Aryan. So we can conclude that Hitler misapplies the scientific terms "species" and "race."

Second, scientific work in genetics would not support the contention that "the offspring will probably stand higher than the racially lower parent, but not as high as the higher one." This argument invites the reader to evaluate the claim from the scientific findings in genetics. Would the standards in the field of genetics approve of this contention? Several specific objections come immediately to mind: (1) Constant inbreeding is more likely to reinforce undesirable traits than racial crossbreeding. (2) Given the operation of dominant and recessive traits, offspring do not stand between the higher and the lower parent. (3) The genetic makeup of any given child is a composite of inherited traits, but the genetic code determining race (skin color) is not related to critical factors like intelligence.

Recall that three key questions are asked in any given situation to discover the standards of validity. Consider each of those questions in relation to this selection from *Mein Kampf*.

1. *Given the circumstances of this dispute, is this argument relevant?* Our analysis of Hitler's text suggested that in fact this argument is not relevant. Hitler has employed a pseudoscientific argument to advance an ideological position. It was only through deception that the argument was made to appear relevant.
2. *Given the circumstances of this dispute, can this argument be adequately supported with evidence?* Our analysis has demonstrated that Hitler's case depends on the science of genetics and that genetic research would not support these claims.
3. *Given the circumstances of this dispute, can the argument's conclusion be reasonably inferred from the argument's premises?* Apart from the lack of scientific documentation, Hitler's key contention did not follow from the reasons he offered. The mistaken equivocation of "species" and "race" supports the entire chain of reasoning.

Now turn to a second example. In the following illustration we analyze an argumentative composition that meets the field-dependent criteria for validity.

EVALUATING ARGUMENTS

Martin Luther King's "Letter from Birmingham Jail"

"Letter from Birmingham Jail" was dated April 16, 1963. Dr. King composed the letter while in the Birmingham Jail as a response to a published statement by eight fellow clergymen from Alabama. Begun on the margins of the newspaper in which the clergymen's letter appeared, the letter was continued on scraps of paper supplied by a friendly black trustee. Finally, the letter was finished on a legal pad supplied by Reverend King's attorneys.

The awarding of the Nobel Peace Prize to Martin Luther King in 1964 attests to his stature in the world community. In particular, this letter has been praised as a classic defense by those who seek to redress political grievances in the face of established opposition.

In such a case, do our proposed standards of validity support the social and historical judgment of this work? We begin by briefly outlining Dr. King's essential arguments.

The chief contention of the eight clergymen was that the protestors were trying to move too fast. "One of the basic points in your statement," King wrote, "is that the action that I and my associates have taken in Birmingham is untimely. Some have asked: 'Why didn't you give the new city administration time to act?' " King took this opportunity not only to address the specifics of the Birmingham situation, but to address all of those who would advise the oppressed to wait. His answer was contained in the following extended excerpt from the "Letter":

> We are sadly mistaken if we feel that the election of Albert Boutwell as mayor will bring the millennium to Birmingham. While Mr. Boutwell is a much more gentle person than Mr. Connor, they are both segregationists, dedicated to maintenance of the status quo. I have hope that Mr. Boutwell will be reasonable enough to see the futility of massive resistance to desegregation. But he will not see this without pressure from devotees of civil rights. My friends, I must say to you that we have not made a single gain in civil rights without determined legal and nonviolent pressure. Lamentably, it is an historical fact that privileged groups seldom give up their privileges voluntarily. Individuals may see the moral light and voluntarily give up their unjust posture; but, as Reinhold Niebuhr has reminded us, groups tend to be more immoral than individuals.
>
>   We know through painful experience that freedom is never voluntarily given by the oppressor; it must be demanded by the oppressed. Frankly, I have yet to engage in a direct-action campaign that was "well-timed" in the view of those who have not suffered unduly from the disease of segregation. For years now I have heard the word "Wait!" It rings in the ear of every Negro with piercing familiarity. This "Wait" has almost always meant "Never." We must come to

see, with one of our distinguished jurists, that "justice too long delayed is justice denied."

We have waited for more than 340 years for our constitutional and God-given rights. The nations of Asia and Africa are moving with jetlike speed toward gaining political independence, but we still creep at horse-and-buggy pace toward gaining a cup of coffee at a lunch counter. Perhaps it is easy for those who have never felt the stinging darts of segregation to say, "Wait." But when you have seen the vicious mobs lynch your mothers and fathers at will and drown your sisters and brothers at whim; when you have seen hate-filled policemen curse, kick and even kill your black brothers and sisters; when you see the vast majority of your twenty million Negro brothers smothering in an airtight cage of poverty in the midst of an affluent society; when you suddenly find your tongue twisted and your speech stammering as you seek to explain to your six-year-old daughter why she can't go to the public amusement park that has just been advertised on television, and see tears welling up in her eyes when she is told that Funtown is closed to colored children, and see ominous clouds of inferiority beginning to form in her little mental sky, and see her beginning to distort her personality by developing an unconscious bitterness toward white people; when you have to concoct an answer for a five-year-old son who is asking: "Daddy, why do white people treat colored people so mean?"; when you take a cross-country drive and find it necessary to sleep night after night in the uncomfortable corners of your automobile because no motel will accept you; when you are humiliated day in and day out by nagging signs reading "white" and "colored"; when your first name becomes "nigger," your middle becomes "boy" (however old you are) and your last becomes "John," and your wife and mother are never given the respected title "Mrs."; when you are harried by day and haunted by night by the fact that you are a Negro, living constantly at tiptoe stance, never quite knowing what to expect next, and are plagued with inner fears and outer resentments; when you are forever fighting a degenerating sense of "nobodiness"—then you will understand why we find it difficult to wait. There comes a time when the cup of endurance runs over, and men are no longer willing to be plunged into the abyss of despair. I hope, sirs, you can understand our legitimate and unavoidable impatience.[13]

Dr. King asks the reader to engage his text in an entirely different manner than Hitler did in *Mein Kampf*. Where Hitler employed the language of science, Dr. King used the political-philosophical-religious language of moral justice. Within that framework, Dr. King argued against those who counseled the civil rights movement to "wait."

The major reasons supporting King's rejection of the argument to wait are the following: (1) The new administration, although different in temperament, is still committed to segregation. (2) History has demonstrated that civil rights have only been realized through the pressure of organized resistance. (3) For defenders of the status quo "wait" is a synonym for "never" and there is never a time that is "well-timed." (4) One cannot expect a people who have suffered the devastating consequences of racism for centuries to endure any longer.

Do these lines of argument and the supporting evidence permit us to label King's argument valid? Consider each of the key validity questions in turn.

1. *Given the circumstances of this dispute, is this argument relevant?* The argument was relevant in the immediate sense because it responded directly to the letter by the eight clergymen. The argument is relevant in the larger sense because it spoke to the moral justification for nonviolent civil disobedience. Finally, the argument is relevant because it addresses the issue of delay on appropriate terms. Dr. King does not hide the moral and political nature of his position. Unlike Hitler, he does not introduce a wholly unrelated domain of knowledge for the sake of deception.

2. *Given the circumstances of this dispute, can this argument be adequately supported with evidence?* Unlike *Mein Kampf,* where it was clear that genetic evidence contradicted the claims, "Letter from Birmingham Jail" requires the reader to evaluate several different kinds of evidence. First, the reader is presented with evidence that the new mayor is a "much more gentle person than Mr. Connor, [yet] they are both segregationists, dedicated to maintenance of the status quo." This is a claim that readers in the City of Birmingham would be in a position to know. King, unlike Hitler, does not appeal to some mysterious law of nature but to the readers' own experience.

   Second, the reader is asked to reflect on the lessons of history. King supports his argument with the "historical fact that privileged groups seldom give up their privileges voluntarily." Notice that this is indeed an issue of fact rather than value. There is no attempt to cover moral commitment with the gloss of objectivity. The text does not state this "fact" categorically but offers the qualifier "seldom." Certainly history is filled with the struggle of the powerless to gain power and secure civil rights. The United States was formed through such a struggle.

   Third, King speaks from both personal experience and the collective experience of his people when he wrote that "wait" has "almost always meant 'Never.'" King acknowledges that he is speaking from a particular perspective and again uses qualifiers to remove the absolutist tone that dominates the prose of *Mein Kampf.*

   Fourth, King vividly summarizes the subjective emotional consequences of segregation for blacks. He is obviously not cataloguing actual specific events but portraying generally the kind of humiliation blacks suffered. Responsible accounts of segregation, whether by journalists or historians, would certainly support this portrait.

3. *Given the circumstances of this dispute, can the argument's conclusion be reasonably inferred from the argument's premises?* The conclusion of King's argument is that the appeal to "wait" is unjustified. Unlike the arguments of the logician, the conclusions of everyday argument do not follow formally from the premises. The link between reason and conclusion is persuasive rather than necessary. With this in mind, ask yourself whether Dr. King's arguments justify the audience's approval of the essay's conclusion.

In retrospect, we know that American society did accept the argument that blacks had suffered too long under the yoke of segregation. But this is really only evidence about effectiveness and not about worthiness. Should the audience have accepted these arguments?

An affirmative answer might be built on the following considerations. First, Dr. King provided arguments that were consistent with our culture's sense of justice. He appealed to standards of judgment, field-dependent criteria, that were widely accepted. He referred to the famous dictum that "justice too long delayed is justice denied." He pictured the terrible conditions of oppression so that the audience could "understand our legitimate and unavoidable impatience." He asked only that his case be judged by the principles of morality that the culture has always revered. Hitler by contrast subverts legitimate standards of validity by confounding issues of political justice with a pseudoscientific appeal to the irrelevant laws of nature.

Martin Luther King built a case that we unhesitatingly label valid. This does not mean that good arguments could not be offered against his point of view or even that the case of the eight clergymen was necessarily invalid, but that Dr. King's position was founded on grounds that are worthy of the audience's acceptance.

CONCLUSIONS

In this chapter, you have been introduced to the various burdens of argument. These burdens are conceptualized as "duties" or "responsibilities" advocates accept when they sincerely argue. When we choose to reason rather than impose our will by force or trickery, these burdens define our obligations to the audience.

Although the burdens of argument exist in all situations, the manner in which our obligations must be carried out differ from one set of circumstances to another. Because these burdens of argument are audience-centered, they are dynamic in character.

The three burdens of argument are presumption and the burden of proof, the burden of rebuttal, and the burden of validity. *Presumption is expressed as an initial approval of pre-occupied ground. Burden of proof is the flip side of presumption. The advocate of change upholds the burden of proof by providing sufficient reasons to overcome presumption.*

Participants in argument take on a second burden, the *burden of rebuttal.* This is the charge to the arguer to *address legitimate opposing arguments.* Those who engage in argumentation have the responsibility to carry the case forward and engage those who raise legitimate objections to their point of view.

The final burden is the *burden of validity.* The speaker has an obligation to advance *arguments worthy of audience approval.* This does not suggest that the advocates' positions will be accepted but only that they ought to conform their arguments to established criteria of worthiness.

Each of these burdens has both *field-invariant* and *field-dependent* features. The burdens exist in all fields and have the same meaning in each field. These are the field-invariant features. However, the criteria for assigning presumption, demanding rebuttal, and judging validity differs from one domain to another. The audience imposes different standards in science than it does in religion, for example.

These burdens represent the very foundation of argumentation. In fact, an exchange that did not exhibit a recognition of the burdens of proof, rebuttal, and validity could hardly be called argumentation at all. These duties are the cornerstone of what we term argument.

NOTES

1. "Burden," *Oxford English Dictionary* (1933).
2. Stephen Toulmin, *An Examination of the Place of Reason in Ethics* (London: Cambridge Univ. Press, 1950), p. 133.
3. These concepts have technical names: "field-invariant" and "field-dependent." These terms were originally used by Stephen Toulmin in *The Uses of Argument* (London: Cambridge Univ. Press, 1958), p. 15.
4. "Presume," *Oxford English Dictionary* (1933).
5. For a detailed discussion of this view, see Ronald Lee and Karen King Lee, "Reconsidering Whately's Folly: An Emotive Treatment of Presumption," *Central States Speech Journal* 36 (1985): 164–177.
6. Richard Whately, *Elements of Rhetoric*, ed. Douglas Ehninger (Carbondale, IL: Southern Illinois Univ. Press, 1963), p. 112.
7. Charles Arthur Willard, *Argumentation and the Social Grounds of Knowledge* (University, AL: Alabama Univ. Press, 1983), p. 133.
8. See Robert C. Rowland, "The Influence of Purpose on Fields of Argument," *Journal of the American Forensic Association* 18 (1982): 228–245.
9. John Stuart Mill, *On Liberty*, ed. Currin V. Shields (Indianapolis: Bobbs-Merrill, 1956), ch. 2.

10. Charles L. Stevenson, *Ethics and Language* (New Haven: Yale Univ. Press, 1944), p. 152.

11. "Valid (logic)," *Dictionary of Philosophy*, ed. Peter A. Angeles (New York: Harper & Row, 1981).

12. From Adolf Hitler, "Nation and Race," in Vol. I of *Mein Kampf*, trans. Ralph Mannheim (New York: Houghton Mifflin, 1943).

13. Martin Luther King, Jr., "Letter from Birmingham Jail, April 16, 1963," in *Why We Can't Wait* (New York: Harper & Row, 1963). Copyright © 1963 by Martin Luther King, Jr. Reprinted by permission of Harper & Row, Publishers, Inc.

RESOURCES FOR ARGUMENT

If you are a student, you quickly learn that "resource" is one of the educational establishment's favorite buzz words. Test scores are falling because schools "lack resources." Administrators are hired who can "manage resources." Instructors are told they are important because they are in charge of the nation's most important "resources" in the title of this section. Somehow "Assets sources."

We hate mind-numbing bureaucratic jargon as much as anybody else, but we still decided to use the word "resources" in the title of section two. Somehow "Assets for Argument" seemed too much like the name of a chapter in a bad self-improvement book.

Unlike the bureaucrat, we chose the word "resource" because when coupled with "argument" it conveys precisely what we mean. Argument resources and natural resources are a good deal alike. Both are discovered and both are a means to an end. Geologists search for oil and when they find it they extract it, refine it, and use it to produce energy. Advocates search for lines of argument and corroborating evidence and when they find them they collect them, structure them, and use them to influence audiences.

Each of the four chapters in this section deals with either the discovery, location, or selection of arguments and evidence. Propositions function to send advocates looking for resources in particular directions. Issues narrow the search to critical questions the audience may pose. Selection of specific kinds of data and particular forms of argument are dictated by the variety of circumstances that surround any persuasive effort.

4

TYPES OF PROPOSITIONS

At what has euphemistically been termed "Friday afternoon seminar," graduate students and faculty members traditionally gather over refreshments to discuss the various burning issues of academic life. As critical consumers of argument, we have often noted that these "seminars" are most remarkable for their failure ever to settle any issue. Why would an ostensibly intelligent group of people, repeatedly covering the same ground, have such difficulty in reasoning toward mutually acceptable conclusions?

Once struck by this strange phenomenon, we felt an urge to investigate further and to pay much closer attention to the development of arguments. When we did this, the problem became clear. There was one central difficulty. No one ever knew for sure what proposition was under discussion. But even those who had a glimmering of a possible proposition were frustrated by the furious switching of topics during the course of the proceedings.

When we pointed this out to our colleagues, we expected them to be grateful for our offering of wisdom and act in ways consistent with our findings. Surprisingly, they seemed little interested in our observations and continued on as unproductively as ever. We now suspect that we have either misinterpreted the purpose of the "seminars" or not taken sufficient account of the effect of the refreshments.

THE FUNCTIONS OF PROPOSITIONS

You probably understand quite well the function of a business or sexual proposition, but may not have nearly as clear a sense of the function of a proposition in argumentation. As you may have gathered from our story of the Friday seminars, a proposition is the point to be discussed or maintained in argument. Usually, the proposition is stated in sentence form at the outset.

The first function of a proposition is to *specify the point of discussion*. It tells the disputants precisely the topic upon which their arguments will focus. In a court of criminal law, this function is fulfilled by the reading of the charges. After this is done, the prosecution, the defendant, the judge, and the jury are all aware of precisely what is to be contested. In candidate debates for political office, everyone understands very well that the overriding proposition is who is best suited for this office. More specific propositions, the issues of the campaign, are debated in order to help the voters ultimately decide the larger question. In formal meetings, the agenda serves the purpose of announcing the propositions that those attending will take up and act upon.

Propositions serve a second function by specifying the *kind of question* under dispute. You may recall that in Chapter One we described the elements of the argumentative situation. One element of the situation was the "topic." We briefly introduced different topic forms. In this chapter, we will take up the three types of topics in considerably greater detail. But for now it is sufficient to note that the second function of a proposition is to specify whether the dispute is essentially over a question of fact, value, or policy.

Third, propositions in more formal settings *assign obligations* to those upholding or opposing the proposition. In other words, the topic determines the affirmative and negative representatives. In a court of law, the charges label one party the prosecution and the other the defense. In addition, these assignments provide one side with the burden of proof and the other with the presumption. Beyond these general assignments of burdens, a whole host of other rules may be invoked. In court, for example, the prosecution is allowed to speak both first and last.

Finally, propositions function to *instruct audiences*. The proposition makes clear what effect the disputants expect to bring about in the audience. Legislative debates in Congress dispute propositions that make clear to the audience that the desired effect is a vote up or down on a specific bill. The charges in criminal cases make clear to the audience (jury) that a vote of guilty or not guilty is expected. A properly worded proposition crystallizes the arguers' end and, consequently, the specific effect they hope to realize in the audience.

KINDS OF PROPOSITIONS

Traditionally, argumentation theorists have identified three types of propositions: fact, value, and policy. These propositional types are distinguished by what they ask the audience to affirm. A proposition of fact requests that the audience affirm a particular *state of affairs*; a proposition of value asks the audience to affirm an *evaluation*; and a proposition of policy asks the audience to approve some *action*.

In what follows, each general propositional type is detailed. First, the defining characteristics of each type are illustrated. The ability to distinguish among the three types of propositions is essential for effective argument. Second, within the broad general categories of propositions there are particular kinds of fact, value, and policy proposi-

positions there are particular kinds of fact, value, and policy propositions. Each subclassification presents special possibilities to users of
argument.

PROPOSITIONS OF FACT

A proposition of fact asks the audience to affirm a particular state of
affairs. A more precise conception of what it means to "affirm a state
of affairs" is gained by examining four different forms of factual propositions. Please examine the following statements:

1. Intelligent life exists in other places in the universe.
2. The United States' provision of medical treatment for the Shah
   was the cause of the Iranian hostage crisis.
3. The movie *Deep Throat* is legally obscene.
4. An effective vaccine to combat AIDS will be developed within
   the next five years.

Proposition 1 asserts *existence*. It states that intelligent life does
exist somewhere else besides earth. This first example represents the
most fundamental factual issue. Before any additional issues can be
resolved, we first must determine whether we are speaking of a real
phenomenon. For example, in a murder trial the first order of business is the establishment of the *corpus delecti*. If there is no reason to
believe that someone died, then there is little point in continuing the
prosecution.

Proposition 2 asserts a *causal* relationship. The audience is asked to
agree that our government's willingness to provide medical treatment
to the Shah precipitated the taking of American hostages in Iran. A
cause-effect relationship asserts that one fact (medical treatment for
the Shah) produced another fact (taking of American hostages). Again
to use a legal analogy, the second item that must be established in a
murder trial is the cause of death. Unless the prosecution can establish
that the deceased died by other than natural causes, then there can be
no justification for prosecution.

Proposition 3 asserts *classification*. It asks the audience to assent
to the fact that the movie *Deep Throat* fits the criteria outlined in the
statutes defining obscenity. To return to our murder trial, the prosecutor must establish that the deceased died in a manner consistent with
the legal definition of homicide. If in fact death occurred but it is
classifiable as an accident, a suicide, or an act of self-defense, then the
state has no cause to bring a homicide indictment.

Proposition 4 asserts the *occurrence* of a future condition. The
advocate of the proposition asks the audience to believe that in the
next five years medical researchers will develop an effective vaccine
against Acquired Immune Deficiency Syndrome. In our murder trial,
the issue of future occurrence would arise in considerations of bail.

Judges must decide whether the defendant is likely to flee the jurisdiction and not return for trial. Judges who make a determination that the defendant is likely to flee either deny bail altogether or set a very high bond.

In sum, a proposition of fact is defined as a statement that may be affirmed or denied through tests of existence, causality, classification, or occurrence.[1] In Chapter Five, we take up the issues that adhere to each of these types of factual propositions.

PROPOSITIONS OF VALUE

Propositions of value ask the audience to make judgments of worth. Values deal with evaluations of good and bad, right and wrong, desirable and undesirable, ugliness and beauty, and so forth. Value propositions have proven the most theoretically troublesome for argumentation scholars because value propositions often resemble fact and policy propositions.

For example, arguers may discuss the existence of a value, the reason (cause) for the value existing, the classification of a phenomenon under a set of value standards, and may predict the occurrence of a value judgment. Actually many of these circumstances are instances of propositions of fact that have values as their subject matter. Consider these examples:

1. Americans value education.
2. Lack of effective contraception was responsible for the moral sanction against premarital sex.
3. Lying to your parents is wrong.
4. The Catholic Church will never regard abortion as moral.

As these statements are currently worded, three of the four propositions are factual. But all of them, with very minor changes in wording or interpretation, could be value propositions.

Proposition 1 states that "Americans value education." This, of course, could be fully determined by an investigation of the facts. We might turn to surveys of American attitudes toward education, examine the amount of resources Americans expend on education, and so forth. This proposition could be wholly established by such procedures. However, if we were to make subtle changes in the wording, it would be transformed into a proposition of value. Consider the following:

1a. Americans ought to value education.
1b. American education is valuable.

Factual material alone cannot establish either proposition 1a or 1b. The facts concerning how Americans do feel about education will not establish how they "ought" to regard education or whether education is "valuable." Facts may help us decide how we ought to regard an object, but they will never tell the whole story. Saying something "is valuable" cannot be established solely by facts. We cannot use any test that will reveal the element of "valuable" in an object. A value is different than some element that we can test through our senses.

Proposition 2 asks the audience to agree that "Lack of effective contraception was responsible for the moral sanction against premarital sex." This is a straightforward proposition of fact that asserts a cause-effect relationship. The cause of the moral sanction against premarital sex was the historic "lack of effective contraception." This is a question that historians and anthropologists are quite capable of addressing. It is typical of the kind of factual questions that guide these disciplines. Again, this proposition can be transformed into a proposition of value with a few word changes:

2a. With the availability of contraception premarital sex ought to be morally acceptable.
2b. Effective contraception makes premarital sex morally acceptable.

Proposition 2a, through the introduction of the word "ought," cannot be established merely by the presence of facts. Facts may establish what "is" but never wholly answer the question what "ought" to be. "Oughts" require evaluative judgments.

Proposition 2b is a closer case. If we interpret the statement as meaning that effective contraception has made most people judge premarital sex as morally acceptable, then it is a factual proposition asserting a causal relationship. But if it is a statement that we interpret as meaning that effective contraception "ought" to make premarital sex morally acceptable then it is a value proposition. The present wording of proposition 2b does not make clear which interpretation is intended.

Proposition 3 reads that "Lying to your parents is wrong." This is a value proposition although it closely resembles the factual proposition of classification. Examine the following two alterations in the statement:

3a. Most people regard children lying to their parents as wrong.
3b. In this culture children lying to their parents is regarded as wrong.

Propositions 3a and 3b make clear that the act of children "lying to parents" is classified as "wrong" by "most people" or by "this culture." These statements are subject to tests of facticity. If you were a basketball referee and saw a player in possession of the ball walk without dribbling, you would have to call a penalty. Your thought processes would involve considering the criteria for advancing the ball set down in the rules and then determining whether this particular incident is classifiable as a violation. This same procedure could be used to establish 3a and 3b.

However, the original proposition 3 does not ask for a simple classification. It may be interpreted as asserting that the audience "ought" to regard "lying to parents" as wrong. The statement of the moral rule has power because it advises the audience about how they "ought" to regard this practice.

Finally, proposition 4 asserts that "The Catholic Church will never regard abortion as moral." If this proposition is regarded as a prediction of the future attitude of the Church, it is a clear case of a factual proposition of occurrence. Examine a rewording of this statement:

4a. The Catholic Church ought never to regard abortion as moral.

This wording of proposition 4a makes it clear that the audience is being asked to make a value judgment about the Church's future moral direction. This is no longer a prediction of a future state of affairs but a moral recommendation.

In summary, all value propositions *recommend an evaluation* to the audience. This is true whether the proposition is worded with "is," such as "Education is valuable" and "Lying to your parents is wrong," or with "ought," such as "Premarital sex ought to be morally permissible" and the "Catholic Church ought never to regard abortion as moral."

PROPOSITIONS OF POLICY

The advocate of a proposition of policy requests the audience's approval of some *future action*. This type of proposition guides deliberations any time decisions about courses of action must be made. The legislature debates policy when it considers the merits of future appropriations, the corporate board when it argues over the wisdom of selling off a division, and the English Department's faculty when it discusses changes in the curriculum.

The object of approval is always future rather than past action. Passing judgment on past action is an evaluation and thus constitutes a proposition of value. Consider the contrast between these two propositions:

1. Congress should cut the deficit this year by $40 billion.
2. Congress acted wisely in passing the Gramm-Rudman-Hollings deficit reduction measure.

The first proposition asks the audience to approve of a future congressional action. The second statement asks the audience to positively judge the wisdom of earlier congressional action. The first is a proposition of policy and the second a proposition of value.

A properly constructed policy proposition contains phrases designating an *agent*, a *verb approving future action*, and a *specific action*. In proposition 1, "Congress" is the agent, "should" is the verb approving future action, and "cut the deficit this year by $40 billion" is the phrase naming the specific action.

In this example, the audience is asked only to approve of an action. In some propositions of policy, the audience itself is asked to take action. A variation on proposition 1 illustrates this change in agent:

1a. You should write letters urging the Congress to cut the deficit this year by $40 billion.

In this variation, "you" is the agent, "should" remains the verb, and the action is now specified as "writ[ing] letters urging the Congress. . . . " Audience members are directed to do more than approve of the action in variation 1a, they are asked to engage in letter writing. In both cases 1 and 1a the statements are considered propositions of policy. Although only variation 1a requires some specific action on the part of the audience, both propositions focus the arguments of the advocate on the wisdom of taking some future action. As you will discover in Chapter Five, the issues adhering to propositions 1 and 1a are the same.

In conclusion, propositions of policy contain an agent, a verb approving of future action, and a specific plan of action. Whenever audience members are asked to implement a policy or pass judgment on some other agent's future action, the focus of debate is a proposition of policy.

FACT, VALUE, AND POLICY CONFUSION

In any protracted discussion on whatever proposition, fact, value, and policy questions will arise. A proposition is the central question in any dispute. The presence of subsidiary issues that are of a different type than the central question does not affect categorization of propositions.

For example, to pass any reasonable judgment on the wisdom of congressional action to cut the budget, the speaker would have to establish facts (economic projections of the deficit, economic effects of the deficit, etc.) and make value judgments (Are the negative consequences of the deficit more or less important than the negative consequences of budget cuts?). However, the defining feature of this dispute is the request for audience approval of a future action. These other issues are merely steps on the way to making a case for the policy to the audience.

The advocate will always find subsidiary issues of a kind different from the main question when arguing for a proposition. Similar issues are discoverable in fact and value propositions. When constructing a proposition, always keep in the foreground of your thinking the request that the advocate is making of the audience. The desired audience response defines propositional types.

Advocates' failure to focus on desired audience response, and the subsequent confusion of propositional types, has polluted a good deal of our public argument. For example, the seeming inability of the pro-life and pro-choice forces to maintain a focus on the overriding question is largely a result of a misinterpretation of fact and value propositions.

The controversy surrounding fetal status has confounded fact and value propositions. One side has focused on the issue of whether "life begins at conception." The other side has focused on "fetal viability outside the womb." These factual contentions are only of interest to the extent that they help address the question of "humanness." At what point in the development of *Homo sapiens* are we justified in applying the label "human"? Of course, the notion of humanness is not a question of fact but an attribution of value. Humanness refers to certain qualities and not merely some argument about organic and inorganic matter or some facts about survival outside the womb. This does not mean that evidence of life and fetal viability may not be used to make an argument about humanness, but that they are subordinate to the central proposition that requests the audience assent to a value claim.

Likewise, the pornography debate is confused by the confounding of fact and policy. The public is subjected to endless discussions of what the social scientific literature has to say about the effects of pornography. With the recent release of the so-called Meese Commission Report, the newspapers were filled with charges and counter charges from members of the Commission who vehemently disagreed with each other about the proper assessment of the research.

Of course, this factual issue of the cause-effect relationship between exposure to pornography and antisocial behavior is important to making an intelligent decision about policy. But the debate has focused so exclusively on this issue that other, perhaps more fundamental, issues are pushed out of the public discussion. This is after all essentially an argument about policy. The Justice Department commissioned a report in order to make determinations about how the government ought to deal with pornography. Because public attention has focused on the social scientific argument about pornography's effects, deliberation about the consequences of any policy that restricts freedom of speech has often been shortchanged.

Many of the advocates in the evolution versus creationism debate have been unwilling to focus on the same proposition. The evolutionists have tried to debate the proposition "Resolved: So-called creationist science is not a science." They outline the presuppositions of science and argue that creationist perspectives fail to meet these criteria.

On the other hand, the supporters of creationism have focused not on the issue of what is a science but have maintained that inclusion of a *Genesis* perspective on the development of humankind is morally right. In other words, the evolutionists are supporting a factual proposition of classification and the creationists are supporting a proposition of value. It is very difficult to make headway in a dispute if the two sides are focusing on different propositions.

INTERPRETING THE PROPOSITION

The proposition lays down the topic over which the dispute will take place, but it does not assure that the audience will adopt a single interpretation. Obviously, advocates who can persuade the audience to "see" the proposition in their terms have a greater chance of achieving a desired end.

At first glance, this problem of propositional interpretation may seem relatively unimportant. However, a great many disputes turn on the definition of key terms and resultant audience interpretation of the topic. In all domains of argument, disputes concerning the proper understanding of terms occur. For example, legislators argue about issues of jurisdiction all the time. If the question was properly interpreted, should the bill be committed to this committee or that one? Is this a legislative issue or a judicial one? Does the Executive have the power to address this question or does Congress have an obligation to consider the action? Jurisdictional judgments turn on definitions of the proposition's key terms.

Besides jurisdictional problems, definitional disputes often determine the scope of a dispute. A few years ago, a particularly thorny issue of interpretation arose that illustrates the relationship between definition and propositional scope. The national high school debate resolution called for the affirmative to uphold a proposition that asked for a significant alteration in the manner in which the United States "selected" presidential and vice-presidential candidates. The verb "select" is such a simple word that it is hard to believe so much fuss was raised by opposing teams disputing the legitimacy of the affirmative's use of the term. Some people held that "select" and "elect" were synonymous terms and others were adamant in maintaining that the two words labeled distinctly different processes. Those committed to the second view said that "select" designates the nominating process and "elect" specifies the process of choosing between candidates in the general election. As you can imagine, the first interpretation allowed those upholding the resolution a good deal more leeway in their construction of cases than did the second interpretation. If you are debating on the negative, it is not to your advantage to give the affirmative any additional room to maneuver.

We will take up the specific issues and argumentative strategies of definition in Chapter Five. It is enough here to become aware that agreement on the content of a proposition does not assure a common understanding of the proposition's terms. How particular words are understood by the audience is often the key to the outcome of a dispute.

CONCLUSIONS

To reasonably pursue arguing for any cause, the advocate must begin with a clear understanding of the central question in dispute. Public and private controversies are often muddled by a failure of the advocates to make the issue in contention clear to the audience.

The proposition is a statement that *specifies the point of discussion*. Not only do propositions specify subject matter, but they serve the second function of designating the *kind of question* under dispute. Third, propositions *assign obligations* to the participants in the argument. It places advocates on one side or the other, assigns argumentative burdens, and often invokes particular procedural rules. Finally, propositions function to *instruct audiences*. The proposition makes clear the effect the arguer seeks from the audience.

There are three kinds of propositions: *fact, value,* and *policy.* These three types are distinguished by the different effect each seeks from the audience. Propositions of fact ask the audience to affirm a particular state of affairs. Propositions of value ask the audience to recommend an evaluation or make a judgment of worth. Propositions of policy ask the audience to take action or to approve of a future action.

The distinctions among these three propositional types are subject to confusion. In any dispute about policy, for example, issues of fact and value will be raised. In any argument over facts, issues of value and policy will become pertinent. Propositions designate the overriding question that the participants in argument hope to resolve, but this does not mean that each subsidiary issue in the dispute will follow the form of the core proposition.

Finally, we advised students of argumentation to carefully consider issues of definition and interpretation. Agreement on the proposition does not necessarily entail common interpretation. Thorny issues of definition often determine which side will prevail with the audience.

Cogent argument is only possible when the propositional content is specified, propositional type is understood, and key propositional terms are clearly interpreted for the audience. These common sense rules of argumentation are frequently violated and controversies devolve from reasoned exchange to emotional shouting matches. Without a clear starting point very little of value is ever accomplished.

NOTES

1. See Wil A. Linkugel, R. R. Allen, and Richard L. Johannesen, *Contemporary American Speeches*, 5th ed. (Dubuque, IA: Kendall/Hunt, 1982), pp. 101–110.

5

DISCOVERY OF ISSUES

The classical writers were concerned with developing guidelines for locating useful arguments and evidence. Aristotle labeled this process of location rhetorical "discovery" and later Roman authors used the Latin term *inventio* or "invention."[1] Obviously, we do not consider the terms "discover" and "invent" equivalent. "To discover" is "to find" and "to invent" is "to create." Electricity was discovered but the light bulb was invented.

In this chapter and the next, we purposely use the term "discovery." Issues and data are found rather than created by an inspired imagination. If issues and data were created anew each time someone engaged in argument, then the enterprise of writing a text on argumentation would be foolhardy. But if location is the essential process, then instruction in argument and evidence can serve as a useful map directing advocates to appropriate materials.

The present chapter is taken up with two tasks. First, we outline an audience-centered philosophy of rhetorical discovery. Second, we explain the concept of issue and discuss the means of locating the issues in any given situation.

APPROACH TO RHETORICAL DISCOVERY

Whatever else the term "rhetoric" might imply, it invariably involves an audience. If you examine the adjective "rhetorical," you will discover that its meaning in any adjective-noun pair suggests a relationship to audience. Consider these combinations: rhetorical effects, rhetorical theory, rhetorical event.

The phrase "rhetorical effects" refers to the effect a given discourse has on an audience. The adjective-noun combination "rhetorical theory" refers to a theoretical construct that explains the relationship between symbol use and audience response. A "rhetorical event" is a situation in which symbols are used to influence an audience.

Without further belaboring the obvious, *rhetorical discovery is the examination of the audience to locate issues and uncover evidentiary requirements*. The present chapter takes up the discovery of issues and Chapter Six examines the procedures for uncovering evidentiary requirements. But before taking up particular strategies of discovery, a general overview of our approach to the process is in order. We proceed by contrast, beginning with those approaches we do not endorse.

The first approach is familiar to all instructors of introductory courses in speaking or writing. Our colleagues affectionately refer to this as the *Time* magazine philosophy of rhetorical discovery. The student most likely to employ this technique often comes to the instructor on the day before the assignment is due and says "I don't know what to talk (or write) about." The following day the student shows up and delivers a speech on (or turns a paper in about) the deployment of Cruise Missiles in Western Europe. When asked why he decided to talk about Cruise Missiles, he replies "I was flipping through *Time* and this topic caught my eye."

The second approach, enjoying an equally infamous reputation among instructors, is the personal hobby perspective to rhetorical discovery. Typically, this student has been playing in a drum and bugle corps since she was eight years old and has decided to tell the class about the raging controversy surrounding the changing of the rules in drum and bugle competition.

The third approach, somewhat more admirable than the first two, is the self-proclaimed expert slant on rhetorical discovery. Advocates committed to this procedure have gone out and mastered as much of the material surrounding the subject as they can. When presenting their findings, they fill their presentations with an impressive array of technical evidence and arguments. They are impressed by their own command of the material and are unconcerned about the audience's ability to comprehend their presentation.

I am sure we all know people who are ready with a bundle of superficial knowledge useful for making small talk at cocktail parties (*Time* magazine approach), people who are completely absorbed by a narrow area of knowledge of little interest to anyone else (hobby perspective), and people who delight in impressing listeners with their knowledge but have little regard for the art of thoughtful explanation (self-proclaimed experts). All of these procedures ultimately fail because they do not begin with a careful consideration of the audience. After all, the purpose of argumentation is effective justification. If advocates do not understand their audiences, their attempts at justification will surely be ineffective.

What does it mean to ground the process of rhetorical discovery in the audience? It means that the advocate begins *not* by asking "what can be said about this topic," but by inquiring "what does the audience require be said about this topic." This change appears as a small wording change, but it is a difference that makes all the difference. Our three students, using the wrong approaches to rhetorical discovery, forgot that argumentation is audience-centered.

Remember that concern for the audience does not entail a slavish commitment to merely tell the audience what it wants to hear. Argumentation is concerned with *effective* and *worthy* justification. Rhetorical discovery is the process of locating arguments and data that will move the audience and move them with good reasons. These good and effective reasons are found in the issues flowing from any given controversy.

ISSUES

The participants in a dispute are ultimately disagreeing about the wisdom of maintaining the proposition. But within the framework of taking sides on the proposition, a number of other levels of disagreement occur. Advocates clash on arguments, issues, and stock issues. The argument is the most specific and the stock issue is the most general point of contention.

The relationship among these three components of contention are related in this sense: Stock issues adhere to all propositions of a given kind and are useful guides to the discovery of issues; issues are vital questions in a controversy that are answered by the use of arguments. Notice that *issue* is the concept that is present in both clauses. Stock issues help us locate the issues. Arguments support our position on the issues.

Issues are the vital points that the advocate must establish to justify adoption of the proposition.[2] Often issues are thought of as questions. The supporter of the proposition must answer yes to these questions. If the audience says no to any of these key questions, the proposition is not justified. These key questions or issues change with circumstances. The audience, occasion, topic, advocates, and propositional type all influence the development of issues.

In the way of example, ponder this all too familiar debate proposition:

Resolved: that the United States should abolish the Electoral College.

Now consider this list of possible issues adhering to the proposition:

1. Does the electoral college undermine the principle of one person, one vote?
2. Is the original purpose for the Electoral College now outdated?
3. Is there any real danger of the Electoral College overturning the popular vote?
4. Is there any real danger of deal making in an election brokered in the House of Representatives?
5. Is the charge that abolition of the Electoral College will decrease minority representation illusionary?

In any given dispute over this proposition, one or more of these questions may become vital to the audience's judgment of the wisdom of abolishing the Electoral College. For example, in the late 1960s and early 1970s the presence of Alabama's Governor George Wallace in the presidential sweepstakes fostered a good deal of argument over issues number 4 and 5. For certain audiences, the possibility of all three candidates receiving fewer than fifty percent of the vote in the Electoral College was acutely troublesome. Those groups concerned with civil rights gains feared the kind of deal George Wallace might cut in a brokered election. Some speculated that he would throw his support to one of the major party candidates in exchange for a roll back in civil rights gains. Yet, others argued that the presence of significant minority populations in key electoral vote states increased black political power beyond the absolute numbers of black voters. At this time, and with audiences seriously committed to civil rights reform, questions 4 and 5 required an affirmative answer for the advocate seeking to establish the wisdom of adopting a policy that ended the Electoral College.

Obviously, for other audiences less concerned with the practical politics of civil rights reform other questions might become issues. For those audiences animated by a commitment to participatory democracy, questions 1 and 3 would constitute the vital issues.

Finally, for those audiences who have adopted traditionally conservative values, question 2 might serve as the deciding point. Conservatives believe that institutions are built up by the slow and cautious move of historical change. People ought to act cautiously when tampering with the product of history. If the advocate can establish that the historical justification for the Electoral College is no longer of any relevance, then the chances of convincing the audience look bright.

In sum, issues are the vital points that the advocate must establish in justifying the proposition. These issues are rhetorical because they change in relationship to the audience and other attendant circumstances.

STOCK ISSUES

Since the earliest works on rhetoric, analysts of argument have searched for aides to the discovery of vital issues. Although most of these schemes have long since been abandoned, one that remains an essential tool of the advocate is the use of *stock issues*. Stock issues "are not the real issues in any particular proposition, but rather a formulation of questions that may prove helpful in finding the real issues."[3] Different sets of stock issues apply to the various propositional types. There are fixed stock issues for fact, value, and policy. We might term the stock issues general points of contention that always adhere to a given propositional type.

In the following sections, we enumerate the stock issues for each propositional type. Each stock issue is accompanied by illustrations of its application for the discovery of actual issues in a real dispute.

STOCK ISSUES IN PROPOSITIONS OF FACT

In Chapter Four, we contended that a proposition of fact is a statement that asks the audience to affirm a particular *state of affairs*. In order to illustrate the use of stock issues, we ask you to reconsider our examples of factual propositions:

1. Intelligent life exists in other places in the universe.
2. The United States' provision of medical treatment for the Shah was the cause of the Iranian hostage crisis.
3. The movie *Deep Throat* is legally obscene.
4. An effective vaccine to combat AIDS will be developed within the next five years.

Each example represents one of the four kinds of factual propositions: existence, cause, classification, and occurrence. Yet, despite these differences of type, the same two stock issues adhere to all propositions of fact. To put it another way, an audience of reasonable people will always be concerned with the answers to these broad questions.

Stock Issue One: *What are the reliable criteria for judging the facticity of the statement?* These criteria are *field-dependent*. The criteria for judgment of proposition 1 will of necessity involve standards of the physical and biological sciences. A list of specific issues might include:

1a. Are there reliable biological criteria for determining life?
1b. Are there reliable psychobiological criteria for determining intelligent life?
1c. Are there reliable criteria for determining the conditions necessary for sustaining intelligent life?
1d. Are there reliable statistical procedures for determining the likelihood that such conditions exist and that they would spawn intelligent life?

Notice that the content of the proposition directs the audience to request that advocates engage certain scientific criteria in the judgment of the proposition. The list 1a through 1d is made up of specific issues, but it was discovered by addressing the general stock issue.

This stock issue can generate field-dependent criteria for each of the other sample propositions. Consider the following issues for proposition 2:

2a. Are there reliable historical criteria for determining the motives of the hostage takers?

2b. Are other causal explanations convincingly confounded by the historical evidence?

Proposition 2 is slightly simpler than proposition 1 because it calls for fewer levels of proof. This causal assertion is placed in the domain of history. Historical tests of argument and evidence are demanded for the establishment of the proposition.

Examine these issues for proposition 3:

3a. Is there a clear definition of legal obscenity?
3b. Can the legal definition of obscenity be reliably applied to particular cases?

Finally, consider these issues for proposition 4:

4a. Are the roadblocks to an AIDS vaccine theoretically surmountable?
4b. Are sufficient resources devoted to AIDS research to allow meeting the five year deadline?
4c. Are there reliable criteria for predicting the pace of medical advances?

Once the advocate has established the presence of reliable criteria for judgment, a second stock issue is operative. Stock Issue Two: *Does the present case meet the reliable criteria of facticity?* In other words, the criteria generated by stock issue one create the key issues the advocate must address under stock issue two. Let's return to our examples in order to demonstrate this process.

Proposition 1 read: "Intelligent life exists in other places in the universe." Under the first stock issue, we located criteria from the physical and biological sciences for the reasonable determination of the factuality of this statement. Now the task is to determine whether this proposition can meet these standards of judgment. For this purpose, consider issue 1c: "Are there reliable criteria for determining the conditions necessary for sustaining intelligent life?" Admitting a lack of scientific sophistication, we assume the following issues would become important:

1-1. Are there other planets that have the desirable mix of atmospheric conditions necessary to sustain intelligent life?
1-2. Are there other planets that have the temperature range necessary to support intelligent life?
1-3. Are there other planets with sufficient water and soil conditions to support the production of food?

Statements 1-1 through 1-3 may represent the criteria that scientists might pose when attempting to judge the truth value of proposition 1. The first stock issue locates reliable criteria for judgment and the second applies that criteria.

The same procedure would apply to each of our propositions. To adequately illustrate without belaboring the obvious, we will consider one additional example. Consider the following issues related to proposition 3. Presently, the courts have employed the criterion of "contemporary community standards" to determine obscenity. Consequently, the key stock issue two question would become:

3-1. Does the film *Deep Throat* violate contemporary community standards in this jurisdiction?

In sum, stock issue one is a guide to the location of *reliable criteria for determining facticity* and stock issue two is a *guide to the application of criteria to the particular case*. The issues that each stock issue generates are field-dependent. In other words, the subject matter of the proposition directs the arguer to particular domains of knowledge. The presence of stock issues is field-invariant. Each factual proposition will elicit the same issue forms even though the content of each issue will depend on the particular subject matter.

STOCK ISSUES IN PROPOSITIONS OF VALUE

The stock issues of value are almost identical in form to the stock issues of fact. Rather than ask the audience to affirm a particular state of affairs, a proposition of value asks the audience to affirm an *evaluation*. Consequently, stock issue one asks *what are the reliable criteria for evaluation* and stock issue two asks *does this particular case meet the criteria of evaluation*.

For the purpose of illustration consider these two propositions of value:

1. American education is valuable.
2. Katherine's use of another student's work is morally wrong.

First, what are the reliable criteria for evaluation? To address this stock issue in proposition 1, we must ask what criteria our culture uses to determine if something is "valuable." We are immediately confronted with a problem because "valuable" is such a general term. Valuable in what way? For instance, one may inquire whether education is "economically valuable" or "psychologically valuable" or "individually valuable." Each of these senses of "valuable" would generate a different list of *reliable criteria*. A determination of the most important sense of "valuable" would depend on the audience and attendant circumstances of the dispute. For some audiences and occasions, the economic sense of valuableness would be most relevant and for other occasions the psychological value of education would work best. Examine these criteria for the economic value of education:

1a. Economically valuable activities raise individual income.
1b. Economically valuable activities spur economic growth.

Now examine proposition 2. Notice that the proposition directs us to issues of "plagiarism." The criteria for passing a judgment of "morally wrong" in plagiarism cases are set down legally in academic settings by university handbooks. In this case the concept of "morally wrong" has been defined by specific field-dependent standards of conduct. In the 1985 edition of the Indiana University *Academic Handbook*, the following passage appears:

> Honesty requires that any ideas or materials taken from another source for either written or oral use must be fully acknowledged. Offering the work of someone else as one's own is plagiarism. The language or ideas thus taken from another may range from isolated formulas, sentences, or paragraphs to entire articles copied from books, periodicals, speeches, or the writings of other students. The offering of materials assembled or collected by others in the form of projects or collections without acknowledgment also is considered plagiarism. Any student who fails to give credit for ideas or materials taken from another source is guilty of plagiarism. (Faculty Council, May 2, 1961)

The criteria for evaluation of "Katherine's" actions as "morally wrong" is clearly spelled out in this passage of the Indiana University *Academic Handbook*. Two particular passages are relevant to stock issue one:

2a. Plagiarism is morally wrong.
2b. Failure to fully acknowledge the work of other students is plagiarism.

Criterion 2a specifies that the act of plagiarism is sufficient to earn the label "morally wrong." The additional criterion 2b provides a more particular standard for determining what constitutes plagiarism.

Stock issue two asks: "Does this particular statement meet the criteria of evaluation?" For proposition 1 the accompanying issues are the following:

1-1. Does a higher level of education raise individual income?
1-2. Do higher aggregate levels of education spur economic growth?

For proposition 2 there is only a single issue relevant to addressing the second stock issue:

2-1. Did Katherine fail to fully acknowledge the work of another student?

Each proposition of value demands the location of reliable and relevant criteria for evaluation and then the application of those criteria to the object of argument. Value propositions often challenge the advocate to locate field-dependent criteria of judgment. Sometimes various fields have differing perspectives on values. The arguer is charged with deciding which set of criteria is most relevant for a given audience and occasion.

STOCK ISSUES OF PROPOSITIONS OF POLICY

Propositions of policy ask the audience to approve some *future action*. Unlike propositions of fact and value, stock issues of policy have a unique set of standards for the judgment of action. *The four stock issues are termed ill, blame, cure, and cost.*

We will use the following two examples of policy propositions to illustrate the stock issues:

1. Congress should adopt a comprehensive program of national health insurance.
2. The states should establish tougher penalties for drunken driving.

ILL. The stock issue of ill asks the question, "Is there a significant reason for change?" A prudent person would not approve a future action if there was no compelling reason to take that action. Every change involves some risk and without any felt difficulty in present circumstances there is little reason to approve the proposition.

Establishing a reason for change typically involves both issues of quality and quantity. Is there some difficulty that is qualitatively significant? Is there some difficulty that is quantitatively significant? Something may occur frequently but the effect is of little consequence. On the other hand, a difficulty of great proportion may occur so infrequently that it does not justify action.

With these considerations in mind, examine specific ill issues for proposition 1:

1a. High medical bills affect thousands of Americans every year.
1b. High medical bills may result in individual bankruptcy.
1c. Cost frequently prevents people from seeking needed medical care.
1d. Delayed medical care increases mortality rates.

Notice that issue 1a describes the widespread effect of high medical bills and 1b details the severity of the effect. Similarly, issue 1c notes that people are frequently deterred form seeking medical care because of cost and 1d lays out the severe consequences of delaying treatment.

A list of ill issues relevant to proposition 2 would take the same form:

2a. Thousands of people drive drunk every day.
2b. Drunk driving is the leading cause of traffic fatalities.

The first statement deals with the pervasiveness of drunk driving and the second with the severity of the consequences of this illegal behavior. Given sufficient supporting data to establish 2a and 2b, the audience would have reason to feel uncomfortable with the present situation. These claims would justify an affirmative answer to the question, "Is there a significant reason to change?"

BLAME. The stock issue of blame inquires, "Is there an inherent reason to change?" "Inherency" is not a term we hear frequently in daily conversation. *If the difficulty is inherent, then present arrangements are incapable of alleviating the ill.*

Several different conditions may account for the inherent nature of an ill. First, structural flaws in current arrangements may preclude alleviation of the problem. Second, present policy may be capable of alleviating the ill but only by incurring unacceptably high costs. Third, present policy may foster attitudes that preclude alleviation of the problem.

Return to our two sample propositions of policy. Not every problem persists for the same reason. Some policies have structural flaws, others work only with unacceptably high costs, and others are resisted by those who are key to their successful operation. At least one example of each type of inherency can be found in our two illustrations:

1e. The third party nature of insurance assures inadequate coverage of catastrophic medical bills.
1f. The premiums necessary to adequately cover catastrophic medical bills would impose an unacceptably high cost on employers.
2c. Judges are consistently unwilling to send drunk drivers to jail.

Condition 1e argues that the present private insurance system is structurally flawed. Because insurers can neither control the price nor the demand for health care, they must impose deductibles, co-payments, customary fee schedules, and payment caps in order to limit their liability. As long as these features exist, catastrophic medical bills will continue to plague consumers.

Condition 1f contends that even if private insurers could provide truly comprehensive coverage, the price of such coverage would drain the resources employers have devoted to the provision of fringe benefits. American companies would sustain devastating economic losses if they were forced to pay for such coverage. Here the advocate is arguing that the present system is structurally capable of meeting the problem, but the consequences make this approach unwise.

Condition 2c explains why the problem of drunk driving continues to persist. Although tough penalties for driving under the influence might work, judges are unwilling to impose harsh sentences on a consistent basis. Here the argument is that the nature of the system permits the attitudes of individuals to preclude solution.

Cure. The cure issue asks, "Is there a solution?" In other words, is there a plan that will alleviate the ill? Obviously any such plan must overcome the problems that have plagued current policy. The proposal must not fall prey to the same difficulties discussed under the stock issue of blame. The advocate ought to present a plan sufficiently detailed to allow meaningful audience evaluation and then demonstrate how the new proposal will overcome the old problems.

In our two examples, the advocate might propose the following:

1h. A federally funded national health insurance program would alleviate the effects of catastrophic medical bills. A full-blown proposal would specify costs, funding, items covered, and forms of administration.

2d. Mandatory jail sentences for drunk driving would reduce traffic fatalities. The presentation of such a plan should include length of terms, the options for fulfilling the sentence, and the manner of dealing with cost and administration.

Plan 1h argues that the problems of private health insurance could be overcome by instituting national health insurance. The advocate may provide evidence of successful foreign experience with national health insurance to demonstrate the policy's viability.

Plan 2d provides for a mandatory sentencing structure that would remove the discretion of judges. The attitudes of individual judges could no longer prevent the imposition of tough penalties.

Cost. The stock issue of cost asks, "Does the policy have more advantages than disadvantages?" In other words, the audience wants to know whether the future action is going to bring new undesirable consequences that outweigh the old problems. The government, for example, could probably eliminate the problem of littering by imposing ten year jail terms on violators. But the obvious injustice of using such a harsh penalty on such a minor offense would preclude any reasonable audience from approving of any such proposal.

Considering the proposals for national health insurance and mandatory jail sentences for drunk drivers, what would advocates of these propositions have to establish in order to satisfy the audience on the stock issue of cure? The advocate would have to show that disadvantages to these proposals were less important than the solution of the ill. Look at the following list of possible disadvantages:

1j. National health insurance would necessitate a massive tax increase.

1k. Without the restraint of cost, the demand for health care would overrun the system.

2e. Drunk driving convictions would outstrip available jail space and force judges to release dangerous felons.

2f. Mandatory sentencing precludes careful consideration of individual circumstances and thus ultimately denies justice.

The advocate faced with this array of objections would have to demonstrate either that these consequences would not come about or that their seriousness has been exaggerated. For example, disadvantage 1j might be refuted by suggesting that the federal government's ability to spread the risk over the entire population would actually make the additional individual tax less than average current health insurance premiums.

Disadvantage 1k might be addressed by demonstrating that increased demand for health care has been managed successfully by other countries employing a national health care system. Perhaps evidence could be offered showing that effective screening methods are presently available.

The respondent to disadvantage 2e might argue that drunk drivers are among the most dangerous criminals. In addition, the types of crimes that might be assigned lesser sentences would not constitute the class labeled "dangerous" felonies.

Finally, disadvantage 2f asks the audience to consider two competing senses of justice. The advocate of this proposition might maintain that equality under the law is best served by equality of sentencing and not by making decisions on a case-by-case basis. In addition, despite the attractiveness of considering individual circumstances in principle, in practice this translates into a weak drunk driving policy.

In summary, the successful advocate of a proposition of policy must establish a significant reason for change (ill), the inherent incapacity of present arrangements (blame), the ability of an alternative policy to solve the problem (cure), and, finally, that the advantages of the proposed policy outweigh the disadvantages (cost).

CONCLUSIONS

In this chapter, we outlined a philosophy of rhetorical discovery. From our perspective, *rhetorical discovery is the examination of the audience for the purpose of locating issues and uncovering evidentiary requirements.* This requirement does not imply a slavish commitment merely to tell the audience what it wants to hear. But rather an obligation to tell the audience what it wants and needs to hear in order to make a reasoned judgment.

Issues are the vital points that the advocate must establish to justify adoption of the proposition. These key points change with the audience, occasion, topic, advocates, and propositional type. *Stock issues are general points of contention that always adhere to a given propositional type.* Stock issues are not the real issues, but rather a formulation of questions that may prove helpful in finding the real issues.

There are two stock issues relevant to a proposition of fact. First, *what are the reliable criteria for determining facticity?* Second, *does the present case meet the reliable criteria of facticity?*

There are also two stock issues applicable to propositions of value. First, *what are the reliable criteria of evaluation?* Second, *does the present case meet the criteria of evaluation?*

Issues in propositions of policy are discovered by examining four stock issues: *ill, blame, cure, and cost.* Each stock issue asks a different question. The stock issue of ill inquires, "Is there a significant reason for change?" The stock issue of blame asks, "Is there an inherent reason for change?" The stock issue of cure asks, "Is there a solution?" Finally, the stock issue of cost inquires, "Does the policy have more advantages than disadvantages?"

Discovery of the key issues is decisive in virtually any dispute. Public argument is filled with instances of failure to recognize the key questions and the vital concerns of the audience. Wasting time disputing peripheral issues nearly always assures defeat of an advocate's case.

Former Senator Howard Baker of Tennessee became a national political figure by continuing to press two questions during the course of the Watergate Hearings. "What did the President know and when did he know it?" His public acclaim was well deserved because he did what all skillful advocates must do: Discover the vital issues.

NOTES

1. See Lane Cooper, *The Rhetoric of Aristotle* (Englewood Cliffs, NJ: Prentice-Hall, 1932), p. 7. Aristotle wrote, "So let Rhetoric be defined as the faculty [power] of discovering in the particular case what are the available means of persuasion" (ca. late fourth century B.C.). The rhetorical canon of *inventio* was first used by the anonymous Roman author of *Rhetorica Ad Herrenium* (ca. 85 B.C.).
2. See James H. McBurney and Glen E. Mills, *Argumentation and Debate*, 2d ed. (New York: Macmillan, 1951), pp. 41–46.
3. Ibid., p. 55.

6

DISCOVERY
OF DATA

In Chapter One, we concluded that the study of justification is the province of argumentation. By justification we mean the process of proving or showing something to be just, right, or reasonable. We turn now to the question of what constitutes proof. A dictionary definition of the word "proof" suggests it is "anything serving or tending to establish the truth of something or to convince one of its truth."[1] This definition, especially the last phrase, highlights the variable nature of the notion. Rather than being static, the proof needed to persuade varies with the audience, the topic, the advocate, and the occasion.

Consider a particular case. A recent newspaper article carried the following headline: "Is proving the terror of global nuclear war a waste of time?"[2] The article reported a continuing controversy between strategic military analysts and antinuclear activists over the consequences of nuclear war. Prompted by an earlier study positing the theory that nuclear explosions would result in fires whose thick smoke would prohibit the sun's heat and light from reaching the earth thus lowering temperatures, killing plant life, and leaving us in the grip of a nuclear winter, debate has focused on the technical soundness of the theory as well as its implications for policy making. What constitutes proof differs for the various parties involved in the controversy.

Even though nuclear winter remains a theory, it has been used as proof both for calls for disarmament and reaffirmation of the strength of deterrence. Jonathan Schell states the case for disarmament in his book *The Abolition*. "The very existence of uncertainty about whether or not a holocaust would extinguish our species should lead us to treat the issue morally and politically as though it were a certainty."[3] To Schell and other abolitionists, the threat overrides all other concerns. Rather than risk the possibility of ecological catastrophe, the bomb should be banned.

Strategic military analysts, while claiming the theory is fraught with scientific uncertainty, do not deny nuclear winter is a possibility. They differ with the abolitionists on two key points. First, they doubt the disaster would be total. According to Harvard professor Joseph Nye Jr., the question is one of risk analysis. "Is defending our way of life worth raising the risk that the species will be destroyed from one in 10,000 to one in 1,000 for a certain period of time?"[4] Most people make such trade-offs everyday on a smaller scale. We accept the risk of riding in an automobile because of the convenience it brings into our lives. Second, the strategists point to the terrible potency of nuclear weapons as strengthening deterrence. Historically, they argue, many arms races have ended without leading to war. Knowing that it will surely be destroyed if it launches a nuclear weapon, a rational government will try as hard as it can never to launch. Furthermore, if an accidental launch occurs, fear of a holocaust may well work to limit the exchange. While coming to different conclusions, both the abolitionists and the strategists relied on data—"facts or figures from which conclusions can be drawn"—interpreted to support their positions.[5]

Data, the raw material of argument, serve as the basis for convincing someone of the reasonableness of a claim. Consequently, as one seeks to discover data, the search must be guided by a clear understanding of the nature and purpose of evidence, the audience, the topic, the advocate, and the occasion.

As indicated previously, audiences have certain expectations about the appropriate manner of justification. These expectations are shared by communities of people and cut against individual idiosyncrasies. Differences in audience expectation influence the kind of data needed to convince them of the reasonableness of a claim. Suppose one were to argue before the medical/scientific community that a certain drug cures AIDS. The medical/scientific community shares the expectation that claims of this sort will be supported with data from rigorous study. Initially, they would expect theoretical data indicating the specific chemical and biological action of the drug. Second, they would expect data from experimental studies showing the effectiveness of the drug on laboratory animals. Finally, they would look for clinical (case study) data supporting the effectiveness of the drug on humans.

If, on the other hand, you were trying to convince AIDS victims to engage in clinical testing of such an experimental drug, the expectations of this audience might be somewhat different. While they, too, would be interested in the action of the drug and the results of its use on laboratory animals, they would also expect data revealing the possible side effects of the drug and their impact on one's quality of life. They might also expect to learn what contribution their participation might make to future research on the cure and control of AIDS.

Topic and question form also influence the nature of data constituting persuasive proof. Recall the discussion of abortion and pornography in Chapter One. Fetal viability was seen as a question best answered by the biological sciences. Data from medical studies and from experts in obstetrics and pediatrics would be required before a critical listener would assent. Likewise, in order to establish a link between pornography and sex crimes, the advocate would most profitably search for data from social scientific studies in criminology, psychology and sociology.

The advocate also shapes the need for and nature of data. An expert may rely, at least in part, on his or her own knowledge as adequate data. Few of us, however, possess the expertise needed to command assent. Instead, we must rely on external data to enhance perception of our credibility. The kind of data constituting persuasive proof will also vary with the occasion. Evidentiary requirements in a court of law are specific and formalized. The rules of interscholastic debate stipulate that data must be from published documents equally accessible to all parties. Informal discussions rarely demand data of this sort.

Guided by an awareness of audience, topic, advocate, and occasion, one is ready to discover the various kinds of data available to the advocate.

KINDS OF DATA

The kinds of data most commonly available may be classified as examples, comparison, testimony, and statistics.

EXAMPLES

Examples establish reality by resort to a particular case. They report or describe real occurrences or observable phenomena in order to establish a claim. Data of this sort may be brief statements or more detailed descriptions sometimes called illustrations. Consider two specific cases included in a report on education and poverty:

EXAMPLE ONE

> At one elementary school in Harlem, an innovative program called the Writing Process helps first- and second-graders read and write by encouraging them to produce their own "books" of original stories. Each class maintains a "library" where children can borrow and read one anothers books as well as a plentiful and well-thumbed stock of standard children's literature.[6]

EXAMPLE TWO

> Kent Amos is a highly successful black businessman. He was a senior executive with the Xerox Corporation for 15 years and now heads his own consulting firm. Six years ago he began transforming the dining room of his elegant home in an exclusive Washington suburb into a study hall for high school students who go to the same inner city school he attended. Mr. Amos opens his home every day after school (and whenever any of his "family" of students need him) to provide tutoring, financial help, and general

fatherly support to a total of more than 40 young people. Of these, more than half have already entered college, and all plan to go. Before they met Amos most of them had never dreamed of it.[7]

Each of these two examples describes real occurrences or observable phenomena. They both aim to establish a claim of reality. The first case establishes what can be done in schools to encourage reading while the second establishes the value of individual effort. The two cases differ in degree of detail.

COMPARISON

Comparison is based on the belief that what is known or believed to be true of one thing will be true of something else as long as it is like the first in all essential characteristics. Comparison may be either direct or indirect. Direct comparison may be labeled as a parallel case and consists of one or more cases similar to the case under consideration. Recent discussions of U.S. support for Nicaraguan "freedom fighters" have compared the situation directly to our experience in Vietnam. To the extent that U.S. intervention in Vietnam failed so also will any similar involvement in Central America.

Indirect comparison posits an implicit but indirect relationship between two cases. Attempts to fine tune the economy through changes in fiscal and monetary policy have been likened to trying to drive an automobile while stepping on the accelerator and the brake at the same time. This is not to suggest that fine tuning the economy and driving are one and the same. Instead, the relationship between manipulating fiscal and monetary policy and accelerating and braking are similar in structure and consequence.

TESTIMONY

Testimony refers to the opinions of experts. Data of this sort usually involve the interpretation and/or evaluation of factual material by an individual who possesses special expertise in the relevant field. Two pieces of actual testimony illustrate the point.

TESTIMONY ONE

Many states have raised their secondary school diploma requirements, says Nancy Young of the National Education Association, the teachers' union based in Washington. While this can't be faulted conceptually, unfortunately, it may have pushed out marginal students. When you raise standards, but you don't give students who need it extra help in meeting those standards, minority students in particular can be hurt.[8]

TESTIMONY TWO

The reform movement is not all bad for low income minority children, asserts Phillis McClure of the NAACP Legal Defense and Education Fund. The big plus for these kids is that many states, predominantly in the South, are for the first time establishing public kindergarten programs. South Carolina is even going to provide preschool education for four-year-olds. These are very positive steps.[9]

Both statements reflect the opinions of experts. Both statements involve the interpretation and/or evaluation of factual material. The testimony of Ms. Young provides data useful in arguing the disadvantages of increasing graduation requirements while Ms. McClure's testimony provides data designed to prove the value of legislative action in education reform.

STATISTICS

Statistics may be looked at simplistically as numerical expressions of a factual nature about a specific population or sample. In more detailed terms statistics "consist of arithmetic and graphic ways for deriving manageable and useful descriptive summaries from large and heterogeneous collections of data; methods for inferring from the observable to the not observable; procedures for testing a wide variety of hypotheses; and techniques for discovering whether and to what degree one set of events is contingent upon or related to another set of events."[10]

Statistics may take the form of raw data such as "federal officials believe the cartel smuggled 58 tons of cocaine into the United States since 1979," or "the war in El Salvadore has claimed an estimated 60,000 lives." They may be expressed in terms of medians, percentages, or other comparative measures. For example, by 1990 salmon farmers will produce about 100,000 metric tons of fish. While that represents only 15 percent of the total salmon harvest, it would be at least 10 times the amount that the 1200 Pacific salmon trollers would be expected to catch.[11]

LOCATING DATA

How does one find the kinds of data described in the previous section? You have grown up amidst what has been termed by many as the "information explosion." The potential sources of data are vast but may be located in two general ways. First, one may turn to the library for research from a wide array of publications. Second, one may find it helpful to do field research in the form of interviews or surveys.

LIBRARY RESEARCH

The topic you are researching and the type of data sought should guide your choice of a library or the section of a library that will be most useful to you. Many colleges and universities have a system of branch or specialized libraries in addition to a main library. You may well find on campus a separate medical, legal, business, education, or music library. Within the main library one may find resources organized by type such as reference materials, books, periodicals, government documents, and microforms. Begin by familiarizing yourself with the library/ libraries to which you have access. Do not hesitate to talk with the library staff, especially the reference staff. They are trained professionals who can be of tremendous assistance.

CARD CATALOGUE.   The card catalogue usually lists the books, periodicals, newspapers, microforms, and media in the library collection. The card catalogue is divided into an Author-Title Catalogue that lists works by author and by title, and a Subject Catalogue that lists works by Library of Congress subject headings. A catalogue card contains the elements presented in figure 6.1.

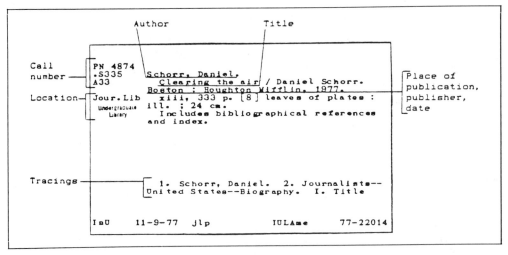

Figure 6.1 Author-Title Catalogue Card

When you find an item of interest, you must record the entire call number from the upper left corner of the card. This number will allow you to locate the appropriate stack area and shelf on which the material is stored.

INDEXES AND ABSTRACTS.   Libraries contain a variety of indexes and abstracts cataloguing newspapers, periodicals, and scholarly journals but also occasionally books. A representative list of indexes would include the *New York Times Index, Business Periodicals Index, Index*

Medicus, Index to Legal Periodicals, Social Science Citation Index, and *The Reader's Guide to Periodical Literature.* These resources are organized alphabetically by subject and by author. An index provides basic information on when and where an article was published. An entry in *The Reader's Guide to Periodical Literature* includes such information as shown in figure 6.2.

Discrimination in employment
> *See also*
> Aged—Employment
> Black women—Employment
> Equal pay for equal work
> Don't be age biased against the young or old. S. Rose. *Work Woman* 12:27+ O '87
> Normal nonsense [reverse discrimination seen in U.S. Employment Service rankings of General Aptitude Test Battery scores] D. Seligman. il *Fortune* 116:165-6 N 9 '87
>
> **Canada**
> When women do men's work [guarding both male and female prisoners] B. Amiel. il *Macleans* 100:9 O 12 '87

Figure 6.2 Entry From *The Readers Guide to Periodical Literature*

Abstracts such as *Psychological Abstracts, Sociological Abstracts, Pollution Abstracts, Criminology Abstracts,* and *Child Development Abstracts and Bibliography,* offer the same basic information plus a short summary of the publication's content. Examine the abstract from *Sociological Abstracts* in figure 6.3.

85Q0105
> Beirne, Piers (U Wisconsin, Madison 53706), **Rent and Rent Legislation in England and Wales 1915-1946,** *The Sociological Review Monograph,* 1976, 23, Dec, 64-82.
> ¶ A discussion of the use & the impact of rent control as a social measure to alleviate the economic condition of the Wcs in England. After briefly reviewing Karl Marx's theory of rent, rent legislation enacted for both the public & private sectors between 1915 & 1946 is examined. Instead of producing the expected improvements, the legislation has only encouraged the expansion of the industrial & financial factions of capital in the process of production. In the interest of social stability, the Wcs' disposable income was increased by a reduction of the rent expenditure, only to be absorbed by other components of the capitalist economy. 21 References. S. Karganovic

Figure 6.3 Entry From *Sociological Abstracts*

SPECIALIZED ENCYCLOPEDIAS, DICTIONARIES, AND FACT BOOKS. Library reference sections include a variety of publications designed to help the researcher explore the background of an issue and understand key concepts. Encyclopedias such as the *Encyclopedia of the Social Sciences,* the *Encyclopedia of Religion and Ethics,* and the *Encyclopedia of Science and Technology,* offer fairly lengthy articles authored by experts in the various fields. Dictionaries such as the *Dictionary of Political Analysis, Concise Science Dictionary,* the *International Relations Dictionary,* and the *Dictionary of Philosophy* offer somewhat more brief discussions of key concepts within specific fields.

Also located in most reference libraries are resources such as *The Statistical Abstract of the United States* and *The World Almanac,* which provide statistical information on a variety of subjects updated each year. *Facts on File,* drawn from magazines and newspapers, provides weekly news updates.

GOVERNMENT DOCUMENTS. U.S. government publications including reference information on all branches of the federal government, congressional reports, committee hearings, texts of public laws, and agency publications are a very rich research tool. Government publications are listed in indexes such as the *Monthly Catalogue of U.S. Government Publications, Index to U.S. Government Periodicals, Congressional Information Services Index (CIS)* and *Government Reports and Announcements Index.*

The *CIS Index,* begun in 1970, is the most easily used of these indexes. Published monthly, CIS is in two parts. The CIS index volume contains subject, title, bill number, report number, and document number indexes. The companion abstract volume contains summaries of publication contents. It is advisable to begin with the index volume. If, for example, you want to find information on or testimony from Secretary of State George P. Schultz concerning terrorism countermeasures, you would consult this index under the appropriate alphabetical listing (see figure 6.4).

Shultz, George P.
  First concurrent budget resolution, FY86,
    foreign aid and foreign policy aspects,
    S251–2.3
  Foreign aid programs, FY85 and
    supplemental FY84 approp, S181–17.1
  Foreign aid programs, FY86 approp,
    H181–82.5
  Foreign aid programs, FY86 authorization,
    H381–49.1, S381–28.1
  Intl narcotics trafficking and foreign policy,
    articles, H381–57.2
  Refugee admission and resettlement
    assistance programs, Admin FY85
    proposal, S521–37.1
  "Southern Africa: Toward an American
    Consensus", S241–19, S381–27.3
  State Dept diplomatic missions security
    enhancement programs, advisory panel
    rpt, H381–79.2
  State Dept programs, FY86 approp,
    H181–34.4
  Terrorism countermeasures, H381–18.5

Figure 6.4 Entry From CIS Index Volume

Upon locating a reference, one must record the abstract citation. This citation begins with the letters S, H, J, or PL, followed by several numerals, a dash, and several more numerals. With this citation number in hand, one turns to the abstract that is organized by letter and then numerically within each letter (see figure 6.5).

H381-18   LEGISLATION TO COMBAT
           INTERNATIONAL
           TERRORISM: 98TH
           CONGRESS.
           Nov. 9, 1983, June 7, 13, 19,
           Sept. 26, 1984.   98-1; 98-2.
           iv+461 p. il.   †   CIS/MF/7
           •Item 1017-A; 1017-B.
           *Y4.F76/1:L52/8.
           MC 85-16260. LC 85-601445.
Hearings before the *Subcom on International Security and Scientific Affairs* to consider the following bills and resolutions to address international terrorism problems:

H. Res. 233 (text, p. 187-188), to urge the President to enter into negotiations with the Soviet Union to provide for mutual cooperation in dealing with the threat of accidental nuclear war caused by acts of terrorism.

H.R. 5612 (draft text, sectional analysis, p. 214-219, text, p. 220-226), the Act for Rewards for Information Concerning Terrorist Acts, an Administration bill, to authorize Justice Dept and State Dept payment of rewards for information leading to prevention of terrorist activities against U.S. persons or property, or for information leading to arrest or conviction of terrorists. Includes provisions for informant eligibility for resident alien status and protection under the Federal Witness Security Program.

H.R. 5613 (draft text, sectional analysis, p. 206-214, text, p. 227-235), the Prohibition Against the Training or Support of Terrorist Oranizations Act of 1984, an Administration bill, to impose criminal penalties on U.S. citizens or businesses providing military or intelligence assistance to international groups or foreign governments that support terrorism.

June 7 and 19 hearings were held jointly with the *Subcom on International Operations.* June 13 and Sept. 26 hearings were held before the full committee.

H381-18.5: June 13, 1984. p. 77-115.

Witness: SHULTZ, George P., Sec, State Dept; accompanied by McGovern, Daniel W., Principal Dep Legal Adviser, Office for Counter-Terrorism and Emergency Planning, State Dept.

Statement and Discussion: Assessment of recent increase in terrorist activities, with explanation of Administration policy response; need for H.R. 5613.

Figure 6.5 Entry From CIS Abstract Volume

After reading the abstract, if you decide the item is relevant and would like to research the actual document, you will need to record the call number. The call number is the long number preceded by an asterisk and usually beginning with a letter such as Y. You must copy this number exactly including slashes and semicolons in order to be able to find the document on the shelf in the stacks.

In addition to U.S. government publications, some libraries also carry state and local publications, publications of foreign governments, and international organizations. Typically, the location of these documents is recorded in a special document card catalogue. If not, inquire about your library's specific cataloguing procedure.

ADVANCED RESEARCH TECHNOLOGY.   Attempts to manage the information explosion have resulted in a variety of technological advances providing researchers greater and more convenient access to resources. An early innovation, *Newsbank*, provides access to the contents of newspapers from over 100 cities around the United States. Articles from the socio-economic, political, international, and scientific fields are screened by trained information specialists. The articles are indexed and then photographed on microfiche. Most of the articles on a topic will appear together on a single microfiche, thus significantly reducing the number of microfiches examined in completing a search. *Newsbank* is updated each month.

Advances in computer technology have lead to the development of a variety of databases. It has been possible for some time to conduct computerized searches of these on-line databases for a fee. More recent advances in laser videodisk technology have resulted in searching systems that are quite "user friendly" and require no prior instruction. *InfoTrac* is the best known of these systems. This database contains bibliographic references to articles appearing in over 1,000 general and business periodicals published since 1982, as well as in the *New York Times* and *The Wall Street Journal* for the previous 60 days. Using *InfoTrac* is much like using any other index. Examine the sample printout on the topic of adoption in figure 6.6.

```
ADOPTION                                        InfoTrac Database
                                                Infotrac 3.23a

            ADOPTING an older child.                DATA DISPLAY
            (book reviews)
         =  by Claudia Jewett
            B  Parents' Magazine-March'85 p42(1)
            26K4488
         ADOPTION
            See also
              ADOPTEES
              BIOLOGICAL PARENTS
              CHILDREN, ADOPTED
              FOSTER HOME CARE
              INTERCOUNTRY ADOPTION
              INTERRACIAL ADOPTION
           -ANALYSIS
         =     Adoption vs. abortion; some pro-choice forces
             embrace a new option.  by Elisa Williams   il
             Newsweek-April 28'86 p39(1)
             33J1188
         =     The adoption option.  (advice for working women)
```

Figure 6.6 Sample InfoTrac Printout

Similar databases exist to search legal periodicals and government documents as well. Advances continue and new databases come on line rapidly. Again, familiarizing yourself fully with the library/libraries you plan to use will make researching efficient and enjoyable.

FIELD RESEARCH

The advocate may find it useful to complement library research with field research.

INTERVIEWS.   It is often possible for the researcher to conduct personal interviews with individuals possessing special expertise on a particular topic. Interviews must be carefully planned. One should schedule an appointment well in advance of when the information is needed. It is of crucial importance that the conduct of the interview be planned. Prepare a list of questions to ask and/or topics to be covered. Take a tape recorder to the interview so that you will be able to accurately retrieve the data you need from the interview.

INFORMAL SURVEYS.   Some topics may lend themselves to primary data collection. For example, one might attempt to assess the feelings of college students toward foreign language requirements by conducting a survey. Even an informal survey of this sort needs to be planned. Decide beforehand what questions you will ask and who you will survey. Once you have conducted the survey, you will have to analyze and interpret the data.

RECORDING AND ORGANIZING DATA

The goal of data discovery is the collection of evidence that can be used to support the claims you make when arguing persuasively. In order to accomplish this goal, the advocate must first record and then organize the data so that they can be used when needed.

RECORDING DATA

The manner in which you record data will depend on what stage of the research process you have achieved and to what end you wish to use the data you are collecting.

BIBLIOGRAPHIC NOTATION.   In the early stages of research, when you are exploring a wide range of potentially useful resources, it is a good idea to keep a listing of the materials you have examined. This listing should include the name of the author, the title of the publication, the place and the date of publication, and relevant page numbers. These bibliographic records will be even more useful if annotated. In order to annotate a bibliographic entry, one includes a brief description or summary of the content of the publication.

SPECIFIC EXCERPTS. There are a variety of methods for recording specific excerpts of data you will actually use when arguing. The actual method of choice is up to each individual as long as it is systematic. Some may prefer to record data on notebook paper while others may find the use of index cards more convenient. Traditionally, debaters record data on either 3 × 5 or 4 × 6 index cards referred to as evidence cards. Most evidence is recorded in the form of a direct quotation from the source. If paraphrasing of lengthy material or interpretation of graphic material is necessary, one must take care that the product of paraphrasing or interpreting accurately represents the intent of the author.

Whether one uses notebook paper or index cards, each specific excerpt or piece of evidence should include certain fundamental items. First, each piece of evidence must have a complete citation. This citation should include basic bibliographic information (author, title, date of publication, page number) and the qualifications of the author. By qualifications we are referring to what it is about the author that makes him or her a good source of information. Qualifications may include academic degrees, special study or personal experience, positions held, and the like. If these qualifications are not readily apparent, one may have to search for them within the context of the publication or in specialized reference materials such as *Who's Who in America, Current Biography,* or *Who's Who* in specific fields like science, political science, or education. Each excerpt should encompass a complete thought. Examine carefully the sample of a specific excerpt in the form of an evidence card used in interscholastic debate (figure 6.7).

Edward B. Jenkinson, Professor of Education, Indiana University, *Dealing with Censorship,* 1979, p. 2.

A recent study indicated that censorship disputes are twice as likely to grow up in large cities (with over 100,000 residents) than in small communities having fewer than 2,500 residents. Large cities were also 50 percent more likely to spawn cases than are either middle sized or small urban communities.

Figure 6.7 Sample Evidence Card

Each piece of evidence recorded must then be organized so that it can be retrieved and used when needed.

ORGANIZING DATA

If the data you have collected is to be used for a single speech, the process of organization requires nothing more than ordering the evidence for the purpose of that persuasive speech. The debater, on the other hand, must be able to use the collected data over and over during the course of a semester or debate season. Consequently, debaters usually develop a system for filing the evidence they record on index cards.

Filing systems are about as varied as debaters. Some debaters will file evidence by stock issues, some will file by subject, and still others develop numerical systems similar to the Dewey decimal system. Each individual must ultimately develop a system that works for him or her. Filing by subject is an easily managed system. In order to create such a file, divide evidence cards into categories by subject. Then label an index card divider with the appropriate subject title and use the dividers to separate each category.

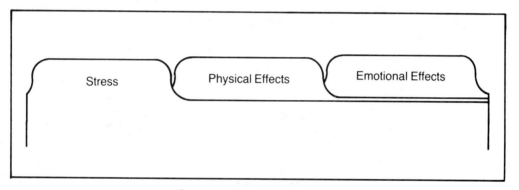

Figure 6.8 Sample Filing System

The cards are then placed in an appropriate file drawer, box, or briefcase. Each time the file is used, data must be replaced or refiled in order to maintain the system of organization.

RHETORICAL SELECTION OF DATA

When you have done a good job of researching a topic, you will have a substantial amount of different kinds of data drawn from a variety of sources. The next task is to select the data you will use to make a given argument. In order to succeed in arguing persuasively, the advocate will have to select not only data that best communicate the intended message but that also meet the needs and expectations of the audience. In other words, the advocate should select the best evidence from the audience or listener's point of view. Understanding the listener's point of view requires consideration of what attitudes the audience holds toward the topic, what values the audience respects, and what knowledge of the topic the listener already possesses. In addition, the advocate should consider the psychological impact of each different kind of evidence.

Examples appear to have strong persuasive appeal. As descriptions, they are characterized by vivid language and easy to comprehend dramatic or narrative structure. Examples tend to be about specific people or events to which an audience can easily relate. They often have strong emotional appeal. Unfortunately, examples are easily denied by counterexamples. So, while they appear essential to building a persuasive argument, one should not rely on examples alone.

Like examples, comparisons have the advantage of making information concrete and understandable. Comparisons accomplish these ends by drawing upon what is familiar to a listener and using that familiarity to relate and explain new concepts. Recall the sample comparison given earlier. Few people understand how fiscal and monetary policy function to fine tune the economy but almost everyone in an adult audience is likely to be a driver and thus understand the function of the accelerator and the brake. Consequently, comparison is vital when dealing with issues that listeners may find complex and/or unfamiliar.

Statistical or numerical data have become an integral part of our daily lives. Most of us have come to expect quantification. If we see a newspaper headline like "Automobile Fatalities Decline," we immediately assume we will read figures indicating the total number of automobile fatalities occurring. Furthermore, we expect to find comparative statistics in the form of percentages indicating the size or significance of the reported decline. Likewise, when an advocate claims seat belts save lives, we expect to be told how many or what percentage of lives are saved.

Even though we expect quantification, statistical and numerical data are not easy to process. The listener is unable to manage large quantities of numerical data in an oral communication setting. The advocate must exercise caution in the use of numerical data and should make an effort to ensure that the data are understandable. Figures can be dramatized by comparing them or casting them in terms easily visualized by the listener.

Testimony is also a valuable source of persuasion. In addition to providing the audience with the insight and evaluation of experts, testimony can create a kind of "halo effect" resulting in enhanced credibility for the advocate. When selecting testimony, be sure the qualifications of the expert are known (you should provide them) and give some thought to audience perception. The listener must share your opinion that the individual quoted is indeed an expert.

Finally, an advocate should provide the listener with variety. Each of the different kinds of data has strengths and weaknesses. None are perfect or guaranteed to persuade. Furthermore, audiences are made up of individuals who perhaps prefer different kinds of data. A persuasive argument can and should be supported by data from a variety of sources.

Consider a debate over the increased stress experienced by children in which it is argued that stress causes suicide. One could support this argument by turning to examples such as the case of an eight-year-old child who deliberately ran in front of a car, or a nine-year-old who tried to hang himself, or a twelve-year-old who took a drug overdose. One might point to statistics such as those indicating that 300 youngsters committed suicide in 1985 and the suicide rate for youths under 15 has tripled since 1960. Testimony from experts like pediatrician T. Berry Brazelton could be provided concluding "Today, preadolescence is more stressful than it used to be." Finally, one might conclude that childhood is gone. "The social changes that have pushed the fast forward button (a comparison to video recording equipment) on children are irreversible."[12]

But does data really make a difference in the persuasiveness of the argument? This is an issue that communication researchers have explored. A number of experimental studies have been conducted to investigate the effect of evidence on attitude change. The results have been mixed. In the 1950s Robert S. Cathcart and Erwin P. Bettinghaus reported the results of studies in which they found that the inclusion of evidence increased the amount of attitude change.[13] Later researchers reported no significant difference in attitude change between a speech including high quality evidence and those including low quality or no evidence.[14] What might account for these mixed results? Communication researchers began to suspect that the effect of evidence might be difficult to assess because of its interaction with other elements in the communication process.

Source credibility was the first communication variable suspected of interacting with evidence. By source credibility we mean audience perceptions of the speaker that may lead the audience to accept or reject the speaker's message. Summarizing the results of research in this area, James C. McCroskey concluded " . . . nine studies provide substantial justification for the generalization that initial credibility and evidence usage interact to produce attitude change and perceived credibility. Briefly stated, the initially high-credible source gains little from including evidence but the initially moderate-to-low credible source can substantially increase his perceived credibility and the attitude change he produces in his audience by including evidence to support his position."[15]

Second, the quality of message presentation or delivery was suspected of interacting with evidence. To test this supposed interaction, Arnold and McCroskey designed an experiment using a single speaker to present an "evidence speech" and a "no-evidence speech" employing both good delivery and poor delivery. The results of the experiment indicated that greater attitude change and higher perceived credibility were produced by the "evidence speech" with good delivery.[16]

Third, the audience interacts with the evidence. The perceived role of the audience may affect audience response to the use of evidence. According to Barry Collins, when a listener assumes the role of a problem solver, he or she is concerned about getting information relevant to the problem under consideration.[17] In this context, evidence becomes the chief material of proof. Likewise, audience opinion is important in assessing the quality of evidence. A study by Luchok and McCroskey revealed that when sources of evidence were good the message was perceived to be of higher quality than when the sources were poor.[18] They further noted that it is detrimental to both attitude change and credibility to use poor evidence. Postexperiment interviews with subjects involved in studies related to evidence suggested that prior audience knowledge of or familiarity with the evidence on a subject might affect audience response. Specifically, McCroskey hypothesized that "presenting evidence to people who previously have been exposed to that evidence will have no effect on either attitude change or credibility, but presenting the same evidence to people who are not familiar with it will significantly increase attitude change."[19] The results of further study confirmed this hypothesis.[20]

Finally, investigations into the effect of evidence as an inhibitor of counter-persuasion are of particular interest and importance to our study of argumentation. Counter-persuasion refers to the presentation of a subsequent message that undermines the persuasive impact of an earlier message. A study by McCroskey assessed the effect of evidence as an inhibitor of counter-persuasion.[21] In this context McCroskey found that evidence did indeed inhibit counter-persuasion. Furthermore, evidence is important to both low- and high-credibility sources. For the low-credibility sources, the presentation of evidence continued to enhance their credibility. For the highly credible sources, the failure to use evidence when a preceding speaker has used evidence results in a loss of credibility.

The results of research on the persuasive influence of evidence are far from definitive. The difficulty stems from the interaction of evidence with other variables in the communication process such as the audience's initial perception of the advocate, the quality of the advocate's delivery, the perceived role of the listeners, and the audience's familiarity with the evidence. Still, there is clear justification for the presentation of evidence. First, low-credibility advocates can expect to increase the audience's initial attitude change with the presentation of evidence. Second, all advocates can assure greater long-term attitude change by using evidence to innoculate audience members against counter-persuasion.

Beyond any consideration of persuasive effect, the presentation of quality evidence is an ethical imperative. Argumentation concerns both the effective and the worthy. Arguments, unsupported by evidence, cannot meet the requisite standards of reasonableness.

CONCLUSIONS

In this chapter, you have been introduced to the discovery of data. Data provide the vital link between the physical world and one's mental interpretation of it. This facilitates analysis, synthesis, and evaluation both on the part of the advocate and the audience as they engage in the argumentative process. The various kinds of data available to the advocate have been classified in terms of examples, comparison, statistics, and testimony. We have also explored the process of locating data through library research, using both traditional and advanced technological research tools, and field research. Once located, data must be recorded and organized. We have described a system of recording that begins with bibliographic annotation and culminates in the transcription of specific excerpts or quotations on index cards. Each of these index cards must then be organized for ease in retrieval and use. The system suggested involves classification and filing by subject.

Finally, we discussed the rhetorical selection of data. Each time the advocate argues, data must be chosen to support the claim being made. Data selection should be made with the audience, the advocate, the topic, and the occasion clearly in mind. Given the topic and the occasion, audiences have certain expectations about what constitutes persuasive proof. Each of the various kinds of data has strengths and weaknesses, each meets different audience needs and expectations. Variety is the key. The advocate should provide the listener with variety both in terms of kinds of data and sources of data.

NOTES

1. "Proof," *Webster's New World Dictionary* (1980).
2. Peter Grier, "Is proving the terror of global nuclear war a waste of time?" *The Christian Science Monitor*, 20 November 1986, p. 3.
3. Jonathan Schell, *The Abolition*, (New York: Avon Publishing, 1984), p. 27.
4. Grier, p. 4.
5. "Data," *Webster's New World Dictionary* (1980).
6. Kristin Helmore, "When Great Expectations Pay Off," *The Christian Science Monitor*, 20 November 1986, p. 33.
7. Ibid., pp. 33–34.

8. Kristin Helmore and Karen Lang, "Exiles Among Us," *The Christian Science Monitor*, 20 November 1986, p. 29.

9. Ibid., p. 29.

10. Barry K. Spiker, Tom D. Daniels and Lawrence M. Bernabo, "The Quantitative Quandary in Forensics: The Use and Abuse of Statistical Evidence," *Journal of the American Forensic Association* 19 (1982): 89.

11. Marshall Ingwerson, "U.S. hopes indictments will induce nations to seize drug smugglers," *The Christian Science Monitor*, 21 November 1986, p. 7; Chris Norton, "Salvador: peace is distant," *The Christian Science Monitor*, 24 November 1986, p. 1; Mark Baumgartner, "Salmon Trollers' gourmet market threatened by fish farms," *The Christian Science Monitor*, 24 November 1986, p. 8.

12. "Children Under Stress," *U.S. News & World Report*, 27 October 1986, pp. 58–63.

13. Robert S. Cathcart, "An Experimental Study of the Relative Effectiveness of Four Methods of Presenting Evidence," *Communication Monographs* 22 (1955): 227–233; and Erwin P. Bettinghaus, Jr., "The Relative Effect of the Use of Testimony in a Persuasive Speech upon the Attitudes of Listeners," unpublished M.A. thesis, Bradley University, Peoria, IL, 1953.

14. Delmar C. Anderson, "The Effects of Various Uses of Authoritative Testimony in Persuasive Speaking," unpublished M.A. thesis, Ohio State University, 1958; Dan L. Costley, "An Experimental Study of the Effectiveness of Quantitative Evidence in Speeches of Advocacy," unpublished M.A. thesis, University of Oklahoma, 1958; William R. Dresser, "Effects of 'Satisfactory' and 'Unsatisfactory' Evidence in a Speech of Advocacy," *Communication Monographs* 20 (1963): 302–306.

15. James C. McCroskey, "A Summary of Experimental Research on the Effects of Evidence in Persuasive Communication," *Quarterly Journal of Speech* 55 (1969): 172.

16. Ibid., 173.

17. Barry E. Collins, *Social Psychology: Social Influence, Attitude Change, Group Processes, and Prejudice* (Menlo Park, CA: Addison-Wesley, 1970), pp. 25–33.

18. Joseph Luchok and James C. McCroskey, "The Effect of Quality of Evidence on Attitude Change and Source Perception," paper presented at the Speech Communication Association Convention, Chicago, IL, 1974.

19. McCroskey, "A Summary of Experimental Research," 174.

20. Ibid.

21. James C. McCroskey, "The Effects of Evidence as an Inhibitor of Counter-Persuasion," *Communication Monographs* 37 (1970): 188–194.

7

FORMS OF ARGUMENT

In Chapter One, we distinguished among three basic concepts: logic, persuasion, and argumentation. In the course of the explanation of these three terms we often used the word "argument" without bothering to provide any definition. The word "argument" is so common in everyday speech that it hardly requires definition. However, in ordinary use the term has two distinct meanings. Confusion often arises, even among argumentation theorists, if these two separate senses are not kept in mind.

A telephone call from an old college buddy of Ron's illustrates the separate senses of argument. Chuck is a lawyer currently working in New York City and he delights in calling Ron and berating him for exhibiting a "new-found provincialism" since moving to "backwater" Indiana. There are people who believe that the only important developments in American life are spawned on one of the two coasts. Chuck, considerably more chauvinistic than that, holds that everything worth experiencing occurs on Manhattan Island.

Chuck's life is guided by two sacred texts, the *New York Times* and the *Village Voice*. When accounts or editorial opinion differ between the two newspapers, Chuck has a strong presumption in favor of the *Voice* because he views it as more politically chic. For instance, on September 1, 1983, a Soviet fighter plane shot down a Korean airliner that had strayed into Soviet air space; all 269 passengers were killed. Considerable controversy surrounded the event, including speculation about the underlying motives for the Soviet action. The *Voice* ran articles purporting to establish that flight KAL 007 had been a spy plane and by implication that the Soviet Union was justified in shooting it down. Whether in fact this was the precise thesis of the story or not is unknown (after all Ron gets his news from the *Bloomington Herald-Telephone*), but this is the gist of Chuck's explanation.

Not surprisingly, Ron was somewhat skeptical about this quite radical revision of the Administration's official account of the incident. As the telephone conversation developed Ron got into a loud and contentious "argument" with Chuck. At one point, he said in a now thoroughly exasperated voice, "You are not listening to my argument. You are attacking an argument that I never made." Some time passed and finally Ron ended the conversation by saying, "There is no point in having an argument with you because you are so stubborn you refuse to consider the evidence for the opposing point of view."

In this chapter, we address the sense of argument used in the phrases "You are not listening to my argument" and "You are attacking an argument that I never made." Specifically, we distinguish between argument₁ and argument₂, explain the concepts of warrant and backing, and, finally, consider formal, material, and logical warrants.

ARGUMENT₁ AND ARGUMENT₂

Daniel O'Keefe has written several essays in which he painstakingly details the differences between "argument" used in the phrases "There is no point in having an argument with you" and "You are not listening to my argument."[1] O'Keefe explained, "In everyday talk the word 'argument' is systematically used to refer to different phenomena.... Crudely put, an argument₁ is something one person makes (or gives or presents or utters), while an argument₂ is something two or more persons have (or engage in). Arguments₁ are thus on a par with promises, commands, apologies, warnings, invitations, orders, and the like. Arguments₂ are classifiable with other species of interactions such as bull sessions, heart-to-heart talks, quarrels, discussions, and so forth."[2]

How do we distinguish an argument₁ from commands, apologies, warnings, invitation, orders, and the like? What are the defining characteristics of arguments as utterances? An argument "is a piece of reasoning in which one or more statements are offered as support for some other statement."[3] Last night Ron and Karen attended an Indiana University basketball game. Forty-five minutes before the game, Karen said "We should leave right now because the traffic to Assembly Hall will be very heavy." This utterance was an argument₁. It meets the criteria for an argument₁ because it provides one statement, "the traffic to Assembly Hall will be very heavy," in support for another statement, "We should leave right now."

The step that permits the leap from one supporting statement to the conclusionary statement is called an "inference." In television movies, which in a kind moment might be labeled "trash," a variant on the following scene is frequently played out:

> CARL: I called home last night from Phoenix and no one answered. I called again after midnight and still there was no answer. Now I find out that you have been taking tennis lessons three times a week from the club pro Brad Jackson.
> KELLY: Just what are you *inferring*!!
> CARL: Don't play innocent with me Kelly. You've been having an affair with that gigolo.

Carl's claim that his wife is having an illicit romance with the tennis pro is supported by her late absence from home and her new found interest in taking tennis lessons. The process of reasoning that permits the leap from information Carl gathered and reports on in his first set of lines is used to reason to or infer the conclusion in his last bit of dialogue.

So an argument (argument₁) is an utterance that infers one statement from another statement or set of statements. But inferences are of different types and qualities. To intelligently evaluate arguments, the critic must understand the different justifications for inference.

WARRANT AND BACKING

We all know people who make crazy inferences. The insanely jealous wife may infer an affair from the evidence that her husband gave his female secretary a card for her birthday or a jealous boyfriend may suspect his girlfriend of romantic duplicity if she studies for a chemistry final with a male classmate. If the use of arguments is to support a reasonable process of justification, understanding the nature of justified inference is critical.

Two facets of the inference process are identified by the terms *warrant* and *backing*. A warrant is hypothetical; backing is substantial. As the names imply, backing backs warrants. Let's take each concept in turn and illustrate its relationship to an inference.

The function of warrant in argument is very close to the familiar meaning of "warranty" or "guarantee." A warranty assures the buyer that the purchased product will be free of certain kinds of defects and that if it is not, the manufacturer will make some form of restitution. In much the same way, an argument warrant licenses the inference. It is the formal statement of the promise that the move from statement one to conclusionary statement two is permissible.

The term "warrant" was popularized in Stephen Toulmin's *The Uses of Argument*. Toulmin wrote, "Our task is...to show that...the step to the original claim or conclusion is an appropriate and legitimate one. At this point, therefore, what are needed are general, hypothetical statements, which can act as bridges, and authorize the sort of step to which our particular argument commits us. These may normally be written very briefly (in the form 'If D, then C'); but...they can profitably be expanded, and made more explicit: 'Data such as D entitle one to draw conclusions, or make claims such as C,' or alternatively 'Given data D, one may take it that C.' Propositions of this kind I shall call *warrants* (W)...."[4]

If we return to the dialogue in our trashy movie and put it in Toulmin's terms, we get something like this:

DATA (D): No one was home when Carl called late last night. Kelly has suddenly started taking tennis lessons three times a week from Brad Jackson.

WARRANT (W): If a wife doesn't come home at night when her husband is out of town and she suddenly starts taking tennis lessons from a good looking club pro, then one may take it that she is having an affair.

CLAIM (C): Kelly is having an affair.

Notice that the warrant is hypothetical as indicated by its "if, then" structure. It serves as a rule in the form: if this condition exists then you may infer that then some second condition exists. But this is an unsatisfying place to leave the problem of inference. So we can create a rule that will warrant the move from one statement to another conclusionary statement, but not all rules are justified. Some rules are wrongheaded and not worth following. What support can be offered for the wisdom of our rule?

The concept of "backing" was coined by Toulmin to designate the support for warrants. Unlike the hypothetical nature of a warrant-rule, backing provides substantial authority for inferences. *Backing is the generalizations that make explicit the body of experience relied on to establish the trustworthiness of the ways of arguing applied in any particular case.*[5] In our example of Carl's accusation that Kelly is having an affair, the backing might take this form:

BACKING (B): Experience has demonstrated that an adulterous mate leaves tell-tale signs of infidelity. These signs include unexplained whereabouts and new pursuits that justify unaccounted for time.

We have come very close to the notion of field-dependent validity introduced in Chapter Three. Backing is field-dependent. The kind of backing necessary to justify Carl's claim of Kelly's infidelity is different than that necessary to support Karen's assertion that we should leave forty-five minutes early for the basketball game. We have taken up in detail the relationship between validity and audience. The same relationship exists between backing and audience.

We have come at this topic again from another direction for a couple of reasons. First, we want to demonstrate that the general burdens of argument are related to the very components of what constitutes an individual argument. Second, in Chapter Three we discussed validity in general terms, but did not consider its specific manifestations in the various types and forms of individual argument.

DEFINITIONAL, MATERIAL, AND PSYCHOLOGICAL BACKING

Return to the definition of backing for a closer look; *backing is the generalizations that make explicit the body of experience relied on to establish the trustworthiness of the ways of arguing applied in any particular case.* The phrase of interest for this section is "body of experience." There are bodies of experience that definitionally, materially, or psychologically support the warrant and thus license the conclusion.

Consider the following three arguments:

1. Harry was born in Bermuda, so presumably he is a British subject.[6]
2. Laura came from a very poor home environment, so she is unlikely to have much academic success.
3. I am furious with you, go to your room.

Consider the following three statements of backing for these three arguments:

B1. British law provides that any person born on British soil is a British subject.
B2. Sociological research demonstrates that children from poor home environments succeed academically much less frequently than children who come from more privileged backgrounds.
B3. I'll get in even more trouble than I'm already in if I don't do what my mother says.

Is there some important difference between these three arguments and their attendant backing? Argument B1 is *definitional*, while B2 is *material*, and B3 is an instance of *psychological* backing.

Definitional backing is dependent on conforming to a closed set of rules. Just as $2 \times 3 = 6$; All men are mortal, Socrates is a man, therefore, Socrates is mortal; are valid by definition, so too is the argument concerning Harry's citizenship. The backing did not depend on experience, which would entail finding out the status of Harry's citizenship by investigating the status of a significant number of people who had been born in Bermuda, but on the rules of law. Harry is a British subject because someone born in Bermuda is defined as a British subject.

Material backing is dependent on tests of experience. It relies upon the results of observation, experimentation, or induction. The body of knowledge that supports material backing was gathered by examining particular cases in order to support the generalization. The generalization in argument B2 is the product of examining a large number of individual cases in order to determine a pattern of behavior.

Psychological backing is dependent upon the listener's subjective reaction. The conclusion "go to your room" can be supported neither by definition nor by experience. In other words, it is not a claim that fits the formal fields of law, mathematics, or logic, nor the material fields of the natural or social sciences. In both arguments 1 and 2 the conclusion consisted of a declarative sentence. The sentence described Harry's status and predicted Laura's academic future. But the conclusion to argument 3 is the command "go to your room." Commands do not describe a current state of affairs, nor do they predict a future state of affairs. Rather, they demand an action be taken. One can speak of "proving a statement" but never of "proving a command." I may offer reasons for following or not following the command, but these would never constitute "proof of the command." In argument B3 the child decides that he is in enough trouble without countermanding his mother's order to go to his room. This consideration of possible consequences had a psychological impact on his deciding to follow the order, but did not definitionally or materially establish that order.

ARGUMENTS BACKED BY DEFINITION

Throughout the text we have provided numerous examples of arguments backed by the rules of formal logic. These arguments are often identified by the terms analytic, deductive, or tautological. These terms have slightly different technical meanings, but they all identify an argument whose inference is backed by appeal to rules rather than experience. As the British philosopher A. J. Ayer pointed out, "a proposition is analytic when its validity depends solely on the definitions of symbols it contains."[7]

ARGUMENTS WITH MATERIAL BACKING

Unlike the arguments whose warrants are formally backed, materially backed warrants support only *probable* arguments. The truths of formal mathematics and logic are certain—after all, their truth is dependent on the definitions of terms—but the arguments from experience are never certain. They are never certain because additional experience may always in theory confound the conclusion.

A scientific hypothesis is a typical case of a materially backed claim. Consider these sample hypotheses:

H_1: Modernization is inversely related to the intensity of a society's religious practice.

H_2: Gender is a significant determinant of income.

H_3: Decreased marginal tax rates lead to increased economic growth.

Social scientists at one time or another have maintained these three hypotheses. We have not worded them as cautiously as the professional historian, sociologist, and economist would, but the general drift ought to be clear.

The social scientist charged with testing these hypotheses would examine the history of a large number of modern societies, observe men and women with similar training and similar occupations in order to chart income levels, and observe the relationship between tax rates and economic growth in a series of countries. After completing their research work, the social scientists would perhaps confirm each of these hypotheses with some degree of confidence. Social scientists can never be certain of these relationships, because future experience may invalidate the hypothesis. Or they may find that some other intervening variable was responsible for the suspected relationship. As simple a claim as "the sun comes up every day," may be confounded tomorrow when it does not come up. It has come up so often and for so long that we are very confident of our claim, but we can never be certain.

There are various forms of materially backed argument: example, analogy, cause, and sign. Each is discussed in turn.

ARGUMENT FROM EXAMPLE

Argument from example is sometimes termed a generalization. To use language even more technical, reasoning from example is often referred to as an *inductive generalization*. The term *inductive* or *induction* is "a method of reasoning by which a general law or principle is inferred from observed particular instances."[8] This form of argument is referred to as both example and generalization because each term is appropriate depending upon whether the speaker is emphasizing the "particular instances" or the "general law or principle."

Consider the following illustrations of arguments from example:

1. Three pieces of blue litmus paper turned red when dipped into acid; we may draw a general conclusion that *all* blue litmus paper dipped in acid will turn red.[9]
2. Eighty out of a hundred doctors would choose aspirin if stranded on a desert island; therefore, most doctors would choose aspirin if stranded on a desert island.
3. "Todd and Curti, in writing their *America's History*, laid the foundations for presenting American history as a class struggle in this way: 'They (the founding fathers) were determined to keep control of the government in the hands of the *well-to-do*, whom they considered more stable, more judicious, and more temperate than the *poorer*, and *less educated people*.' This is the Marxist view of American history, first propagated early in this

century by Charles Beard in *An Economic Interpretation of the Constitution*. It is followed blindly today by most textbook writers, even though Beard later repented and repudiated his interpretation as faulty."[10]

In each of these cases, individual instances of experience are used to justify a general claim. In example 1 the claim is that all litmus paper will turn red if dipped in acid; in 2 that most doctors would prefer aspirin if stranded on a desert island; and in 3 that the Marxist view of American history is followed blindly by most American textbook writers. Obviously, the strength of the general claim is dependent on the quality of the individual instances. Certainly, it would occur to all of us to ask of advocates employing arguments 2 and 3 whether the instances were typical of all those of the class. Were these hundred doctors representative of all doctors? Is *America's History* by Todd and Curti typical of all American textbooks? The specific tests of argument are taken up in greater detail in Chapter Nine.

ARGUMENT FROM ANALOGY

Argument from analogy is often referred to by the more familiar name *comparison*. We argue from the more familiar instance to the less familiar instance. The following illustration is a typical case of analogical reasoning:

S1. My grandparents were married very happily for 63 years. They were both devoutly religious, came from similar backgrounds, and were considerate of one another's feelings.
S2. My wife and I are both devoutly religious, come from similar backgrounds, and are considerate of one another's feelings.
C1. My wife and I will have a long and happy marriage.

Careful consideration of this illustration will reveal the very close similarity between argument from analogy and argument from example. Where arguments from example move from particular cases to generalize about all cases of a class, arguments from analogy move from a particular case(s) to another particular case. Analogical reasoning infers that because two things have some qualities in common they will have another quality in common. Because the two marriages shared these qualities in common, the advocate felt comfortable in asserting that an additional quality would also be shared.

Notice, too, that the obvious worrisome question about this argument is nearly the same as the one we addressed to the supporters of our arguments from examples. In argument from example, the question is whether the specific instances are representative of the whole class. In argument from analogy, the question is whether the like qualities are the relevant qualities. Just as an argument from example may go haywire because the specific instances were misleading, so too may the analogy collapse if the essential qualities are misidentified.

ARGUMENT FROM CAUSE

An argument from cause asserts the existence of a "relationship between two events or states of affairs such that the first brings about the second."[11] The recent controversy surrounding the loss of the space shuttle Challenger was filled with arguments from cause.

1. The mechanical explanation for the explosion of Challenger was the failure of the O-rings on the solid rocket booster.
2. The reason for the failure of the O-rings was the cold weather, which impeded the sealing effect of the rings.
3. The reason the shuttle was launched in these cold conditions was due to a bureaucratic commitment to keep an ambitious schedule of shuttle flights.

Each of these arguments maintains that an effect—explosion of the Challenger, failure of the O-rings to seal, launch in cold weather—was the result of a specific cause—failure of the O-rings, cold weather, bureaucratic commitment. This is not merely an assertion that two events occurred simultaneously but that the one was the result of the other. All kinds of things occur at the same time, but do not causally interact with one another.

The status of causation has been a lively topic in the history of philosophy. We will maintain that it is a form of inductive reasoning. Through experience we learn whether one event caused another. The purpose of controlled experimentation is to determine which variable is responsible for a given result. The Food and Drug Administration requires double-blind studies to document the effectiveness of a new medicine. Typically, a number of patients afflicted with a medical condition are divided into two groups; half the patients are given a placebo and the other half the real drug. Neither group knows whether they have the placebo or the real drug. The experimenters then compare the progress of the patients in each group. If the group taking the drug shows significantly better progress than the placebo group, then there is sufficient justification to assert that the drug was responsible for this improvement. This double-blind procedure is the means by which medical scientists separate causal relationships from coincidental relationships.

Our explanation so far makes causation seem very straightforward. But not all causal arguments fit the paradigm of experimental science. Theological arguments based on causal reasoning initially appear to rest on a different type of warrant-backing relationship.

The "argument to design" is "by far the most popular and widely

persuasive of all the traditional arguments for the existence of God."[12]
Those who support this position reason through the following steps:

1. Observations of the natural world reveal an extraordinary degree of regularity and integration.
2. Even the most universal and fundamental regularities uncovered by scientists cannot be intrinsic to the Universe itself.
3. Therefore, order must be imposed and sustained by a Designer (God).

This contention is close to another theological argument for the existence of God. Every event is caused, but the first event must have been uncaused. Therefore, the first cause must be the result of God.

These arguments rely on our understanding of causal argument. In both our examples of scientific and theological argument, the investigators are reasoning back from observed result to cause. In the example of the drug efficacy test, the investigator reasoned back from the change in condition between the experimental and control group to the conclusion that the drug caused or failed to cause a therapeutic effect. In the theological example, philosophers reason back from the observation that the universe is ordered or that all events are caused to the conclusion that God must be a primary cause. In both the medical and theological examples, the argument depends on inductive reasoning. Obviously, theological argument is not subject to the same kind of experimentation as biological arguments, but the nature of causal reasoning remains the same. Although there are fields of causal argument that appear not to rely on material backing, we believe that close examination will always reveal the argument's inductive character.

ARGUMENT FROM SIGN

Argument from sign is easier to illustrate than define. Examine samples of sign argument and then we will proceed to a conceptual definition of this argument type.

S1. The flags on federal buildings are flying at half-mast; therefore, someone important must have died recently.
S2. Bobby Knight tossed a chair onto the basketball court during a game; therefore, one of the officials must have made a bad call.
S3. High ice cream sales are a sign of high rates of juvenile delinquency.

Complicating any definition of sign argument is its confusing kinship with argument from cause. Two of our three examples might be turned into arguments from cause, but the third cannot:

C1. The death of someone important caused the federal government to order all flags flown at half-mast.

C2. A bad call by an official caused Bobby Knight to toss a chair onto the basketball court during a game.

C3. High rates of juvenile delinquency cause ice cream sales to increase.

"All arguments from sign," James McBurney and Glen Mills wrote, "are based on the assumption that two or more variables are related in such a way that the presence or absence of one may be taken as an indication of the presence or absence of the other."[13] The key difference between sign and cause is that sign does give an indication that the proposition is true without attempting to explain why it is true.[14] In other words, argument from sign does not explain why the two variables are related. The arguments C1 and C2 explain why there is a relationship between flags and deaths of important persons and between bad calls and tossed chairs. You will notice that argument C3 is a sign that cannot be converted to a causal argument. The mediating variable of temperature is missing. Argument C3 would make sense if we argued that "warm temperatures cause people to buy more ice cream" and "warm temperatures send more children into the streets and lead to an increase in juvenile delinquency." The arguments S1–S3 assert the presence of an important person's death, an official's bad call, and high rates of juvenile delinquency, but fail to explain how the presence of these phenomena are related to flags, chairs, and ice cream sales.

Some signs are *reciprocal* and others are *nonreciprocal*. In other words, reciprocal signs exist where each variable can serve as a sign of the other. Nonreciprocal signs exist when only one variable can serve as the sign of the other. Consider our three examples, S1–S3, in this regard:

S1-R. Someone important just died; therefore, the flags on federal buildings are flying at half-mast.

S2-R. One of the officials made a bad call; therefore, Bobby Knight tossed a chair onto the basketball court during a game.

S3-R. Juvenile delinquency is on the increase; therefore, ice cream sales must be on the upswing.

S1-R makes as much sense as S1 because both flags and deaths of important persons are signs of one another. Notice, however, that example S2-R is nonreciprocal; if the coach threw a chair during a game it would suggest the presence of a bad call, but every bad call would not predict the presence of a tossed chair. Example S3-R works as a reciprocal sign. Juvenile delinquency rates and ice cream sales are signs of each other.

There are argumentation theorists who dispute the inductive-material nature of signs.[15] But it seems intuitively obvious to us that arguments from sign are warranted by backing that testifies to the constant conjunction in experience between two phenomena.

ARGUMENTS WITH PSYCHOLOGICAL BACKING

Up to this point, we have discussed reasons that support descriptive statements, either descriptions supported by definitions or by observation of material circumstances. But how do you support conclusions that are not descriptive statements? A couple of options are open. You might say that we have defined argument in terms of "statements" and that sentences that are not declarative sentences are not statements. So by definition this problem goes away because we are no longer talking about arguments as defined at the beginning of this chapter. Or, as we advocate, you may think of a statement as something someone stated. I can "state my suggestion," "state the orders," and "state my advice." We give reasons to follow orders, suggestions, and advice all the time. The car salesman gives us "three reasons to buy the car," our academic advisor gave "good reasons to take a Shakespeare course," and the Marine drill instructor made it very clear that "following orders would be a good idea."

Persuasion is concerned with wielding influence. When we persuade, we are trying to get our listeners to change attitudes, beliefs, and behaviors. We advise, suggest, and order to exert influence on an audience. But it makes little sense to discuss formally or materially backing a suggestion. Suggestions are not validated by descriptions of definitions or observations in the world. They cannot be because they are not declarative sentences that assert a description.

However, suggestions, orders, commands, and the like are given rhetorical force by offering reasons. These reasons support these speech acts psychologically. In later chapters, we will demonstrate that this form of argument is critical to discussion of value and policy. For now, we are content to exemplify some forms of argument that psychologically support nondescriptive conclusions.

All of these forms of argument that we will illustrate have force because they fit into a "psycho-logic." The arguers' ability to discover reasons a particular audience will find compelling is the basis of a psycho-logic. The reasons offered will fit into the audience's pre-existing structure of beliefs, attitudes, values, and behaviors. Because we are socialized to accept that consistency is a defining quality of a reasonable person, the advocate is able to wield influence by using reasons that force us to admit that following a particular suggestion, order, piece of advice, etc. is consistent with our psycho-logic. Or, the advocate may suggest that failure to act on such appeals is inconsistent with our psycho-logic. Because our experience is so varied, there are numerous forms of argument that may fit into this category of psycho-logic. Here we are going to look at three general categories of appeal to consistency.

CONSISTENCY AND AUTHORITY

We may follow advice, commands, and suggestions because we respect the advisor, commander, or the person making the suggestion. The credibility of the source has a tremendous influence on us. When this appeal to credibility is transformed into an argument, it often resembles the following illustrations:

1. The Surgeon General urged Americans to stop smoking and protect themselves from cancer; therefore, I ought to stop smoking.
2. My family doctor confirmed the specialist's diagnosis and urged me to have the operation; therefore, I ought to have the operation.
3. My wife contended that wearing a black tuxedo with brown shoes was laughable; therefore, I should wear black shoes.

In the first example, there is an inconsistency between a behavior and a source. The listener respects the source but is engaging in a behavior the source decries. In order to remain consistent, the listener must either devalue the source or the behavior. Of course, in this case the advocate is hoping that the smoker will move in the direction advocated and cease smoking.

In example 2, the patient did not want to have the operation. She did not have a personal relationship with the specialist and it was easy to dismiss his advice. However, she had been going to the family doctor for years and, in fact, he had delivered her two children and pulled her elderly father out of a dangerous bout of pneumonia two years ago. It was very difficult to act inconsistently with the advice of such a respected person.

Although the male author would not wear a black tuxedo with brown shoes, he is completely ignorant of fashion conventions in almost all other areas. He has come to have faith in his wife's judgment about these matters because he has made a great deal fewer fashion blunders since his marriage. Even though he finds his own taste pleasing, he has come to respect his spouse's judgment and thus is moved to follow her advice.

Arguments based on the tension between an existing belief, value, attitude, and a respected source are very common. Note that these arguments can also work in the other direction. One might well argue against taking advice from people because they hold positions with which the listener disagrees.

CONSISTENCY AND BELIEF

We are using the term "belief" to stand for beliefs, values, and attitudes. Persuasive arguments are often built on the inconsistency between these in-head phenomena. Consider the following arguments:

1. You oppose abortion because you believe life is sacred; so how can you possibly support capital punishment. I suggest you reconsider your position on capital punishment.
2. You profess to be a fundamentalist and yet you raise your children based on permissive principles from child psychology. The Bible preaches "spare the rod, spoil the child." I suggest you reassess your child-rearing practices.

In both arguments 1 and 2 the advocate is attempting to change the position of the listener on an important issue. This is accomplished by making hearers uncomfortable with the inconsistencies in their structure of beliefs, values, and attitudes. In argument 1 the advocate explains that the two positions held by the hearer rest on inconsistent premises. In argument 2 the arguer is pointing out that it is inconsistent to hold that the Bible is to be interpreted literally, rather than allegorically, and accept the teachings of modern child psychology.

CONSISTENCY AND BEHAVIOR

This section deals with two different sources of appeals to consistency. First, the advocate may point out inconsistencies between two behaviors. Second, the advocate may point out inconsistencies between behavior and beliefs, values, and attitudes. Consider each type in the following illustrations:

1. You are an avid exerciser and yet you are a heavy smoker. These are inconsistent behaviors because they work at cross purposes. You ought to quit smoking.
2. Despite the fact that you are convinced that fried foods increase your blood cholesterol level and that an increase in blood cholesterol significantly increases your chance of a heart attack, deep fried entrees continue as the main staple of your diet. You ought to reform your eating habits.

In argument 1 the auditor is apprised of behavioral inconsistencies. How can a person feel strongly about good health and exhibit that attitude through regular exercise and yet countermand this concern with health by chain smoking? Of course, highlighting this inconsistency ought to increase the listener's psychological discomfort.

In illustration 2 the listener is accused of acting in ways that he knows are foolhardy. He knows that cholesterol is dangerous; he values his life; yet, he is a glutton for fried foods. The persuasive emphasis on inconsistency presses the audience to confront its irrationality.

There are many more variations on the use of consistency as a psychological foundation for argument. Additional development of this concept will appear in later chapters.

A CAUTIONARY NOTE

The trouble with categories is that they are almost always only partially accurate. You choose one feature to emphasize in an organizing scheme and inevitably overlook some other contrary feature. Ron teaches a class in political communication. During the recent primary season, he asked the members of the class to rank on a liberal-conservative continuum the various presidential candidates. Of course, student judgments differed widely depending on the features they chose to stress.

The tripartite division among definitional, material, and psychological backing is a paradigm case of the dangers of drawing rigid distinctions. These categories were designed to emphasize a particular distinguishing feature of the warrant-backing relationship, but in so doing they ran roughshod over some subtler commonalities. One problem with our category system requires clarification.

All warrant-backing relationships are psychological. Because we are concerned with audiences' adherence to claims, argumentation is inherently psychological. The selection of one definition over another or the choice of an analogy rather than a sign, will certainly have psychological consequences for the audience.

Our point of emphasis is that definitional and material backing are deductively and inductively related to the proposition. These processes are much closer to the typical reasoning found in mathematics and science than the relationship detailed under psychological backing. In this last case, the process resembles neither induction nor deduction because the object is to support a cause of action rather than a description.

CONCLUSIONS

In this chapter, we have moved from the larger perspective of argumentation to a narrower discussion of the structure of individual arguments. *Arguments₁, the utterance of an argument, are defined as a piece of reasoning in which one or more statements are offered as support for some other statement.* The step that permits *the leap from supporting statements to a conclusion is called an inference.*

All inferences are not worthy of acceptance. Some people give reasons that do not adequately support their conclusions. We judge an inference by the quality of its *warrant* and *backing.* A *warrant is a rule that authorizes the move from reason to conclusion.* Backing is the substantive support for the warrant-rule. Stephen Toulmin defines *backing as the generalizations that make explicit the body of experience relied on to establish the trustworthiness of the ways of arguing applied in any particular case.* Backing is field-dependent because the support for a warrant depends on the particular "body of experience" from which the argument is drawn.

The remainder of the chapter took up three general types of backing. Although each individual argument is backed by reference to a specific field, the relationship between reason and conclusion is licensed by one of the general types of backing. Some arguments are backed by appeal to formal rules (logic and mathematics, for example), others by observation of material circumstances, and still others by psychologically-based backing.

Definitional backing is dependent on conforming to a closed set of rules. Arguments of this type are deductive.

Material backing is dependent on tests of experience. It relies upon the results of observation, experimentation, or induction. Material backed arguments are probable rather than certain, because new evidence from experience may always confute the conclusion of a materially backed argument. Reasoning of this type includes arguments from *example, analogy, cause,* and *sign.*

Arguments that are backed psychologically support persuasive attempts to wield influence. *Psychological backing is dependent upon the listeners' subjective reaction to the reason supporting the conclusion.* This mode of reasoning supports conclusions that are not declarative statements but instances of suggestion, command, or advice. The arguer supports these conclusions by employing arguments that appeal to the audience's "psycho-logic." We learn to define reasonableness with a commitment to consistency among our cherished sources, beliefs, and behaviors. By demonstrating that attending to a particular persuasive appeal will provide consistency and alleviate inconsistency, the advocate is able to use arguments that have rhetorical force.

NOTES

1. See Daniel J. O'Keefe, "Two Concepts of Argument," *Journal of the American Forensic Association* 13 (1977): 121–128; and Daniel J. O'Keefe, "The Concepts of Argument and Arguing," in *Advances in Argumentation Theory and Research*, ed. J. R. Cox and C. A. Willard (Carbondale, IL: Southern Illinois Univ. Press, 1982), pp. 3–23.

2. O'Keefe, "Two Concepts of Argument," p. 121.
3. S. Morris Engel, *With Good Reason: An Introduction to Informal Fallacies* (New York: St. Martin's Press, 1976), p. 6.
4. Stephen Toulmin, *The Uses of Argument* (London: Cambridge Univ. Press, 1958), p. 98.
5. Stephen Toulmin, Richard Rieke, and Allan Janik, *An Introduction to Reasoning* (New York: Macmillan, 1979), p. 57.
6. This example is borrowed from Toulmin's *The Uses of Argument*, p. 102.
7. A. J. Ayer, *Language, Truth and Logic* (New York: Dover, 1952), p. 78.
8. "Induction," *A Dictionary of Philosophy* (1979).
9. This illustration was borrowed from Irving M. Copi's *Introduction to Logic*, 3d ed. (New York: Macmillan, 1968), p. 326.
10. John Stormer, *None Dare Call It Treason* (Florissant, MO: Liberty Bell Press, 1964), p. 107.
11. "Causation," *A Dictionary of Philosophy* (1979).
12. "Argument from (or to) Design," *A Dictionary of Philosophy* (1978).
13. James H. McBurney and Glen E. Mills, *Argumentation and Debate*, 2d ed. (New York: Macmillan, 1964), pp. 119–120.
14. See McBurney and Mills, p. 119.
15. See, for example, George W. Ziegelmueller and Charles A. Dause, *Argumentation: Inquiry and Advocacy* (Englewood Cliffs, NJ: Prentice-Hall, 1975), pp. 104–106.

TESTS OF ARGUMENT

All students experience variations of the same recurring nightmare. Typically, in this dream the student is completing the final semester before graduation. The Big Test is scheduled for eight o'clock in the morning in Dr. Ogre's class. You have already been hired for a great job or accepted into a prestigious graduate program. You get to the room on time and prepare to begin the test. You read the questions and begin marking your responses down on the answer sheet. Just before the test is over, you realize that you have systematically marked each answer in the wrong space. The answer to question two is in the space for question three, three in four, four in five, and so on. Dr. Ogre won't give you more time to fix your mistake. You lose your job, get rejected by the graduate school, break up with your intimate other, and end up on skid row.

When you wake up from this nightmare screaming, your roommate calmly explains that there are hardly any Dr. Ogres in the world; almost all schools have procedures for appeal; you can always take the class over again in the summer; and the result of a single test has almost never put anyone on skid row. The nightmare was merely an exaggeration of normal anxiety.

Unfortunately, failing the tests of argument is a great deal closer to the nightmare. Demagoguery persists because political resentment blinds citizens to deception. Racism continues on the shoulders of claptrap masquerading as evidence. Savings are lost in get-rich-quick schemes because wishing obscures reasoning.

Chapters Eight and Nine provide standard tests of evidence and reasoning. They explain the process of matching the norms of the reasonable to actual cases of advocacy.

8

EVALUATION
OF SUPPORTING
MATERIAL

"A lie," says New York University President John Brademas. "Bennett's so-called facts are lies."[1] Brademas was referring to U.S. Secretary of Education William Bennett's contention that thousands of students receiving federally financed student loans came from families with annual incomes above $100,000 a year. What are we to make of this heated exchange between a respected university president and a high ranking government official? Did Secretary Bennett "make up" his comment or does he have data to support his contention? What reason does President Brademas have to doubt Bennett's conclusion? This conflict illustrates the importance of supporting material and underscores the need to evaluate evidence before accepting it as proof of an argument.

In Chapter Six, we discussed the discovery of data and argued that data are used as supporting materials for positions we choose to advocate. Proof, we suggested, is any material serving or tending to establish the truth of something. Such a definition highlights two notions critical to the evaluation of supporting material. First, it is unlikely that advocates will find incontrovertible evidence to support a given position. Rather, data may be found that *tend* to establish the probable truth of a claim or seem *sufficient to convince* someone of the truthfulness of a particular claim. Second, because very little evidence is incontrovertible, the data used to support an argument should be carefully examined by the advocate to assess worthiness and effectiveness.

GENERAL TESTS OF PROOF

The process of evaluating supporting material involves close examination of data. The standard of relevance is the most general test of proof. The supporting material used to substantiate a claim should bear a strong and direct relationship to the claim. Consider the following:

CLAIM: There is a worldwide epidemic of AIDS.
SUPPORTING MATERIAL: As of the end of 1986, 29,000 Americans had contracted AIDS.[2]

The supporting material clearly discusses the problem of AIDS. But, is it relevant to the claim? The claim is that AIDS is a worldwide epidemic but the supporting material makes reference only to the number of cases found in the United States in 1986. There is neither a direct nor a strong relationship between the claim and the data. Consider some alternative pieces of supporting material:

1. 21 cases of AIDS have been reported in Japan and 12 in the Soviet Union.
2. There have been 548 cases of AIDS in Great Britain, 806 cases in France, 675 in West Germany, 170 in Switzerland, and 15 percent of the Zambian population carry the AIDS virus.[3]

The first piece of evidence is more directly related to the original claim because it includes both Japan and the Soviet Union, but it still does not bear a very strong relationship to the claim because it focuses on only two countries in the world. The second piece is directly related to the claim and is more strongly related because it encompasses a much larger segment of the world.

The notion of relevance can be viewed in both field-invariant and field-dependent terms. We assume that all fields require that evidence be relevant to the claims being made. At the same time, what constitutes relevant evidence may vary from field to field. Biblical quotations may be regarded as relevant evidence in a debate about the creation but might be considered irrelevant in a scientific discussion of evolution.

Judging supporting material relevant does not end the process of evaluation. Once the standard of relevancy has been met, the advocate should examine the supporting material in more specific field-dependent terms.

DISCOVERING FIELD-DEPENDENT
PROOF REQUIREMENTS

In Chapter Two, we defined a "field" as roughly equivalent to an area of study such as an academic discipline. Each field, we suggested, is further defined by principles that govern the conduct of those operating in the field. One such principle specifies what counts as adequate data or supporting material for a particular position advanced in a given field. When making an argument, the advocate must discover the field-dependent proof requirements and attempt to insure that the data used to support the argument meet those requirements.

Unfortunately, not all fields are as straightforwardly conventional as academic disciplines. Furthermore, many arguments cross fields or encompass more than one field. Consequently, advocates should first identify what field(s) they are entering with a given argument. The recent public debate over the wisdom of surrogate motherhood illustrates the complexity of field determination. Each year hundreds of women sign agreements to bear children whom they then surrender to the other contracting party in return for monetary compensation. But what happens if the surrogate mother changes her mind and refuses to surrender the child after birth?

To whom does the child belong? An answer to this question depends, in part, on issues within the field of law. Initially, is the contract binding? In arguing the binding nature of the contract, several proof requirements might be considered. First, is there existing legislation that regulates the practice of surrogacy? Second, are there precedents that have been established in other similar legal cases? Third, was the contract entered into freely and honestly by all parties? Fourth, were provisions of the contract violated by any of the parties? In addition to the issue of contract fidelity, this case also raises the issue of legal custody. In a custody case, the argument focuses on who is the better parent, which calls into play a different set of proof requirements. Here, the advocate would be required to provide evidence indicating that one or the other party to the contract was physically or morally unfit for parenthood, or financially unable to provide adequate care for the child.

Beyond these legal issues, this case also raises social and ethical issues that cannot begin to be resolved without turning to other fields such as sociology, psychology, and moral philosophy. Rapid advances in reproductive technology challenge traditional definitions of parenthood. From the field of sociology, advocates might seek to explore such questions as: If conceiving and bearing a child does not make a woman a mother, then what does? Does society approve of surrogacy? Are surrogates mothers, or manufacturers of a product? Is an infant a person or a product? The field of psychology is an appropriate vantage point for the consideration of such issues as: Should women be encouraged to conceive children they will never raise? Can maternal instinct be suppressed without psychological damage? Can psychological testing insure that a surrogate mother will not change her mind? Finally, within the field of moral philosophy, the advocate is invited to examine the ethical aspects of baby selling, or the possible creation of a class of "breeder" women.

Once the appropriate field(s) is identified, advocates should discover what counts as acceptable proof within each field. It is not feasible for us to provide a list of field-dependent proof requirements for all possible fields. Rather, advocates should be reminded that each field is guided by traditions that govern the conduct of those operating in the field. The specific proof requirements are usually easily discernible. Each of the questions raised should be answered with supporting material appropriate to the field.

MEETING THE EVIDENTIARY DEMANDS OF THE FIELD

Consider the social and ethical questions raised in the previous discussion of surrogate motherhood. Suppose we were to argue that society approves of surrogacy. What evidentiary demands does the field of sociology impose? Sociology is a social science guided by the notion that whatever is said about behavior is reasoned from systematic observation and is tested and retested by observation. Consequently, in order to sustain that society approves of surrogacy, we should provide evidence documenting societal attitudes toward surrogate motherhood. Such evidence can be found in surveys of public opinion. The Gallup Organization conducted such a survey and concluded that in 1983, 39 percent of a polling sample approved of surrogate motherhood. As the public has become more familiar with the idea, the approval rating has increased. In 1987, 41 percent of those polled approved of surrogate motherhood.[4]

In comparison, moral philosophy does not demand empirical data on public opinion toward "baby selling." In fact, moralists often stand against the unethical behavior of recent fashion. Instead, advocates arguing in this field are required to provide evidence of a fundamental principle within the accepted moral code that is violated by surrogacy. For example, we might argue that an infant is a human being and human beings in our society are not bought and sold. If, however, society is undergoing social change causing it to question the applicability or restrictiveness of the previously accepted social code, advocates will have to provide evidence attesting to the probable immoral consequences of the act. Thus, we might argue as does Barbara Katz Rothman in *The Tentative Pregnancy*, that the technical revolution in methods of contraception "makes it possible to create a 'breeder' class of women, probably poor women, who would rent their wombs to wealthier people."[5]

Whatever the particular field-dependent proof requirement, meeting those evidentiary demands will usually require use of the various types of data discussed in Chapter Six. Each type of evidence is unique in the procedures used to create the data and the conclusions that can legitimately be drawn from the data. As a result, in addition to providing data that meet the evidentiary demands of the field, advocates should attempt to provide the highest quality supporting material available. In order to do this, advocates must judge evidence against standards for the particular data type.

SPECIFIC TESTS OF PROOF

Chapter Six delineates four types of data: example, comparison, testimony and statistics. Each data type is evaluated via a set of unique standards.

TESTS OF EXAMPLES

Examples establish claims by reference to the particular case. They report or describe observable phenomena in order to establish a more general claim.

> CLAIM: Japanese students do better in school than American students because they spend more time in school and study harder.
>
> EXAMPLE: Kenji Yokozawa, 11, of Kawasaki, Japan, sees nothing unusual in a weekday schedule that includes eight hours of public school, one-and-a-half hours of private "cram" school and a nightly round of homework. "I can play an hour with my friends before cram school," he says. And he can ease up on weekends. There's no cram school then, and public classes end at noon on Saturday.[6]

Since examples are reports or descriptions of observable phenomena, the first three tests of examples assess the circumstances of the observation.

1. Is the source (observer) qualified to make the observation?
2. What was the attitude of the observer toward the subject?
3. How recent was the observation?

Let us evaluate the previous example in light of these three standards.

1. The source for the example was *U.S. News and World Report*. The article indicates that three reporters working out of Tokyo were responsible for making the particular observation reported in the example. It seems reasonable to assume that these reporters were qualified to make such an observation.
2. While it is impossible to know precisely what the attitude of the observers was toward the subject, we can get some feeling for that attitude given what we know about reporters and from reading the entire article. Journalists are imbued with the standards of professional objectivity. In this case, reading the entire article provides the impression that the reporters were engaged in responsible journalistic reporting.
3. Again, it is impossible to know the exact date of the observation. We know the article appeared in the January 19, 1987 issue of the magazine, so we know the observation took place sometime prior to that date. It seems reasonable to assume that the observation was reasonably recent. Recency is an important standard only in situations where the advocate's claim might be altered over time. Historical examples are rarely faulted for lack of recency.

The last three tests of examples confront the nature of the example and its relationship to the claim.

4. Is the example representative?
5. Have contradictory examples been accounted for?
6. Have a sufficient number of examples been provided?

Let us continue our evaluation.

4. Here, we begin to see some problems with the example. We know that this is a typical day for Kenji Yokozawa but we do not know how typical Kenji is of all Japanese students. We may assume that his eight hours of public school each day is typical because we know that Japan has a system of universal public education. We cannot, however, assume that his attendance at a private "cram" school is typical. We would need more data. The problem of representativeness might be overcome by more encompassing studies of attendance at "cram" schools.

5. At this point, we are unaware of any contradictory examples. However, the advocate should be prepared to explain any contradictory examples that might arise.

6. Recall that the example is used to support a claim. The claim in this instance is that Japanese students do better in school than American students because they spend more time in school and study harder. Do we have a sufficient number of examples to justify the claim? The answer is no. We have an example of only one Japanese student. We have no examples of American students and thus no reason to believe they are spending significantly less time attending school or studying after school.

So, while this is an interesting and useful example that meets some of the specific tests of example, it does not meet all of the suggested tests. Specifically, the example alone is not sufficient to establish the claim. The advocate needs to provide additional examples or combine this example with other types of data to adequately support the claim.

TESTS OF COMPARISON

Comparison assumes that what is known or believed to be true of one thing will be true of something else as long as it is like the first in all essential characteristics. Comparison may be direct, such as a parallel case, or indirect. Return for a moment to our earlier discussion of surrogate motherhood.

CLAIM: Surrogate motherhood is moral.
COMPARISON: "One lady my family knows called me a high-class hooker. . . . My comeback when churchgoers criticized me — 'Mary was a surrogate for God.'"[7]

Typically, comparisons, whether direct or indirect, are evaluated in terms of three specific tests.

1. Are the items of comparison familiar and understandable?
2. Are the compared characteristics accurately described?
3. Are the compared cases alike in all essential regards?

Actually, the illustration above contains two comparisons. First, the surrogate mother is compared to a high-class hooker. Second, the surrogate mother is compared to Mary, the mother of Jesus.[8] Let us submit each comparison to the tests outlined above.

1. The comparisons made appear to be familiar and understand-able. Most of us are familiar with the term "hooker" and under-stand it as equivalent to the term "prostitute." Most of us are familiar with Mary, the mother of Jesus, and understand the story surrounding the conception of Jesus.

2. In this illustration, none of the compared characteristics are actually described. Instead, we are left to fill in the description ourselves. Is serving as a surrogate mother accurately described as similar to engaging in prostitution? Here we begin to see some weaknesses in the comparison. While a prostitute may actually engage in sexual intercourse in return for payment, a surrogate mother does not engage in sexual intercourse. The child is conceived through artificial insemination. Is the surro-gate mother accurately characterized as similar to Mary? While the surrogate mother actively seeks to conceive a child for another, Mary did not. Unlike the surrogate who will be reim-bursed for her services, Mary was not.

3. Again, since very little description of the compared cases is provided, we are on our own in evaluating whether the com-pared cases are alike in all essential regards. Both the prostitute and the surrogate are motivated by money. A case could also be made to suggest that both are motivated by altruism. But, there are also some important differences between the hooker and the surrogate mother. As we have already mentioned, the surrogate mother does not engage in sexual intercourse. While the prostitute may engage in her work repeatedly, the surrogate mother rarely performs her job more than once. Likewise, while it may be true that both Mary and the surrogate mother con-ceived a child without sexual intercourse and that the father of the child was someone other than their husband, the circum-stances are significantly different. The surrogate makes a choice to conceive. Mary was surprised. The surrogate surrenders the child at birth to another set of parents. Mary raised Jesus in her own family.

If we find the comparison between the surrogate and the hooker deficient in terms of these tests and the comparison between Mary and the surrogate adequate, we might then conclude that surrogate motherhood is moral. However, in this particular instance, both comparisons are found to be deficient when evaluated with regard to the accuracy of description and the similarity of essential characteristics.

TESTS OF AUTHORITATIVE TESTIMONY

Authoritative testimony refers to the opinions of experts. Supporting material of this sort usually involves the interpretation and/or evaluation of factual material by an individual who possesses special expertise in the relevant field. There are three tests of authoritative testimony.

1. Is the authority qualified to present testimony?
2. Is the authority capable of presenting testimony?
3. Is the testimony presented consistent?

Each of these tests isolate a broad category of consideration. What does it mean to be qualified to present testimony? Answering this question yields a variety of subtests that might be used to evaluate the supporting material.

1q. Is the authority formally educated or trained in the field?
2q. Is the authority considered an expert in the field?
3q. Is the authority highly regarded by colleagues in the field?

Likewise, what does it mean to be capable of presenting testimony?

1c. Has the authority carefully observed and/or investigated the issue?
2c. Does the authority have preconceived expectations or biases?
3c. Is the authority truthful and of good moral character?

What do we mean by consistency?

1s. Is the authority internally consistent? Are earlier positions supported or contradicted?
2s. Is the authority externally consistent? Do other experts agree with the testimony presented?

Let us evaluate authoritative testimony in terms of these three tests. The recent concern over the AIDS crisis has led to a heated debate over government involvement and responsibility. Consider two pieces of authoritative testimony.

TESTIMONY ONE

"Federal prevention programs have been in almost total disarray the last few years," says Gary McDonald, executive director of AIDS Action Council, a nonprofit advocacy group that represents over 250 AIDS social service groups around the country.[9]

TESTIMONY TWO

The National Academy report reaches a similar conclusion, and blames it on lack of presidential leadership. "We need Reagan to focus public attention on the problem and to give the campaign much-needed direction and coordination," says June Osborn, Dean of the School of Public Health at the University of Michigan.[10]

1. Are the authorities testifying qualified? Have they had formal education or training in the field? Are they considered experts? Are they highly regarded by their colleagues? Both authorities appear to be qualified to testify. We know that June Osborn is the Dean of the School of Public Health. We know that to achieve that position she must have had formal training in the field of public health. We are reasonably safe in assuming, since she was selected Dean of the school and since she was a member of the National Academy, she is considered an expert and is highly regarded by her colleagues. In the second case, we know much less about Gary McDonald. We do not know what his formal education or training might be, but we assume he would not be selected to head a national advocacy group without some training in the field. Again, by virtue of his position we assume he is competent at what he does and is well regarded in the field.

2. Are the authorities capable of presenting testimony? Have they had an opportunity for careful observation and/or investigation? Do they have preconceived expectations or biases? Are they truthful and of good moral character? Given what we know, we have no reason to doubt the truthfulness or the moral character of either authority. While both have an interest in the field, we have no reason to assume bias. Both have had an opportunity to observe the operation of existing programs. June Osborn has had the further opportunity, as a result of her involvement with the National Academy, to engage in a detailed investigation of current government efforts to deal with AIDS.

3. Are the authorities consistent? They are certainly externally consistent. Each agrees with the other that current programs lack leadership and direction. Given what we know, it is impossible to determine whether they are internally consistent. We have no knowledge of past positions taken by either authority on the subject of AIDS.

Both pieces of testimony appear to be of relatively high quality. They both meet the three broad tests of testimony.

TESTS OF STATISTICS

Statistics are numerical expressions of a factual nature about a specific population or sample. Three broad questions may be asked in an attempt to begin evaluating statistics as supporting material.

1. Have the concepts been properly measured?
2. Was the investigation properly designed?
3. Are the results properly interpreted?

Each of these questions call into play a series of more specific questions designed to test the worthiness of the statistics. What do we mean by proper measurement?

1m. Is it really possible to measure and quantify the claim?
2m. Is the measurement valid? Is the measuring instrument actually measuring the concept in question and measuring it accurately?
3m. Is the measurement reliable? Is there consistency of measurement?

How is the investigation designed?

1d. What is the design and methodology of the study?
2d. What is the size of the sample?
3d. Is the sample representative?
4d. Are the units of comparison comparable?

When we ask if the results are properly interpreted, we are exploring the relationship between the results and the conclusion being drawn. Two subtests emerge.

1i. Is there a clear relationship between the claim and the data collected?
2i. Are the results statistically significant?

It is important that advocates understand proper measurement, design, and interpretation. All too often, we use statistics as supporting material without any understanding of how they came to be. Admittedly, some sophisticated experimental design and advanced statistical techniques are difficult for the layman to comprehend and explain. Still, it is possible to grasp the basics.

Recent investigations into the problem of sexual abuse have uncovered some interesting statistical data. The results of two studies illustrate the importance of methodology and procedures.

STUDY ONE

Sociologist Diana Russell of Mills College sent trained interviewers around San Francisco to interview 930 randomly selected women face to face. She found that 357 or 38 percent reported at least one instance of having been sexually abused in childhood.[11]

STUDY TWO

In August 1985, the *Los Angeles Times* published the results of a national telephone survey of 2,627 randomly selected adults. Overall, 22 percent of the respondents confided they had experienced as children what they now identify as sexual abuse.[12]

Consider the first broad question focusing on proper measurement. Examine each of the subareas.

1m. It is, of course, possible to quantify claims concerning the amount of or extent of sexual abuse of children.
2m. The measuring instruments, face to face and telephone interviews, appear valid. That is, they are capable of measuring the concept in question and measuring it accurately. Of course, we must allow for the possibility that not everyone may be truthful in these interview situations.
3m. The two measurement instruments appear reliable in that they produce consistent measurement.

Fortunately, each of these studies provides some details concerning the design of the investigation.

1d. The first study utilized face-to-face interviews, while the second employed an anonymous telephone survey. Each technique has some drawbacks. Some individuals in the second study might have been reluctant to tell a stranger on the phone something so personal and intimate. Similarly, some individuals in the first study may have been too embarrassed by the face-to-face situation to admit to having experienced sexual abuse. Both studies fail to specify an important design feature. How was sexual abuse defined? Whether sexual abuse is defined as sexual advances, fondling, or actual sexual intercourse changes how the data are interpreted.
2d. Both studies specify sample size. The second study was considerably larger than the first.
3d. The first study selected individuals randomly, but only in San Francisco. The second study appears more representative because it was nationwide.
4d. Neither of these studies attempt to compare statistics.

The current furor over the quality of education has created a flurry of statistical data. Consider the following:

CLAIM: American schools are failing to properly educate our children.
SUPPORTING MATERIAL: The Scholastic Aptitude Test (SAT) is the best known measure of school performance. The average SAT

scores fell sharply for 20 years, from 969 in 1961 to 890 in 1981, after which it staged a small rally. This year's average was a flat 906.[13]

Are these statistics properly interpreted in the claim?

1i. The relationship between SAT scores and the effectiveness of schools is not clearly established. In fact, those responsible for developing and administering the test continually caution that it is not a measure of school performance.

2i. We have no way of knowing from this piece of evidence whether the drop in scores is really statistically significant. Certainly a drop of 79 points seems large, but we would need to know much more about the measurement instrument and the design of the study before we could assume statistical significance.

In this section, we have discussed standards for the evaluation of four specific types of data: examples, comparison, testimony, and statistics. Advocates should apply these standards in two ways. First, they should use the standards as a guide when selecting the highest quality material to support their own arguments. Second, they should use these standards as a way of testing the quality of their opponents' supporting material.

RHETORICALLY EFFECTIVE USE OF PROOF

Up to this point, we have focused on general tests of evidence that all reasonable people will demand before acknowledging evidence as worthy of acceptance. But beyond these general guidelines, there are standards of proof that vary from audience to audience. The advocate's audience will dictate the strategies of using evidence. Of course, each specific adjustment required for every possible audience is well beyond the scope of any text, but some general considerations of rhetorical adaptation are worth outlining.

Source credibility: Credibility, of course, refers to qualifications that we have already discussed. In addition, studies have uncovered a general personality dimension and the influence of perceptions of dynamism. Consequently, some sources have built up a tremendous reserve of positive feeling among audiences even though judging on the basis of expert credentials alone they may not merit such response. For example, Billy Graham may well have considerably greater credibility on religious matters than a very distinguished theologian. The advocate's responsibility is to make judgments that balance the tensions between worthiness and effectiveness.

Source-Proposition Imbalances: In Chapter Seven, we discussed the relationship between authority and consistency. When making decisions about the use of evidence, particularly in cases where the advocate is addressing an audience unfavorably predisposed to the proposition, the choice to employ reluctant testimony can be critical. Even well qualified sources that are strongly associated with a particular position may have a limited effect on influencing hostile audiences. Conversely, sources previously connected with the opposing position who now identify with the advocate's position can be effectively utilized. This situation exploits what have been termed source-proposition imbalances. The audience positively evaluates the source but has a negative attitude toward the proposition supported by the arguer. This psychological imbalance is uncomfortable for the audience and may force a readjustment in attitude favorable to the advocate's cause.

The advent of feminists joining the antipornography fray is an illustration of a topic area rich in potential source-proposition imbalances. Feminists are traditionally identified with liberalism and liberal causes. Obviously, liberals have traditionally been strong advocates of free speech and supporters of progressive literary works. The spectre of liberal feminists calling for controls on the expression of sexuality in film and print must set up source-proposition imbalances for a number of audiences identified with the women's movement. Certainly, this situation presents rhetorical opportunities for enlarging the antipornography constituency as advocates reach out to previously hostile liberal audiences. On the other hand, advocates could argue that this self-serving abandonment of basic First Amendment free speech principles by so-called "liberal" feminists demonstrates the shallowness of their cause: Source-proposition imbalances can just as easily be resolved by denigrating the source as by altering the proposition.

Diversification of Supporting Materials: There are at least two justifications for diversifying supporting materials; one reason deals with the makeup of particular audiences and the other with the general emotional appeal of the advocate's case. Let us discuss each in turn.

Often, we talk as if audiences are homogeneous in their attitude toward the proposition under discussion. But audiences come together for a variety of different reasons and under a number of different circumstances. These various audiences have been codified into a typology: pedestrian, passive, selected, and concerted audiences. Pedestrian audiences are typified by the sidewalk preacher. The speaker attracts an audience by gaining the attention of those who walk by. The passive audience's attention is assured by the rules of order but the audience is not assembled because of a necessary interest in the speaker's remarks. This situation is usually found in a public speaking class. Students are required to come and listen to their classmates give speeches, but because students did not choose to come to a speech because of their interest in the topic, student involvement in individual speeches may vary widely. Members of a selected audience come to a speech because of their interest in the topic, but all the members do not have the same attitude toward the topic. This is the situation with many public lectures on a college campus. Students come to listen to speakers because of their general interest in the subject, but the audience members may have various attitudes toward the topic. Finally, the concerted audience is made up of members who come together with a single unified attitude toward the speaker's proposition. The authors recently attended a meeting to discuss a response to the University's failure to address apartheid effectively. All the people who came to the meeting were opposed to apartheid and favored divestment of the University's economic interest in South Africa.

The point of this extended discussion of audiences is to demonstrate the variety of circumstances in which the advocate confronts a heterogeneous audience. In these cases, it is critical to the success of the persuasive effort to look for a variety of supporting materials that will appeal to the different predispositions various segments of the audience bring to the proposition.

For example, the surrogate mother controversy outlined a whole variety of argumentative positions and evidence forms. For some, quantification that statistical evidence can provide will prove decisive, and for others the impassioned plea of a moral philosopher would work effectively.

The second reason for diversification is to create an emotional texture to the presentation that is critical to persuasive success. Examples provide concrete instances that build emotional identification. Comparisons can explain unfamiliar material by relating it to concepts that the audience recognizes. Testimony provides interpretation of which none of the other forms of supporting material are capable. Authorities may explain, for example, subtleties of motive that escape other forms of evidence. Finally, statistics are able to quantify through aggregate numbers and precisely specify correlations. Unfortunately, statistics also lack the passion of emotional identification that the other evidence types provide. A mix of materials best makes an effective case for an audience.

There are, of course, other rhetorical considerations when judging the usefulness of individual pieces of supporting material. But these broad issues of source-proposition consistency, source credibility, and diversification of supporting materials are key tests of rhetorical effectiveness.

CONCLUSIONS

In this chapter, we have focused on the evaluation of supporting material. We began with a discussion of general tests of proof. The *standard of relevance* is the most general test of proof. The supporting material used to substantiate a claim should be a strong and direct relationship to the claim. Once the standard of relevance has been met, advocates should examine their supporting material in terms of the *field-dependent proof requirements*. Advocates must first identify what field(s) they are entering with a given argument. Having identified the field(s), advocates should attempt to discover what counts as acceptable proof within each field. Each field is guided by traditions that govern the conduct of those operating in the field. The specific proof requirements should be discoverable from an investigation of those traditions.

In order to be effective, advocates will have to *meet the evidentiary demands of the field*. In the process, they will most likely resort to the use of data such as examples, comparison, authoritative testimony, and statistics. Each of these types of data should meet *specific tests of proof* outlined in this chapter.

Finally, we shifted our discussion from tests of proof to a consideration of standards of proof and strategies for using evidence that vary from audience to audience. Here we examined *source credibility*, *source-proposition imbalances*, and the *diversification of supporting materials* as general considerations in the process of adapting supporting material to the audience in order to enhance effectiveness.

NOTES

1. Peter Brimelow, "Are We Spending Too Much on Education," *Forbes*, 29 December 1986, p. 73.
2. The figure 29,000 was reported in "AIDS: At the Dawn of Fear," *U.S. News and World Report*, 12 January 1987, p. 60.
3. See, "The Bind that Ties All Nations," *U.S. News and World Report*, 12 January 1987, p. 64.
4. "Who Keeps 'Baby M'?" *Newsweek*, 19 January 1987, p. 45.
5. Ibid., p. 46.
6. "The Brain Battle," *U.S. News and World Report*, 19 January 1987, p. 58.
7. "Who Keeps 'Baby M'?" *Newsweek*, 19 January 1987, p. 46.
8. Whatever our own religious beliefs may be, most of us are probably familiar with the Christian belief that Mary was the mother of Jesus, and we understand the story surrounding the conception of Jesus.
9. "AIDS: At the Dawn of Fear," *U.S. News and World Report*, 12 January 1987, p. 63.
10. Ibid.
11. Alfie Kohn, "Shattered Innocence," *Psychology Today*, February 1987, p. 56.
12. Ibid.
13. Peter Brimelow, "Are We Spending Too Much on Education?" *Forbes*, 29 December 1986, p. 76.

9

EVALUATION
OF ARGUMENT

Ron acquired his driver's license in 1968 when he was sixteen years old. Like all graduates of high school programs in driver's education, he was taught a very complex system of parallel parking. Memory of the exact procedure has faded now but inaccurate snatches of the instructions remain: "Line the door up with the rear fender"; "Turn the steering wheel two-and-a-half turns"; and "Back up until the front fender is even with the other car's back fender."

Now, you certainly are entitled to wonder what the male co-author's musings about his adolescence have to do with argumentation. Instruction in argument often resembles this lesson in parallel parking. The history of scholarship in argumentation and logic has produced a whole library worth of volumes that list countless fallacies of reasoning. To make the memorization of these rational defects even more cumbersome, many fallacies are known by Latin names such as *post hoc ergo propter hoc, non sequiter, ad hominem, ad populum,* and others a good deal more obscure.[1]

Ron is not a particularly outstanding driver, but he is a great parallel parker. Yet, he is quite sure that he never follows consciously any of the instructions about parking he was taught in driver's education. We seriously doubt that any experienced driver ever parks by following these directions. Similarly, we are quite sure that few competent advocates, outside the ranks of the professional logician, run a list of Latin-named fallacies through their minds when confronted with a persuasive argument in everday life.[2]

If this appeal to utility were not alone a sufficient reason to adopt a different approach, our move to legitimize arguments that are neither formally nor materially backed but psychologically warranted would demand some nontraditional procedures for evaluating flaws in reasoning. These previous works were concerned with the *rational,* and the present project explores the standards of the *reasonable.* As we explained in Chapter One, "Argumentation is distinguished from logic because it deals with those issues that grow out of the context of concrete situations. Most disputes are not resolved by appeal to formal procedures, but must be *tested against communal concepts of reasonableness.* These standards spring from the particulars of audience, topic, advocate, and occasion."

This shift to the standard of reasonableness has two immediate implications for the evaluation of argument: First, a wider variety of arguments are legitimized by this standard; and, second, the norms of evaluation are ultimately dependent on the elements of context. Let's begin by addressing each of these implications in turn.

LEGITIMIZING A WIDER VARIETY OF ARGUMENTS

The easiest way to support the contention that a much larger variety of arguments are legitimized under a reasonableness standard is to proceed by example. None of the illustrations that follow could meet the standards of strict rationality; in fact, most are examples of reasoning labeled as fallacious in logicians' textbooks. Our categories of illustration cannot exhaust all of these newly legitimized arguments, but they should exemplify the type of argument that is reasonable but not rational.

ARGUMENTS TO AUTHORITY

EXAMPLE ONE

> While out on patrol the squad engaged the enemy and was involved in a prolonged fire fight. The platoon sergeant ordered Corporal Jones to take three men and protect the flank. He enquired of the sergeant why he should do this. The sergeant replied, "Because I said so."

EXAMPLE TWO

> A heart patient was advised by her cardiologist to have bypass surgery. In order to confirm the doctor's diagnosis, the patient traveled a hundred miles to the state's university medical school. The eminent chair of cardiology failed to confirm the first doctor's diagnosis and instead suggested a program of lifestyle changes and drug therapy. The university cardiologist argued that her condition was not presently severe enough to warrant the risk of surgery. Confronted with two conflicting opinions, the patient pondered the respective prestige of each doctor and decided against the surgery.

ARGUMENTS TO TRADITION

EXAMPLE ONE

> With the arrival of their first child Bill and Kristin had an extended argument over what to name the baby. Kristin did not really put up much resistance to the first name of "Christopher," but wanted

the child to have the middle name of her maternal grandparents. But the name "Tatchell" sounded odd to Bill. Kristin argued that there had been no sons to carry on the name and that using it as Christopher's middle name was important for family tradition.

EXAMPLE TWO

Ideological conservatives hold that history is the accumulated repository of a civilization's wisdom. Existing institutions and arrangements represent the product of history. Consequently, conservatives argue for slow and careful change because any radical departure cuts against inherited tradition.

ARGUMENTS TO THE PERSON

EXAMPLE ONE

A: "C's courtesy to his elder friend is admirable."
B: "Perhaps you would speak with less assurance, if you knew how anxious he is to have that elderly friend take him into his business."
A: "Yes, that puts the matter in another light."[3]

EXAMPLE TWO

"Jack," Ruth said, "how can you continue to think that your two-pack-a-day cigarette habit will not harm your health?" Jack replied, "I just read a report from the Tobacco Institute that refuted much of the medical evidence on the harmful effects of smoking." "But," Ruth argued, "99 percent of the reputable medical authorities in the world believe smoking is the leading preventable cause of death. Go and ask anybody on the street and they will confirm what I am telling you."

ANALYSIS OF NONTRADITIONAL ARGUMENTS

Each example category could be assigned a Latin name denoting a fallacious argument: *argumentum ad verecundiam* (appeal to authority or tradition), *argumentum ad hominem* (argument against the person), and *argumentum ad populum* (appeal to the crowd).

But given the situation in each case, are these arguments really fallacious? We believe in each case an audience would find these arguments reasonable under the circumstances. This is not to claim that these are knockdown arguments that clinch the case, but only that they are worthy of consideration in the contexts in which they are presented.

ARGUMENTS TO AUTHORITY.   In example one, the sergeant finds himself in a situation in which providing a rationale for a given combat strategy is beside the point. The overriding issue is one of taking effective action. In terms of reasoned discussion of strategy, the response "Because I said so" is obviously inappropriate. In the context of combat, "Because I said so" is undoubtedly the only reasonable justification. Example one resembles another argument often labeled fallacious; *argumentum ad baculum* (appeal to force). There is embedded in the sergeant's response the implied threat that not to follow orders in combat may bring serious punitive sanctions. But again, in this situation such an appeal seems quite reasonable.

In example two, a patient who is in no position to exercise an independent judgment about her medical condition must rely on the advice of experts. In this case, the two experts she has consulted offer opposing treatment regimens. In such a case, it seems perfectly reasonable to follow the counsel of the physician with the most impressive credentials. Obviously, such arguments do not appear valid for providing conclusive biological evidence of the patient's condition, but these arguments are certainly reasonable considerations for determining what action ought to be taken by the cardiac patient.

ARGUMENTS TO TRADITION.   In the first example, tradition is a reasonable consideration in selecting a child's name. One of the purposes of names is to place a child in a line of ancestral succession. To carry on a family name should not strike anyone as an invalid consideration in this circumstance.

In the second example, a fuller understanding of conservatism should render this a reasonable appeal to tradition. The world is an uncertain place and new institutional arrangements bring uncertain results. The wisdom of any group of people in a given time is subject to the vagaries of temporary fashion and popular whim. To argue that the product of history is a stable guide and ought to serve as a standard of judgment does not seem unreasonable.

ARGUMENTS TO THE PERSON.   The two examples under this heading represent two different forms of appeal. The first is an attack on the person and the second is an appeal to popular sentiment. Each is an appeal to persons rather than to the specifics of the argument.

In the first example, listeners would undoubtedly find this line of argument convincing because we all consider motives in making moral evaluations. Why someone acted in a particular way can make a major difference in our assessment of that person. Whether people act out of self-interest or altruism is an important standard of moral evaluation. Mother Teresa and Albert Schweitzer are cultural heroes because they selflessly cared for others without thought to personal gain. The worst brand of television evangelist is scorned for amassing a personal fortune in the name of a God who commanded us to act for spiritual rather than material motives. In the present case, our evaluation of C changes when we find that C is not acting on the basis of higher principle but the grubby motive of pecuniary self-interest.

In our second sample case, Ruth is engaged in an argument with her husband about the wisdom of continuing to smoke. She is trying to strip away his rationalizations by appealing to the consensus of authority and general lay opinion. Of course, this argument does nothing to establish any particular line of scientific investigation about the effects of smoking. But this argument does go a long way to impeach the Tobacco Institute's credibility and provide some firm ground for decision making. A physician or biologist could make independent scientific judgments based on the data, but the lay person is in no position to make such evaluations and must rely on informed opinion.

REASONABILITY AND THE NORMS FOR GOOD ARGUMENT

If the implications of our parallel parking analogy were carried out to their logical conclusion, we would have to stop writing this chapter at this point. Ron cannot really explain the precise procedure he uses for parallel parking; it seems merely a matter of instinct. Although argument evaluation is not usefully understood as a formal procedure of fallacy identification, it is more than instinct. Good judgment is learned.

But if standards of evaluation are context bound, or more technically field-dependent, how can any textbook provide specific guidelines for the countless number of situations in which argumentation takes place? Of course, the answer is that no book could possibly accomplish such a task.

To use another analogy, understanding the norms of argument is much like learning the rules of a language. Once the grammar of a language is understood, a finite number of rules may be used to critique an infinite number of sentences. There are a few rules of chess, but billions of move combinations. A chess game that involved a series of moves never seen before could still be critiqued if one of the players moved a pawn ahead three spaces on the board. A pawn may only move one or two spaces.

The task before us is to identify a similar "grammar" of argument norms which will insightfully guide the advocate. The obvious place to start is with the standard that governs all argumentation: reasonableness.

In the course of our discussion, a *reasonable* argument has been conceptualized as a claim sufficiently justified to warrant audience approval. The standards of reasonable justification change as the circumstances of advocacy change. To enrich the concept of "reasonable," consider the definition of David Zarefsky: "A reasonable argument is one which most people would accept when they were exercising their critical judgment."[4]

Understanding the concept of critical thinking, applying its principles, and avoiding the obstacles that promote rash judgment represent the grammar of reasonableness. In other words, there are procedures for good judgment in all contexts, although the specific standards of worthy argument differ from field to field.

What is critical thinking? "Critical thinking," Edward D'Angelo wrote, "is the process of evaluating statements, arguments, and experience. An operational definition of critical thinking would consist of all the attitudes and skills used in the evaluating process."[5] The key words are "attitudes" and "skills." Sincere argumentation has a characteristic attitude that the interlocutors bring to the dispute. Since few claims are certain and most are materially or psychologically backed, the arguer must be willing to bring a *critical attitude* to the exchange of views.

The late Douglas Ehninger observed, "Appeals to printed data are indecisive, experimental procedures are inapplicable, and the premises required for [logical] proofs may themselves be matters of contention." Consequently, in the end judgment of worthy argumentation "always is dependent on the cooperativeness and good will of those persons whom a controversy concerns and in this sense consists of neither more nor less than a moral obligation on their part."[6]

This culture has created a list of names for those who engage in argument without the requisite critical attitude: dogmatic, closed-minded, stubborn, gullible, naive, and so on. The persons, processes, and products that foster an uncritical attitude toward argumentation have likewise been assigned pejorative names: indoctrination, propaganda, manipulation, cults, brainwashing, disinformation, and others.

It is one thing to brand these behaviors unethical and another to provide skills of critical thinking that can arm the advocate against the strategies of the propagandist.[7] In what follows, we have outlined dimensions of the critical attitude, skills of critical thinking, and analysis of arguments that attempt to subvert critical inspection. These concepts, attitudes, and skills are general and ought to be brought to all argumentation in whatever field.

REASONABILITY AND THE CRITICAL ATTITUDE

The critical attitude is best understood in terms of ideal cultural roles. Reflect on the habits of mind expected of the philosopher, scientist, detective, teacher, diplomat, jurist, and journalist. The term "ideal" is employed not to emphasize the average or actual thinking habits of those who populate these professions, but to focus on the societal aspirations for those who assume these professional roles. The habits of mind are the same for each ideal professional role. Of course, the scientist and the diplomat do not address similar problems, use the same subject matter standards of judgment, turn to the same kinds of evidence, or use arguments of similar types; yet, it is very comfortable to assert that both exhibit habits of mind that encompass the critical attitude.

Inevitably, this kind of discussion, no matter how hard the writer labors to avoid it, involves a list. But unlike the lists of fallacies that were featured for so many centuries by logicians, this list features *dimensions of attitude*. These dimensions compose a standpoint rather than a mental checklist of argument defects. One adopts a standpoint and struggles to act in ways ethically consistent with it. A standpoint is intensely personal and subjective; a checklist of fallacies is impersonal and objective. With the conclusion of our exhortation, consider the following features of the critical standpoint:[8]

1. *Intellectual curiosity.* This is the opposite of what is sometimes referred to as "dogmatic slumber." The intellectually curious seek answers to various kinds of questions and problems. They investigate explanations by probing for answers.

The escape from superstition, identified with the classical Greek tradition, was mounted by philosophers consumed by intellectual curiosity. The Socratic dialogues, the archetype of the western intellectual tradition, are marked by relentless questioning in order to evaluate accepted explanation. Centuries later Descartes' rationalist philosophy questioned the presuppositions of the age. On the philosophic back of John Stuart Mill, a classical liberalism was spawned that celebrated the "marketplace of ideas" where unfettered speech was held as the best environment for the discovery of truth. Democratic institutions of public deliberation and legal advocacy are built on the bulwark of intellectual curiosity. These institutions can function only with citizens who seek answers and challenge easy explanations.

2. *Open-mindedness.* "The risk that the open-minded person takes," the philosopher Henry Johnstone has argued, "is that of having his belief or conduct altered. This risk, of course, is strictly correlative to the risk the arguer takes that his arguments might fail."[9]

The pointlessness of arguing with the close-minded was captured in the story of the philosopher meeting the bigot:

> Striking up acquaintances with fellow men in the course of our travels is supposed to be one of the far-from-home-ly joys of the wayfarer. On a recent trip such a boon companion initiated the conversation by asking where I was from. When I told him I lived in North Carolina, he said, "The niggers are certainly taking over the South, aren't they?" Now where does one begin his answer? Is this

to be a vignette for the *Reader's Digest* in which I plant a few friendly ideas in the raw soil of my friend's mind, those spanking new fresh seeds which his local library will water, those sudden inspirational shoots to be nurtured by a subscription to the Anti-Defamation League biweekly newsletter? Is it to be a "Let's define our terms" approach? Or is it not the case that an immense weariness informs the scene, an old and burdened haunting of bad faith which makes it practically impossible to have an argument at all. The difficulty is not in finding arguments, lines of argument, etc. Rather, it is the pointlessness of such procedures that makes for weariness here. One knows that a style of mind is already in operation and will never be stopped.... The situation of the man in question permits no openness, and the situation defines the possibility of argument. It is conceivable that one of us might convince the other of some limited aspect of the total problem, but such convincing would be limited precisely because the basic self, the person involved, would be really not at issue.[10]

If prejudice has so shrouded the mind that appeal to reason is no longer capable of penetration, then argument itself is fruitless. The form of argument—the exchange of supported claims—might be carried out, but with the absence of the essential critical attitude nothing can be accomplished. The critical attitude demands a person open to the possibility of reason.

This does not mean that we ought to live as radical skeptics willing to continuously risk all our most cherished intellectual anchors. No one can live in such a world. We would be paralyzed by uncertainty. Even Descartes, history's most systematic doubter, had to maintain faith in certain fundamental beliefs. But the critical attitude does imply that the person is willing to listen, consider, and investigate the position of others.

3. *Flexibility.* The term "flexibility" may refer to a number of different critical characteristics, but here the emphasis is on *methodological flexibility*. A variety of "isms," taken to radical extreme, identify the methodological dogmatist. Radical empiricism, rationalism, historicism, spiritualism, behaviorism, and so forth disrupt critical inquiry.

In the twentieth century, methodological inflexibility has led to curious results. The view held by many radical empiricists was that respectable knowledge consisted of either logical demonstration or sense data. Of course, the domain of ethics is subject neither to logical nor scientific demonstration. The results of the deprecation of the ethical realm have been intellectually severe.[11]

The battles between religion and science have been typical of this inflexible methodological attitude. The evolution/creationism debate has often slipped into dogmatic commitments to inappropriate methods of inquiry. For example, the suggestion that creation ought to be taught as an alternative to evolution may have merit. On the other hand, the suggestion, by those who label themselves as practitioners of creation science, that public schools should teach creationism as biology is an example of methodological dogmatism. Creation may have theological merit, but it is not science. Evolution may have scientific merit, but it is not theology. This dispute often flounders in an argumentative quagmire because advocates on each side insist on methodological hegemony for scientific or theistic perspectives.

The essence of the field approach advocated in this text is that various perspectives are called for in different situations. The literary critic does not employ the methods of the mathematician, but the conclusions of the works of each are reasonable.

4. *Being systematic.* A systematic thinker is committed to following a line of reasoning to its conclusion. A commitment to the systematic involves the adoption of an attitude that avoids the tangents and irrelevancies that can cloud the issue.

The application of strict rules of evidence in the courtroom are designed to assure the systematic development of arguments. Our own habits of mind, undisciplined by imposed rules of procedure, may wander from following the critical thread of inquiry.

We all have friends who make us wonder why they cannot solve persistent problems in their lives. The husband and wife never seem to settle a dispute about how to raise their children, handle their finances, or share domestic chores. Close examination would probably reveal a truckload of emotional baggage that prevents systematic reasoning. Psychological therapy has as a major objective the assistance of clients in developing ways to reason to the solution of their own problems. In other words, therapists help people reason systematically with minimum interference from distracting side issues.

5. *Persistence and decisiveness.* Persistence and decisiveness represent opposite sides of the same coin. People have to make decisions on what evidence is available. In most venues of life, choices are made with very limited evidence. Yet, making a choice, choosing a side, or adopting a point of view is not justification for failing to persist in critical inquiry.

In an emergency, a physician must act quickly and make educated judgments about treatment. Having decided on treatment does not justify halting the administration of additional tests that may shed more light on the patient's condition. Decisions should never end critical thinking.

In the wake of the explosion of the shuttle Challenger, one wonders about the relation between decision and the persistence of critical thinking. We know from the investigation that there were engineers who persisted in their critical evaluation of the launch. But the bureaucratic fact of prior decision seemed to act as a symbol that the time for critical evaluation was over. Once the decision was made, NASA did not want to entertain the arguments of doubters.

6. *Respect for other viewpoints*. This may strike you at first reading as a redundant category. After all, what are open-mindedness and flexibility if they do not embody a respect for other viewpoints? This, of course, is correct. But under this category we feature another aspect that has not received its due.

A certain kind of *tolerance* is the hallmark of the critical attitude. Not a tolerance of error, dogmatism, manipulation, or any other defect in judgment, but rather a recognition that several different competing viewpoints are deserving of the respect afforded by the label reasonable. This does not mean that you should hold each view with equal intensity or give up attempts to strengthen the case for one over another, but it does suggest that the other be held with respect.

For instance, in the continuing debates over political philosophy it is difficult to imagine the appearance of a knockdown argument that could ever resolve liberal/conservative controversy. Each outlook represents two fundamentally different views of human nature. Some people will find one creed more persuasive than another. Yet, each side ought to respect the views of the other. Remain tolerant enough to suppose that each has something interesting and informative to report about the human condition.

THREATS TO CRITICAL THINKING

In an ideal world all those who engaged in argument would enter arenas of dispute with the requisite critical attitude. Unfortunately, the very conditions of dispute create incentives for manipulation, deception, and coercion by the self-interested. Persuasion is the avocation of the unscrupulous. Sincere arguers may fall prey to the techniques of manipulation and find their critical thinking processes short-circuited.

Two interesting books, George Steiner's *In Bluebeard's Castle* and Claus Mueller's *The Politics of Communication*, from separate angles enquire into the causes of European fascism and the German final solution. Analysts of every academic stripe have puzzled over the nightmare of Nazism and wonder how it could have happened at the very center of Western Civilization. It did not occur in a primitive region of the world, but incubated in a nation of great philosophers, writers, composers, and theologians. The carnage was all the greater when the bureaucratic and technical sophistication of an advanced society was put to work for the end of genocide.[12]

Providing a quick diagnosis for these horrific events would constitute intellectual quackery of the highest order. This was not a case explained simply as a rational defect in the thinking of individuals, but the product of a profound cultural decay. But the public justifications for fascism were composed with all the techniques of the propagandist. The appeals were designed to derail critical inquiry. Even in America advocates of racial and religious hatred still find audiences. During the writing of this chapter, the vice-president of the Los Angeles Dodgers baseball club went on *Nightline* and told Ted Koppel that blacks lacked the "necessities" for management and are not great swimmers because they lack "buoyancy." Surprisingly, a good number of ball players in the Dodger organization came to Al Campanis's defense; not excusing his statements but providing testimonials to the kind of person he is. Campanis has a portrait of Jackie Robinson in his home. The failure to apply critical skills to the claptrap of racism learned in a continuing ignorant narrative exacts a high price. Even good people are trampled by the persistence of the clichés of intolerance.

Perhaps these examples represent the darkest moments of suspended critical judgment, but the other cases are no less mind numbing. Everywhere we can find a public dialogue trampled by the work of the unscrupulous or ignorant. Only the assumption of a critical attitude and the relentless application of the skills of critical thinking can guarantee a vibrant public conversation.

The subversion of the reasonable is accomplished in three general ways, through the misuse of language, the control of information, and the privileging of decision making. Each of these techniques will be taken up in turn.

MISUSE OF LANGUAGE

We begin with illustrations of language manipulation and move to skills for undermining the objectives of language misuse. Our examples are political ones because they have drawn the lion's share of attention from analysts of propaganda.

In an analysis of Nazi Germany, Claus Mueller discovered that "dictionaries and encyclopedias were revised by deleting terms, adding new ones, and redefining others. These alterations constituted a direct intervention in the use of language. A revised encyclopedia, *Meyers Lexicon*, was published in 1936." The examples of redefinition are chilling:

PREFASCIST AND FASCIST DEFINITIONS

I—definition of term during the Weimar Republic
II—definition of term during the Third Reich

Abstammungsnach-	I	"see under 'cattle breeding'"
weis	II	"genealogical certificate of Aryan origin"
Arbeitsdienst	I	"see under 'constraint to work'"

	II	"great educational institution for the National Socialist people's community."
Blutschande	I	"incest"
	II	"intimate relation with a non-Aryan"
Blutvergiftung	I	"toxema; blood poisoning"
	II	"appearance of decay in people and races"
fanatisch	I	fanatic; adjective that has negative connotations
	II	fanatic; adjective that has positive connotations
hart	I	hard; adjective that has negative connotations
	II	hard; adjective that has positive connotations
Intellect	I	"creative capacity"
	II	"as distinguished from instinct . . . a term denoting a critical, subversive, and destructive quality."
Konzentrationslager	I	" . . . camps established by Great Britain for the Boers . . . where women and children perished in masses."
	II	"Better term to be used is 'Detention and Education Camps.' . . . They have the purpose of educating the enemies of the National Socialist State . . . of making them harmless and transforming them into useful members of the community (Volksgenossen)."
organisch	I	organic
	II	"a positive attribute . . . denoting what has been grown from blood and soil, e.g., organic philosophy which eludes the tyranny of the schemes of reason."
rücksichtslos	I	inconsiderate
	II	" . . . a term that has a positive meaning denoting resoluteness and energy. Describing the enemy, it preserves its old connotations."
Hass	I	hate
	II	hate has a positive meaning if applied to the right side. "The heroic hate of the Nordic race is strongly contradictory to the cowardly hate of the Jewry."

Zuchtung	I	breeding
	II	breeding. "There really has been a rebirth of the nation because of the conscious breeding of a new man."[13]

Such an imposed systematic redefining of language is unlikely in this country, but the persuasive misuse of terms is still used to undercut critical thought. The defense against such techniques is an understanding of the distorting process and a close questioning of the justification of language choice.

There certainly is no wired relationship between the physical world and symbols. If responsible word use consisted entirely of terms anchored in sensible reality, our vocabulary would shrink considerably. The same object viewed from different perspectives will elicit various descriptions. The symbols of quality are not readily apparent to the senses. The languages of religion, metaphysics, ethics, and aesthetics are largely built on concepts that are invisible.

But, fortunately, we do not live in Humpty Dumpty's world:

"When I use a word," Humpty Dumpty said, in a rather scornful tone, "it means just what I choose it to mean. Neither more nor less."

"The question is," said Alice, "whether you can make words mean so many different things."

"The question is," said Humpty Dumpty, "who is to be master. That is all."[14]

Words are not so plastic that they may be fashioned for whatever purpose the advocate desires. Words have a history and, consequently, have boundaries of justifiable use. Within particular contexts the boundaries of usage become even more precise. The following lines of inquiry ought to clarify the meaning of language.

1. *Field-dependent definitions of terms.* You might remember from Chapter Three that we analyzed a section of Hitler's "Nation and Race." Specifically, it was clear that the term "race" was misused in its genetic context. "Race" was subsituted for "species."

The distinguished political theorist Murray Edelman in his book *Political Language* catalogues a number of misleading words in our political vocabulary that structure our perceptions and interfere with thoughtful analysis. Specifically, in his analysis of the language of the helping professions he discovers systematic language use that focuses attention on the individual rather than society as the cause of poverty. "Quiescent public acceptance of poverty as a fact of social life," Edelman maintains, "depends upon how it is defined, far more than upon its severity. To define it, and therefore perceive it, in terms of the inherent inadequacy of the poor person is to treat its symptoms in individuals, usually in ways that ensure high rates of recidivism, whether the treatment consists of welfare benefits, imprisonment for crime, or hospitalization for emotional disturbance."[15]

The apparently innocuous, what Edelman calls "banal," language of social welfare creates particular perceptions of poverty. The focus on "training programs," for example, reinforces the notion that poor people must fix themselves. Case workers provide "counseling" and "guidance" for the recipients of welfare in order to correct their behavior. This constellation of helping terms turns our attention from defects in economic structure to defects in human nature.[16] Ultimately, this use of language cuts off enquiry into systemic causes of poverty. Our language has structured our pattern of thinking. In this case, looking at the individual is appropriate to the field, but it is not solely appropriate. In asking whether the definition of terms is consistent with the field, the consumer of argument must also ask whether the definitions are the *only* appropriate meanings for the terms.

2. *Analyzing the arguer's intent in employing terms.* Words function for different purposes. Some phrases describe, others command, promise, evaluate, advise, warn, and so forth. The cloaking of the arguer's intent in the guise of inappropriate functional phrases often leads to very unfortunate results.

Fact and value confusion, or put differently, the use of descriptive and evaluative functions, is problematic. To assign a description is in a sense to evaluate. Consider two examples:

> Today, as it seems to have been throughout the years, our conceptions of honor are widely divergent in their viewpoint. That is the reason the majority of people are misled by a fundamental fallacy in regard to their conception of honor. Many people consider honor as a material thing, much in the same way you consider your money, job, and home as material things.
>
> Honor, however, is not like that. You can be deprived of your money, your job, and your home by someone else, but, remember, that no one can ever take away your honor....
>
> After all, what is honor? It is your own personality, and true honor depends on the standards which a man will set up for himself and by which he will endeavor to live.[17]

A: He has had little formal education, as is plainly evident from his conversation. His sentences are often roughly cast, his historical and literary references rather obvious, and his thinking is wanting in that subtlety and sophistication which mark a trained intellect. He is definitely lacking in culture.

B: Much of what you say is true, but I should call him a man of culture notwithstanding.

A: Aren't the characteristics I mention the antithesis of culture, contrary to the very meaning of the term?

B: By no means. You are stressing the outward forms, simply the empty shell of culture. In the true and full sense of the term, "culture" means *imaginative sensitivity* and *originality*. These qualities he has; and so I say, and indeed with no little humility, that he is a man of far deeper culture than many of us who have had superior advantages in education.[18]

These two illustrations make clear the difficulty with words like "honor" and "culture." They appear straightforwardly descriptive, but the terms hide a range of attitudes toward their objects. Unanalyzed these loaded terms can lead to misunderstanding and uncritical acceptance of evaluative judgments. In both the excerpts above, the troublesome terms are probed in order to determine the intent of the user. Once this intent is clear, the audience is in a position to make considered judgments.

3. *Analyzing clichés.* Very often our thinking is directed by the cliché. Sometimes these clichés are unspoken but their folk wisdom is so ingrained in our thinking that they direct our judgment.

Two events occurred recently in which the appeal to the cliché influenced public debate. These clichés were unexamined but their influence was pervasive.

Event One

The Iran-Contra affair has percolated in the national press for some months. The *Tower Commission Report* revealed that the President could not recall key episodes and that he appeared quite detached from the day-to-day operation of American foreign policy. Some months before, at the President's last news conference, he had stumbled badly in explaining the sale of arms to Iran. President Reagan had made comments that were quickly disavowed by the White House.

In his speech addressing the recommendations of the Tower Commission, the President discussed a number of changes he would institute in the running of the National Security Council. He committed himself to a careful scrutiny of procedures and personnel. He reassured the country that he was fully engaged in matters of foreign policy.

The press largely began to view these episodes and evaluate the President's later explanations through the lens of an old cliché. "You can't teach old dogs new tricks." Ronald Reagan was the oldest sitting President in the nation's history. He has throughout his career adopted a particular management style. Could such a man change his manner of operation at this late date in his public career? Although this episode raised serious questions, the underlying cliché went largely unexamined.

EVENT TWO

The authors of this book teach at Indiana University in Blooming-ton. The male author is a basketball fanatic and the female author humors this fanaticism by feigning interest in the sport. In 1987 Indiana University captured its fifth NCAA basketball cham-pionship and the third in the past eleven years.

During the course of the tournament Indiana played and de-feated the #1-ranked team in the nation, University of Nevada-Las Vegas. UNLV's coach and program are controversial to say the least. In Ron's frenzy for victory he began to pump up himself and his basketball cohorts with uncomplimentary judgments about the nature of the UNLV basketball program. On reflection, in a cir-cumstance less consumed with passion, he came to see that his claims rested on a single cliché. "Where there is smoke, there is fire." In fact, Ron is not in possession of any evidence that is satisfactory to substantiate allegations of misconduct.

Embedded in our arguments, used as warrants and backing, are uncritically accepted clichés. They are unexamined because we accept them as common sense or because we use language that submerges them below the surface. Asking the question "Why?" can alter the whole course of an argument.

CONTROL OF INFORMATION

Information control may take two general forms: censorship and dis-information. Critical thinking is short-circuited by the lack of relevant information and by the production of misinformation.

1. *Analyzing argument in a censorship environment*. Since the Second World War two events have most disturbed American faith in govern-ment. Both the Vietnam War and the Watergate scandal involved decision making in an environment of restricted information.

Arguments are often persuasive because they are made from the authority of privileged information. Many of the initially effective argu-ments for continuing the prosecution of the war in Southeast Asia turned on the supposition that the President and his advisors were privy to confidential information that justified American involvement in the name of the "national interest." Perhaps this is why the Admin-istration fought so hard against the publication of the so-called Penta-gon Papers. William Safire recounts the episode in these words: "In 1971 the *New York Times* published selections from a secret 47-volume study of the origins of the Vietnamese war, which they labeled 'Viet-nam Archive' but which promptly became known as the 'Pentagon Papers.' After the series began, the government moved to enjoin pub-lication; the Supreme Court ultimately upheld the right of the *Times* and other newspapers to publish the documents."[19]

What the Pentagon Papers revealed was that the Emperor was wearing no clothes. In fact, the same doubts that had found currency among the ranks of the Administration's critics were held by those in the very highest levels of the government's foreign policy establishment. In fact, the argument from privileged information was more smoke screen than anything else.

"The doctrine of Executive privilege is well established," President Nixon said publicly on March 12, 1973, as the Watergate case was about to break.[20] This became the cloak behind which Nixon tried to hide the evidence of official misconduct in the affair. Reporters, prosecutors, and other investigators were able to penetrate the wall of secrecy because the alleged explanations could not explain the available information.

The argumentative principle of *external consistency* is the key to critical thought in this kind of environment. What could such privileged information show that could explain away all the contradictory information? This information could not be externally consistent with other available data. Reliable information meets the test of external consistency.

2. *Analyzing disinformation.* Censorship and disinformation are definitionally distinct but in practice they almost always occur together. Where information is restricted for reasons not justified by the public interest, we can usually assume that the purpose of secrecy is to protect some official explanation. In other words, censorship of information makes the practice of disinformation more effective.

"Disinformation" is a term coined to denote false information that is given official credibility. Of course, argumentative environments polluted by the deliberate production of misinformation is not restricted to government. But the analysis of the disinformative situation has been most thoroughly analyzed in this context.

The tests of *motive* and *consistency* remain the best defense against disinformation. If the information appears inconsistent with other accounts, you must ask whether there is a motive for disinformation. In both the Vietnam and Watergate cases external inconsistencies existed with other sources of information, and there were clear political motives for lying.

PRIVILEGED SPHERES OF DECISION MAKING

Professor G. Thomas Goodnight has identified three spheres of argument: personal, technical, and public. We view some issues as appropriate for personal decision making, others for deliberation by experts, and still others for general discussion by the public.

"Some disagreements are created," Goodnight contends, "in such a way as to require only the most informal demands for evidence, proof sequences, claim establishment, and language use. These may typify arguments in the *personal sphere* where the subject matter and consequences of the dispute are up to the participants involved." Yet, other "disagreements are created in such a way as to narrow the range of permissible subject matter while requiring more specialized forms of reasoning. These typify the *technical sphere* where more limited rules of evidence, presentation, and judgment are stipulated in order to identify arguers of the field and facilitate the pursuit of their interests." Finally, the *public sphere* "is discrete insofar as it provides forums with customs, traditions, and requirements for arguers in recognition that the consequences of dispute extend beyond the personal and technical spheres."[21]

Spheres of argument are cultural and time bound. In some societies, the range of public interest extends through yard's gate and in the front door. Issues that are regarded as highly personal in the United States are part of the state's business in other societies. Even in America, the boundaries are changing. At one time, the control of private property was sacrosanct. With the agitation for civil rights, public accommodation and fair housing laws made certain decisions about the use of privately owned property a matter of public concern. Once regulation of private sectors of the economy was either not done or the specific regulations were subject to vigorous public debate. With the advent of independent regulatory agencies, the burden of decision making has shifted from the public to the technical sphere.[22]

Often long-term and bitter controversies turn on the notion of sphere of decision making. Liberals hold that the viewing or reading of erotica is a personal decision; some conservatives suggest that the control of pornography is the public's business. Liberals hold that abortion is a personal choice between a woman and her doctor; conservatives hold that abortion is a public decision because the fetus is endowed with civil rights. Liberals hold that gun control ought to be a public decision; conservatives hold that gun ownership is a private decision. In all these controversies, there is a tension involving the technical spheres. Liberals, particularly, often favor leaving issues of fundamental rights to the technical expertise of the courts and conservatives ask for action (often action to preclude court jurisdiction) by bodies of public deliberation.

But these arguments are not threats to critical thinking. These controversies, by and large, have exposed their presuppositions and the key premises are open to public critique. The danger comes when manipulation is used to remove our power of decision. Consider the following cases:

CASE ONE

A doctor comes in to talk to a patient. Putting on a most officious manner, she tells her patient to leave everything in "her hands." Trading on superior position and knowledge, as well as the vulnerability of a sick patient, the doctor makes all the decisions about medical treatment.

CASE TWO

United States law requires that congressional intelligence committees must be kept abreast of covert operations. In the Iran-Contra affair, critics suspect that the Director of Central Intelligence, William Casey, did not discharge this duty. Apparently, the Executive acted without meaningful consultation with Congress.

CASE THREE

"This memorandum," Dean wrote on August 16, 1971, "addresses the matter of how we can maximize the fact of our incumbency in dealing with persons known to be active in their opposition to our Administration. Stated a bit more bluntly—how we can use the available federal machinery to screw our political enemies." John Dean, an advisor to President Nixon, was suggesting the use of the IRS, among other agencies, to harrass not criminals but merely opponents of Nixon. Among the names on the "enemies list" were a respected labor leader (Leonard Woodcock), a distinguished black congressman (John Conyers), and an eminent journalist (Daniel Schorr).[23]

In case one, the doctor has unjustifiably denied the patient the right to decision. The doctor ought to lend her expert advice to the discussion, but the decision is ultimately the patient's. The patient's ability to exercise critical judgment is derailed by the doctor's presumption that treatment decisions are a matter for the technical rather than personal sphere.

In case two, the law has established public control over intelligence agencies. The means of exercising this control is through a process of congressional consultation. Members of Congress are the people's representatives in this matter. Of course, the President as head of the Executive branch is also the people's representative. But to the extent that the Executive branch disregards consultation, intelligence matters become increasingly an issue for the technical sphere of professionals and less a matter subject to the control of the public through congressional deliberation.

In case three, the President used public spheres of power for personal ends. These agencies were no longer under the control of representative bodies making judgments for the public good, but were now the tool of personal ambition with complete disregard for the public interest.

The consumer of argument must remain vigilant, for the self-interested frequently sidestep critical examination by asserting that they are operating in a sphere that privileges their arguments. Recognition of the socially sanctioned spheres of decision making provides the ammunition necessary to refute such claims.

CONCLUSIONS

A good deal of ground has been covered in our attempt to explore the evaluation of argument. First, evaluation of argumentation was distinguished from traditional checklists of logical defects. Few people ever utilize these arcane Latin-named fallacies in their daily confrontation with practical argument. But even if they did try to use these methods, the results would prove unsatisfactory. The defects of rationality disregard the importance of context. Certain formally defective arguments are perfectly reasonable in given contexts.

Second, this text is built on the theoretical bedrock of argument fields. How could any text possibly review all the possible fields of argument and review each relevant standard of judgment? Such a volume, even if possible, would certainly prove useless. Can you imagine trying to master all of the specific material in such an enormous work? Consequently, we looked for a grammar of the reasonable that cut across all contexts of argument and, yet, gave the arguer equipment for detecting and avoiding the pitfalls of assenting to unworthy claims. This grammar exists in a deeper understanding of the standard of reasonableness. To borrow the definition of David Zarefsky, "A reasonable argument is one which most people would accept when they were exercising their critical judgment."[24]

Critical judgment is operationalized in terms of requisite attitudes and skills. The participant in a dispute must bring a critical attitude and an inventory of critical skills to argument. The dimensions of critical attitude include intellectual curiosity, open-mindedness, methodological flexibility, a commitment to systematic reasoning, persistence and decisiveness, and a respect for other viewpoints.

The skills of critical thinking encompass a defense against the misuse of language, the control of information, and the privileging of decision making. The misuse of language is uncovered by a determination to assess the meaning of terms. The consumer of argument ought to consider the field-dependent definitions of terms, analyze the arguer's intent in employing particular terms, and critically evaluate clichés.

The control of information involves censorship and disinformation. Critical thinking is difficult in an environment polluted by lack of information or misinformation. Here the arguer must employ tests of external consistency in order to judge disinformation against other sources of data and question the motives of those who offer the "official" story.

Finally, critical thinking requires skills to penetrate claims of privileged spheres of decision making. Argument occurs in personal, technical, and public spheres. Unscrupulous persuaders frequently find it to their benefit to contend that a given decision is not the business of the audience. Individual autonomy is eroded by the physician who claims a patient's treatment is in the technical sphere. Public dialogue decays when presidents circumvent public dialogue through the use of power for personal gain. The ever growing cult of the expert has diminished the issues appropriate for public discussion. These procedures slowly constrict choice and make us more and more dependent on the judgments of others. The defense against such encroachment is a recognition of the accepted boundaries of the technical, personal, and public spheres. It is only through awareness that the arguer can effectively critique the efforts of the propagandist.

NOTES

1. For a conventional treatment of fallacies, see Irving M. Copi, *Introduction to Logic*, 3d ed. (New York: Macmillan, 1968), pp. 59–88.
2. For those interested in the history of communication theory, it is worth noting that similar attacks were frequently made against the elaborate schemes of topics that composed systems of rhetorical invention.
3. Charles L. Stevenson, *Ethics and Language* (New Haven: Yale Univ. Press, 1944), p. 121.
4. David Zarefsky, "Persistent Questions in the Theory of Argument Fields," *Journal of the American Forensic Association* 18 (1982): 204.
5. Edward D'Angelo, *The Teaching of Critical Thinking* (Amsterdam: B. R. Gruner, 1971), p. 7.
6. Douglas Ehninger, "Validity as Moral Obligation," *Southern Speech Communication Journal* 33 (1968): 215, 222. This view has been promoted by a number of important argumentation theorists. See, for example, Henry W. Johnstone, Jr., *Validity and Rhetoric in Philosophical Argument* (University Park, PA: Dialogue Press of Man and World, 1978); Maurice Natanson, "The Claims of Immediacy," in *Philosophy, Rhetoric and Argumentation*, eds. Maurice Natanson and Henry W. Johnstone, Jr. (University Park: Pennsylvania State Univ. Press, 1970), pp. 10–19; and Wayne Brockriede, "Arguers as Lovers," *Philosophy and Rhetoric* 5 (1972): 1–11.
7. For an ethical analysis of deception, manipulation, and coercion, see Chapter Three.
8. This list is taken in part from Edward D'Angelo's *The Teaching of Critical Thinking*, pp. 7–8. Our commitments to a philosophy of argumentation forced us to abandon D'Angelo's third feature, "objectivity," and substantially modify the fifth item on his list, "intellectual skepticism."
9. Henry W. Johnstone, Jr., "Some Reflections on Argumentation," in *Validity and Rhetoric in Philosophical Argument*, p. 109.
10. Maurice Natanson, "The Claims of Immediacy," pp. 11–12. Copyright © 1965

by the Pennsylvania State University Press. Reprinted by permission of the Pennsylvania State University Press, University Park, PA, 16802.

11. A work representative of this view is A. J. Ayer, *Language, Truth and Logic* (New York: Dover, 1952), esp. ch. 6. The unfortunate results of this approach are persuasively chronicled by Alasdair MacIntyre in *After Virtue* (Notre Dame: Univ. of Notre Dame Press, 1981).

12. George Steiner, *In Bluebeard's Castle* (London: Faber, 1971); and Claus Mueller, *The Politics of Communication* (New York: Oxford Univ. Press, 1973).

13. Mueller, pp. 27–28.

14. Lewis Carroll, *Through the Looking Glass* (New York: St. Martin's Press, 1977), p. 130.

15. Murray Edelman, *Political Language* (New York: Academic Press, 1977), p. 7.

16. See Edelman, pp. 16–20.

17. *New York Times*, 5 December 1938, p. 20. Reprinted in Charles Stevenson, *Ethics and Language*, pp. 279–280.

18. Stevenson, p. 211.

19. "Right to Know," *Safire's Political Dictionary* (1978).

20. "Executive Privilege," *Safire's Political Dictionary* (1978).

21. G. Thomas Goodnight, "The Personal, Technical, and Public Spheres of Argument: A Speculative Inquiry into the Art of Public Deliberation," *Journal of the American Forensic Association* 18 (1982): 220.

22. This move to the technical sphere is insightfully analyzed by Theodore Lowi, *The End of Liberalism: The Second Republic of the United States*, 2d ed. (New York: W. W. Norton, 1979).

23. "Enemies List," *Safire's Political Dictionary* (1978).

24. Zarefsky, 204.

PRESENTATION OF ARGUMENT

A friend of ours described to us one December how he selects Christmas presents: "I never go shopping more than two days before Christmas, but I get up early on the twenty-third and make sure I am the first person at K-Mart. I get a booth in the cafeteria, enjoy a cup of coffee and a piece of pie, and wait for the first blue light special." This largely explains why our friend gave us Vanna White's autobiography and twenty-five feet of garden hose last Christmas.

Coincidentally, and this has remained a mystery to our friend, he frequently breaks up with girlfriends just after Christmas. We think Cynthia was especially disappointed by the plumber's starting kit. In some serious sense, our friend has never appreciated the social expectations surrounding presents. He has never understood that the selection of a gift symbolized the relationship between the giver and the receiver.

Circumstances dictate different kinds of presents. Just as few marriages can survive buying the wife a can opener for her anniversary, few argumentative efforts can survive a haphazard presentation. The decisions surrounding selection require thoughtful consideration.

The four chapters in this section describe the boundaries of presentational choice in building cases, launching refutation, and asking questions. What "presents" the advocate brings to the audience determine the course of their relationship.

10

THE AFFIRMATIVE CASE

The term "case" is frequently accompanied by the language of the building trades. A case is "constructed" or "built." The case materials—arguments—are "made" or "manufactured." The case strategy is "designed." None of us would find the following sentences unusual: "The District Attorney's Office built a strong case. The assistant DA made a particularly telling argument about the issue of motivation. Overall, I thought the prosecution's strategy was very well designed."

A second metaphor follows "case" through our language: the container. We buy cases of beer, put our papers in a briefcase, and pack the suitcase for a weekend getaway. Likewise, the phrase "the prosecutor's case contained some very telling lines of argument" trickles easily off the tongue and sounds fine to the ear.

As both the construction and container metaphors suggest, a "case" is the larger structure in which arguments are placed. Consequently, the case is concerned with the architecture of advocacy. These features include at least the following:

1. An argumentative structure that meets the requirements of the given propositional type.
2. A presentational strategy that packages the arguments to appeal to the audience.

To carry the metaphor beyond the reader's tolerance, the first feature is an issue of engineering, and the second of design. First, the architect must meet the client's functional requirements as well as the city's building code; and second, the design must please the client's aesthetic sense. Obviously, the two requirements are only analytically distinct. Function and aesthetics interact so intensely that the issues are hardly separate. Similarly, the rhetorical equivalents, substance and style, are so interwoven that separation is more theoretical than practical.

In this chapter and the next, we lay out functional requirements and presentational strategies for different case types. In this chapter, the concept of "affirmative" is explained; critical examination of controversial cases of public advocacy are examined; and requirements and presentational options for propositions of fact, value, and policy are explored.

DESIGNATING THE AFFIRMATIVE

The affirmative upholds the burden of proof by providing sufficient reason to overcome presumption. Recall that presumption is expressed as an initial approval of pre-occupied ground. Because pre-occupied ground is defined differently in various fields, the affirmative is designated in accordance with particular circumstances.

For example, in criminal trials the prosecution is the affirmative because it advocates change. The verdict of guilty asks for the creation of a new condition apart from the pre-occupied ground of innocence.

In experimental science, the null hypothesis represents pre-occupied ground. The investigator is an advocate for the affirmative and the affirmative's position is encompassed in the experimental hypothesis.

In other situations, the very same position is designated the affirmative in one situation and the negative in another. Advocates of the death penalty are on the negative in judicial disputes because the courts have legitimized the use of capital punishment. At an American Civil Liberties Union convention, advocates who argue that the ACLU ought to adopt a pro-death penalty policy are affirmative because that organization currently is opposed to capital punishment.

CONSTRUCTING THE AFFIRMATIVE CASE: PROPOSITIONS OF FACT

A proposition of fact is defined as a statement that may be affirmed or denied through tests of existence, causality, classification, or occurrence. Our concern here is to explain the strategies of case construction for affirming a proposition of fact.

Rather than begin with abstract guidelines, we have chosen to illustrate this form of case construction with an analysis of the *Final Report of the Attorney General's Commission on Pornography*. The Commission released the Report in July 1986. Chapter Five in Part Two of the document represents an interesting example of a case affirming a proposition of fact. The Commission's conclusions, as you may know, stirred up considerable controversy. Other members of the Commission, as well as outside commentators, have harshly criticized the findings.

The excerpted section of the Report confronts the reader with issues of human dignity. The American college campus has become a hotbed for the discussion of pornography. Students and administrators have clashed over the wisdom of showing sexually explicit films on campus. Women's groups have strongly objected to the production of images that degrade females. The problem of sexual assault has drawn attention to the possible link between pornography and violence against women.

The following section is an essentially verbatim transcript of a portion of the Report.[1] Read this selection carefully and pay special attention to the organization of the overall case.

Resolved: substantial exposure to sexually violent materials is causally related to antisocial acts of sexual violence.

Increasingly, the most prevalent forms of explicit material fit the description of sexually violent pornography. Some of this material involves sado-masochistic themes, with the standard accoutrements of the genre, including whips, chains, devices of torture, and so on. But another theme of some of this material is not sado-masochistic, but involves instead the recurrent theme of a man making some sort of sexual advance to a woman, being rebuffed, and then raping the woman or in some other way violently forcing himself on the woman. In almost all of this material, whether in magazine or motion picture form, the woman eventually becomes aroused and ecstatic about the initially forced sexual activity, and usually is portrayed as begging for more.

When clinical and experimental research has focused primarily on sexually violent material, the conclusions have been virtually unanimous. In both clinical and experimental settings, exposure to sexually violent materials has indicated an increase in the likelihood of aggression. More specifically, the research shows a causal relationship between exposure to material of this type and aggressive behavior towards women.

Finding a link between aggressive behavior towards women and sexual violence, whether lawful or unlawful, requires assumptions not found exclusively in the experimental evidence. We see no reason, however, not to make these assumptions. The assumption that increased aggressive behavior towards women is causally related, for an aggregate population, to increased sexual violence is significantly supported by the clinical evidence, as well as by much of the less scientific evidence. They are . . . assumptions that are plainly justified by our own common sense. This is not to say that all people with heightened levels of aggression will commit acts of sexual violence. But it is to say that over a sufficiently large number of cases we are confident in asserting that an increase in aggressive behavior directed at women will cause an increase in the level of sexual violence directed at women.

Thus we reach our conclusions by combining the results of the research with highly justifiable assumptions about the generalizability of more limited research results. Since the clinical and experimental evidence supports the conclusion that there is a causal relationship between exposure to sexually violent materials and an increase in aggregate aggressive behavior directed towards women, and since we believe that an increase in aggressive behavior towards women will in a population increase the incidence of sexual violence in that population, we have reached the conclusion, unanimously and confidently, that the available evidence strongly supports the hypothesis that substantial exposure to sexually violent materials as described here bears a causal relationship to antisocial acts of sexual violence and, for some subgroups, possibly to unlawful acts of sexual violence.

ANALYSIS: CASE REQUIREMENTS

DEFINITIONS. To support any proposition, the advocate must make clear to the audience what the key terms mean. In this case, pornography is defined as "sexually violent material." This phrase is given precision by describing two genres: sadomasochism and forced sex.

The case requires a second definition. Not only must the causal agent, in this case sexually violent material, be defined but the effect must be specified. What are "antisocial acts of sexual violence"? It is clear from the Commission's conclusions that these acts may include "unlawful acts" and may also refer to other antisocial acts of aggression against women.

RELIABLE CRITERIA. Recall from Chapter Five the first stock issue of fact: *What are the reliable criteria for judging the facticity of the statement?* These criteria are field-dependent. In other words, the subject domain of pornography, the question of causality, and the social context of the issue points to certain fields.

The Commission argues that the relevant fields are in the behavioral sciences. Within this broad area, the specific standards of experimentation and clinical observation are most relevant. Two standards of proof are established:

1. Do controlled experiments demonstrate a significant relationship between exposure to violent sexual material and an increase in the likelihood of aggressive behavior toward women?
2. Does clinical experience demonstrate that an increase in aggressive behavior toward women will in a population increase the incidence of sexual violence?

Because of the rules governing the use of human subjects in experiments, laboratory evidence alone cannot establish a direct link to sexual violence. "The difficulty with experimental evidence of this variety," the Commission concluded elsewhere in the Report, "is that it is virtually impossible to conduct group experiments outside of the laboratory setting . . . . Perhaps more significantly, enormous ethical problems surround control group experiments involving actual antisocial conduct . . . . With respect to any experiment of this variety, drawing conclusions requires making assumptions between, for example, measured aggression and an actual increase in the likelihood of commmitting offenses."[2]

Clinical evidence gathered from observations of mental health professionals can say little about the extent of a problem because those in therapy represent a restricted population, but "it . . . is [a] sensitive professional evaluation of how *some* people behave, what causes them to behave in that manner, and what, if anything, might change their behavior."[3]

The combination of experimental evidence, demonstrating a general link between violent pornography and heightened aggression, and clinical observation, establishing a particular link between aggression in specific patients and violent antisocial behavior, makes the case for the proposition. Each form of evidence is subject to the standards of the respective domains of social science.

MEETING THE CRITERIA. The second stock issue reads: *Does the present case meet the reliable criteria of facticity?* The Report declared, "When clinical and experimental research has focused primarily on sexually violent material, the conclusions have been virtually unanimous." Put differently, the Commission holds that specialists in the relevant fields consistently approve of the evidence for the argument.

ANALYSIS: PRESENTATIONAL STRATEGIES (I)

Our concern is not with narrow stylistic issues. You should turn to other sources for suggestions about introductions, conclusions, word choice, persuasive order, and so forth. Any number of standard texts can provide sage counsel about the microdecisions of discourse construction.

Here the issues are broader. What latitude does the framework of argumentation allow? It demands definitions, reliable criteria, and evidence that the criteria have been met. But working within this general framework, the advocate has freedom.

The essence of presentational freedom is the freedom to *include* and *exclude*. What does the audience demand to worthily assent to this proposition? To answer this question other more specific issues are addressed. What is already granted assent? On what points is there confusion? Which arguments are most controversial? Are there technical issues beyond the interest or comprehension of this audience?

"[S]ince argumentation aims at securing the adherence of those to whom it is addressed," Perelman reminds us, "it is, in its entirety, relative to the audience to be influenced."[4] For the sake of discussion, re-examine the extended excerpt from the *Final Report of the Attorney General's Commission on Pornography*. The Report's intended audience, those the Commission wished to influence, is revealed in the strategies of presentational choice.

1. The Commission wanted to emphasize the prevalence of sexually violent pornography. The members pressed to define this

sort of material beyond the stereotype of "whips and chains."
2. The Commission pressed areas in which researchers had agreed. The relationship between sexually violent images and heightened measures of aggression are consistently noted in the social scientific literature.
3. The Commission begins to make extrascientific appeals in arguing that heightened measures of male aggression in laboratory settings translate into increases in sexual violence. Here words like "common sense" appear. The word "assumption" appears frequently. There is no quantification of the increased number of sexually violent episodes expected in a population exposed to this form of pornography.
4. The Commission admits that "combining the results" of different forms of research are necessary and yet the members feel comfortable in the "generalizability of more limited research results."
5. The Report hedges between the definition of causal outcome as "unlawful acts" and other unspecificied forms of antisocial behavior.

As one would gather from the very nature of such government commissions, this Report was designed as a political document. And as such, the members of the Commission forged a discourse directed at multiple audiences. First, the Reagan Administration has a conservative constituency. Second, the purpose of a report of this type is to generate arguments relevant for various legislative bodies. Third, the Report, particularly on a subject as controversial as pornography, could expect wide public airing. A variety of groups—religious, feminist, legal—are intensely interested in this topic.

Notice how the presentational choices, even in this small excerpt, mirror these concerns. If one is going to build an argument against explicit sexual material, it is much easier to do it if highly deviant images are viewed as prevalent. Even strong defenders of a broadly interpreted First Amendment find it very difficult to defend "rape" and "torture." The discussion is moved as far away from descriptions that might neutrally be labeled "erotica" as possible. The definitions define the area of argument. These definitions play to the most vocal anti-pornography groups and emphasize a kind of pornography that is distasteful to even the most ardent civil libertarians.

The Commission, knowing the highly controversial nature of the research, focused on areas of unanimity. This allowed them to rest the starting point of the argument on firm findings in social science. The more troublesome move was to proceed beyond experimental findings on heightened aggression and to argue for a causal link to violent sexual acts. At this point, the Report moved from the language of social science to the populist vocabulary of politics. Assumptions were embraced as "common sense." The anecdotal evidence of "clinical" experience is sufficient for making conclusions.

Finally, the Commission members move beyond "unlawful" outcomes to suggest that the audience knows that other forms of antisocial activities are undoubtedly linked to sexually violent pornography. The audience is allowed to read in any number of interpretations. Perhaps this material fosters attitudes and behavior that are at odds with the dominant form of moral conscience.[5]

Presentational choices are adjustments to audience within the framework of the propositional requirements. The Commission addressed the stock issues of a proposition of fact, but it did so with an eye toward the audiences it wished to influence.

ANALYSIS: PRESENTATIONAL STRATEGIES (II)

This is less a second analysis than an opportunity to stress the two separate presentational strategies that were utilized in the Attorney General's Report. We think it is clear from our explanation that the Commission addressed controversies concerning both the standards of evaluation and whether sexually explicit material met those standards. In other words, there is controversy concerning both the appropriate scientific standards of investigation and whether investigations of the effects of pornography meet those standards.

Often, only one of the stock issues is central to the controversy. For example, in arguing the therapeutic effect of a new drug it is likely that both parties will accept traditional standards. The regimen of testing is very well understood by everyone in the drug industry.

In other cases, the entity is very well understood but the standards are the subject of dispute. In a recent controversial case in Bloomington, Indiana, a couple allowed their newborn infant to die because it had serious medical problems. This became known as the "Baby Doe" case. The specifics of the incident were not in question. The relevant standards for handling such an incident were the subject of intense controversy.

Our point is really quite simple. Not all cases involve emphasis on both establishing and meeting the criteria. Some, such as the pornography case, are highly complex and involve both, but others demand that the advocate focus on only one of the key stock issues.

CONSTRUCTING THE AFFIRMATIVE CASE: PROPOSITIONS OF VALUE

Propositions of value ask the audience to make judgments of worth. Values deal with evaluations of good and bad, right and wrong, desirable and undesirable, ugliness and beauty, and so forth.

We have chosen to illustrate the construction of this case form with an analysis of the United States Supreme Court's decision in a recent Georgia capital punishment case. On a 5–4 decision, the Court found for the State of Georgia and affirmed the constitutionality of its capital punishment system.

The affirmative case in this situation is found in the dissenting opinion of Justice Brennan. Because the Court upheld the Georgia law, the majority opinion of Justice Powell argued for the negative or pre-occupied ground.

Some details of the circumstances are important for understanding the various judicial opinions. The *New York Times* offered the following background description:

> It was around 2 o'clock in the afternoon of May 13, 1978, when Warren McCleskey and three other armed men went into the Dixie Furniture Store near downtown Atlanta, ordered the customers to lie down on the floor, tied up the employees and began searching for money.
>
> A few minutes later Officer Frank Schlatt, a five-year veteran of the Atlanta Police Department, responded to a silent alarm reporting a robbery in progress.
>
> When the 31-year-old police officer walked into the store he was struck by two bullets from a .38-caliber Rossi revolver. One of the bullets struck him in the right eye, killing him.
>
> Mr. McCleskey was arrested several weeks later on an unrelated charge and, according to police, confessed to participating in the robbery. He and his accomplices were tried separately. The others received prison terms of varying lengths.
>
> At his trial in October 1978, one of the accomplices identified Mr. McCleskey, who was then 30 years old, as the man who shot Officer Schlatt. Two other witnesses testified that they had overheard Mr. McCleskey brag about killing the officer.
>
> On Oct. 12, a jury of 11 whites and one black convicted him of two counts of armed robbery and one count of murder. After a hearing in the penalty phase of the trial, he was sentenced to die in Georgia's electric chair.
>
> After Mr. McCleskey lost two rounds of appeals in the state courts, the NAACP Legal Defense and Educational Fund Inc. took over the case. Among other things, attorneys for the legal defense fund challenged the constitutionality of the death penalty on the ground that it was administered in a racially discriminatory manner in Georgia.
>
> A study concluded that those who killed whites were much more likely to be sentenced to death than those who killed blacks. Mr. McCleskey is black; Officer Schlatt was white.[6]

The Supreme Court is ordinarily regarded as making judgments of constitutionality and thus concerned with propositions of fact. Was the given decision by the lower courts consistent with the Constitution or not? At other times, we look at the Supreme Court as arguing for particular types of remedies—school busing, affirmative action, and so forth—and in this light they argue over propositions of policy. In the present decision, we have focused on Justice Brennan's *evaluative assessment* of the Georgia sentencing system. In his dissenting opinion, he has portrayed that system as "irrational." In the following section, excerpts from Justice Brennan's opinion are quoted at length.

> Resolved: the application of the death penalty under the State of Georgia's capital punishment system is irrational.

I would reverse the Court of Appeals, for petitioner...Mc-Cleskey has demonstrated precisely the type of risk of irrationality in sentencing that we have consistently condemned in our Eighth Amendment jurisprudence.

At some point in this case, Warren McCleskey doubtless asked his lawyer whether a jury was likely to sentence him to die. A candid reply to this question would have been disturbing. First, counsel would have to tell McCleskey that few of the details of the crime or of McCleskey's past criminal conduct were more important than the fact that his victim was white....Furthermore, counsel would feel bound to tell McCleskey that defendants charged with killing white victims in Georgia are 4.3 times as likely to be sentenced to death as defendants charged with killing blacks....In addition, frankness would compel the disclosure that it was more likely than not that the race of McCleskey's victim would determine whether he received a death sentence: 6 out of every 11 defendants convicted of killing a white person would not have received the death penalty if their victims had been black....Finally, the assessment would not be complete without the information that cases involving black defendants and white victims are more likely to result in a death sentence than cases featuring any other racial combination of defendant and victim. The story could be told in a variety of ways, but McCleskey could not fail to grasp its essential narrative line: There was a significant chance that race would play a prominent role in determining if he lived or died....

Defendants challenging their death sentences...never have had to prove that impermissible considerations have actually infected sentencing decisions. We have required instead that they establish that the system under which they were sentenced posed a significant risk of such an occurrence. McCleskey's claim does differ, however, in one respect from earlier cases: it is the first to base a challenge not on speculation about how a system *might* operate, but on empirical documentation of how it *does* operate.

...Close analysis of the Baldus study...in light of both statistical principles and human experience, reveals that the risk that race influenced McCleskey's sentence is intolerable by any imaginable standard.[7]

ANALYSIS: CASE REQUIREMENTS

DEFINITIONS.   Closely inspect the phrasing of our proposition: "The application of the death penalty under the State of Georgia's capital punishment system is irrational." The term upon which Justice Brennan's analysis turns is "irrational." The other words are either well understood or do not constitute the point of controversy.

The term "irrationality" appears in the following sentence: "McCleskey has demonstrated precisely the type of risk of *irrationality* in sentencing that we have consistently condemned in our Eighth Amendment jurisprudence." For legal scholars this may have very particular meaning, but for the average reader of the daily newspaper "irrationality" is still ambiguous.

Perhaps because of the nature of the forum in which the term appears, we could safely assume that "irrationality" equates with "injustice." The Court's business is to assure justice and to right injustice. We assume that principles of justice follow some rational course.

RELIABLE CRITERIA.   The first stock issue for propositions of value is: *What are the reliable criteria for evaluation?* The reliable criteria come from operationalizing the key value term: "irrational." In this case, Justice Brennan has clearly equated sentencing based either on the race of the victim or the accused as "irrational." Only those factors directly concerned with the nature of the crime or the criminal history of the defendant are rationally relevant. Skin color is a factor that is entirely apart from these concerns. The standard of judgment for Brennan was revealed in this line of his decision: "McCleskey's claim does differ, however, in one respect from these earlier cases: It is the first to base a challenge not on speculation about how a system might operate, but on empirical documentation of how it does operate." From this strain of argument, the following criterion emerged:

> Is there reliable empirical documentation for the racially
> discriminatory application of the death penalty?

MEETING THE CRITERIA.   Justice Brennan applied the standards of statistical analysis in concluding that "...Close analysis of the Baldus study...in light of both statistical principles and human experience, reveals that the risk that race influenced McCleskey's sentence is intolerable by any imaginable standard."

In a later section, which we did not include in the excerpt, the opinion provided a detailed defense of the Baldus study:

> The Baldus study indicates that after taking into account some 230 nonracial factors that might legitimately influence a sentencer, the jury *more likely than not* would have spared McCleskey's life had his victim been black. The study distinguishes between those cases in

which (1) the jury exercises virtually no discretion because the strength or weakness of aggravating factors usually suggests that only one outcome is appropriate; and (2) cases reflecting an "intermediate" level of aggravation, in which the jury has considerable discretion in choosing a sentence. McCleskey's case falls into the intermediate range. In such cases, death is imposed in 34 percent of white-victim crimes and 14 percent of black-victim crimes, a difference of 139 percent in the rate of imposition of the death penalty.[8]

It is quite clear from this passage that Justice Brennan believed that the Baldus study constituted reliable empirical documentation that supported the contention of racial application of the death penalty in the State of Georgia. This evidence of racism was sufficient to support a judgment that the capital punishment system in Georgia was irrational in its operation.

ANALYSIS: PRESENTATIONAL STRATEGIES (I)

In this first section, we characterize the strategy of Justice Brennan's dissenting opinion in the Georgia death penalty case. In the following section, we examine a wholly different approach appropriate in other circumstances.

In the present judicial opinion Brennan laid out a widely accepted standard and then attempted to show that the facts in the case fell under that standard. The standard itself was not the point of contention but rather whether the facts fit the standard. Consider the following comparison:

INSTRUCTOR: "What you did was wrong."

STUDENT: "Why do you say that?"

INSTRUCTOR: "Plagiarism constitutes academic dishonesty and is consequently morally wrong."

STUDENT: "I am not guilty of plagiarism. The paper you have in front of you is my own work. I can show you my earlier drafts, my notes from the list of sources I consulted, and bring in witnesses that can testify to the long hours I spent composing this monograph."

The instructor and the student both agree that plagiarism constitutes a moral wrong. The question is whether the student's behavior fits the definition of plagiarism. The student's defense consists of offering documents and witnesses that will attest to the source of the work.

Similarly, Justice Brennan does not spend any time developing the argument that racially motivated sentencing is unjust, but instead demonstrates that the evidence of racism is sufficient to conclude that Warren McCleskey was unjustly sentenced. This position is made clear in the first sentence of the excerpted opinion: "McCleskey has demonstrated precisely the type of risk of irrationality in sentencing that we have consistently condemned in our Eighth Amendment jurisprudence." The majority opinion written by Justice Powell and the dissenting opinion of Justice Brennan clash on the issue of what is necessary to prove racially discriminatory sentencing in a particular case. Both agree that racial discrimination is a standard for overturning a sentencing decision. In a part of the decision we did not include, Brennan reinforces the pre-existing status of the standard in these words: "Since *Furman v. Georgia*, (1972), the Court has been concerned with the *risk* of the imposition of an arbitrary sentence . . . ."[9]

Justice Brennan is arguing in a circumstance where there is a settled code of values. Precedent has established racial discrimination as an evil and, in addition, as an element that is sufficient to overturn a sentence. What remains is arguments over the second stock issue of value. The Court split 5 to 4 over differing views of what evidence was required to establish convincingly that racial discrimination was present.

ANALYSIS: PRESENTATIONAL STRATEGIES (II)

In other circumstances, stock issue one—the establishment of reliable criteria—is not simply understood but becomes the very focus of the controversy. Under normal circumstances people agree on settled standards of evaluation. But inevitably change creates stress and forces reassessment of settled standards. Constructing a case for a proposition of value in such a situation demands an altogether different set of presentational strategies. The stock issues remain the same, but the audience demands different rhetorical choices.

For the sake of illustration, examine a brief exchange between two parties. You will notice that their disagreement is quite different in form from the Supreme Court opinion we have just discussed.

A: Extramarital sexual intercourse is sinful.
B: But only consider why you say so. You are influenced by others, who follow the authority of others still. On back in this chain of authorities there were unquestionably a great many people who were impelled to the view by a need of giving children a secure social status. But these people lived in a time when there were no effective means of birth control. With birth control, extramarital intercourse need no longer have anything to do with illegitimate children and must be viewed in a new moral light.
A: What you say of the origin of my feelings may be quite true. But meanwhile you overestimate the effectiveness of present birth control methods, and people's ability to make intelligent

use of them. And again, you overlook all the more subtle consequences. You reckon without jealousy, and without considering that intercourse brings with it emotional ties that are not easily broken. These are matters that lead me to continue my unfavorable attitude, regardless of how my attitude may originally have been formed.[10]

In the example of the instructor-student disagreement concerning plagiarism both parties accepted the statement that "plagiarism is wrong." The question was whether what the student had done was wrong. This turned not on the standard but on the facts of the student's behavior in composing the essay. But in the present exchange, the very issue is whether "extramarital sexual intercourse is sinful."

What is the reliable standard for evaluation of sinfulness? This becomes the central issue. Is the standard of sinfulness time bound since technology has provided ways to avoid the unfortunate result of pregnancy?

Interlocutor A does not want to give up the pregnancy result as a justification for the label sinfulness. A explains that B's characterization of birth control is much too optimistic. Beyond the technical problems, the human element will always assure out-of-wedlock pregnancies. In addition, other more fundamental consequences justify the label "sinfulness." Irresponsible sexuality leads to jealousy and other harmful emotional outcomes.

The case for the change in the moral code is based on arguments from consequence. A code of values is designed to harmonize interests in a community. A argues that birth control has removed worries of unfortunate consequences and B denies this and lists other consequences that are beyond technical control.

CONSTRUCTING THE AFFIRMATIVE CASE: PROPOSITIONS OF POLICY

The advocate of a proposition of policy requests the audience's approval of some future action. This type of proposition guides deliberation any time decisions about courses of action take place.

In the course of writing this book, the American trade deficit reached historic levels. Because Congress became increasingly impatient with what they viewed as the Reagan administration's passive posture on the issue, Democrats began to formulate and introduce their own trade legislation. Representative Gephardt from Missouri received national attention for his bold trade proposals. Congressman Gephardt made trade legislation one of the centerpieces of his run for the Democratic presidential nomination.

The Gephardt plan was presented in the form of an amendment to the Trade Act of 1974. The plan is officially designated "Sec. 126. Mandatory Negotiations and Action Regarding Foreign Countries having Excessive and Unwarranted Trade Surpluses with the United States." This proposal was popularly termed the Gephardt amendment.

The amendment was introduced on the floor of the House on April 29, 1987. In what follows, we have included excerpts from speeches by supporters of the legislation.

> Resolved: Congress should adopt the Gephardt amendment to the Trade Act of 1974.

Since 1981, over 13 million jobs have been lost because of unprecedented and uncontrolled trade deficits. In 1986 alone, 2.5 million American workers saw their jobs exported to countries that undermine international trade laws and ignore basic workers' rights. In my own district, statistical unemployment remains in double digits because imported steel has crippled America's steel and coal industries.

In fact, the United States is now the world's largest exporter of jobs as well as the largest debtor nation. Our protectionist trade rivals are winning the economic war for the future.

This rampant protectionism abroad requires a firm response. We cannot accept a global marketplace where we are free to buy but not to sell. In today's world marketplace this is too often the case, however, we are powerless to respond. There are no provisions in present U.S. trade law which mandate comprehesive negotiations or actions with regard to countries that maintain patterns of unjustifiable and unfair trade policies.

Consequently, our trade officials have had to rely almost exlusively on multilateral negotiations established by the General Agreement on Tariffs and Trade [GATT] to pursue our trade objectives. But while the GATT system was adequate when we ruled the economic roost and tariffs were the principal trade barriers, it has failed to provide a defense for nontariff barriers that predominate in the new world economy.

The Gephardt amendment seeks to bring our trade policy into this new world of international trade. It targets foreign protectionist countries that use unfair and discriminatory trade priorities to build up large surpluses with us. Countries with an "excessive trade surplus," 75 percent of imports over export, would be identified by the International Trade Commission. The USTR must then determine if that country has a pattern of unjustified, unreasonable, or discriminatory trade practices that have a significant impact on U.S. commerce. Only if these two essential conditions are met, does the Gephardt amendment apply. If both criteria do exist, the USTR and then the President are given 8 months to negotiate a reduction in the deficit. If the deficit slips below the 75 percent rate, or the country eliminates its unfair trade practices, there is no further action required. However, if a nation fails to meet these requirements, the President must reduce the bilateral deficit by 10 percent.

The emphasis on results is critical. American workers will no longer tolerate carrying the burden of a $170 billion trade deficit. American business will no longer tolerate paying the price of closed markets. And Congress must no longer tolerate a failed trade policy. The time to act is now. I urge the adoption of the Gephardt amendment.[11]

ANALYSIS: CASE REQUIREMENTS

DEFINITIONS. The agent of change—the Congress—and the object of change—the Trade Act of 1974—are understood as entities. During the course of this debate, other related concepts demanded definition. What is the difference between "protectionism" and "fair trade"? These emotional buzz words came to separate the two sides in the dispute.

ILL. The stock issue of ill asks the question, "Is there a significant reason for change?" A prudent person would not approve a future action if there was no compelling reason to take that action.

The advocates of the Gephardt amendment identified one key problem. The United States, they argue, is losing millions of domestic jobs as a result of unfair foreign trade practices. As the speaker said, "Since 1981, over 13 million jobs have been lost because of unprecedented and uncontrolled trade deficits."

BLAME. The stock issue of blame inquires, "Is there an inherent reason to change?" If the difficulty is inherent, then present arrangements are incapable of alleviating the ill.

The loss of jobs is traceable to unfair foreign trade practices. Major United States trading partners erect a variety of barriers that discourage exporters from entering their markets.

Current mechanisms for dealing with foreign protectionism are no longer adequate. The GATT mechanisms do not work in an environment where nontariff barriers are the principle means by which markets are kept closed. The advocate argued, "[GATT] has failed to provide a defense for nontariff barriers that predominate in the new world economy."

CURE. The cure issue asks, "Is there a solution?" In other words, is there a plan that will alleviate the ill?

Obviously, the affirmative believes that the Gephardt amendment is the solution to the problem. By identifying and targeting countries with both "excessive trade surpluses" and a "pattern of unjustified, unreasonable, or discriminatory trade practices," the Gephardt amendment will provide the administration with the necessary leverage to protect American interests. In a section we did not include, Representative Gephardt said, "The bottom line is pressure . . . . My belief is that we will not get change in behavior by the Japanese, the Taiwanese, the South Koreans, and many of the European nations who would qualify under this amendment if we do not apply pressure. Unless they understand that, unless they open their markets, there will be definitive action taken by the United States."[12]

The supporters of the Gephardt amendment met both conditions for fulfilling the requirements of the cure issue. First, a plan was presented. Second, lines of argument were advanced that established the workability of the new proposal.

COST.   The stock issue of cost asks, "Does the policy have more advantages than disadvantages?" In other words, the audience wants to know whether the new proposal is going to bring new undesirable consequences that are more serious than the old problems.

Unlike the stock issues of ill, blame, and cure, the cost issue is often not fully developed by the advocate. Disadvantages are frequently first presented by those who oppose the adoption of the new policy, and then in response the affirmative addresses the issue of cost. For example, later in the debate Congressman Richardson spoke in defense of the amendment, "It is not going to provoke a trade war; it is not going to provoke massive retaliation. It sends a message to the rest of the world and our trading partners that America wants an equal playing field, that we are not patsies anymore, that we want fair trade."

ANALYSIS: PRESENTATIONAL STRATEGIES (I)

There are a wider variety of standard presentational approaches for propositions of policy than for the other case forms we have examined. We are not certain of the reason for this, but two explanations seem most persuasive. First, policy propositions have a larger number of stock issues and, therefore, are subject to greater presentational variation. Second, controversies over action intersect with a variety of decision-making philosophies. As an obvious example, liberals and conservatives have different views of change. Arguments are put in particular frameworks to appeal to these various perspectives on change.

In the excerpt you read, the case for the Gephardt amendment was cast in a format called the *needs case*. The rhetorical emphasis in this kind of case is on the seriousness of the problem and the inability of the current system to solve that problem. Examine the following outline:

I. The enormous United States trade deficit has cost the country millions of jobs.
II. The limitations of the General Agreement on Tariffs and Trade prevent effective action against unfair foreign trade practices.

A. The trade deficit is largely the result of unfair foreign trade practices.

B. GATT is ineffective in pressuring foreign nations to open up their domestic markets.

PLAN OUTLINE:

1. Countries with huge bilateral trade surpluses are placed on a list of "excessive surplus countries"—countries that export 75 percent more to the U.S. than they import.

2. USTR examines the trading practices of each excessive surplus country to determine whether that country has a pattern of unfair trade practices that has a significant adverse effect on U.S. trade—unwarranted trade surplus countries.

3. A six month negotiating period begins with excessive and unwarranted surplus countries.

   a. Successful negotiation: USTR will reevaluate on a yearly basis whether that country has eliminated unfair trading practices. If so, no further action is required.

   b. Unsuccessful negotiation: The U.S. will retaliate dollar-for-dollar against the value of the unfair trading practices that that country maintains.

4. A yearly reevaluation of the practices of that country would occur to determine whether it has in fact eliminated unfair trading practices and whether an excess surplus remains.

5. If that country fails to eliminate its unfair trading practices still has a huge surplus, it would be faced with a bilateral surplus reduction requirement of 10 percent for each of four years.[13]

III. The Gephardt amendment will promote fair trade.

The Gephardt amendment was written to address a specific problem. Consequently, one way to design a case in its support is to emphasize the problem, the causes of the problem, and the solution to the problem.

ANALYSIS: PRESENTATIONAL STRATEGIES (II)

A second policy approach emphasizes the *comparative advantages* of the new approach over the old scheme. Here the assumption is that the present way of doing things is working toward the intended goal, but that a new approach could reach this goal more quickly, effectively, and/or with less cost.

All the stock issues—ill, blame, cure, cost—are addressed, but with a different rhetorical emphasis. If the advocates of the Gephardt amendment had followed the comparative advantages model, the framework of the case would have looked something like this:

PLAN OUTLINE:

1. Countries with huge bilateral trade surpluses are placed on a list of "excessive surplus countries"—countries that export 75 percent more to the U.S. than they import.
2. USTR examines the trading practices of each excessive surplus country to determine whether that country has a pattern of unfair trade practices that has a significant adverse effect on U.S. trade —unwarranted trade surplus countries.
3. A six month negotiating period begins with excessive and unwarranted surplus countries.
   a. Successful negotiation: USTR will reevaluate on a yearly basis whether that country has eliminated unfair trading practices. If so, no further action is required.
   b. Unsuccessful negotiation: The U.S. will retaliate dollar-for-dollar against the value of the unfair trading practices that that country maintains.
4. A yearly reevaluation of the practices of that country would occur to determine whether it has in fact eliminated unfair trading practices and whether an excess surplus remains.
5. If that country fails to eliminate its unfair trading practices and still has a huge surplus, it would be faced with a bilateral surplus reduction requirement of 10 percent for each of four years.

I. The Gephardt amendment would more quickly decrease the American trade deficit.
   A. The enormous United States trade deficit has cost the country millions of jobs.
   B. The limitations of the General Agreement on Tariffs and Trade prevent effective action against unfair foreign trade practices.
      1. The trade deficit is largely the result of unfair foreign trade practices.
      2. GATT is ineffective in pressuring foreign nations to open up their domestic markets.
   C. The Gephardt amendment will more effectively pressure foreign nations to open their domestic markets.

The comparative advantages approach begins by presenting the proposal. It is from the comparison of the new proposal with the old arrangements that the advocate derives the comparative advantage.

Notice that the language in contention I and in IC is in the comparative case. The phrasing stresses a quicker decrease in the trade deficit. This is consistent with a vision of doing the job better. This structure fits comfortably with the trade issue. The country has had some successes in negotiating trade packages with our chief trading partners, but citizens have been frustrated by the very slow and piecemeal progress of existing approaches. There is only a slight difference in wording between focusing on what "is wrong" and what could "go better," but the effect on the audience is quite substantial.

ANALYSIS: PRESENTATIONAL STRATEGIES (III)

A third affirmative policy approach is called the *goals–criteria* case. The goals–criteria case emphasizes the proposal's consistency with a set of established principles. This case form is appropriate when the present system has a well understood set of guidelines that must be met by any new proposal. Usually, this is an approach best suited for an analysis that wishes to focus on process rather than outcome.

Following our previous pattern, we have constructed a goals–criteria case for the Gephardt amendment:

I. American trade policy should operate on the following criteria:
  A. American trade policy must encompass a free trade philosophy.
  B. American trade policy must strive for international economic fairness.

PLAN OUTLINE:

1. Countries with huge bilateral trade surpluses are placed on a list of "excessive surplus countries"—countries that export 75 percent more to the U.S. than they import.
2. USTR examines the trading practices of each excessive surplus country to determine whether that country has a pattern of unfair trade practices that has a significant adverse effect on U.S. trade—unwarranted trade surplus countries.
3. A six month negotiating period begins with excessive and unwarranted surplus countries.
  a. Successful negotiation: USTR will reevaluate on a yearly basis whether that country has eliminated unfair trading practices. If so, no further action is required.
  b. Unsuccessful negotiation: The U.S. will retaliate dollar-for-dollar against the value of the unfair trading practices that that country maintains.
4. A yearly reevaluation of the practices of that country would occur to determine whether it has in fact eliminated unfair trading practices and whether an excess surplus remains.
5. If that country fails to eliminate its unfair trading prctices and still has a huge surplus, it would be faced with a bilateral surplus reduction requirement of 10 percent for each of four years.

I. The Gephardt amendment promotes free trade.
  A. Present reliance on GATT has failed to open foreign markets.
  B. The Gephardt amendment's combination of negotiation and economic pressure will open foreign markets and promote free trade.

II. The Gephardt amendment promotes international economic fairness.
   A. Present trade agreements perpetuate unfair foreign trade advantages.
   B. The Gephardt proposal demands that the United States and her major trading partners work under the same set of rules.

You can see that the goals-criteria format deemphasizes the substantive ill. Rather, this case form focuses on the relationship between principle and policy. In a democratic society, we often demand that our public policies meet certain standards of operation.

This form of presentation would have proven useful in the recent trade debate. Conservatives demanded a continued commitment to free trade and vigorously objected to any bill that resembled protectionist legislation. This goals-criteria format emphasizes the Gephardt amendment's commitment to free market principles.

CONCLUSIONS

A case is the larger structure in which arguments and evidence are placed. First, the advocate must construct a case that meets the functional requirements for sustaining the proposition. Second, the advocate must adopt presentational strategies that effectively appeal to the audience. The set of functional demands are met by addressing the stock issues of a given proposition. The presentational demands are met by determining the most persuasive framework of argument for a given context.

This chapter was concerned with the affirmative case. The affirmative upholds the burden of proof by providing sufficient reason to overcome presumption. Presumption is expressed as an initial approval of pre-occupied ground. Because pre-occupied ground is defined differently in various fields, the affirmative is designated in accordance with circumstances.

The functional affirmative case requirements for propositions of fact and value require the advocate to define key terms, to explain the reliable criteria for judgment, and to demonstrate that the present case meets the criteria.

The essence of presentational strategy is the freedom to include and exclude. The advocate must decide what is well understood, what is taken-for-granted, and what is contested. In many cases, the standards of judgment are well understood. Then, the advocate focuses on demonstrating that the present case can meet these accepted standards. In other situations, the present case is well understood but the standards of judgment have become the issue of contention. The circumstances of a given controversy provide the guidelines for making these rhetorical judgments.

The functional affirmative case requirements for policy are some-what more complex. The advocate must define key terms and address the stock issues of ill, blame, cure, and cost. There are three general presentational schemes for managing this task. The first is called the *needs case*. The needs case emphasizes the problem, the cause of the problem, and the recommended solutions to the problem. The *comparative advantages* case focuses on a comparison between the old and new plan. In this case type the assumption is that the present policy is meeting the intended goal, but not as quickly, effectively, and/or efficiently as it might. Finally, the *goals-criteria* case stresses the new proposal's consistency with established principles. The emphasis is less on outcome and more on following expected procedures.

NOTES

1. *Final Report of the Attorney General's Commission on Pornography* (Washington, D.C.: U.S. Government Printing Office, 1986), pp. 323–326.
2. *Attorney General's Commission*, pp. 318–319.
3. Ibid. p. 315.
4. Chaim Perelman and L. Olbrechts-Tyteca, *The New Rhetoric*, trans. John Wilkinson and Purcell Weaver (Notre Dame: Univ. of Notre Dame Press, 1969), p. 19.
5. An earlier section of the Report suggests this wider sense of harm: "And we certainly reject the view that the only noticeable harm is one that causes physical or financial harm to identifiable individuals. An environment, physical, cultural, moral, or aesthetic, can be harmed, and so can a community, organization or group be harmed independent of identifiable harms to members of that community." A paragraph later this sentence is found: "[T]here are acts that must be condemned not because the evils of the world will thereby be eliminated, but because conscience demands it." (p. 303)
6. "Court Case: How It Began," *The New York Times*, 23 April 1987, p. 12. Copyright © 1987 by The New York Times Company. Reprinted by permission.
7. *McCleskey v. Kemp*, 84-6811, U.S. Sup. Ct., April 22, 1987.
8. Ibid.
9. Ibid.
10. Charles L. Stevenson, *Ethics and Language* (New Haven: Yale Univ. Press, 1944), pp. 123–124.
11. *Congressional Record*, 29 April 1987, p. H2759.
12. Richard Gephardt, *Congressional Record*, 29 April 1987, p. H2757.
13. This summary of the Gephardt proposal was taken from Pierre A. Rinfret, *Congressional Record*, 29 April 1987, p. H2762.

11

THE NEGATIVE CASE

Growing up in America, we are socialized into a culture of positive thinkers. The 1980s image of the entrepreneur as hero attests to the prized social value of aggressiveness and risk-taking. We award the bold with acclaim. A whole new generation of political candidates is running on a platform of new ideas. Each succeeding administration talks about a New Deal, a New Frontier, or a Great Society.

Where in all this cultural noise of the new, different, innovative, and bold is there room for the negative? We all aspire to see ourselves as "progressive, " "forward thinking," and "visionary." The negative is reserved for the unduly prudish, the timid paralyzed by caution, and the professional nay sayer who dispenses pessimism like aspirin.

But there are heroes of the negative. There are those who staunchly defended traditional values in the face of zealotry. There are those who adhered to reason when some wished to trample all that had been accomplished in a burst of passion. There are those who resisted Hitler's rise, Joseph McCarthy's Red Scare, limits on First Amendment freedoms, and the enthusiasm of the moment to counsel caution. Don't we all wish there had been a capable negative when John Kennedy decided to go ahead with the Bay of Pigs operation, when Lyndon Johnson first began escalating the Vietnam War, when Richard Nixon planned the invasion of Cambodia, when Jimmy Carter allowed the Shah admission to the United States, and when Ronald Reagan decided to trade arms to Iran for the return of hostages in Lebanon?

The competent negative is essential to an ordered society. The critic demands that advocates of change live up to the requirements of proof and reasonable argument. The responsible critic demands adherence to the standards of critical thinking in each controversy.

In this chapter, we will follow a pattern of organization that mirrors Chapter Ten. First, specific guidelines for the designation of the negative are offered. Second, the options for the construction of the negative case for fact, value, and policy propositions are explored.

DESIGNATING THE NEGATIVE

The negative enjoys presumption. Recall that presumption is expressed as an initial approval of pre-occupied ground. Pre-occupied ground is defined according to the commitments of a particular field.

This presumption provides a number of persuasive advantages to the negative. The defender of pre-occupied ground can triumph not only by presenting a constructive case for a particular view, but by demonstrating the failure of the affirmative to meet the reasonable standards of advocacy. In the legal context, prosecutors must prove their case, and without that proof the defense wins by default. In science, investigators must demonstrate the validity of their findings and without such demonstration the null hypothesis continues to reign.

Second, because there is already "initial approval" the defender of pre-occupied ground enjoys existing points of agreement upon which to build arguments. There are certain accepted facts and values upon which presumption rests that permit the negative to identify with the audience.

Third, the negative enjoys the advantage of exploiting the risk of change. The new, though often tantalizing, is fraught with uncertainty. This uncertainty is a rhetorical resource that the negative can effectively employ.

CONSTRUCTING THE NEGATIVE CASE: PROPOSITIONS OF FACT

In Chapter Ten we chose to illustrate an affirmative case for a proposition of fact with an analysis of the *Final Report of the Attorney General's Commission on Pornography*. The so-called Meese Commission Report drew sharp criticism from a number of quarters.

A representative negative critique of the Commission's findings was published by Christie Hefner, President of Playboy Enterprises, Inc., in a 1987 issue of *The Humanist*.[1] In what follows, we have extracted excerpts from the article that focus on the key issues of the contested proposition of fact.

> Resolved: substantial exposure to sexually violent materials is causally related to antisocial acts of sexual violence.

> [T]he commission members focus much of their effort on those parts of sexual imagery that are the most violent and hateful, which gives you an impression . . . very different from, in fact, what is *really* out there. This problem of faulty methodology was attacked by the two commissioners who filed a dissenting report, Dr. Judith Becker of Columbia University . . . and Ellen Levin. One of the things they wrote in the dissenting opinion was, "that the evidence brought to the panel was skewed to the very violent and extremely degrading."

> [T]he commission ignored the evidence that points to just the *opposite* conclusion. For example, one of the very few pieces of original research that the commission did was to look . . . at the thirteen

best-selling men's magazines to find what percentage of their material was violent. . . . [T]he actual amount proved to be *less than one percent*. [T]his statistic is amazingly missing from the final report. . . .

. . . When you read the headlines from the report, you may not see what's behind them: . . . the problem in [defining] the word *harm*, as in "pornography causes harm." . . . I think we would all like to know that the basis for censorship is that the material is harmful and that the harm is both real and serious. What does the commission have to say about this? Well, according to Commissioner Becker in the dissenting opinion, "The commission began with the ultra-conservative premise that a majority considered masturbation, oral/genital sex, premarital sex, to be harmful and anti-social behavior."

. . . I don't think the Meese commission proved there *is* a link [between pornography and violent crime]. The *Los Angeles Times* put it even more strongly than I might have when it wrote: "The kindest thing that can be said about the two thousand page report of the Attorney General's Commission on Pornography is that it's a joke, not funny, but a joke. The commission's scholarship is ludicrous, its conclusions unsupported, its methodology zany."

Scientific data exist in a variety of arenas that . . . could have pointed to a very different conclusion. First of all, there's evidence from other countries which has been conveniently ignored by the commission. . . . In Japan, themes of bondage and rape in their printed material are much more prevalent than in this country, but the incidence of rape in Japan is one-sixteenth that in the United States. There's scientific research that has been done on the potential causes of violence and sexual abuse against women and children, and there isn't a single study that suggests that pornography is a cause, let alone a substantial cause, of this violence.

Dr. Becker . . . says, "No serious body of evidence of a causal connection between pornography and crime exists. I believe some of the commissioners are simply attempting to legislate their own personal morality." Dr. Edward Donnerstein, who is one of the experts called in front of the commission, says, "[W]e have to conclude there is no evidence for any harm related effects." Murray Strauss, who was also a witness in front of the commission, says, "The fundamental problem is there's a wide consensus about the issue of violence, but the commission's concern was sex, and as a means of getting at sex, they said sex promotes violence, but that's crazy."

. . . The report fails to focus on violence as distinct from sexuality, even though all scientific evidence indicates that when you're talking about sexually violent material, it's the violent component—not the sexual component—that has an adverse effect on people's attitudes. When you show people hardcore sexual material without a violent context, you see a neutral effect. When you show them violent material without a sexual context, you see negative results.

. . . [P]art of the problem with the commission's report is that it simply runs counter to the experience of millions of Americans. More X-rated video cassettes were rented during 1985 than there were people who voted for Ronald Reagan. Millions of poeple have seen sexual material in magazines and films, and they have not become violent. Moreover, if one examines countries that have serious problems of violence and abuse against women—such as South Africa, Iran, or the Soviet Union—you discover that these are countries that are not only politically repressive but sexually repressive in their approach to materials as well.

. . . [T]he final public policy danger and tragedy of the Meese Report [is that]: *it misdirects sincere people's attention away from thinking about the real causes of violence and abuse.*

. . . When the commission relies upon unfortunate victims who give anecdotal testimony and are encouraged to blame pornography for their personal problems, what they are doing is disregarding the real causes of their problems—be they family pathology, sexual ignorance due to repression, poverty, drug or alcohol abuse— and the commission, therefore, opts for the rhetoric instead of the serious inquiry that's necessary.

. . . When the murderer of Harvey Milk and Mayor George Moscone says that Twinkies made him do it, we don't let him off. When a psychopath pulls a sword on the Staten Island Ferry and kills two people and says, "God made me do it," that isn't an alibi. Why is it so different when we deal with areas of sexuality and sexual imagery? We don't let someone blame alcohol for drunk driving. We say *you* are responsible if you become abusive.

ANALYSIS: CASE REQUIREMENTS

DEFINITIONS.   The ability to define terms is a powerful advantage in any dispute. Particularly in controversies over matters of fact, the manner in which the key words are specified is often decisive.

In the present case, Hefner made two moves worth noticing. First, she addressed the causal agent, "sexually violent materials," by seriously questioning its scope. The Report had argued that "the most prevalent forms of explicit material fit the description of sexually violent pornography." She turned to scientific data that contradicted this claim. And, moreover, she provided evidence, both from the testimony of dissenting Commissioners and from an examination of data left out of the final report, that the Meese Commission had purposely slanted the findings.

Now this first attack did not directly refute the meaning of the words "sexually violent materials," but rather suggested that other investigators have been unable to draw the conclusion that violent sexual activity is the "most prevalent form" of pornography. The audience is left to conclude either that the Commission's definition was unduly broad or that the Report's conclusions were based on biased applications of the definition.

Second, Hefner disputed the Commission's definition of the term "harm." Recall that the Commission defined harm not just as "unlawful acts" but as "anti-social acts." One of the dissenting commissioners labeled this definition "ultra-conservative" and asserted that it was based on an overly strict conception of sexual morality. In other words, Hefner argued that the definition of harm was at odds with standard definitions in the field.

RELIABLE CRITERIA.   Both advocates and critics of the Report agreed that scientific evaluation of the pornography-violence link was appropriate. But, in addition to reliance on experimental data, the Commission tried to justify key findings with clinical evidence. Here Hefner cried foul.

She maintained that such anecdotal evidence is inherently unreliable. She wrote, "When the commission relies upon unfortunate victims who give anecdotal testimony and are encouraged to blame pornography for their personal problems, what they are doing is disregarding the real causes of their problems—be they family pathology, sexual ignorance due to repression, poverty, drug or alcohol abuse—and the commission, therefore, opts for the rhetoric instead of the serious inquiry that's necessary." In other words, there is always a tendency to look for reasons to escape personal responsibility for one's actions. The urge to rationalize makes this form of evidence highly unreliable.

Beyond the issue of psychological reliability, Hefner argued that the use of this form of evidence was unprecedented. She drew the following comparisons: "When the murderer of Harvey Milk and Mayor George Moscone says that Twinkies made him do it, we don't let him off. When a psychopath pulls a sword on the Staten Island Ferry and kills two people and says, 'God made me do it,' that isn't an alibi. Why is it so different when we deal with areas of sexuality and sexual imagery? We don't let someone blame alcohol for drunk driving. We say *you* are responsible if you become abusive." In fields that render judgments of responsibility, the focus is on the individual rather than elements of the environment that may influence personal choice.

MEETING THE CRITERIA: This was where Hefner placed the lion's share of her criticism. Her objections emphasized the Meese Commission's failure to meet the standards of social scientific investigation.

First, scientific investigation demands impartiality. Stacking the deck is propaganda, not social science. Through a series of examples, Hefner contended that counterevidence and alternative explanations were systematically excluded from consideration. A report cannot carry the label "scientific" if it does not impartially weigh the available evidence.

Second, scientific establishment of causality demands an account of intervening variables. Hefner wrote that the "violence" not the "sex" was responsible for the "adverse effect on people's attitudes."

She argued, "When you show people hardcore sexual material without a violent context, you see a neutral effect. When you show them violent material without a sexual context, you see negative results." In other words, pornography—characterized as sexually explicit material—does not lead to violent acts. Hefner asserted that the Commission, in a move violating the canons of social science, failed to account for the independent effect of violence.

Third, sound scientific scholarship demands an explanation of contrary findings. In this case, Hefner emphasized the contrary findings from experience in Denmark, Japan, South Africa, Iran, and the Soviet Union. More specifically she challenged the Commission to explain why "millions of people have seen sexual material in magazines and films, and they have not become violent."

ANALYSIS: PRESENTATIONAL STRATEGIES (I)

Recall that presentational strategies for our purpose are characterized as the patterns of inclusion and exclusion. Presentation in this broad sense concerns the arguer's judgment about what is important and what is peripheral for a specific audience.

Upholding the negative affords a great deal more freedom than is granted the affirmative. The affirmative, shackled with the burden of proof, must establish all the relevant stock issues. Now the audience may already agree on particular issues and not force the affirmative to do much work in a particular area. However, theoretically the affirmative is responsible for the establishment of all key issues in the case. By contrast, negatives are free to pick their spots. With the capture of a single critical issue, the negative justifies a favorable decision.

In this first section on presentational strategy, we want to emphasize the negative focus on reliable criteria. As you might imagine, the audience for a publication entitled *The Humanist* is going to have strong feelings about anything that smacks of censorship. In addition, *The Humanist* reader is likely to have serious reservations about the Reagan agenda.

"Science" is not the god term for conservatives that it is for liberals. In fact, much of the social conservative agenda highlights political-scientific antagonism. These conflicts are exemplified by conflicts with the medical community over abortion, with science educators over creationism, and with medical ethicists over practices of passive euthanasia. Consequently, Hefner's liberal audience was probably highly motivated to hold the Commission's findings up to the most rigorous standards of social science.

In sections we did not excerpt from Hefner's essay and in many other published critiques of the Meese Commission, critics focused on the issue of censorship. The assumption is that such a Report is funded in order to justify some form of legislative action. This working premise allowed those who rejected the Report to make a very strong case for exceptionally vigorous application of standards of proof. To justify restriction of freedom, the proof of danger must be clear and convincing. Hefner wrote, "I think we would all like to know that the basis for censorship is that the material is harmful and that the harm is both real and serious."

Where the Commission appealed to "common sense" and reasonable "assumptions," critics demanded that these so-called common sense assumptions meet social scientific standards. The move from studies that show acquisition of aggressive attitudes to conclusions that assert a causal connection to sexually violent behavior was not allowed by the negative. This did not strike critics as anything approaching common sense. Appeals to anecdotal evidence from clinical experience was no longer given a pass by the critics. For an audience not imbued with an antipornography presumption, each of the Meese Commission's moves are intensely examined.

In an interesting move Hefner compares the use of pornography as an explanation of violent behavior to criminal trials in which defendants have made other claims of powerful environmental influences. She makes an impassioned plea for individual responsibility. Yet, conservatives typically focus on individual responsibility and liberals traditionally put a good deal greater emphasis on the environment. This, in fact, is a turn-the-tables argument. It is an argument that appeals to conservatives using their own first premise. Yet, it is also an argument that beckons back to the issue of legality. Control of pornography is a legal issue and, consequently, the case for censorship must meet both scientific and legal criteria.

To put the point succinctly, understanding Hefner's audience makes the presentational strategy intelligible. The choice of emphasis is always a function of the audience the advocate is trying to influence.

ANALYSIS: PRESENTATIONAL STRATEGIES (II)

In "Presentational Strategies (II)" we examine Hefner's refutation of the second stock issue of fact. Does the Meese Commission Report meet the reliable criteria of facticity? Of course, Christie Hefner argued that the Report falls short of meeting the required standards of proof.

Now in an earlier section, "Analysis: Case Requirements," we pointed out the lines of arguments that were pursued on this issue. Here we are not concerned with "case requirements" but with presentational choices. In other words, we shift from arguments necessary to fulfill the standards of the reasonable to an examination of strategies of audience adaptation. Two strategic questions demand answers: Why did Hefner choose to place the essay's greatest emphasis on the refutation of the second stock issue? Why did she choose these particular arguments to use in addressing the issue?

One would suppose that the best reason for emphasizing a particular issue is because you believe your opponent's case is weakest at this point. An infantry commander seeks the weakest part of the enemy's defense to attack; the chess master seeks the most effective line of attack against a particular defense; and the football coach draws up an offensive game plan that has the best chance of exploiting the other team's defensive vulnerabilities.

Having said this, what in the rhetorical situation that confronted Hefner led her to judge that this second stock issue was the soft underbelly of the antipornography forces? Let's try to construct the situation as Hefner probably viewed it:

1. Any critic of the Meese Commission would find the following passage enticing: "Finding a link between aggressive behavior towards women and sexual violence, whether lawful or unlawful, requires assumptions not found exclusively in the experimental evidence. We see no reason, however, not to make these assumptions.... They are... assumptions that are plainly justified by our common sense."[2]

2. Note this highly inviting sentence: "The assumption that increased aggressive behavior towards women is causally related, for an aggregate population, to increased sexual violence is significantly supported by the *clinical evidence, as well as by much of the less scientific evidence* (our emphasis)."[3]

3. Given the dissenting opinions of some commissioners and the presence of contrary evidence, the critic might well find this claim highly provocative: "[W]e have reached the conclusion, *unanimously and confidently* (our emphasis), that the available evidence strongly supports the hypothesis...."

4. Christie Hefner's own situation, as president and chief operating officer of Playboy Enterprises, Inc., made the choice to focus on violence rather than sex as the key variable a good strategic choice. Clearly, Playboy's interests are in maintaining a marketplace where publication of erotica is unrestricted.

5. With an audience already predisposed to view the actions of Edwin Meese with considerable suspicion, the focus on political motives that undermined impartiality seemed like a wise rhetorical choice.

6. Although the Meese Commission hedges on the issue of scientific standards, it is still quite clear that the Report seeks to back findings with social scientific research wherever possible. They move to other kinds of "extrascientific data" only when forced.

These six considerations make the choice to emphasize the second stock issue fit comfortably into a considered persuasive strategy. Given the affirmative case, the readership of *The Humanist*, and Hefner's own interests, the selection of specific lines of argument make excellent strategic sense.

The audience is ready to hold the Report to strict standards of proof. First, liberals traditionally have ideological commitments to science. Second, the strong anticensorship presumption among this audience operates to insist on the most rigorous standard of proof for any case that is linked to restrictions of First Amendment freedoms. Third, dissent among the Meese commissioners undermines the confidence that the public is likely to have in the conclusions. Four, a liberal audience is likely to have suspicions about a very conservative Attorney General, and by association, about any commission operating in his name.

The very equivocation of the Commission's own phrasing of conclusions suggests that a skeptical audience will not judge the Report as meeting the strictest standards of proof. In sum, the forum, the audience, the affirmative case, and the writer's own inclinations created imperatives that structured this negative response to the Meese Commission Report.

CONSTRUCTING THE NEGATIVE CASE: PROPOSITIONS OF VALUE

In Chapter Ten we illustrated an affirmative case for a proposition of value with an analysis of the Supreme Court decision in the McCleskey case. The affirmative was represented by the opinion of Justice William Brennan. Although the opinion was a dissent, it represented the affirmative because it argued for a change in the existing state of affairs. Brennan maintained that the Georgia capital punishment system was applied irrationally.

The negative, or the defense of present values, was offered by Justice Lewis Powell writing for the majority. In the following section, excerpts from Justice Powell's opinion are quoted at length.

> Resolved: the application of the death penalty under the State of Georgia's capital punishment system is irrational.
>
> Our analysis begins with the basic principle that a defendant . . . has the burden of proving "the existence of purposeful discrimination." . . . A corollary to this principle is that a criminal defendant must prove the purposeful discrimination "had a discriminatory effect" on him. . . . Thus, to prevail under the Equal Protection Clause, McCleskey must prove that the decision makers in his case acted with discriminatory purpose. . . .
>
> McCleskey's claim that these statistics are sufficient proof of discrimination, without regard to the facts of a particular case, would extend to all capital cases in Georgia, at least where the victim was white and the defendant is black.

The Court has accepted statistics as proof of intent to discriminate in certain limited contexts . . . .

But . . . the application of an inference drawn from the general statistics to a specific decision in a trial and sentencing simply is not comparable to the application of an inference drawn from general statistics to a specific venire selection or Title VII case. In those cases, the statistics relate to fewer entities, and fewer variables are relevant to the challenged decisions . . . .

Finally, McCleskey's statistical proffer must be viewed in the context of his challenge. McCleskey challenges decisions at the heart of the state's criminal justice system. "[O]ne of the society's most basic tasks is that of protecting the lives of its citizens and one of the most basic ways in which it achieves the task is through criminal laws against murder." . . . Implementation of these laws necessarily requires discretionary judgments. Because discretion is essential to the criminal justice process, we would demand exceptionally clear proof before we would infer that the discretion has been abused. The unique nature of the decisions at issue in this case also counsel against adopting such an inference from the disparities indicated by the Baldus study. Accordingly, we hold that the Baldus study is clearly insufficient to support an inference that any of the decision makers in McCleskey's case acted with discriminatory purpose.

McCleskey also argues that the Baldus study demonstrates that the Georgia capital sentencing system violates the Eighth Amendment . . . .

McCleskey argues that the sentence in his case is disproportionate to the sentences in other murder cases . . . . [H]e further contends that the Georgia capital punishment system is arbitrary and capricious in *application*, and therefore his sentence is excessive, because racial considerations may influence capital sentencing decisions in Georgia . . . .

To evaluate McCleskey's challenge, we must examine exactly what the Baldus study may show. Even Professor Baldus does not contend that his statistics *prove* that race enters into any capital sentencing decisions or that race was a factor in McCleskey's particular case. Statistics at most may show only a likelihood that a particular factor entered into some decisions. There is, of course, some risk of racial prejudice influencing a jury's decision in a criminal case . . . .

Because of the risk that the factor of race may enter the criminal justice process, we have engaged in "unceasing efforts" to eradicate racial prejudice from our criminal justice system. . . . [I]t is the jury that is a criminal defendant's fundamental "protection of life and liberty against race or color prejudice." . . .

The capital sentencing decision requires the individual jurors to focus their collective judgment on the unique characteristics of a particular criminal defendant. It is not surprising that such collective judgments often are difficult to explain. But the inherent lack of predictability of jury decisions does not justify their condemnation. On the contrary, it is the jury's function to make the difficult and uniquely human judgments that defy codification and that "buil[d] discretion, equity, and flexibility into a legal system."

McCleskey's argument that the Constitution condemns the discretion allowed decision makers in the Georgia capital-sentencing system is antithetical to the fundamental role of discretion in our criminal justice system....

...In light of the safeguards designed to minimize racial bias in the process, the fundamental value of jury trial in our criminal justice system, and the benefits that discretion provides to criminal defendants, we hold that the Baldus study does not demonstrate a constitutionally significant risk of racial bias affecting the Georgia capital-sentencing process.[4]

ANALYSIS: CASE REQUIREMENTS

DEFINITIONS. Justice Powell certainly did agree with Justice Brennan that "irrational" in the sense of "unjust" constituted grounds for overturning the decision. However, definition still became an issue if only by indirection.

Powell was concerned with the word "discretion." He was adamant in his contention that "discretion" is not synonymous with irrationality. This point turns up at several junctures of the opinion: "Implementation of these laws necessarily requires discretionary judgments"; "discretion is essential to the criminal justice process"; "demand exceptionally clear proof...that the discretion has been abused"; "the jury's function...'[to] build discretion...into a legal system'"; and "antithetical to the fundamental role of discretion in our criminal justice system."

It is enough for now to highlight the emphasis on the distinction. In the next section, we will demonstrate how this distinction shapes the criteria for evaluation.

RELIABLE CRITERIA. What are the reliable criteria for evaluation? The reliable criteria for Justice Brennan, upholding the affirmative, came from operationalizing the key value term "irrational," but for Justice Powell an alternative set of criteria are drawn from operationalizing the term "discretionary."

To put it simply, mindful of the danger of oversimplification, Brennan's criteria for determining irrationality turned on outcome but Powell's criteria for determining tolerable discretion turned on process. The very fact of the statistical differences between white and black sentences established for Brennan the racial application of the death penalty and thus an "irrational" system of capital punishment in Georgia. Powell, on the other hand, did not seek uniformity in outcome but turned to the legal process as standard. If the process was followed faithfully, we should not be concerned with juries rendering "uniquely human judgments that defy codification."

Consequently, Brennan is satisfied with aggregate statistics that demonstrate a racially skewed sentencing system. Powell demands evidence that the process in the McCleskey trial was corrupted. Powell held, "In light of the safeguards designed to minimize racial bias in the process . . . we hold that the Baldus study does not demonstrate a constitutionally significant risk of racial bias affecting the Georgia capital-sentencing process."

MEETING THE CRITERIA. Given that the two opinions use different criteria, it is not surprising that each arrives at different conclusions about meeting their respective standards. This case did not turn essentially on issues of fact, but rather on the appropriate standards of evaluation.

Brennan argued that "rationality" was determined by equitable outcome. The Baldus study demonstrated a system-wide racial disparity in sentencing. Consequently, the system is irrational and the proposition is upheld.

Powell argued that "rationality" turned on following a process. The process was followed and therefore the McCleskey decision was just. Consequently, the proposition is rejected. For Powell, evidence of a system-wide difference in outcome said nothing about what happened in this particular case. Without evidence that the procedural safeguards were violated, there is no reason to suspect any racial influence.

ANALYSIS: PRESENTATIONAL STRATEGIES (I)

Following our pattern, the first section on presentational strategy focuses on the negative case that strikes at the "reliable criteria for evaluation." Since we have already argued that this is the primary point of issue in *McCleskey v. Kemp*, our illustration should serve the cause quite well.

In the previous section, we noted that Brennan turned to equality of outcome and Powell to the safeguards of procedure. Have we merely got two justices passing in the night or is there some way they can actually argue over the correctness of criteria? If we answered "no," settling propositions of value would resort to some nonrational procedure. So, of course, we hope to demonstrate that this conflict is subject to reasonable standards of resolution.

Brennan's claim was founded upon the following premise: "Defendants challenging their death sentences . . . have never had to prove that impermissible considerations have actually infected sentencing decisions. We have required instead that they establish that the system under which they were sentenced posed a significant risk of such an occurrence."

Quite to the contrary, Powell asserted, "[A] criminal defendant must prove that a purposeful discrimination 'had a discriminatory effect' on him . . . McCleskey must prove that the decision makers in this case acted with discriminatory purpose." He went on to contend that "the Court has accepted statistics as proof of intent to discriminate in certain limited contexts."

We have now arrived at an impasse due not to the limits of reason but to the authors' ignorance of law. This chapter was written soon after the decision was handed down and, consequently, scholarly commentaries are not yet available.

With that said, we will offer some possibilities. It is obvious that both Brennan and Powell rely on precedent to back their claims. Brennan found precedent for overturning sentencing decisions based on a demonstrated risk of discrimination in the system. Powell found precedent for overturning a sentence only when discrimination was demonstrated in the specific case. He argued that only in other more limited circumstances have statistical analyses been appropriate for a discriminatory finding.

Powell emphasizes that the criminal defendant has a significant burden of proof in these cases. By implication he infers that other discrimination cases—perhaps busing, hiring, athletics, and so forth—were of a different kind.

We are confident, however, that these arguments make sense to lawyers. Legal scholars examine opinions and critique them on their merits all the time. The reasonableness of each justice's appeal to precedent is subject to evaluation by those schooled in the law.

ANALYSIS: PRESENTATIONAL STRATEGIES (II)

In this case, the standards of judgment were more important than the facts in the case. The Baldus study's findings became an issue, but the negative, represented by Lewis Powell, did not spend much energy on disputing the figures. Given his evaluative standards, the Baldus' figures did not represent anything crucial.

In fact, this situation is least often the case. In most situations, the standard is understood and the facts are disputed. We universally understand that murder is wrong, but we often dispute the application of the term in a given case.

Assume for a moment that Powell and Brennan agreed on the standards for "rational" sentencing. For instance, assume that Powell acquiesced to Brennan's focus on sentencing outcome. In such a case, the quality of the Baldus study would become the lynch pin of the decision. At present, Powell only mentions the Baldus study to demonstrate that it has nothing to say about race as a factor in the particular case of Mr. McCleskey. Powell wrote, "[W]e hold that the Baldus study is clearly insufficient to support an inference that any of the decision makers in McCleskey's case acted with discriminatory purpose."

Notice that a value dispute that turns on stock issue two is transformed into a factual dispute. Are the facts of the case such that they meet the criteria of evaluation? This has led some ethical philosophers to suggest that most disagreements in value turn on issues of facts.[5]

CONSTRUCTING THE NEGATIVE CASE: PROPOSITIONS OF POLICY

In Chapter Ten we illustrated an affirmative case for a proposition of policy with an analysis of the congressional speeches in support of the Gephardt amendment to the Trade Act of 1974. The affirmative called for adoption of the amendment, because the amendment represented a significant departure from reliance on international agreements (principally GATT).

The *New York Times* took exception to Mr. Gephardt's proposal. In an editorial, The *Times* argued against the following proposition of policy:

> Resolved: Congress should adopt the Gephardt amendment.
>
> The party that launched a half-century of world trade expansion now threatens to take America back to tit-for-tat protectionism. That's what the House leadership's amendments to the foreign trade bill would do, and it spells trouble.
>
> The offensive amendment comes from the Democratic whip, Richard Gephardt, who has made trade the key issue in his Presidential Campaign. He's right to do that, but comes out, with full support from Speaker Wright, on the wrong side.
>
> The amendment would authorize—virtually compel—severe curbs on imports from Japan, West Germany, South Korea, Taiwan and perhaps others. It is inconceivable that these countries would take such humiliation without fighting back. This is the path to less trade.
>
> Mr. Gephardt targets countries that use "unfair trade practices" and have large export surpluses in their American trade. Since all countries, including our own, are guilty of some unfairness, the amendment essentially penalizes surpluses that Washington deems "excessive." There's nothing wrong with cracking down on unfair tactics; there are already international procedures for that. But cracking down on "too much" is too much.
>
> The amendment prescribes brief negotiations aimed at eliminating alleged unfair practices and reducing the surpluses. If they fail, Washington would limit imports from that country enough to cut the imbalance 10 percent a year; for Japan, a $6 billion hit each year.
>
> Mr. Gephardt's approach appeals to unions and others who are certain that foreigners have caused America's huge trade deficit. They are wrong; the trade deficit stems mostly from huge budget deficits and the unattended upsurge of the dollar. Far from restoring competitiveness, protectionist restrictions only protect inefficiency.

> Current law already authorizes adequate penalties on countries that discriminate against American goods....The Gephardt amendment would not solve the trade problem, would worsen relations with good friends and would hurt, not help, trade expansion. President Reagan rightly threatens a veto; Congress would do well to defeat it long before.[6]

ANALYSIS: CASE REQUIREMENTS

DEFINITIONS.   There was no real disagreement over the specific terms of the resolution. However, the characterization of the bill as "protectionism" was surely an issue of contention. The notion of protectionism harkens back to unpleasant experiences with trade legislation in the early part of the century. In addition, protectionism does not strike a sympathetic chord in a country that views itself as a haven of free market economics. Like the term "pornography," "protectionism" is pejorative. Gephardt, we are certain, would describe the amendment as a "fair trade bill." He would argue that "fair trade" does not equate with "protectionism."

This fight was, perhaps, not terribly important for the substance of the argument, but was critical for the response the *Times* editors were trying to elicit. Language powerfully influences our perceptions, especially our perceptions of something as distant from personal inspection as trade legislation.

ILL.   The issue of ill inquires, "Is there a significant reason for change?" Notice that the negative did not contest this issue. There is no suggestion that the trade imbalance is not a serious problem. In fact, the editorial praised Mr. Gephardt for making trade the centerpiece of his presidential bid. The *New York Times* viewed trade as a serious problem, but disagreed with the Gephardt approach.

BLAME.   Recall that the blame issue addresses the question, "Is there an inherent reason to change?" Demonstrating an inherent problem entails establishing that present arrangements are incapable of alleviating the ill. This does not mean that the negative must demonstrate that the ill is being alleviated, only that it could be eliminated by use of current mechanisms.

The *Times* placed a good deal of emphasis on this stock issue. In two separate sections of the editorial, we find these claims: "There's nothing wrong with cracking down on unfair tactics; there are already international procedures for that"; and "Current law already authorizes adequate penalties on countries that discriminate against American goods." These two contentions argue that international structures exist for dealing with unfair trade practices and that domestic legislation is already on the books that addresses these practices.

Notice that in its consideration of the blame issue, the *Times* strengthened its case for labeling Gephardt's bill protectionist. In essence, the editorial maintained that legislation exists for dealing with "unfair trade practices" but that Gephardt's hidden agenda is to deal with "surpluses that Washington deems 'excessive.'" Even if our trading partners are acting within the boundaries of fairness, so the *Times* implied, they are subject to restrictions just because they sell too many products in the United States. So, the real issue is "protectionism" and not "fair trade." The "fair trade" problem is not inherent because structures for dealing with this issue are already available.

CURE.   The issue of cure asks, "Is there a solution." Certainly, the *New York Times* did not believe that the Gephardt proposal would solve the trade problem. The editors advanced two reasons for this viewpoint: first, this bill would restrict rather than expand trade; and, second, the real causes of the mounting trade deficit would remain unaddressed. Consider each in turn.

First, the Gephardt amendment assumes that our trading partners would stand passively by while we instituted restrictive measures. This scenario is unrealistic. In fact, "It is inconceivable that these countries would take such humiliation without fighting back. This is the path to less trade." Keep in mind that there are two paths to balanced trade; increase exports and decrease imports. Decreasing imports, while suffering a concomitant decrease in exports, will not solve the trade problem. Since the Gephardt amendment will ultimately aggravate the export situation by fostering retaliation, the bill is not a solution to the ill.

Second, the Gephardt amendment fails to address the real causes of the trade deficit. The editorialists wrote in part, "Mr. Gephardt's approach appeals to unions and others who are certain that foreigners have caused America's huge trade deficit. They are wrong; the trade deficit extends mostly from huge budget deficits and the unattended upsurge of the dollar." The plan will not solve the problem because the underlying economic conditions that created the trade deficit are not dealt with in the Gephardt legislation.

COST.   Consideration of cost involves the question, "Does the policy have more advantages than disadvantages?" Will the Gephardt amendment's benefits outweigh the new undesirable consequences that may result? The *New York Times* answered with an emphatic "No!"

Two lines of argument were forwarded for this position. The first disadvantage dealt with the possibility that relations with important allies would suffer. The paper claimed, "The Gephardt amendment...would worsen relations with good friends." Because editorial space is small, the *Times* did not elaborate. However, the clear implication is that America's staunchest allies in Europe and the Far East are the likely targets of the bill's penalties. To undermine foreign relations with Japan, Korea, Taiwan, and West Germany is far too great a price to exact.

Second, the editorial suggested that "[f]ar from restoring competitiveness, protectionist restrictions only protect inefficiency." A serious problem in American industry is the failure to invest at adequate levels in new plants and equipment. In addition, American industry has been plagued with bloated corporate bureaucracies and an underproductive work force. The key to solving these difficulties is the application of the penalties of the marketplace. Competitive pressures from foreign competition force American companies to increase quality and efficiency. The Gephardt legislation would protect poorly performing companies from market forces and, consequently, undermine efforts to improve American competitiveness. The American consumer may suffer as a result. Protectionism leads to reduced product choice, higher prices, and lower quality goods.

ANALYSIS: PRESENTATIONAL STRATEGIES (I)

Recall in Chapter Ten that we indicated that there were a larger variety of standard affirmative presentational strategies for policy than for any other propositional type. Correspondingly, there are a larger number of stock negative approaches to policy.

In this section and the next three, we will discuss the strategic options of defense of the present system, direct refutation, minor repairs, and counterplans. In the present section, we will begin with a discussion of *defense of the present system*. This is essentially the stance taken by the *New York Times* in the editorial excerpted here.

Making the rhetorical choice to defend existing policy depends on a careful assessment of situation and audience. First, does the present policy deserve defense? Advocates must always ask whether in good conscience they can defend the system. Certainly there are circumstances in which a bankrupt policy could be successfully defended in front of a particular audience, but advocates that would take on such a task would pay a high moral price. Second, does an approach that defends the present system have any chance of success with the intended audience? If a speaker were called on to address the United Auto Workers concerning the Gephardt amendment, it is highly unlikely that defending the present system would prove successful. This audience probably could be convinced that the Gephardt bill was bad legislation, but it is unlikely that union members would be receptive to a defense of Reagan administration trade policy.

What features of the editorial lead to the categorization of the essay as a defense of the present system? First, the *Times* defended an antiprotectionist trade philosophy. This philosophy is consistent with the commitments of the present administration. Second, the editorial defended the efficacy of current mechanisms to insure fair trade.

You notice that the editorial did not suggest that the present system is a panacea. In fact, the editors were quick to point out that there were problems with the deficit and the dollar that required attention. But with regard to trade policy per se, the *New York Times* endorsed maintaining existing arrangements.

ANALYSIS: PRESENTATIONAL STRATEGIES (II)

The second strategy is known as *direct refutation*. This approach is characterized by an unwillingness to defend any alternative policy. The stance of the negative employing direct refutation is simply that the affirmative policy is wrongheaded.

The most obvious parallel to this approach is the strategy of a defense counsel to attack the prosecutor's case without making any attempt to constructively build a case for the defendant's innocence. The defense attorney demonstrates that the prosecution cannot fulfill the burden of demonstrating the defendant guilty beyond reasonable doubt and thus that is all that is necessary for a verdict of not guilty. The lawyer in these circumstances may have grave reservations about letting his client take the stand. Or, the prosecution's case may be so demonstrably weak that direct refutation is all that is required. Or, the case is such that there is very little good evidence on either side and, consequently, the defendant's constructive case for innocence is not particularly strong. Finally, at times there is a rhetorical advantage in adopting the *persona* of the attacker. Taking on the burden of defending the defendant's story requires a more passive and vulnerable rhetorical stance.

If the *New York Times* had decided to adopt the strategy of direct refutation, how would such a strategic choice affect the content of the editorial? The single major difference would appear in the refutation of the blame issue. Rather than defend the present system's maze of domestic legislation and international trade agreements, the editorialists would have focused only on the failure of the Gephardt bill. They may have pointed out that existing legislation accomplished the same thing, but they would do this in the spirit of undermining Gephardt rather than defending an antiprotectionist philosophy.

The arguments launched against the stock issues of cure and cost could remain in tact. These positions do not constitute a defense of the present system. In fact, in the discussion of the cure issue the *Times* points out that the present system has not dealt effectively with the deficit or the dollar.

ANALYSIS: PRESENTATIONAL STRATEGIES (III)

The third negative approach to policy is called *minor repairs*. The minor repairs approach relates specifically to the blame issue. The advocate adopting this strategy admits that there is something amiss with the present system that prevents it from effectively addressing the ill. However, the defect in the present system is not an inherent flaw. The defect is fixable without changing the dominant structure or philosophy of the present system.

This concept is most easily explained by example. A good policy is often undermined by inadequate resources, poor administration, or uncoordinated parallel policies. These impediments to effectiveness do not require a change of policy, but rather some modification that may include provision of adequate resources, better personnel, or superior coordination.

If the *New York Times* had adopted this position, it would have advanced its arguments with a slightly different twist. Rather than merely suggest that existing legislation could address the problem of unfair trade, the newspaper would argue that present legislation could be invigorated with changes in administration, coordination, resources, personnel, and so forth.

Second, the editorial now points out that deficit reduction and an unusually high dollar have created problems. The editors may have suggested that the administration use existing mechanisms to more vigorously pursue these underlying causes of the trade deficit. Here the minor repair would constitute an alteration of policy focus without a call for new legislation.

The rhetorical advantage of this approach is fairly obvious. The advocate can deflect the audience's hostility toward present arrangements and yet capitalize on the fear of unpredictable change. It is a strategy that is both bold and conservative at the same time. Consequently, it defends an existing policy while simultaneously providing hope for an improved outcome.

ANALYSIS: PRESENTATIONAL STRATEGIES (IV)

The final negative strategy is the *counterplan*. The counterplan is the riskiest of the four approaches we have discussed. Here the negative takes on the burden of presenting an alternative proposal that breaks with both the affirmative plan and the present system.

The advocate makes the judgment that the usual advantage in attacking the affirmative and/or defending existing arrangements does not exist in this situation. This judgment may come from an examination of conscience that dictates an abandonment of both the existing system and the affirmative proposal. Or, the negative may believe that mere refutation without a constructive alternative is irresponsible. Or, the audience in a particular circumstance may harbor insurmountable hostility to present policy. If these circumstances obtain, the negative should consider the counterplan strategy.

The requirements of the counterplan are:

1. The counterplan must not fit within the boundaries of the proposition. Propositions are frequently worded broadly enough that more than one proposal can fulfill the requirements. The negative is opposed to the proposition and not merely the specific affirmative plan. Consequently, any negative counterplan that fits within the framework of the proposition would in essence advocate the affirmative.
2. Can the counterplan address the affirmative ills? By counterplanning the negative admits that the present system cannot address the serious problems that presently exist. However, the negative advocate maintains that an alternative policy can do a better job than the affirmative policy. If there are significant ills that the counterplan cannot deal with, then there is considerable reason to prefer the affirmative policy.
3. Can the counterplan avoid serious disadvantages? Even if the counterplan cannot solve all the affirmative ills, it still may be preferable if it avoids specific disadvantages.
4. Does the counterplan have unique advantages? The audience may judge the counterplan superior because it brings with it additional benefits over the affirmative proposal.

If the editors of the *New York Times* had adopted a counterplan strategy in their Gephardt editorial, they might have advanced some of the following arguments. First, they probably would have expanded the section dealing with the alternative causes of the trade problem. This might have entailed proposing an entirely new policy to deal with the budget deficit and the high dollar. Second, this would permit them to argue that they would solve the problem of the trade imbalance and avoid all the disadvantages of protectionism. Third, any proposal that could in fact reduce the budget deficit would certainly provide additional benefits beyond trade. Such a policy would probably stimulate economic growth, reduce interest rates, and assure low inflation levels.

Notice that a proposal directed at deficits and the high dollar is strikingly different from the Gephardt amendment and certainly could not be construed as falling under its boundaries. Therefore, it is clear that such a proposal is on negative ground and does not support the proposition.

CONCLUSIONS

This chapter dealt with the requirements and strategies for upholding the negative. The negative is designated by presumption. The negative is assigned to the side that enjoys pre-occupied ground. Of course, presumption provides the advocate with a number of rhetorical advantages. These may include the choice to attack the opposition without defending a constructive position, exploiting initial points of agreement that presumption presupposes, and, finally, appealing to the risk inherent in any significant change.

In a proposition of fact, the negative may choose to engage the opposition's definitions, criteria for facticity, or claim that the present case meets the criteria. In the analysis of the Meese Commission, we demonstrated that each issue was exploited. Although, it was clear that Hefner focused primarily on the failure of the Commission to live up to its own social scientific standards of proof.

In a proposition of value, the negative may attack definitions, criteria, or the claim that the present case meets the criteria. In the analysis of Justice Powell's opinion in *McCleskey v. Kemp*, it was obvious that the fiercest battle was waged over the issue of appropriate criteria. Powell and Brennan interpreted the legal precedents differently and formulated distinct standards of evaluation. However, given the stable value system in most cultures, value disputes will turn more frequently on whether the current case meets the established standards of evaluation.

Negative approaches to policy are more numerous. The negative advocate may choose to defend the present system, defend nothing and directly refute the affirmative, defend a series of minor repairs that effectively address the problems identified by the affirmative, or abandon both the present system and the affirmative in order to defend a counterplan. The choice of strategy depends on the personal commitments of the advocate, the quality of both the present system and the affirmative proposal, the availability of reasonable alternatives, and the predisposition of the audience.

We often view adopting the *persona* of the negative as unexciting work. After all, few of us relish the pejorative label "obstructionist," "traditionalist," or "timid conservative." By examining specific illustrative cases and detailing the wide range of available strategies, we hope to have dispelled these unwarranted stereotypes.

NOTES

1. Christie Hefner, "The Meese Commission: Sex, Violence, and Censorship," *The Humanist*, Jan./Feb. 1987, pp. 25–29, 46. Copyright © 1987 by Christie Hefner. Reprinted by permission of Christie Hefner.
2. *Final Report of the Attorney General's Commission on Pornography*, July 1986, p. 325.
3. Ibid.
4. *McCleskey v. Kemp*, 84-6811, U.S. Sup. Ct., April 22, 1987.
5. See A. J. Ayer, *Language, Truth, and Logic* (New York: Dover, 1952), ch. 5; and Charles Stevenson, "The Emotive Meaning of Ethical Terms," in *Logical Positivism*, ed. A. J. Ayer (New York: Free Press, 1959), pp. 264–281.
6. "What Mr. Gephardt Would Protect," *New York Times*, 23 April 1987, p. 24. Copyright © 1987 by The New York Times Company. Reprinted by permission.

12

STRATEGIES
OF REFUTATION

During the 1984 campaign season Ronald Reagan was widely perceived to have performed below expectations during the first presidential debate with Walter Mondale. You may recall that the President "drew criticism for giving stumbling, unfocused responses to some questions."[1]

In the weeks between the first and second debate, public speculation began about the effect Reagan's advancing years were having on his ability to govern. The so-called age issue became the major threat to the President's campaign. The public's concern over age was more troublesome than other political issues because it would be very difficult for the President to address directly. Since it was unlikely that Walter Mondale would ever attack the President on the age issue *explicitly*, devising a strategy was a vexing rhetorical problem.

Fortunately for the Reagan forces, an opportunity for response presented itself at the midway point of the second Reagan-Mondale debate.

> MR. HENRY L. TREWHITT, *The Baltimore Sun*: Mr. President, I want to raise an issue that I think has been lurking out there for two or three weeks, and cast it specifically in national security terms. You already are the oldest President in history, and some of your staff say you were tired after your most recent encounter with Mister . . . Mr. Mondale. I recall, yet, that President Kennedy, who had to go for days on end with very little sleep during the Cuba missile crisis. . . . Is there any doubt in your mind that you would be able to function in such circumstances?
>
> MR. REAGAN: Not at all, Mr. Trewhitt. And I want you to know that also, I will not make age an issue of this campaign. I am not going to exploit, for political purposes, my opponent's youth and inexperience. [Laughter] [Applause]
>
> If I still have time, I might add, Mr. Trewhitt, I might add that it was Seneca or it was Cicero—I don't know which—that said, "If it was not for the elders correcting the mistakes of the young there would be no state."[2]

Was Reagan's quip effective? Several pieces of evidence support the contention that the President's strategy was in fact very effective.

First, Walter Mondale agreed to dismiss age as an issue. Note Mr. Mondale's response to the same question during the debate:

> Mr. Trewhitt: Mr. Mondale, I'm going to hang in there. Should the President's age and stamina be an issue in the political campaign.
>
> Mr. Mondale: No, and I have not made it an issue, nor should it be. What's at issue here is the President's application of his authority to understand what a President must know to lead this nation, secure our defense, and make decisions and the judgments that are necessary.[3]

Second, media commentators began to report that Reagan had effectively handled the question of age. For example, the *Congressional Quarterly* wrote, "In the debate's most memorable moment, Reagan tried to deflate much of the age issue. Asked if he would be able to function during a crisis, Reagan quipped, 'I will not make age an issue of this campaign. I am not going to exploit, for political purposes, my opponent's youth and inexperience.'" The publication concluded that "Reagan's performance . . . seemed to deflect questions about his age and competence that had been raised by his debate showing two weeks before."[4]

Third, whether or not this episode was critical to the Reagan victory, it was certainly a turning point in the contest. The Mondale campaign never again achieved the kind of momentum it enjoyed in the weeks after the first debate. Ronald Reagan went on to win a second term as President in a landslide electoral victory.

In sum, a critical issue arose among the public and press, although not articulated by the opposing candidate, and it was disposed of with a 24 word jest. How are students of argumentation supposed to account for such an episode?

THE NATURE OF REFUTATION

We grow up with a linear conception of rationality. We are taught that logical, disciplined thinkers follow careful *lines* of argument.

Argument——Counterargument——Response——Counterresponse

An argument is advanced; a counterargument is offered in opposition; the original argument is defended by a response to the counterargument; the counterargument is defended by offering a counterresponse to the original response, etc.

In formal school debates formats are established that facilitate use of this pattern of argument.

1st Aff——1st Neg——2nd Aff——2nd Neg

Debates are recorded and judged by using flow sheets that follow the development of a given argument through stages of argument/counterargument, response/counterresponse during the course of the contest. At the debate's conclusion, the judges trace their fingers across these lines of argument to see which side most successfully practiced the art of *refutation*.

If you looked up the synonyms for the term "refute," you would find a list that included "disprove," "answer," or "prove false."[5] These equivalent terms reinforce the linear sense of argument development. An argument is presented; the argument is "answered"; the answer is "disproven"; and the argument that was claimed to "disprove" is "proven false."

This represents the Marquis of Queensbury pattern of refutation. Just as the rules of boxing define a "fair fight," this ideal pattern of refutation designates procedures for a "rational dispute." Unfortunately, neither street fights nor real world instances of argumentation follow the rules very closely. The contingencies of situation seem to disrupt the "fair fight" and the "rational dispute."

For a moment consider Reagan's strategy for dealing with the age issue in the linear pattern:

Reagan's age is adversely affecting his ability to govern.	—— Quip: "I am not going to exploit my opponent's youth and inexperience."

There is no sense in which we could say that Reagan had "disproved" the claim that his age was affecting his ability to govern by offering a quip about his "opponent's youth and inexperience."

What is required is a conception of "refutation" that fits the larger framework of argumentation and yet maintains a reasonably close relationship to its typical meaning. We certainly want to avoid the use of abusive definitions, which merely assign meanings arbitrarily. *The object of refutation is to decrease the strength of the opponent's arguments.* The phrase "strength of arguments" refers to the intensity of the audience's adherence to a claim. "Since argumentation concerns theses to which different audiences adhere with variable intensity," Chaim Perelman wrote, "the status of elements which enter into argumentation cannot be fixed as it would be in a formal system: this status depends on the real or presumed adherence of the audience."[6] Some arguments are strongly held by the audience and others are held with only nominal intensity.

The term "refutation" is not fully defined merely by specifying its object. "Refutation" demarcates a process. Would anyone describe jury tampering as an effective strategy for refuting the prosecution's case?

Or, would it sound reasonable to argue that the Soviet invasion of Afghanistan was an effective refutation of the case for national self-determination? *Because refutation is an argumentative process it involves the presentation of effective and worthy justifications for decreasing adherence to an opponent's claims.* What counts as a worthy justification will, of course, be determined by the particular field within which the discourse resides.

Where does this leave us? What effect will this conception of refutation have on an evaluation of Ronald Reagan's strategy for dealing with the age issue in the 1984 campaign? We think it makes a good deal of difference. There are many ways of diminishing the adherence to a particular argument that do not involve disproving the claim. And in specific circumstances, these strategies are perfectly acceptable.

Return to the second Mondale-Reagan debate with this broader notion of refutation in mind. What is the purpose of the presidential debates? Can anyone seriously argue that the presidential debates are set up to provide contests similar to formal interscholastic debates? The so-called candidate debates are really joint news conferences where the voters get a chance to compare the merits of each candidate. Although the format is structured to provide some time for the candidates to address their opponent's position, this is certainly not required. Typically, candidates have taken the opportunity to stress important themes of their campaign and have not focused on a point by point counter of the opponent's case. And, after a number of such debates, the public has come to understand the nature of political debates.

Beyond the format of the these debates, we need to reflect on the nature of the age issue. In the very brief time allotted Reagan to address Mr. Trewhitt's question, what else could we have expected him to say? Is it reasonable to assume that he is going to run through a medical history or present detailed studies on the effects of aging? Surely this is not a reasonable expectation.

Third, could Reagan afford to give this issue too much credit by taking it very seriously? Perelman and Olbrechts-Tyteca have made some interesting observations about this strategic difficulty:

> Any refutation—whether it be of an accepted proposition, of one's opponent's argument, of an unexpressed argument, or of an objection to an argument—implies an attribution to what is refuted of a certain force deserving attention and effort. To make the refutation of consequence and deserving of consideration, one has to make a sufficiently high estimate of what one is attacking: This is necessary not only for purposes of prestige, but in order to better gain the attention of the audience and secure certain strength for the future for the arguments one uses. And one has to make a sufficiently low estimate of what one is attacking, so that the refutation is strong enough.[7]

If Reagan had presented a full-fledged formal response to the age issue, the effect would have been to elevate its importance in the mind of the audience. The media would have treated it as a serious charge that required detailed analysis. By joking about it, Reagan refuted the age argument by dismissing it as a serious political question. As if to say, "In this society we choose Presidents on the basis of their accomplishments not on the year of their birth."

Finally, even if we become convinced that Reagan's response was effective in this situation, are we prepared to say that it was worthy refutation? Certainly, if we followed the ideal model of rationality, Reagan's response would have to be judged unworthy. The President's quip was not an argument at all in the classic sense. His jest was not backed up by any convincing evidence. In fact, he ignored Mr. Trewhitt's question altogether. To phrase the issue differently, does the field of electoral politics license the worthiness of such a humorous rejoinder to a serious issue?

Recall that humor has been Ronald Reagan's consistent strategy in reassuring the American people at critical times. When he was challenging Jimmy Carter in the 1980 presidential election, he responded to accusations about his record in California with the phrase "there you go again." During the critical hours of his medical treatment following the assassination attempt, Reagan jested with doctors saying "I forgot to duck" and "I hope you are Republicans." He opened his first major address following his recuperation by reading a humorous letter that a child had sent him.

In all of these cases, the President's good humor has reassured the electorate. People say to themselves, "if the President can laugh about it then we shouldn't worry." In the Mondale-Reagan debate, the quip humorously reminded people that through history age and wisdom were thought to go together. This stratagem worked because the American people have come to expect our political conversation to be marked by humor. We cannot even imagine the number of political speeches given each year that refer to humorous political insights by Mark Twain or Will Rogers.

APPROACHES TO REFUTATION

The fields of argument are so varied that it would prove impossible to categorize all the strategies of refutation. However, there are certain loci of refutation that cross all field boundaries. Understanding these loci permits classification of refutation strategies and yields a better understanding of argumentation.

The term "loci" is the plural of the Latin-derived word "locus." The term simply means "place or location." We are interested in discovering the rhetorical angles from which refutation may be launched. Recall from Chapter One that the elements of the argumentative situation include audience, topic, advocate, and occasion. The loci of refutation correspond to these elements.

AUDIENCE AS LOCUS OF REFUTATION

Mistakenly, various elements in the argumentative situation are frequently pictured as fixed. Consequently, the audience is understood as pre-existing the message. The audience exhibits some set of characteristics and the message will or will not work effectively in respect to these characteristics. What is missing in this model is the possibility that the message may re-form the audience. In a real sense, the message may actually create the audience.

How can an audience react to an argument before it knows what kind of audience it is? The answer is, of course, that it cannot. By shaping the identity of the audience an advocate has a potent place from which to launch lines of refutation.

Rather than spend additional space on abstract descriptions of this process, consider an example. On November 13, 1969, then Vice-President Spiro Agnew delivered a speech at the Midwest Regional Republican Committee in Des Moines, Iowa. The Vice-President began his remarks by saying:

> Tonight I want to discuss the importance of the television news medium to the American people. No nation depends more on the intelligent judgment of its citizens. No medium has a more profound influence over public opinion. Nowhere in our system are there fewer checks on vast power. So, nowhere should there be more conscientious responsibility exercised than by the news media. The question is, are we demanding enough of our television news presentations? And are the men of this medium demanding enough of themselves?[8]

This speech was widely understood by the news industry as a direct attack by government on the First Amendment freedoms enjoyed by network journalists. Because television is a federally licensed medium, public criticism from the Vice-President was interpreted as an attempt to chill vigorous political reporting and commentary.

A rejoinder to the Vice-President's remarks was delivered by Frank Stanton, then president of CBS, before the International Radio and Television Society in New York City on November 25, 1969. His refutation engaged the Vice-President's remarks from many different vantage points, but his focus on constructing the audience is of particular importance here. Consider the following excerpts:

> [America] is not a consensus society. It is a questioning, searching society—unsure, groping, running to extremes, abrasive, often vio-

lent even in its reactions to the violence of others. Students and faculties are challenging time-honored traditions in the universities. Young clergy are challenging ancient practices and even dogma of the churches. Labor union members are challenging their leaderships. Scientists, artists, businessmen, politicians—all are drawn into the fray. Frequently, because everyone is clamoring for attention, views are set forth in extreme terms....

But no healthy society and no governing authorities worth their salt have to fear the reporting of dissenting or even of hostile voices. What a healthy society and a self-respecting government have to fear—at the price of their vitality if not of their life—is the suppression of such reporting....

Dwight D. Eisenhower said, "I believe the United States is strong enough to expose to the world its differing viewpoints...."

Criticism is an essential ingredient in that mix. It is central, not tangential, to a free society. It is always a free society's strength and often its salvation....

Let me, in conclusion, invoke [Learned] Hand in more revealing words: "Our democracy rests upon the assumption that, set free, the common man can manage his own fate; that errors will cancel each other by open discussion; that the interests of each when unguided from above, will not diverge too radically from the interests of all...."[9]

In the speech by Vice-President Agnew, the phrase, "No nation depends more on the intelligent judgment of its citizens," suggested a description of the American people. The audience is part of a nation where the "intelligent judgment" of citizens is essential. Frank Stanton seized on this description to discredit Agnew's arguments. Intelligent citizens with good judgment are not sheep that can be led by a few journalists on the network news. Stanton describes the citizenry of the country in these words: "It is a questioning, searching society"; "...no healthy society and no governing authorities worth their salt have to fear the reporting of dissenting or even of hostile voices"; "...the United States is strong enough to expose to the world its differing viewpoints"; "[Criticism] is always a free society's strength and often its salvation"; and "Our democracy rests upon the assumption that, set free, the common man can manage his own fate; that errors will cancel each other by open discussion."

If American citizens are intelligent then we do not have to fear the critical voices of journalism; only if they are unthinking followers do we have to fear the influence of the network news. Stanton refuted Agnew's case, in part, by reinforcing for the audience members what kind of people they are. They are not the kind of people that will find the links in Agnew's argument persuasive.

Consider a second illustration. In an address delivered at the

Southern Baptist Convention Christian Life Commission Annual Meeting in Atlanta, Georgia on March 23, 1982, Jerry Falwell spoke on the topic "Strengthening Families in the Nation." One extended passage is of interest:

> Our President said last January in his Inaugural Address what many presidents have said and what many members of Congress and the judiciary have said, that his is a nation under God. He didn't say it's a Christian nation. He didn't say it's a Jewish nation. He said it's a nation under God. A nation built upon the Judeo-Christian ethic. We hear a lot about the Judeo-Christian ethic. That just means in lay language principles out of the Old Testament—Judeo—and the New Testament—Christian. And those Old and New Testament principles are the cornerstone upon which this great republic was built. Our founding fathers were by no means all godly men. But they were influenced by godly principles, by Pilgrims and Puritans and men and women of God insomuch that history supports the fact that we have a Constitution and a Declaration of Independence and a Bill of Rights that are definitely, strongly Judeo-Christian ethic in premise.[10]

Once the audience defined itself as part of a Judeo-Christian society, then the arguments that followed about evolution, abortion, and pornography were claims that such an audience would accept. Those who would refute this position would characterize the American people in some other way. Notice that the description of the American people in the Frank Stanton speech highlights different qualities. The Stanton definition of audience would not suit the Reverend Falwell's message.

Finally, we explore a third example. In a trial the jury is the essential audience. The jury is made up of men and women empowered to decide the question of guilt or innocence. Despite all the procedures for selecting jurors, there is no set of individuals that is going to be completely free of prejudices, stereotypes, and other preconceived ideas. The system works because the law tells jurors what kind of audience they are supposed to become. Consequently, jurors, taking their responsibility seriously, try to approximate that which they are commissioned to be. Think of how hard it must have been for the jury to return a not guilty by reason of insanity verdict in the trial of the man who attempted to assassinate Ronald Reagan.

Many of you probably have served on award committees, membership committees, or on some deliberative body. Responsible members try to put their personal feelings aside and become the kind of decision makers the organization charter specifies. This process is facilitated by messages that encourage audience members to take on the proper *personae*.

In summary, refutation may take place by focusing on the relationship of the audience to the key premises of opposing arguments. If the advocate can convince audience members that they are not the type of people that could accept such premises, refutation will be successful.

TOPIC AS LOCUS OF REFUTATION

Directed from the perspective of topic, refutation centers on issues of jurisdiction. The advocate refutes arguments by demonstrating that they are irrelevant to the subject matter or the form of the question under discussion. In one way or another, the upshot of the refutation is to convince the audience that the opponent's arguments are "beside the point."

Because the rules of procedure are so thoroughly codified, jurisdictional issues in the law provide clear illustrations of this refutation strategy. Legal issues must be brought to the proper tribunal. Civil and criminal cases are referred to different courts. State and federal issues are addressed before different judges. Legal concerns dealing with military justice, bankruptcy, or juvenile crime are handled by special courts. It is always appropriate to ask for dismissal based on improper jurisdiction. Once a cause is located in the proper jurisdiction, additional rules exist for determining which lines of argument are relevant to the cause of action. Questions not pertinent to the cause of action are not permitted.

Jurisdictional issues are not limited to formal legal proceedings. All of us, at one time or another, have been chided for bringing irrelevant points into the discussion. All of us have undoubtedly been irritated by speakers or writers who wander off on some tangent unrelated to the topic. Pointing out the inappropriateness of an argument to the subject under discussion is a frequently used refutation strategy. Not all jurisdictional violations are obvious. Many require careful attention and are only clear to an audience when pointed out by a skilled advocate.

Consider several different disputes in which one of the key strategies of refutation focused on jurisdiction:

EXAMPLE ONE

> The old saw of criminal defense attorneys goes something like this: "Try the victim, the state, society, or the prosecutor; try anyone but the defendant." The prosecutor charged with refuting a case built on such a strategy has to demonstrate to the jury that the defendant's case, although emotionally involving, is irrelevant to the critical issues of law.

EXAMPLE TWO

> The struggle between therapists committed to Freudian psychoanalysis and clinical psychologists has turned on what counts as science. Freud had claimed for psychoanalysis the title of science

of the mind. Freud's detractors have argued that psychoanalysis is ideology not science. Psychoanalysis, they maintain, is a system of values about how people ought to live and not a description of the way the mind works. Psychoanalysis may have value but not scientific value.

EXAMPLE THREE

As this book is nearing completion, public debate is heating up over the nomination of Federal Appeals Court Judge Robert Bork to the Supreme Court. Those who oppose Bork argue that his reputed judicial conservatism is out of step with the views of the American people. Bork opponents hope the United States Senate will deny the Bork nomination on ideological grounds. Defenders of Bork, by and large, argue that the Senate hearings ought to focus on questions of ethics and qualifications, not ideology. The President, they contend, should have the prerogative to choose someone who fits in with his philosophical vision of the Court.

In example one, the topic of dispute asks the factual question of whether or not the defendant committed a crime. Defense counsel, uncomfortable trying the case narrowly on the merits, raises a series of side-issues that serve to emotionally confuse the jury. Jurors feel sorry for a defendant victimized by society's neglect. They begin to feel outraged at the despicable person who was the victim of the crime. The prosecutor's summation and the judge's instructions serve to focus the jury's attention on what is relevant to the legal and factual issues in the case. The defense counsel's case is refuted by emphasizing that the main lines of argument do not fit within the boundary of legitimate issues.

In example two, the subject of dispute is whether psychoanalysis is scientifically supported. The evidence offered by psychoanalysts to support the contention is condemned as irrelevant by psychologists. The products of case studies, dream interpretation, free association, and the like are not viewed as meeting the rigorous standards of experimental science. This evidence may be interesting, but it cannot count as scientific demonstration.

In example three, the proposition directs the disputants to determine whether the United States Senate should certify Robert Bork's fitness to serve on the Supreme Court. Opponents of Bork's nomination choose to debate the merits of his judicial philosophy. Are his positions on affirmative action, abortion, and free speech desirable? Although willing to engage in debate on the desirability of such positions, proponents strongly argue that these considerations are not appropriate issues for the Senate to take up under the "advise and consent" provisions. Proponents of Bork claim that these arguments are out of the rightful jurisdiction of the Senate.

Issues of jurisdiction are both macro and micro. In other words, jurisdiction addresses both the larger issue of whether the case falls within the boundaries of the topic and the more specific question of whether a given argument is on point. Following our legal analogy, the macro issue is finding the proper tribunal to hear the case and the micro issue is developing lines of argument relevant to deciding the issue in dispute. For the sake of convenience we will call the macro-jurisdictional issues *questions of topicality* and microjurisdictional issues *questions of relevance*. Particular refutational strategies are available under each broad category.

QUESTION OF DEFINITION.   Topics, of course, establish the boundaries of argument. The meanings of key words in topics convey limits. Most issues of topicality turn on the interpretation of a particular term.

Recently, the furor over the Iran-Contra affair highlighted the relationship between jurisdiction and definition. You may recall that the diversion of funds to the Contras was supposedly prohibited by the Boland Amendment. However, the wording of the Boland Amendment was sufficiently ambiguous to permit Colonel Oliver North to argue that the National Security Council was not covered by the congressional prohibition against military assistance to the Contras. The relevant section of the law reads as follows:

> SEC. 8066. (a) During fiscal year 1985, no funds available to the Central Intelligence Agency, the Department of Defense, or any other agency or entity of the United States involved in intelligence activities may be obligated or expended for the purpose or which would have the effect of supporting, directly or indirectly, military or paramilitary operations in Nicaragua by any nation, group, organization, movement, or individual.[11]

Administration defenders argued that the phrase "any other agency or entity of the United States involved in intelligence activities" did not designate the National Security Council and its staff operations. Since the NSC is not an intelligence agency, its efforts to fund the Contras did not violate the letter of the Boland Amendment.

In litigating the dispute over the meaning of the Boland language a number of arguments will undoubtedly be advanced. Some will argue that the language just means what it means. Each of the words has a particular denotative meaning and that is what ought to be determining. But others will suggest that Congress had a clear purpose in mind when passing the amendment and, consequently, legislative intent ought to be an important element in deciding on an interpretation.

Definitional issue arise when either topicality or relevance is questioned. In the struggle between psychoanalysts and clinical psychologists, the definition of science determines the relevance of given evidence. In a hearing to consider a Supreme Court nominee the meaning of "advise and consent" determines what is appropriately within the jurisdiction of the Senate.

QUESTION OF TRADITION. There are rules that exist but are never formally written down. These rules are not invoked by the force of law, but enforced by social sanction. Children who do not internalize the social rules of play will soon be shunned by playmates. Adults who do not understand that friendship entails confidential communication will soon be lonely. Analogously, certain arguments are deemed by social tradition as out of bounds in particular contexts. The advocate who points out that an opponent has violated these rules will effectively refute the argument.

Our concern here is the relationship of these rules to given topics. Because of America's commitment to pluralism, there have long been social rules that govern discussion of issues of race, religion, and gender in politics. We are certain that some people's votes are influenced by a candidate's race, religion, or gender, but in the campaign itself it would be inappropriate for opponents to raise these issues.

What would have been the political fallout if George Bush had argued that Geraldine Ferraro should not be Vice-President because she is a woman? Or, if the primary opponents of Jesse Jackson argued that his color made him unsuitable for high political office? Or, if a legitimate political spokesperson declared that Jews were unfit for elective office? The press, responsible public leaders, and many others would cry foul. Such arguments simply have no place in the mainstream of the American public dialogue. Any politician who used such arguments would be excoriated by the public.

There are countless rules, built on a long social tradition, that adhere to particular topics. They are learned by advocates as they are socialized into the rules of civil discourse. The force of these rules is to declare certain arguments jurisdictional violations.

ADVOCATE AS LOCUS OF REFUTATION

Since the time of Aristotle, rhetorical theorists have understood that the audience's perception of the advocate's good sense, moral character, and good will were important determinants of successful persuasion. The ancients used the Greek word *ethos* to explain this phenomenon, but in the modern communication literature the term source credibility is used.

Madison Avenue advertising executives expend huge sums of money obtaining the right spokespersons for their clients. Lee Iacocca started doing his own automobile ads after his successful turnaround of the Chrysler Corporation's financial fortunes. The quick repayment of Chrysler's federal loan, the revitalization of a large corporation, and the perceived improvement in product served to turn Iacocca into a highly credible source.

Retired General Chuck Yeager is the spokesperson for AC-Delco. The producers of the spots show him against the backdrop of military fighter aircraft. The book and movie *The Right Stuff* presented to the public, in heroic detail, Yeager's exploits in breaking the sound barrier. Consequently, AC-Delco thought a man who spent his life testing and trusting technology was a good choice as spokesperson for an automobile accessory company.

But just as perceptions of credibility support persuasive efforts, it is also a profitable angle of refutation. To the extent that the audience mistrusts the advocate of argument, we would expect a concomitant decrease in the audience's adherence to the speaker's claims. In recent months, examples of shattered reputations have littered the headlines.

Jim and Tammy Faye Bakker's television ministry, known as the PTL Club, was in shambles following revelations about his adulterous affair, her drug dependency, and the extravagant use of church funds to support a wealthy lifestyle. Ministers and their families are expected to live lives that are consistent with the principles they preach. This scandal has had a traumatic financial effect on nearly all television ministries. The public has become increasingly cynical about the use of donated funds that are supposedly intended for supporting good works.

Senator Gary Hart was forced from the 1988 presidential race when revelations of his relationship with Miami model and actress Donna Rice were uncovered. The picture of Ms. Rice sitting on the Senator's lap aboard the yacht "Monkey Business" in a Bimini harbor is forever etched in the American memory. Questions of personal fidelity bleed over into the electorate's confidence in a candidate's public fidelity. A public perception of a public servant's good character is a necessary prerequisite for election to President.

Both the Bakker and Hart scandals dealt with a general demise of reputation. In the refutation of argument, the credibility issues are narrower. Rarely, if ever, will you find yourself in a situation where dredging up opponents' sexual and financial history is appropriate. Rather, refutation will focus on questions of *character* and *competence* that directly relate to the issue in dispute. Character and competence are manifested in a variety of ways. Each of these ways is a wedge to decrease the audience's adherence to an opponent's claim.

Motive.   Charles Stevenson in his book *Ethics and Language* provided this illustration of argument from motive:

A: You ought to vote for him, by all means.
B: Your motives for urging me are clear. You think that he will give you the city contracts.[12]

In this example, the focus of attack is not on the speaker. However, the same form of refutation is directed at advocates. For instance, the Tobacco Institute commissions a number of scientific studies on the relationship between health and smoking. Some of these studies have been used to argue that the link between smoking and disease is not as strong as the Surgeon General has suggested. But studies underwritten by tobacco companies are often thought suspect by many people. Does the source of the money influence the outcome of the studies?

The underlying assumption of this refutation strategy is that audiences will suspect the objectivity of any advocate who has a vested interest in the outcome of the dispute. Pointing out to the audience the particulars of the advocate's self-interest may effectively refute the case.

CONSISTENCY.   This strategy does not refer to the process of exploiting logical inconsistencies, but rather to an argumentative strategy that leads the audience to question the character of the advocate. Has the advocate consistently held this position? Has the advocate acted in ways that are consistent with his message?

Interestingly, Vice-Presidents are rarely elected President. Harry Truman and Lyndon Johnson were elected to second terms after inheriting the Presidency through death. Richard Nixon failed to win the office in 1960 after serving Dwight Eisenhower as Vice-President for eight years. Hubert Humphrey failed after serving Lyndon Johnson. Walter Mondale failed after serving Jimmy Carter.

Why is this? One possible reason is that former Vice-Presidents are caught in rhetorically awkward positions. The job of the Vice-President is to defend the program of the President. Loyalty to the boss is the first quality listed on the job description. Under such strictures, former Vice-Presidents find it very hard to develop their own programs. Was it possible to perceive Hubert Humphrey as a peace candidate after he had served as a Johnson spokesman for four years? Is it going to be possible for George Bush to argue credibly for a new approach to deficit reduction after his eight years with Reagan? Former Vice-Presidents are caught in a bind between their rhetoric as spokesman for the administration and their discourse as presidential candidates. Political opponents are more than ready to point out these inconsistencies to the voters.

The word hypocrite refers to the feigning of qualities one does not have. The clearest symptom of hypocrisy is inconsistency between words and actions. Many of us find the advice to lose weight and stop smoking unconvincing coming from a doctor who is a chain smoker and thirty-five pounds overweight.

Most of the time word-action inconsistency is not immediately present. The opponent must bring these inconsistencies to the attention of the audience. The social satirist and comedian Dick Gregory has written about the inconsistency between the words and actions of the church. In this excerpt from "America Is My Momma," you can get a feel for his argument:

> A popular song in the church is "The Battle Hymn of the Republic." Really listen to the words of that song and you will realize that very few people have the right to sing it. The day a person does decide to sing it should be the last day of his life. That is what the words of the song imply: "As He died to make men holy, let us die to make men free." If the Enforcer swept through the church today and said, "Put up or shut up," I only know about five folks who could sing that song and mean it. And three of them are already dead.
>
> "As He died to make men holy, let us die to make men free." We do just the reverse. We will try to *kill* to make men free. But the song doesn't say that. It says, "Let us *die* to make men free." This refusal to live by our words makes a laughingstock of the church, Good Friday, and Easter. Another song which amuses me is "Onward, Christian Soldiers." Church folks seem to think a Christian soldier is a Marine who prays. When you sing, "Onward, Christian Soldiers," you are not *really* talking about a man who will follow the cause of right to his death.[13]

Most social satire is built on the foundation of exploiting societal hypocrisy. This form of argument is at the disposal of all arguers engaged in refutation.

CREDENTIALS. In Chapter Eight, we discussed various tests of evidence. These tests parallel, in most respects, the refutational strategies any disputant may use to discredit an opponent's competence. Does the advocate have the training and background necessary to competently render judgments in the area under discussion? Even if the proponent of an argument has used qualified sources, there remains a question of competence to interpret the evidence. All kinds of people glibly quote passages from the Bible without the requisite understanding of their theological significance. In any discipline, there are people who feign the appearance of knowledge by referring to sacred sources without the necessary background to place these references in a meaningful context.

In the movie *An American Gigolo*, the main character, played by Richard Gere, had all the trappings of culture without the deep understanding that marks the well-educated. He was appearance without substance. His job was to create a fantasy for his clients so that they could pretend the encounter was in some sense genuine.

Even if the advocate's credentials are adequate, they may represent a systematic bias of viewpoint. For example, a psychiatrist will much more likely look for physiological causes for mental disturbance than a psychotherapist. The training in each specialty emphasizes differing perspectives.

KNOWLEDGE AND EXPERIENCE. There are people that have expertise without the accompanying formal training. There are also people who have formal training but do not possess the requisite knowledge and experience. Finally, there are areas of knowledge that do not lend themselves to judgments based on training and credentials.

There are several avenues of argument that may exploit the inadequacy of an opponent's knowledge and experience. Does the advocate have a track record that merits the audience's confidence? In political campaigns, the opponent's record is nearly always a focus. In a local Bloomington race for County Sheriff, the incumbent's track record was the key issue in the election. Traditionally, few voters follow local races very closely. In this case, however, the newspapers had chronicled a series of prisoner escapes through the fence enclosing the exercise yard. In addition, a great deal was made over the poor quality of the food given to prisoners. As a result, the track record of the incumbent was used to undercut his case for re-election. His claims were not persuasive because he had demonstrated that he did not possess sufficient knowledge and experience for the job.

Faced with two conflicting medical opinions from two physicians with all the requisite credentials, experience may well become the critical element of decision. Which doctor has handled more of these cases? The backlog of an advocate's experience may be used as a persuasive argument to favor a particular course of action.

JUDGMENT. During the writing of this book, one of the most controversial Supreme Court nominations in the nation's history was contested. The Senate debated Judge Bork's qualifications to sit on the high court. Interestingly, there was no question of credentials or experience. Bork had been an eminent law professor at Yale where he had held two named chairs. Bork had served as Solicitor General under Richard Nixon. He was currently a sitting judge on the very prestigious Federal Court of Appeals in the District of Columbia circuit.

The Bork question dealt with issues of judgment or good sense. Was Bork's philosophy out of the judicial mainstream? Was he out of step with the views and values of the vast majority of the American public? Would a Justice Bork conduct himself on the Supreme Court in ways that would serve the public good? These are ultimately questions of judgment. Many brilliant people have no sense.

Questions of character and competence are always relevant issues. These issues focus on the advocate. Does the advocate have the attributes that foster trust and confidence? If not, the opponent may use arguments directed at credibility to decrease the audience's adherence to an opposing position.

OCCASION AS LOCUS OF REFUTATION

The broadest conception of occasion may encompass all the other elements of the argumentative situation. Here, however, we refer to *occasion as the place and time of advocacy and refutation*.

Social rules have sprung around considerations of occasion. A cursory reading of the syndicated etiquette column titled "Miss Manners" reveals the close relationship between occasion and the norms of polite society. A particular form of dress is required for each occasion. A particular kind of meal is appropriate for different occasions. Proper speech style, roaming from formal to informal, is determined by occasion. Likewise, the strictures of occasion provide opportunities for criticizing improper argumentation.

Situations are so varied that a catalogue of refutational strategies built on the concept of occasion is impossible. But we are confident that arguers socialized into this society understand the boundaries of appropriateness on given occasions. In what follows, several controversial cases underscore considerations of occasion as a locus of refutation.

Case One

> Many occasions are classifiable as public or private. The circumference of the private is not fixed at a single boundary. Private may refer to the domain of the individual—private thoughts; may refer to the domain of a group—members only; or may refer to a domain free of government control—private enterprise.
>
> Gary Hart was forced to withdraw from the Presidential race because of allegations of philandering. Hart has maintained that this was improper. Arguments against his candidacy ought to focus on his public not his private life. In other words, he attempted to refute these allegations not by denying his personal indiscretions but by denying that a political occasion is an appropriate place to air private issues. He contended that his sexual life ought only to concern his family and was of no relevance to the nation at large.
>
> Geraldine Ferraro was strongly attacked by some officials of the Roman Catholic Church for her public stand on abortion during her 1984 vice-presidential campaign. Ferraro, herself a Roman Catholic, maintained that although she was personally opposed to abortion she would support a woman's right to make up her own mind. Put differently, Ferraro followed the teaching of the Church in her private life, but did not feel that Roman Catholic doctrine ought to be imposed as a public law. The Church did not find this distinction persuasive; moral law transcends public and private.
>
> The Family Protection Act was a proposed statute sponsored by legislators seeking to draw much clearer boundaries between

the private space of the family and the public space of government. Sponsors of this legislation are increasingly concerned with intrusive regulations on the family. They fear that such continued government meddling will disrupt the prerogatives of parents to raise and educate children as they see fit. They do not so much deny the merits of trying to solve issues of family pathology, but they believe that arguments that favor intrusion are simply out of order.

CASE TWO

Often occasions are defined as either public or professional. Professional occasions are identified as a time and place where non-professional perspectives are out of order. Because certain tasks are difficult and technical, society assigns these jobs to experts.

The emotional issue of book banning turns on the definition of the occasion. Is the selection of books that populate school libraries a task exclusively for the trained librarian or is it a task that rightly belongs to the elected representatives of the school district? Those who claim to oppose banning really oppose the agency that does the banning. All schools must select from the available books the ones that they believe are most helpful. When political representatives influence the selection process, this is labeled as "book banning." When librarians employing professional criteria select books, that is not book banning. The anti–book ban forces maintain that political considerations have no place in decisions about books. This is a single example of a whole range of academic freedom issues that turn on the distinction between circumstances regarded as public or professional.

In Bloomington, Indiana, there has been an extended controversy over the clean up of PCBs. PCB is a toxin that has contaminated various parts of the Bloomington environment. Tremendous public anxiety was created by the private negotiations between the city government and the responsible corporation. A plan was drawn up and, after a brief period for public comment, was adopted through a consent decree. This issue created a clash between the technical and public sphere. Citizens in Bloomington were very concerned that their health rested only on a kind of blind faith in professional judgment. Popular arguments were refuted by references to technical findings.

Recently, a number of religious denominations, most notably Lutherans and Southern Baptists, have experienced divisive disputes that have turned on the authority of biblical interpretation. Is the Bible clear and understandable to all who read it or is theology in the realm of the professional? Increasingly, academic theologians find themselves at odds with the members of the denomination. They feel that their training privileges their interpretations of scripture. Others argue that the Bible is perfectly obvious to those who read it and tortured interpretive treatments are not acceptable.

CASE THREE

There is a whole raft of legal doctrine designating the appropriate places for certain types of activity. Without trying to sort out the often complex rulings of the courts, we offer some illustrations of litigation that turned on a notion of appropriate place and time.

The modern shopping mall has been responsible for a number of landmark free speech cases. The critical legal question deals with the relationship between the freedom to speak and access to convenient forums of speech. Do striking employees have the right to picket a store inside the mall? Do political protestors have the right to hand out leaflets in the shopping center? There is a clash between public function and private property.

Church and state disputes frequently turn on considerations of time and place. The courts have held that displaying the Ten Commandments inside a public school is inappropriate. The display of the Christmas nativity scene in the town square is inappropriate. All forms of public prayer have been deemed inappropriate in public schools.

The Courts have consistently upheld statutes that require parade permits. Free speech is guaranteed, but the place and timing of the speech may be controlled for safety, comfort, and convenience of the citizenry.

These three cases demonstrate that the strictures of occasion determine appropriateness. As a refutation strategy, arguments from occasion have the force of ruling the opponents claims out of order. Whether or not the opposition's message has merit, it ought not to have persuasive impact in this place and at this time.

CONCLUSIONS

We purposely have not discussed the message as a locus of refutation. In Chapters Eight and Nine, we describe the various approaches to evaluating evidence and argument. Each argumentative field will have particular criteria relevant to assessing the strength of the material offered in support of a claim. Here, we have suggested that there are other angles of refutation that focus not on the message alone, but the message's relationship to the other components of the argumentative situation. These components are not rigid, fixed points in a communication model with the message serving as the only malleable element. Persuasive characterizations of audiences, topics, advocates, and occasions may effectively refute arguments.

The object of refutation is to decreate the strength of the opponent's arguments. The phrase "strength of arguments" denotes the intensity of the audience's adherence to a claim. A weak audience commitment is tantamount to a weak argument. But because refutation is an argumentative process it involves the presentation of effective and worthy justifications for decreasing the adherence to claims. Worthy refutational strategies are subject to the same tests of reasonableness that any other argumentative claim must meet.

There are particular loci of refutation that exist in all fields. These loci are places or locations for refutation. In other words, refutational loci provide angles from which to launch criticisms of opposing arguments. Each locus of refutation corresponds to one of the elements of the argumentative situation.

Refutation may take place by exploiting the relationship between the *audience* and key premises of opposing arguments. The advocate may so define the audience as to convince members of the audience that they are not the kind of people that could accept such premises. Audiences can be formed by effective rhetorical characterizations.

Social rules are often built around particular *topics*. We learn these rules when we are socialized into the norms of civil discourse. The force of these rules is to declare certain arguments out-of-bounds. These rules, by and large, govern jurisdiction. Refutation launched from this locus contends that opposition arguments are off the topic.

The *advocate* of argument is frequently the target of refutation. The arguer's credibility is nearly always an important persuasion variable. Audiences tend to adhere more strongly to arguments from advocates they perceive as competent and of good character. Opponents may expose advocates' lack of credibility by attacking motives, lack of consistency, lack of credentials, gaps in knowledge and experience, and failure of judgment.

The locus of *occasion* launches refutation based on consideration of place and time of advocacy. The nature of the occasion often determines the appropriateness of argument. For example, public occasions may rule out arguments relevant to private lives.

Again, argumentation's operation in the realm of the reasonable is expanded well beyond the linear rationality that has been the paradigm of so-called logical thought. Consequently, the various dimensions of the argumentative situation provide loci of refutation. The audience, topic, advocate, and occasion are all capable of rhetorical adjustment. How the audience comes to see itself, the topic, the advocate, and the occasion is often critical to success.

NOTES

1. "Reagan-Mondale, Round 2: No Clear-Cut Win," *Congressional Quarterly*, 27 Oct. 1984, p. 2827.
2. "Candidates Debate on Defense, Foreign Policy," *Congressional Quarterly*, 27 Oct. 1984, p. 2832.
3. Ibid.
4. "Reagan-Mondale, Round 2," p. 2827.
5. "Refute," *Webster's New World Thesaurus* (1974).
6. Chaim Perelman, *The Realm of Rhetoric*, trans. William Kluback (Notre Dame, IN: Univ. of Notre Dame Press, 1982), p. 48.
7. Chaim Perelman and L. Olbrechts-Tyteca, *The New Rhetoric: A Treatise on Argumentation*, trans. John Wilkinson and Purcell Weaver (Notre Dame, IN: Univ. of Notre Dame Press, 1969), p. 470.
8. Spiro Theodore Agnew, "Television News Coverage," in *American Rhetoric from Roosevelt to Reagan*, ed. Halford Ross Ryan (Prospect Heights, IL: Waveland Press, 1983), p. 206.
9. Frank Stanton, "A Reply to the Vice-President," in *American Rhetoric from Roosevelt to Reagan*, pp. 215–16, 216, 220, 221. Reprinted by permission of the author.
10. Jerry Falwell, "Strengthening Families in the Nation," in *American Rhetoric from Roosevelt to Reagan*, p. 257.
11. Public Law 98-473, October 12, 1984.
12. Charles L. Stevenson, *Ethics and Language* (New Haven: Yale Univ. Press, 1944), p. 128.
13. Dick Gregory, *The Shadow That Scares Me* (Garden City, NY: Doubleday, 1968), pp. 63–64.

13

STRATEGIES OF QUESTIONING

In the final courtroom scene of Erle Stanley Gardner's *The Case of the Sun Bather's Diary*, Perry Mason is called to the witness stand by District Attorney Hamilton Burger. The questioning begins:

> "All right," Hamilton Burger said. "I'll ask you again point blank, did you go out to Jordan L. Ballard's house on the night of Wednesday, the tenth?"
> "Yes."
> "Did you go to the window in the front of the living room?"
> "Yes."
> "Did you lower and raise the roller shade?"
> "Yes. Certainly."
> "What!" Burger shouted. "You admit that now?"
> "Certainly I admit it."
> "You denied it before the grand jury."
> "I did nothing of the sort," Mason said. "You asked me if I had lowered and raised the roller shade as a signal to the defendant. I told you I had not. You asked me if I lowered and raised it as a signal to anyone. I told you I did not."
> "But you now admit you lowered and raised the roller curtain?"
> "Certainly."
> "Why didn't you say so before the grand jury?"
> "Because you didn't ask me."
> "I've asked you now."
> "I've told you now."[1]

Not unlike Hamilton Burger, many of us learned our earliest lessons in cross-examination from the likes of Perry Mason or some other fictional lawyer. While the courtroom is not the only context within which questioning is an important tool, it is probably the oldest. In fact, the notion of questioning or cross-examination has a rich history.[2]

The rise, during the fifth century, of the Greek Republic along with its popular assembly and system of courts is often cited as creating the conditions necessary for the development of persuasive discourse. Toward the end of the fifth century, Zenon of Elea developed the first systematized use of the question and answer method. Labeled eristic speech, Zenon's method was described as "the art of subtle discussion between professional debaters."[3] His teachings were passed on to his student Socrates who relabeled the method dialectic, a conversational method of argument involving question and answer, and passed it along to his pupil Plato.

Through more than two dozen philosophical dialogues, Plato used dialectic to give an account of how life should be lived. In the *Gorgias*, Plato has Socrates question Gorgias about the persuasiveness of the orator.

SOCRATES: Do you declare that you are able to make a rhetorician out of anyone who comes to you to learn?

GORGIAS: Quite so.

SOCRATES: I believe you said just now that the orator will be more persuasive than the physician even on the subject of health.

GORGIAS: Yes, but I added "in a crowd."

SOCRATES: Then the qualification "in a crowd" means "among the ignorant?" For surely the orator will not be more persuasive than the doctor among those who really know.

GORGIAS: That is true.

SOCRATES: And so, if he is to be more persuasive than the doctor, he becomes more persuasive than one who really knows?

GORGIAS: Surely.

SOCRATES: Though he is not a doctor himself? Is this true?

GORGIAS: Yes.

SOCRATES: And one who is not a doctor is, of course, ignorant of a doctor's knowledge?

GORGIAS: Obviously.

SOCRATES: So when the rhetorician is more persuasive than the doctor, it is a case of the ignorant being more persuasive than the expert in the company of the ignorant. Is that the way of it or is it not?

GORGIAS: That is, of course, the way of it in this case.[4]

While the dialectical method is rarely used in modern philosophical discourse, questioning remains important. It is important not only for the philosopher and the lawyer but for all of us who endeavor to make decisions in the world of practical affairs. This chapter explores the rhetorical functions of questioning, preparation for questioning, and the practice of questioning.

RHETORICAL FUNCTIONS OF QUESTIONING

When cross-questioning was introduced into academic debate in the 1920s, debate was viewed not just as a laboratory in which students developed and practiced skills but as an activity designed to instruct and interest an audience. The power of the interrogative has long been recognized. Interrogation facilitates more than the search for information. Questioning is a way to initiate lines of argument and to secure agreement. It is inherently audience involving. When we speak of the rhetorical functions of questioning, we are referring to the ability of the advocate to use questions to aid in the process of persuading an audience.

While the specific objective of questioning will vary with the subject, audience, and the occasion, two general patterns of questioning are clear. The most familiar pattern is *cross-examination*. This type of questioning is used to undermine existing proof. In the courtroom, for example, cross-examination is "intended to whittle down your trial adversary to damage your client and neutralize or dilute them sub-against your client, to take testimony and exhibits intended by your adversary to demage your client and neutralize or dilute them substantially."[5] Specifically, the lawyer attempts to discredit the witness, discredit the witness's testimony, or obtain helpful admissions.

In comparison, *direct examination* is used to enhance or establish proof. The substantive definition of direct examination of a witness is "the propounding of questions to him for the purpose of eliciting answers establishing the existence of facts favorable to the contentions of the questioner."[6] More specifically, direct examination presents facts highlighting the strengths and minimizing the weaknesses of the case, limits the opponent's case by causing the jury or judge to adopt a favorable theory of the case and thus challenge the opponent to disprove it, and, perhaps, leads an opponent, on cross-examination, into traps that have been laid.

The distinction between direct and cross-examination is largely one of purpose. Direct examination seeks to enhance or establish proof while cross-examination seeks to undermine existing proof. It is not difficult to envision instances in which both question types are employed simultaneously. Even in the restricted arena of the courtroom, Spellman is able to identify the strategy of "direct examination during cross-examination."[7] Certainly, as we argue persuasively in a variety of contexts, questioning of both types is appropriate.[8] Consider the following discussion between a student and her academic adviser.

ADVISER: So, Alice, how are your plans for law school shaping up?
STUDENT: I'd like to go to Notre Dame but I'm applying to Indiana too.
ADVISER: Is there some reason you are only applying to two schools and both of them are in Indiana?
STUDENT: Yes, I really want to stay reasonably close to my home town in Northern Indiana.
ADVISER: I'm surprised Notre Dame would be your first choice. I thought you were interested in international law. Do they have a strong program in international law?

STUDENT: I am interested in international law. My understanding
is that there are a good number of courses in international law
at Notre Dame but they are not known for their expertise in
that area.

ADVISER: Have you considered the University of Michigan?

STUDENT: No.

ADVISER: I understand they have a very fine law school especially
in the area of international law. Are you familiar with their
program?

STUDENT: I have heard that the University of Michigan law school
is excellent. It is well respected and, I've heard, hard to get
into.

ADVISER: What is your grade point average?

STUDENT: 3.88.

ADVISER: How did you do on the LSAT?

STUDENT: My score was 44.

ADVISER: I'd say 44 out of 48 is quite good. I really think you ought
to consider applying to Michigan. Do you know how far the
University of Michigan is from your hometown?

STUDENT: No, I don't. My hometown is Angola, Indiana.

ADVISER: I doubt that it is much farther from Angola to Ann Arbor
than from Angola to South Bend. Is there some reason you
need to be within a certain distance of home?

STUDENT: No, it is just a personal preference.

ADVISER: Well, it seems to me you should at least apply to
Michigan. It has the specific program your interested in, you
seem to have grades and test scores that make you a good
candidate, and the distance is not that much farther from
home.

Notice how both direct and cross-examination are used simultaneously. In determining why Notre Dame is Alice's first choice, the
adviser first cross-examined Alice about the reason for her choice and
then later about why it is important to stay close to home. In arguing
that she ought to apply to the University of Michigan, the adviser used
direct examination to establish that Michigan has a strong program in
international law, that Alice's grades and test scores make her a good
candidate, and that the distance from home issue is minor.

Employing one or both of these patterns, the advocate can use
questioning to accomplish a number of specific rhetorical functions.
First, the advocate may use questioning to clarify the position or
evidence of an adversary. Consider the Scopes trial in which Clarence
Darrow and William Jennings Bryan matched wits. At one point Mr.
Darrow questioned Dr. Maynard M. Metcalf, a Congregationalist and a
professor of zoology at Johns Hopkins University, about the beginning
of life.

DARROW: Where do you think life began?

METCALF: I think probably the animal and plant life began at the border between sea and land. For very long periods, however, there was no such thing as land life, plant or animals, it was all marine. Conditions of life in the ocean are very easy for organisms containing green coloring. That enables them to absorb energy from the sun and they are bathed in a solution of all useful minerals. When terrestrial life began new conditions and necessities arose and developed means adequate to them. Needs are the agents to develop structures.

DARROW: Have any animals returned to the sea?

METCALF: I am confident that the whale has gone back.[9]

Darrow's questioning of Dr. Metcalf allowed the professor to clarify his position concerning the beginnings of life.

Second, questioning may be used to challenge the position of the witness. On August 22, 1973, President Nixon held a news conference during which the following exchange took place.

Q: Mr. President, in your Cambodian invasion Speech of April 1970, you reported to the American people that the United States had been strictly observing the neutrality of Cambodia. I'm wondering if you, in light of what we now know, that there were 15 months of bombing in Cambodia previous to your statement, whether you owe an apology to the American people?

A: Certainly not, and certainly not to the Cambodian people. Because, as far as this area is concerned, the area of approximately 10 miles—which was bombed during this period—no Cambodians had been in it for years.[10]

The questioner, in this instance, is able to point out the inconsistency in Nixon's previous statements and challenge the truthfulness of his position.

Third, questioning may be used to explore the connection between the argument and the supporting evidence. In a scholastic debate on political reform, the affirmative argued that political corruption was a significant problem. The negative inquired in the following manner.

Q: How many candidates are corrupt?

A: I did not specify a number.

Q: Well, if there isn't a specific and significant number, how do we know there is a harm?

A: Well, there is definitely a significant number.[11]

The examiner used questioning to make the point that the evidence presented by the affirmative was insufficient to prove the claim.

Fourth, questioning may be used to investigate the credibility of evidence. Initially, the examiner may be interested in finding out the qualifications of the source of a particular piece of evidence. Such was the case in a debate focusing on the issue of organized crime.

Q: Okay, on organized crime you spent much of your time talking about a book, *The Mafia Is Not An Equal Opportunity Employer*.

A: That's true.

Q: Who wrote that?

A: Nicholas Gates, 1971.

Q: What are his qualifications?

A: I'm not entirely sure what they are.

Q: Your whole organized crime block is built on a guy you don't know. Right?[12]

The examiner may also be interested in determining by whom and in what particular manner a given piece of evidence was collected. This is especially useful when dealing with statistical evidence or evidence that is the product of an empirical study. On a topic concerned with scarce world resources, an exchange about the quality of a study became the focus of the following line of questioning:

Q: Who did the study about 460 million people?

A: I don't know. We can give you a series of studies.

Q: No. I want to know who did that study. Do you know?

A: I specifically can't tell you.[13]

Finally, the examiner may be interested in questioning the context within which a particular piece of evidence is understandable.

Q: What source supported your argument that it would be structurally impossible for the affirmative plan to function?

A: It is from Mr. Glassen.

Q: And Mr. Glassen's qualifications are?

A: He is the former president of the NRA (National Rifle Association).

Q: In his quotation Mr. Glassen was not discussing the specific affirmative plan, was he?

A: No.

Q: In fact, he was not discussing a proposal which involved confiscation of guns on a nationwide scale at all, was he?

A: No.[14]

Fifth, questioning may be used to build argumentative premises. In the previous discussion of direct examination, we indicated that questioning may be used to establish facts or premises favorable to the contentions of the questioner. This was done quite well by Clarence Darrow as he questioned William Jennings Bryan during the Scopes trial.

> DARROW: Then when the Bible said, for instance, "And God called the Firmament Heaven, And the evening and the morning were the second day,"—that does not necessarily mean twenty-four hours?
>
> BRYAN: I do not think it necessarily does.
>
> DARROW: Do you think it does or does not?
>
> BRYAN: I know a great many think so.
>
> DARROW: What do you think?
>
> BRYAN: I do not think it does.
>
> DARROW: You think these were not literal days?
>
> BRYAN: I do not think they were twenty-four hour days.[15]

Darrow established that for Bryan at least, not everything in the Bible is literal. This was a premise he used later to argue against a biblical interpretation of creation.

Beyond gaining information, questioning should be used to persuade. By using questioning to clarify positions or evidence, to challenge the position of an adversary, to explore the connection between argument and evidence, to investigate the credibility of evidence and to build argumentative premises, the advocate involves the opponent and the audience in the process of interrogation. The outcome is the acceptance or rejection of claims and data that serve as the basis for persuasive argument.

PREPARING FOR QUESTIONING

Preparation is the key to effective questioning. While it often appears, especially in television dramatizations, that successful questioners are struck suddenly with brilliant insights allowing them to ask the telling question, such is rarely the case. Instead, "it is true for most of us that our clever ideas refuse to come on demand, they have to be wooed...."[16] How then do we woo clever ideas?

In the most general terms, preparation begins with a thorough understanding of both sides of the case. Initially, advocates must know their case. This knowledge should extend beyond the facts of the case to an understanding of the strengths and weaknesses of the case. Similarly, advocates must understand their opponents' case. It is necessary to put yourself in your adversary's position and anticipate what arguments will be made and what proof needs to be offered to adequately support the arguments.

It is true that the exact content of the adversary's position is not known until it's revealed. Consequently, it is neither wise nor possible to prepare a script of the questioning in advance of the actual encounter. Still, it is possible to formulate a fairly specific plan for questioning. The examiner should begin by making an outline of the intended examination. The outline should begin with a consideration of the general purpose of the questioning. Typically this will involve a decision concerning focus. Do you intend to use the questioning to undermine existing proof, enhance or build an argument of your own, or some combination of the two? Second, the outline should include a consideration of the specific objectives of the questioning. For example, you might want to undermine existing proof by denying the credibility of the evidence. Finally, the outline ought to include a consideration of all substantive subject areas including possible questions that might be asked in each area.

This working outline along with thorough notes on the opponent's actual presentation are the materials from which the advocate will formulate questions during examination period. At this point, we are ready to consider the manner in which questioning should be conducted.

THE PRACTICE OF QUESTIONING

In this section we focus on the psychological and substantive aspects of interrogation as they influence the practice of questioning for the examiner and the witness.

PSYCHOLOGICAL FACTORS

The practice of questioning requires direct confrontation between examiner and witness. This confrontation is focused toward the audience. The cross-examination period is the only time when the audience is able to observe the advocates directly interacting. During this time, the audience is very likely to form opinions that will influence their perception of both the advocates and their arguments. Consequently, both those asking questions and those answering them need to be aware of the impression they would like to convey to the audience.

Let's consider the examiner first. What impression does the questioner want to convey when asking questions? First and foremost, the examiner wants to be perceived as in control. In order to control the witness, the examiner must control the questions. This is why preparation is so important. The examiner must have formulated a plan for questioning in advance and must proceed through that plan in an organized and coherent fashion. Second, the examiner wants to appear knowledgeable and confident. It is not a good idea to ask a question unless you have a pretty good idea of the answer. Third, the examiner wants to appear to be seeking the truth rather than attempting to trick or trap the witness.

Similarly, the witness wants to convey a favorable impression to the audience. Ideally, the witness wants to be perceived first as honest and open, as someone who is willing to cooperate with the examiner in the quest for truth. Second, the witness wants to appear more knowledgeable about the arguments than the examiner. Finally, the witness wants to appear confident. While the examiner controls the cross-examination period, the witness should not allow badgering.

The importance of these psychological factors should not be underestimated. An audience can be as easily disenchanted by an examiner who intimidates a witness as by a witness who allows it to happen. A very telling cross-examination may lose impact because the audience is put off by arrogance or the appearance of deception. A knowledgeable witness may appear uninformed by failing to answer questions fully. While the content of questions and answers is critical, the manner in which they are asked or answered is at least as important.

SUBSTANTIVE FACTORS

How can questioning convey the desired impression? In our previous discussion of preparation, we advised the advocate to prepare an outline of substantive subject areas along with possible questions. It is the phrasing of questions and answers that allows participants to convey desired impressions to an audience.

When asking questions, the examiner should begin in a calm and friendly manner. It is a good idea to begin with easy questions. This permits questioners to convey the image of truth seeker, puts witnesses at ease, and increases the likelihood of unguarded and cooperative answers. The examiner should ask clearly focused and concise questions. This is essential to maintaining control. If the examiner asks, "What do you know about the shortage of food in Africa?," witnesses are free to respond with an answer ranging from "Nothing," to a full blown explanation, lasting well beyond the time limits, of all that they know about the food shortage. In either case, the examiner has lost control of the witness. If, instead, the examiner asks, "Is there a food shortage in Africa?" witnesses are liable to respond yes or no and the issue can be pursued further with equally concise follow-up questions. Finally, the examiner ought to ask meaningful questions that move the argument forward. While some questions are asked for the purpose of clarification, the majority of questions should advance audience understanding. Questions of this sort make the examiner appear knowledgeable.

When answering, witnesses should consider the question carefully. Witnesses ought to take enough time to formulate an adequate response without appearing hesitant. Answering too quickly or taking too long both affect audience perceptions of witness competence. Witnesses should answer clearly and concisely. Beating around the bush or wasting time are perceived as strategies for noncooperation. It is in the best interest of respondents to appear cooperative and confident. This does not mean respondents are obliged to answer every question yes or no, even if that is the examiner's preference. It is perfectly acceptable for a witness to qualify an answer. Should the witness choose to qualify an answer, it is best to state the qualification first. So, if the witness is asked, "Is there a food shortage in Africa?", it is acceptable to respond, "If you are referring to a shortage of grain, yes." In this way, the witness can qualify the answer and still provide the desired yes or no.

By paying careful attention to these substantive matters when phrasing questions and answers, examiners and witnesses maximize their rhetorical effectiveness in these exchanges. Audience members formulate impressions of the adversaries and gain information that will aid decision making.

CONCLUSIONS

Cross-questioning is a vital component of arguing persuasively. Throughout history, across a variety of disciplines, and in a variety of contexts, the question-and-answer method of communication has been used effectively. This chapter explored questioning as an important tool for decision making in the world of practical affairs.

Initially, we examined the rhetorical functions of questioning. Here, we argued that interrogation facilitates more than the search for information. Questioning is a way to initiate lines of argument and to secure agreement. It is inherently audience involving.

We discussed two general patterns of questioning. Direct examination is used to enhance proof by establishing facts or premises favorable to the questioner. Cross-examination is used to undermine existing proof. One or both patterns of questioning may be used to accomplish five specific rhetorical or persuasive functions.

Questioning may clarify the position or evidence of an adversary, challenge the position of the witness, explore the connection between argument and evidence, investigate the credibility of evidence, and build argumentative premises. Each function aids in the acceptance or rejection of claims and data that serve as the foundation for persuasion.

Second, we described preparation for questioning. This process is built on the assumption that while questioning cannot be scripted in advance, a very specific plan can be formulated by considering both sides of the case thoroughly, by anticipating the arguments and evidence of the opponent, and by preparing possible questions in each subject area.

Finally, the psychological and substantive aspects of presentation were explored for both the examiner and the witness. Questioning requires direct confrontation. It is during these confrontations that the audience has an opportunity to assess the adversaries and formulate impressions. As a result, it is very important that both the examiner and the witness are mindful of the impressions they wish to convey to the audience. It is equally important that both participants employ presentational techniques that facilitate creation of the desired impression.

NOTES

1. Erle Stanley Gardner, "The Case of the Sun Bather's Diary," in *A Perry Mason Omnibus* (New York: William Morrow, 1978), pp. 390–391.
2. For a detailed review of this history, see Raymond Standish Beard, "A Survey of the Theories and Trends in Cross-Examination from Ancient Times to Modern," unpublished Ph.D. dissertation, Northwestern University, 1954.
3. Alfred Croiset, *An Abridged History of Greek Literature*, trans. George F. Heffelbower (New York: Macmillan, 1904), p. 282.
4. Plato, *Gorgias*, trans. W. C. Helmbold (Indianapolis, IN: Bobbs-Merrill, 1952), p. 18.
5. John Nicholas Iannuzzi, *Cross-Examination: The Mosaic Art* (Englewood Cliffs, NJ: Prentice-Hall, 1982), p. 6.
6. Howard Hilton Spellman, *Direct Examination of Witnesses* (Englewood Cliffs, NJ: Prentice-Hall, 1968), p. 3.
7. Ibid., p. 72.
8. For a discussion of the use of both question types in interscholastic debate, see Ronald Lee, "An Application and Adaptation of Schwartz's Legal Model of Examination for Interscholastic Debate," Master's Thesis, Wayne State Univ., 1976.
9. Leslie H. Allen, ed., *Bryan and Darrow at Dayton* (New York: Russell & Russell, 1967), p. 55.
10. *The Watergate Hearings* (New York: Bantam Books, Inc., 1973), p. 733.
11. James J. Unger and James M. Copeland, *Second Thoughts: The Question of Political Reform* (Skokie, IL: National Textbook, 1975), p. 144.
12. Unger and Copeland, *Second Thoughts: On the Question of Poverty in the United States* (Skokie, IL: National Textbook, 1973), p. 123.
13. Unger and Copeland, *Second Thoughts: On the Question of World Resources* (Skokie, IL: National Textbook, 1975), pp. 107–108.
14. William M. Reynolds and James J. Unger, *Second Thoughts: On the Question of Manpower and National Security* (Skokie, IL: National Textbook, 1968), p. 63.
15. *Bryan and Darrow at Dayton*, p.153.
16. Roy A. Redfield, *Cross Examination and the Witness*, (Mundelein, IL: Callaghan, 1963), p. 188.

PERFORMANCE OF ARGUMENT

Woody Allen *presented* and *performed* in the movie *Annie Hall*. Are the verbs "presented" and "performed" redundant in this sentence? On reflection, we think you will discover that each word has a distinctly different meaning. To present is "to show." Motion picture presenters are producers, directors, writers, and even theatre owners. To perform is "to carry into effect." Motion picture performers are the actors that bring the script alive. It is the difference between the architect and the carpenter, the planner and the craftsman.

Argumentation is not merely a course of study but a human activity. You may study history and read literature without much thought to making history or writing fiction, but you can hardly study argumentation without considering the exercise of advocacy.

In the final three chapters of *Arguing Persuasively*, we have included useful material for the development of advocacy skills. The most convenient forum for argumentative practice is debate. We provide outlines of formats, rules of procedure, and annotated transcripts of debates. Because debates are formalized, they are inevitably somewhat artificial representations of everyday argument. Yet, the participants are frequently thoughtful advocates who exemplify argumentative practices that are worthy of imitation.

14

DEBATE FORMATS AND SPEAKER DUTIES

Twenty-seven years after presidential hopefuls Richard M. Nixon and John F. Kennedy squared off in Chicago, televised political debates are commonplace. The public had an opportunity to view contests between presidential and vice-presidential candidates during the 1976, 1980, and 1984 campaigns. But are these meetings really debates? Many would say no. They view the meetings more like news or press conferences. One analyst even labeled the contests "The Counterfeit Debates."[1] What does it take to make a real debate?

A debate consists of contestants arguing opposite sides of a specific proposition or resolution in order to win the adherence of listeners. These fundamental elements may be organized in different ways and adapted to different occasions to create a variety of debate formats. Each format guides the conduct of the debate and the duties of the speakers in the debate.

FORMATS

Two broad categories of debate formats will be addressed in this chapter. Each category represents different occasions for or contexts within which debates take place. They also involve different types of audiences. The first category is academic debate and the second is public debate.

ACADEMIC DEBATE FORMATS

Academic debate is practiced at both the high school and college level. It is designed to provide students with an opportunity to develop skills in argumentation and to provide a forum for competition. Because academic debate is a competitive activity, a critic-judge listens to each debate and makes a decision as to who wins.

Standard debate is the most traditional academic format. This method of debating involves two teams with two contestants on each team. The disputants present a series of speeches adhering to the following order and time limitations.

Standard Debate Format

First Affirmative Constructive Speech	10 minutes
First Negative Constructive Speech	10 minutes
Second Affirmative Constructive Speech	10 minutes
Second Negative Constructive Speech	10 minutes
First Negative Rebuttal Speech	5 minutes
First Affirmative Rebuttal Speech	5 minutes
Second Negative Rebuttal Speech	5 minutes
Second Affirmative Rebuttal Speech	5 minutes

While this style of debate was used exclusively for many years, the majority of academic contests today employ a cross-examination style of debate. Current cross-examination formats combine elements of the standard format with elements of the Oregon style of debate. The original Oregon style of debate began with an affirmative constructive followed by a negative constructive. After the constructives each side was allowed to cross-examine the other. Finally, each side was allowed one rebuttal speech. Modern cross-examination formats preserve the standard notion of four constructives and four rebuttals and allow each of the four participants in an academic debate to ask and answer questions.

Cross-Examination Debate Format

First Affirmative Constructive Speech	10 minutes
Cross-Examination by the Negative	3 minutes
First Negative Constructive Speech	10 minutes
Cross-Examination by the Affirmative	3 minutes
Second Affirmative Constructive Speech	10 minutes
Cross-Examination by the Negative	3 minutes
Second Negative Constructive Speech	10 minutes
Cross-Examination by the Affirmative	3 minutes
First Negative Rebuttal Speech	5 minutes
First Affirmative Rebuttal Speech	5 minutes
Second Negative Rebuttal Speech	5 minutes
Second Affirmative Rebuttal Speech	5 minutes

The National Debate Tournament [NDT Debate] at the college level uses the format outlined above. The Cross-Examination Debate Association [CEDA Debate] at the college level and the National Forensic League at the high school level use a format identical to the one outlined above with the exception of shortened time limits. They limit constructive speeches to eight minutes, cross-examinations remain three minutes in length, and rebuttal speeches are shortened to four minutes. The academic debate in Chapter Fifteen uses the Cross-Examination Debate Association [CEDA] format.

Not all academic debate is designed for a two-person team. The Lincoln-Douglas debate format allows one individual to confront another in a dispute over a specific resolution. As the name suggests, this format has been adapted from that originally used by Abraham Lincoln and Stephen A. Douglas in a series of debates throughout Illinois in 1858. In these historic contests, the first speaker gave a speech one hour in length, the opponent then received one hour and thirty minutes for his reply, and the original speaker than closed with a speech of thirty minutes. As currently practiced in academic contests, Lincoln-Douglas debate employs shorter speaking times and includes cross-examination.

Lincoln-Douglas Debate Format

Affirmative Constructive Speech	6 minutes
Cross-Examination by the Negative	3 minutes
Negative Constructive Speech	7 minutes
Cross-Examination by the Affirmative	3 minutes
Affirmative Rebuttal	4 minutes
Negative Rebuttal	6 minutes
Affirmative Rebuttal	3 minutes

The time limits, of course, can be adjusted. Some prefer to allow eight minutes for each constructive speech, four minutes for each cross-examination, four minutes for the affirmative rebuttal, seven minutes for the negative rebuttal, and three minutes for the last affirmative rebuttal.

Each of these academic formats, while constructed for tournament use, can be adapted for classroom use by altering the time limits for each speech and cross-examination period so that the total length of the debate does not exceed the length of the class period. In making those adjustments, it is only important to preserve the equality of speaking time and the order of the speeches. Cross-examination is always an optional element that can be eliminated.

PUBLIC DEBATE FORMATS

Recall our earlier discussion of televised political debates. Why were they referred to as "counterfeit debates"? One explanation focuses on format. The political debates failed to organize the key elements of a debate into an acceptable pattern. Rather than engage in a direct confrontation with an opponent on a specific proposition or resolution, Presidential and Vice-Presidential candidates choose to employ a format much more akin to a joint press conference. Instead of arguing with each other, the candidates respond to questions posed by reporters. Instead of focusing on a specific proposition or resolution, reporters are asked to confine their questions to broad subject areas such as domestic policy or foreign policy.

The importance of format is most apparent in the production diaries for the debates. In 1960, for example, it took twelve meetings to iron out the details of the format Kennedy and Nixon would use in their contests. The Oregon-style debate format was suggested but it was rejected on the grounds that it would not hold an audience.[2] In 1976, the Oregon format was again suggested. This time the networks and representatives for Carter and Ford rejected the suggestion on the grounds that it did not generate excitement.[3]

Is it possible to have a public dispute that includes all of the elements of a real debate? The answer, of course, is yes. In fact, such an event occurred in 1948 when Harold E. Stassen, former governor of Minnesota, and Thomas E. Dewey, governor of New York, both candidates for the Republican party presidential nomination debated the proposition "Shall the Communist Party in the United States be Outlawed?" Stassen argued the affirmative and Dewey the negative. The debate was broadcast over the Mutual, NBC, and Blue radio networks at 6:00 PM on Monday, May 17, 1948.[4]

Public debate encompasses much more than these broadcast events. Public debates occur almost daily in a variety of different contexts. Because public debates take place before an audience, formats that stimulate audience interest and, perhaps even allow for audience participation, should be employed. One of the most popular formats for public debates is a modified Parliamentary style debate. This format is designed for teams, one supporting the affirmative and one supporting the negative.

Parliamentary Debate Format

First Affirmative Constructive Speech	10 minutes
First Negative Constructive Speech	10 minutes
Second Affirmative Constructive Speech	7 minutes
Second Negative Constructive Speech	7 minutes
Open Audience Comments/Questions	
Division of the House or Vote	

The amount of time devoted to audience comments/questions can vary depending on the length of the program.

Debates in which heckling is allowed also stimulate audience interest and involvement. In this debate format, the audience and/or opponents are allowed to interrupt speakers for the purpose of heckling. The guidelines for this type of debate usually specify that a speaker may not be interrupted during the first three minutes and the last two minutes of the speech. It is also a good idea to specify the number of interruptions that will be allowed during each speech.

Heckling Debate Format

First Affirmative Constructive	10 minutes
First Negative Constructive	10 minutes
Second Negative Constructive	10 minutes
Second Affirmative Constructive	10 minutes

This format can easily be adapted for use by individuals rather than teams. In so doing, the affirmative would be given a fifteen minute speech followed by a fifteen minute speech by the negative. Then, each speaker would be allowed a five minute rebuttal.

The various formats discussed in terms of academic debate can also be used for audience debates. The Cross-Examination Debate format, because it includes direct clash between opponents during the questioning periods, is lively and stimulates audience interest. When the debate includes two individuals rather than teams, the Lincoln-Douglas Debate format can be adapted to include audience participation.

Modified Lincoln-Douglas Debate Format

Affirmative Constructive Speech	15 minutes
Negative Constructive Speech	15 minutes
Open Audience Comments/Questions	
or	
Audience Questions of the Affirmative	
Audience Questions of the Negative	
Negative Summary	5 minutes
Affirmative Summary	5 minutes

The open audience comments and questions option provides more give and take among audience members while the questioning of each side by the audience tends to preserve structure. If direct audience involvement is not desired, it is possible to allow the participants to question one another. The public debate in Chapter Sixteen employs a format that begins with each of the two participants delivering a constructive speech. Then each participant presents a rebuttal before going head-to-head in cross-examination. The amount of time allotted to audience comments/questions or participant cross-examination can vary depending on the length of the program.

SPEAKER DUTIES

The duties of each speaker in a debate are determined in part by the format and in part by the type of proposition. The duties of each speaker in academic debate are much more rigidly prescribed than are the duties of the speakers in an audience debate.

ACADEMIC DEBATE

Academic debate formats allow for both team and individual debate. Both policy and value propositions are debated using the various academic formats. Consequently, as we discuss the duties of speakers, we will distinguish between team and individual debate and between debating policy and value propositions.

Standard or Cross-Examination Team Debate

In team debate, each of the four speakers presents a constructive speech and a rebuttal speech. The debate begins with the *first affirmative constructive speech*. This speech is the only speech in the debate that is written out in advance of the debate and delivered from manuscript. The first affirmative speaker is responsible for interpreting the resolution and presenting a prima facie case. A prima facie case is one that includes all of the arguments and evidence necessary to establish the proposition. Generally, the speech is divided into three parts.

First, the speaker should begin with an introduction, state the specific resolution being debated and provide definitions of key terms in the resolution. Second, the speaker should present the "case." By "case" we mean the reasons for change or justification for adopting the resolution. When arguing a proposition of policy, the case will focus on a discussion of the stock issues of ill (harms and significance) and blame (inherency). When arguing a value proposition, the case will typically include an identification and definition of the core value, a discussion of the reliable criteria for making the value judgment, and an analysis of how the proposition meets the criteria. Third, when a proposition of policy is being debated, a specific plan for implementing the resolution is proposed.

All of the remaining speeches in the debate are delivered extemporaneously from notes, evidence cards and/or argument briefs. The *first negative constructive speech* is intended to respond to the affirmative case. The speaker usually begins with a statement of philosophy. This philosophy typically summarizes the negative position on the resolution. Second, the speaker may elect to challenge the affirmative definition of terms. Third, the speaker should provide arguments and evidence that clash with those of the affirmative. When arguing a proposition of policy, the first negative speaker will focus on the stock issue of ill or blame. When arguing a value proposition, the speaker may challenge the definition of the value, and will dispute the criteria for evaluating the value judgment as well as the analysis of whether the proposition meets the criteria. Notice that the first negative speaker arguing a proposition of policy does not discuss the proposed plan for implementing the resolution.

The *second affirmative constructive speech* defends and extends the case analysis presented by the first affirmative speaker. By defending the case, we mean that the second affirmative should answer the arguments of the first negative speaker. If these answers include new, more detailed analysis, and additional evidence, the case will be extended or advanced beyond the original analysis. The duty of the second affirmative does not differ with the type of proposition.

The last constructive speech in an academic debate is the *second negative constructive speech*. While the previous speakers have clashed directly with one another on case issues, the second negative presents arguments that are considered to be off-case. When debating a proposition of policy, the second negative presents arguments and evidence focusing on the proposed plan for implementing the resolution. These arguments are usually of three types. Workability arguments claim that the plan will not work for some technical reason. Plan meet need or plan meet advantage arguments claim that even if the plan were workable, it would not solve the problem or accrue the alleged advantages. Disadvantages, by far the most important second negative arguments, claim that adopting the plan would lead to harmful consequences. When arguing a value proposition, the second negative focuses on the consequences of accepting the value claimed by the proposition.

Notice that regardless of the proposition type, second negative constructive speakers confine their argumentation to off-case issues. The rationale for this behavior has to do with format and strategy. The first rebuttal speech in the debate is the *first negative rebuttal*. Consequently, the second negative and the first negative are speaking back to back, creating what is typically referred to as the "negative block." This block in the middle of the debate is designed strategically to place pressure on the affirmative and to compensate for the fact that the affirmative gives both the first and the last speech in the debate. In order to use the block effectively, the negative wants to make certain that the arguments presented in the two speeches do not overlap. The first negative rebuttal speech should return to case issues. The speaker should attempt to synthesize what has gone on in the debate up to this point making choices as to which arguments are key to securing agreement from the judge. By isolating and extending those arguments, the first negative rebuttalist is able to focus the debate on ground favorable to the negative.

The *first affirmative rebuttal* speech is one of the most difficult speeches in the debate. This speaker is responsible for answering all of the arguments presented in the second negative constructive speech as well as those argued in the first negative rebuttal. Economy of language and grouping of arguments are critical skills for the first affirmative rebuttalist. It is most important that the off-case arguments of the second negative constructive be covered because they have not been addressed by previous affirmative speakers. The first affirmative rebuttal speaker will usually have only a brief amount of time to return to case arguments.

The last two speeches in the debate, the *second negative rebuttal* and the *second affirmative rebuttal*, must cover both case and off-case arguments. Obviously, neither of these speakers will be able to cover every argument that has been presented in the debate. Consequently, as each of these speakers attempts to synthesize arguments and make choices, each should reflect on the stock issues for the type of proposition being debated. The goal of each of these speakers is to persuade the critic-judge to vote for or against the resolution.

Lincoln-Douglas Debate

Lincoln-Douglas debate, as previously explained, involves only one speaker on each side. The propositions used in academic contests of this type are always propositions of value. As in any debate, the *affirmative constructive* must develop a case that justifies the resolution. This speaker typically identifies and defines the core value, presents arguments and evidence concerning the criteria that apply to the value and discusses how the resolution meets those criteria. The *negative constructive* may offer alternative definitions of the value, challenge the criteria applied to the value, and test the ramifications of accepting the value judgment.

The rebuttal speeches in a Lincoln-Douglas debate address the arguments presented in the constructive speeches. In the *first affirmative rebuttal*, the speaker should devote equal time to a defense of the value and refutation of the alleged ramifications of accepting the value. The *negative rebuttal* should also cover both issues but may want to spend more time defending and extending the ramifications of accepting the value, thereby making a strong appeal to reject the resolution. The final *affirmative rebuttal* should summarize the significance of the value in comparison to the possible ramifications of adopting the resolution, thus making a strong appeal to accept the resolution.

PUBLIC DEBATE

The speaker duties in public debates are much less regimented and will depend to a large extent on the nature of the topic and type of proposition being debated. If a team format is used, and the proposition is one of policy or value, the speaker duties outlined above under "Standard or Cross-Examination Team Debate" may be used. If a proposition of fact is being debated, the speaker duties would be similar with the exception of the second negative. Since a proposition of fact would not require a plan, the second negative would not be able to present off-case or plan arguments. Instead, the second negative would continue to present arguments and evidence related to the determination of the fact. These arguments should be different from those of the first negative and should be defended and extended in the second negative rebuttal.

If an individual format is used, the speaker duties outlined above under "Lincoln-Douglas Debate" would be appropriate for a proposition of value or fact. If a proposition of policy is debated, the negative constructive would have to divide time between case arguments and off-case or plan arguments. Finally, if audience participation is allowed either in the form of questions or comments during the debate, the rebuttal speeches should address not only the arguments of the opponent but also those of the audience.

NOTES

1. J. Jeffery Auer, "The Counterfeit Debates," in *The Great Debates: Kennedy vs. Nixon 1960*, ed. Sidney Kraus (Bloomington, IN: Indiana Univ. Press, 1977), pp. 142–150.
2. Herbert A. Seltz and Richard D. Yoakam, "Production Diary of the Debates," in *The Great Debates: Kennedy vs. Nixon 1960*, ed. Sidney Kraus (Bloomington, IN: Indiana Univ. Press, 1977), pp. 73–126.
3. Seltz and Yoakam, "Production Diary of the Debates," in *The Great Debates: Carter vs. Ford 1976*, ed. Sidney Kraus (Bloomington, IN: The Indiana Univ. Press, 1979), pp. 110–157.
4. Tom Swafford, "The Last Real Presidential Debate," *American Heritage*, Jan./Feb. 1986, pp. 67–71.

15

AN INTERCOLLEGIATE
DEBATE

The following debate took place in the final round of the first National CEDA Debate Tournament sponsored by the Cross-Examination Debate Association and hosted by Wichita State University on April 5–7, 1986. The debate was transcribed and edited by James R. Brey from a cassette tape recording. Evidence used in the debate was supplied to the editor immediately following the round. Sources of the evidence have been verified as indicated in the section labeled "Works Cited." The appropriate page numbers of each source have been included in parentheses following the text extract or in-text quote. Endnotes supply the exact quotation and other information when necessary. When the source was not available to the editor or was not located after a reasonable search, the term "source indicated" is in the endnote together with any additional information provided by the debaters. The debate was originally published in *1986 Championship Debates and Speeches* edited by John K. Boaz and James R. Brey. We are grateful to the American Forensic Association for granting us permission to reprint the debate.

The resolution being debated is "Resolved that membership in the United Nations is no longer beneficial to the United States." Anne C. Crenshaw and Miguel Delao, undergraduate students from Florida State University, argue in favor of the resolution. Molly McGinnis and Paul Benson, undergraduate students from Macalester College, argue against the resolution. This was an academic debate using the cross-examination format. Constructive speeches were eight minutes; cross-examination periods were three minutes; and rebuttals were four minutes.

Seven judges listened to this debate; five voted in favor of the negative team from Macalester College and two for the affirmative team from Florida State University.

Comments to the right and the left of the transcript have been added by the authors of this text to highlight and exemplify concepts and issues discussed earlier in the book.

FIRST AFFIRMATIVE CONSTRUCTIVE:
Carrie Crenshaw, Florida State University

Miguel and I stand resolved: That membership in the United Nations is no longer beneficial to the United States. Proposition of value

In beginning our affirmation of the resolution we wish first to note one observation. Observation number one. Criteria for evaluation of the resolution. (A) subpoint, definitions. Initially, we'd like to note that the affirmative has the right to reasonably define terms because otherwise the negative could always define the affirmative as falling outside the scope of the resolution. Establishing reliable criteria for evaluating the resolution

The term *United Nations* implies only the General Assembly, the Security Council, and the Secretariat. Thomas Franck, Director of Research for UNITAR, the UN's think tank, explains what the UN is, in 1985:

> This impression [of disillusionment and disappointment with the UN] cannot be rebutted by reference to public opinion polls demonstrating continued support for selected UN activities such as help to developing countries, the eradication of malaria, or the useful activities of the World Bank and the International Postal Union. The American public is sophisticated enough to know that these praiseworthy activities are carried out by agencies that are largely independent of the principal insitutions of the UN. When the laity think of the United Nations, they have in mind the organs which deal with highly visible political disputes: the Security Council, the Secretariat, and especially the General assembly. [These three organs] which deal with the big political disputes . . . are essential core of the system. (6–7)

In fact, Mr. Franck argues that membership to the UN is only really confined to those three areas when he writes:

> Between World Wars I and II the United States belonged to some specialized agencies, such as the International Labour Organization, even while refusing to join the League of Nations. Even now, we could continue to belong to the best of the functional bodies such as the World Health Organization and the World Food Programme, even if we decided to withdraw from the UN itself because of the initiatives of the core political organs no longer coincided with the US national interests. (7)

The final term needing definition, of course, is beneficial. According to *Webster's New World Dictionary* in 1979, beneficial means: For one's own interest.[1] Thus, we support the contention that beneficiality should be evaluated according to the United States' national interests. Key term to define is "beneficial"

Additionally we'd like to note subpoint (B). The US national interest defined. George Kennan, noted International Relations expert

According to this affirmative the most reliable criteria for evaluating the resolution is national security

and Professor at Princeton, quoted in the December 16th 1985 issue of *Newsweek* gives guidelines by which to determine the US national interest, "[T]he United States should be guided by three basic concerns—military security, the integrity of its political life, and the well being of the American people." (47) Thus if we succeed in proving that the UN no longer acts to serve the interests set forth by Professor Keenan, the resolution can be affirmed.

Meeting the criteria for evaluating the resolution

The grounds for our claim are offered in contention one. United States military security is endangered by conflict. Subpoint (A) conflict control ensures military security. If we wish military security then we must limit conflict. Michael Klare, analyst at the Institute for Policy Studies notes in 1984: "Looking at the world as it is, and wishing to avert a global catastrophe, our goal must be more expedient: the deterrence, containment, and control of military conflict." (247)

Subpoint (B) small conflicts pose the greatest threat of global disaster. Former President Nixon points out this first in his 1984 book *Real Peace*: "The greatest threat to peace comes not from the possibility of a direct conflict between the United States and the Soviet Union, but from the chance that a small war in the Third World will drag in the two super powers and escalate into a world war." (73)

While it may seem obvious that conflict control is in everyone's interest, the UN only exacerbates conflict. Note contention two, the UN heightens conflict. The reason stems from how the UN functions. Please note subpoint (A), the UN is used to blow off steam. The original purpose of the UN was to provide the countries of the world a place where they could vent their frustrations in the hope that the pressures which build up due to unsettled disputes would be relieved without the necessity of blood and agony. Mr. Tugwell, of the Center for Crisis Studies establishes this in 1984: "[A]s Winston Churchill expressed it, 'better jaw, jaw than war, war' . . . . The UN is the one place in the world where representatives of nearly all countries— regardless of size, wealth or power—are freely heard on a broad range of world issues. In this regard . . . the General Assembly is the principal forum for blowing off steam." (158)

However, things haven't turned out quite as Mr. Churchill expected. Subpoint (B), venting sows the seeds for war. The General Assembly is used to mobilize emotions, which cause conflicts. Mr. Tugwell continues in 1984:

> It cannot be said that this beneficial outcome has never occurred. It must also be said that in today's General Assembly, such occurrences are very rare. All evidence points to the safety valve theory being hypocritical, stage-managed and conflict-oriented. Far from cooling passions, the techniques of name-calling and lying are intended to mobilize the Assembly on the side of the speaker, to discredit and isolate adversaries, and to cultivate climates of opinion inhospitable to national argument. (163)

UN involvement in every problem only causes conflict to become extended. Jeane Kirkpatrick, former US ambassador to the UN, examines this reality in 1983:

> In the process of being transformed from actual problems outside the United Nations to United Nations issues, the number of parties to a conflict is dramatically extended. A great many countries who would never be involved at all in the issue of the Golan Heights, for example, become involved in that issue as the conflict is extended inside the United Nations to become a matter of concern to all the world. The United Nations is an arena in which many countries are brought into conflicts they might not otherwise become involved in. (96–7)

As the conflict becomes extended, everyone must choose sides in the issue and this causes more conflict. Professors Yeselson and Gaglione of Rutgers University explain in 1974:

> If a particular black African state wishes to maintain a neutral and helpful position vis-a-vis the Arab-Israeli dispute, it must consider the risk of alienating other Afro-Asian states in respect to issues on which it seeks their support. Politics at the UN, by constantly forcing states to choose up sides, progressively destroys neutral havens, which may mean the difference between war and peace. (175)

This conflict extension precludes the UN from peaceful settlement of conflict. Subpoint (C), venting precludes peacemaking. Mr. Tugwell continues in 1984:

> Nor is the UN's record in controlling regional conflict very impressive. In the Middle East, for example, fluttering blue and white UN flags and contingents of UN observers or peacekeepers never once prevented an Arab military or terrorist attack on Israel . . . . In recent years, undisguised UN hostility toward Israel has effectively disqualified that organization from its supposed pacific role in the Middle East. Significantly, the latest peacekeeping force in the region was sponsored outside the UN. (160)

We note subpoint (D), the UN is used to mobilize for war. The UN may be intended to cool emotions, and plenty of lip service may be given by its supporters to that goal, but the actual participants of the UN use it for mobilizing war efforts. Professors Yeselson and Gaglione of Rutgers explain:

> [The UN] is a weapon in international relations and should be recognized as such. As part of the armory of nations in conflict, the United Nations contributes about as much to peace as a battleship or an atomic bomb. Disputes are brought into the UN in order to weaken

an opponent, strengthen one's own side, prepare for war, and support a war effort. (x)

While the UN would be a good forum for discussing the solution to real problems, it is instead exploited for the mobilization of war efforts. Mr. Tugwell agrees, "The plight of Palestine Arabs is real the UN ought to be a good forum for reconciliation, compromise and settlement. However, instead of venting steam one day and returning the next to contribute to rational debate, the supposedly injured parties in these disputes vent steam to mobilize for war." (165)

While the past has been more successful than portrayed here, that is only the past. Please note finally subpoint (E), the UN has had successes but is now an enemy of peace. Kurt Waldheim notes in 1984: "The system on paper is impressive. It has frequently helped to avoid or contain international violence. Yet in recent years it has seemed to cope less and less effectively with international conflicts of various kinds, and its capabilities in other areas of international cooperation have also seemed to dwindle." (93)

In addition, any past success cannot be taken as indicating of any future trend. Mr. Tugwell explains:

> The UN has enjoyed some success in peace-maintenance, particularly in the prevention of escalation and in helping parties in a dispute to disengage. Although nuclear war has been avoided, this is more to NATO's deterrence policy than efforts in the UN. Moreover, a reluctance on the UN's part to recognize or address the reality of Soviet expansionist policy, coupled with disarmament proposals that may undermine deterrence, could diminish rather than strengthen the preservation of peace in the future. (157)

The only conclusion Miguel and I can reach is that peace can be better assured by not employing the UN in conflicts. Yeselson and Gaglione note: The overwhelming majority of quarrels among allies are settled secretly or bilaterally. Even states basically at odds with each other forego the UN when they are unwilling to exacerbate tensions.[2] (165)

We now ask you to stand resolved that membership in the United Nations is no longer beneficial to the United States.

CROSS-EXAMINATION
Paul Benson questioning Crenshaw

Clarifying a position — **BENSON:** The UN then consists only of the three major organs, correct?

CRENSHAW: Yes.

BENSON: OK, now, do the other areas of the UN contribute to the beneficiality of the UN?

CRENSHAW: Well, we're talking about membership in the United Nations according to the resolution. And membership in the United Nations only includes those three.

BENSON: So only those three. But do the other organizations contribute to our beneficiality of being in that particular organization.

CRENSHAW: I really don't know, and I would contend that is irrelevant, because it is not—

BENSON: That is irrelevant?

CRENSHAW: Yes, it does not fit under the topic in any way. It is not a resolutional discussion.

BENSON: OK. Now the CIA was established by Congress, correct?

CRENSHAW: That's correct.

Building an argumentative premise

BENSON: OK, and when we discuss the beneficiality of Congress would we not look at the actions of the CIA as part of that?

CRENSHAW: No, you wouldn't. In fact, that's the analogy that Miguel uses most of the time. He says—

BENSON: Yeah, I know.

CRENSHAW: Oh, good.

BENSON: Miguel is a nice guy.

CRENSHAW: If you're a member of the CIA, that does not mean you are a representative or a senator.

BENSON: That's irrelevant. I mean, doesn't, when you're evaluating beneficiality of Congress, would you not consider then—

CRENSHAW: But, you see—

BENSON: The actions of the CIA in that, you know, on balance calculus?

CRENSHAW: No, you must take the resolution as a whole.

BENSON: Resolution as a whole? Wouldn't we be taking the resolution as a whole if we did this?

CRENSHAW: No, you wouldn't because you have to deal only with membership in the United Nations. That is the only way you determine the benefits. That is the only thing that you are determining the beneficiality of.

BENSON: OK. I need the national interest (A) subpoint. And all of contention one.

BENSON: Now, the UN escalates these conflicts? Right? How many has it empirically escalated?

Exploring the connection between argument and evidence

CRENSHAW: I think there is one example of the Arab-Israeli.

BENSON: The Arab-Israeli dispute? Which one? (laughter)

CRENSHAW: The conflict in that area.

BENSON: In that area. I mean there are all kinds of conflict. Are we talking, like—

CRENSHAW: Israel and the PLO is what I believe Mr. Tugwell is—

BENSON: Israel and the PLO? Is that like UNIFIL? Is that what you're going to defend?

CRENSHAW: That was a peacekeeping operation. We're talking about venting. The blowing off of steam in the general assembly debate.

BENSON: OK. So blowing off steam is the impact then?

CRENSHAW: That is the link.

BENSON: That is the link to the impact. And the impact is what?

CRENSHAW: The fact that the UN exacerbates conflict and it contributes to—

BENSON: Well, what's the impact of exacerbating the conflicts? Are we talking war here or what?

CRENSHAW: The nations use the UN to mobilize their war efforts, in fact Professors Yeselson and Gaglione say that—

BENSON: Yeselson and Gaglione in '74, right? That's '74 evidence, correct?

CRENSHAW: Yes it is.

Investigating the credibility of the evidence

BENSON: Now you argue that, you know, we have to talk about current examples. OK. Now if that's true, how does this Yeselson and Gaglione even matter. It's twelve years old.

CRENSHAW: Well, you know, if you want to press the evidence.

BENSON: Why, I am. Will you answer my question please?

CRENSHAW: Well, it is 1974. Yes, it is.

BENSON: OK, the Tugwell evidence. Tugwell's Heritage Foundation, correct?

CRENSHAW: No, he is not. He's from the Center for Crisis Studies.

BENSON: Isn't he published in *The World Without a UN*?

CRENSHAW: Yes, he is, but that does not—

BENSON: And isn't that where you got the cite?

CRENSHAW: Yes, but that does not mean that is where he is from.

FIRST NEGATIVE CONSTRUCTIVE:
Molly McGinnis, Macalester College

We were told we would get time for thank yous so I'd like to do that first. Macalester College is very proud to be in the first final round of the National CEDA Debate Tournament. We would like to thank the members of the team that are here with us: Grant, Barb, Peter, Brenda, Steve and Chris,[3] and our coaches Dick Lesicko, Tim Baker, John Jackson, and Dr. Scott Nobles.

Overview number one is that membership is inherently benefi- Challenging the cial. (A) subpoint is that on balance, membership is beneficial and I'll resolution cross-apply to their criteria on case side. Richard Gardner, Professor of Law at Columbia, 1982. "[W]hen we look at the activities of the United Nations *as a whole*, the evidence leads us to the unavoidable conclusion that the advantages of the UN to our national interest outweigh the disadvantages." (50–1)

(B) subpoint is that no US means no UN. *Harpers* in January of '84 cites an anonymous high official of the administration who says "With us out, our Western allies would soon follow . . . along with many pro-Western countries in the third world . . . and the UN would soon collapse." (29)

(C) subpoint is that specialized agencies go too. Thomas Franck, who they cite, says in '85: As for wider withdrawal from the entire UN, the State Department has pointed out, that financial loss would constrain UN organization drastically and force them to cut back programs, including many regarded as especially important; refugee, health, and technical programs, for example.[4] (264–5)

Overview number two is that they suffer from lofty expectations. And lofty expectations says that they expect too much out of the peacekeeping forces and it's not surprising that they conclude that they fail. (A) subpoint is the purpose of peacekeeping mission. Donald J. Puchala, professor of government, University of South Carolina, in 1983: The primary purpose of these UN missions has been to deter the renewed fighting, to gain time for diplomacy, and to discourage external and especially superpower intervention that could lead to . . . escalate to larger wars.[5] (578)

(B) subpoint is that they are not supposed to shift parties. Alan James, Professor of International Relations in '83: "But if the parties refuse to move, it is not the peacekeepers' job to shift them." (633)

(C) subpoint is failure is the fault of outside diplomacy. Indar Rikhye, professor of political science at Yale in '84: (Which takes out their final argument on Yeselson and Gaglione which indicates they are becoming other than the UN). "The lack of peaceful resolution of conflict has more often been due to the failure of diplomacy outside." (224)

OK, overview number two or overview number three, excuse me, Specifying a is that the UN slows proliferation of nuclear weapons. (A) subpoint is benefit of that US is key to the IAEA [International Atomic Energy Agency]. Dr. the UN Scheinman announced in '85 that to insure an effective agency, a leadership role by the United States is needed.[6] (67)

(B) IAEA benefits the US. Robert Keohane, government professor at Harvard in Fall of '85: "[A]n international regime discouraging proliferation has greatly aided American policy . . . ." (152)

(C) subpoint, key to the regime. Joseph Nye, professor of government at Harvard in Summer of '85: The main norms and practices of this antiproliferation regime are found in the NPT, the nuclear non-proliferation treaty, and the IAEA.[7]

Debra Miller, a political science professor at Columbia says in 1983 that the UN itself has also contributed to the articulation of norms against the use of nuclear weapons. The reluctance of weaker states to use nuclear weapons in local disputes may derive in part from the U.N.'s norm against such an action from the perception that sanctions would be employed.[8] (136)

(D) subpoint is that the regime is effective. Leonard Spector from Carnegie Endowment for Peace in 1985. Safeguards probably detect most illegal uses of these plants and therefore pose a significant deterrent to proliferation.[9] (55)

(E) subpoint it slows the prolif rate. Lewis Dunn is from the ACDA in October of '84: "Without the NPT, political constraint to the bomb's spread would be undermined . . . ." (15)

Finally, subpoint (F) and it says that proliferation is disastrous. Scheinman says in '85: "The proliferation of nuclear weapons to more countries would increase prospects for their use, risk involving the superpowers, and raise the possibility of cataclysmic nuclear war." (1)

Challenging definitions

I'm on their observation number one now. (A) subpoint says definitions, that they have the right to be reasonable. First argument here is we will argue that they need to realistically define. And when the overview argues, you know that there is a link between the United Nations and the specialized agencies in terms of funding, that is realistic.

They argue only General Assembly. First argument is parallel to Congress. Now when Congress debates and decides that something needs to be done they delegate that to an agency which they set up, or a commission which they set up, and that's a delegation of responsibility. And we argue that there's the same delegation within the United Nations.

They argue from Franck in '85 that talks about political disputes. First argument is why is the affirmative definition distinct? Why is that the only definition? Why is the analysis I give above inappropriate? They argue that between World War One and World War Two we still belonged to these things. First argument is that a poor analogy between the League of Nations and the United Nations, because we argue now that the funding of both is inextricably tied.

They argue that beneficial means to be in one's own interest. And that's on observation two, the (A) point, where they talk about the definition of benefit. First argument is who is "one's own interest"? I mean is that your interest, or my interest, and how do you weigh those things? Second argument is we will maintain on balance. That you divvy up the costs and benefits of the United States membership in the United Nations and we will conclude that we win. Third argument is how do you weigh? If they prove a benefit and we prove a cost, or vice versa I guess would be the case, you know, how would we decide who wins? Who is the individual cited in their definition?

The (B) subpoint is from Mr. Kennan is 1985. He says that we should be guided by military security, the integrity of political life and the well being of American people. First argument is what are sub-definitions? That is, what is the integrity of the American people? What is military security? And those things are not defined, and if you're not certain whether or not the U.N. hurts those or helps those, then there can be no assertion of whether or not the UN is beneficial or not.

Request for additional definitions

Second argument is why only this? Why can't we talk about health, welfare, and all that? Then they would argue that's within their third definition, which only, which illustrates my point that they need subdefinitions before you can argue it. Third argument is how do you weigh? And that goes back to the balance criterion above.

Challenging the reliable criteria for evaluating the resolution

I am on contention number one, (A) point. They talk about how conflict control; the need for conflict control. First argument is they do not identify third world conflict. Second argument is they do not identify UN fostered conflict, in fact there is no mention of the UN at all in the card. Which would indicate that Klare is not really concerned about the UN conflict in particular, but just about conflict. Fourth argument is not only peacekeeping. Which would indicate that we will argue that peacekeeping is not the only [unintelligible] to peace, nor should peace be the only thing that is discussed because that's not what Kennan discusses only.

Denying that the affirmative meets the reliable criteria for evaluating the resolution

On the (B) point they talk about how small conflicts are the greatest risk. First argument is what are the scenarios? I mean, what does this author assume about what would be the greatest risk? Second argument is how large of a conflict is needed before this harm arose? And third, is this fostered by the UN? Does this piece of evidence indicate that such things are fostered by the United Nations?

Their contention number two. (A) subpoint says that the UN is used to blow off steam. Tugwell in '84. First argument is he's from the Heritage Foundation, and we would indict him in particular. *Atlantic Monthly* says in January of '86. "We're not here to be some kind of Ph.D. committee giving equal time, says Berton Pines, a vice president of the Heritage [Foundation]. Our role is to provide conservative public policy makers with arguments to bolster our side." (Easterbrook, 72) They reach their conclusion first.

Second argument is that debate is a substitute for war. Elliot Richardson is the Representative to the Law of the Sea in 1985. "[T]he long-winded debates are often surrogate for war . . . ." (Fasulo, vi) Third argument is the war is over arms. C. Maxwell Stanley, from the Stanley Foundation in '82: "In the area of peace and security, the General Assembly provides a neutral forum where parties to a dispute can fight with words rather than weapons." (105) Third argument, excuse me, fourth argument is that third world gets to vent their aggressions. Seymour Finger says in '85 that "Sometimes, too, fiery statements at the UN by Third World countries are a substitute for redeeming their pride by going to war when they know going to war would be disastrous." (Fasulo 65) OK?

Final argument is that there are no empirical examples. No indication of where the UN has fostered this sort of thing.

On the (B) point they state it equals the seeds for war. First argument is that they have a good track record. A. LeRoy Bennett, of the University of Delaware in 1984: "[T]he record of the UN in conflict resolution is surprisingly encouraging. Of more than 150 disputes considered by the Council and the Assembly, not more than a dozen remain." (130)

Second argument, nope that's enough there. On the next argument from Kirkpatrick, they talk about how (unintelligible) is extended. First argument is, even if it is prolonged it's better than no peacekeeping. K. Venkata Raman, professor of law at Queens, in 1983 says that "It is true that in some situations . . . indefinitely extended peacekeeping operations have not served to produce a settlement. But the absence of peacekeeping would have aggravated the situation much further." (376)

Next card is from Yeselson and Gaglione. They argue that they choose sides. First argument is 1974 evidence, and they better show some empiricals since then in the twelve intervening years. Second argument is that the empirical needs to be the standard. We argue that the empirically peacekeeping is good. Third argument is that does not talk about the superpowers which means they don't win the Nixon argument above. Fourth argument is that they do not show a snowball. That is Yeselson and Gaglione do not say that these conflicts escalate into the types of things the impacts come off.

(C) subpoint they talk about how peacekeeping does not prevent. First argument is this is only talking about Israel. OK? And that's the Tugwell evidence again, the indicts cross-apply here.

They argue that outside the United Nations work. First argument is the MNF was not peacekeeping it was war. Indar Rikhye, in '84: "The President thus categorically stated that MNF was helping to train and organize the Lebanese army and was needed to back it in maintaining order because Lebanon lacked the forces (to) do so" (235). Meaning we had to put a peacekeeping troop back in order to get these things to work.

Second argument is failure justifies UN. Dr. Cannon, from the board of Governors of the UN in 1984: "In the fall of 1982 the US organized . . . a MNF, outside of the UN, for Lebanon. It failed . . . . The US should have learned that the UN peacekeeping forces are truly international and relatively impartial—a major advantage in seeking to resolve peacefully." (30)

On the lip service argument next from Yeselson and Gaglione. Again 1974 and they need to indicate that the present would be truly the same. Raimo Vayrynen, professor of political science, from the University of Helsinki, in 1985. Peacekeeping forces are advocated both within and outside the UN. Peacekeeping will in the next decade and likely beyond by applied more frequently and with greater variety and complexity.[10] (193)

On the (E) subpoint they talk about how there have been success, but its not enough. J. G. Ruggie, he's a professor of political science at Columbia 1985. "On the whole, peacekeeping has been a success story for the United Nations as even some of the fiercest critics of the organization are obliged to concede." (347)

CROSS-EXAMINATION:
Carrie Crenshaw questioning McGinnis

CRENSHAW: You argue that the UN causes a proliferation of nuclear weapons, is that correct?

McGINNIS: No. We argue that the United Nations' norms and the United Nations' agencies help to slow the rate of proliferation of nuclear weapons in the world.

CRENSHAW: So that's (D) subpoint that says it slows the proliferation rate?

McGINNIS: Right.

CRENSHAW: Does the impact evidence deal with the rate of proliferation or does it deal with just whether or not proliferation is bad?

Exploring the connection between argument and evidence

McGINNIS: It talks about whether or not proliferation is bad. Though we would indicate from the (E) point that, the (E) point is also impact, which says that a fast rate of proliferation is not appropriate for a safe world.

CRENSHAW: Can I see that piece of evidence?

McGINNIS: Well, I just gave it all back. Hang on a second.

CRENSHAW: Because I believe on your next subpoint the only piece of evidence that you read was that proliferation in general is bad.

McGINNIS: Right. That's the (F) subpoint from Schienman. Right.

CRENSHAW: Could I see the (E) subpoint?

McGINNIS: Yeah, (E) subpoint is right here.

CRENSHAW: Why is it that a rate of fast proliferation is worse than a rate of slow proliferation?

McGINNIS: It is the making of the 1NC argument about prolif that more nuclear weapons are not a good thing. And that the move toward that has been halted or slowed by the UN.

Clarifying the
evidence

CRENSHAW: Could you read this piece of evidence for me again please?

McGINNIS: Any one in particular? Oh, the (E) subpoint. Lewis Dunn in '84 says that without the NPT, political constraint to the bomb's spread would be undermined. That's all the card says.

CRENSHAW: What does that say about the rate of the spread?

McGINNIS: We argue that were it not for this organization, more people would have the bomb. That's all we argue.

CRENSHAW: But, you just argued that the rate of proliferation has something to do with this argument.

McGINNIS: Maybe the words I used were inappropriate then, all I'm saying on this subpoint is that, were it not for the UN, more people would have the bomb than do now. That's all I'm claiming.

CRENSHAW: OK. So the rate of the—

McGINNIS: No,—

CRENSHAW: The rate of the—

McGINNIS: All I need— All I need by, not that it's irrelevant, all I'm arguing on this subpoint is that fewer people have the bomb. That's all I'm arguing.

CRENSHAW: OK. Why is it that the United Nations spreads nuclear weapons?

McGINNIS: Why is it that they spread nuclear weapons?

CRENSHAW: 'Cause your link said that—

McGINNIS: I don't argue that they do spread nuclear weapons.

CRENSHAW: Wait now. OK. Correct me if I'm wrong, but didn't you just say that if it were not for the United Nations, then less people would have the bomb?

McGINNIS: No. Were it not for the United Nations, more people would have the bomb than do now. I argue that—

CRENSHAW: OK, I'm sorry. Correct. OK.

CRENSHAW: So the United Nations promotes the spread of nuclear weapons?

McGINNIS: No.

CRENSHAW: It decreases the spread of nuclear weapons?

McGINNIS: Yes.

CRENSHAW: OK. I'm getting sleepy, obviously. Why is that? Through which agency? The International Atomic Energy Agency?

McGINNIS: Two ways. First, the United Nations itself sets the norms against such use.

CRENSHAW: What, the General Assembly?

McGINNIS: Right. The norms generated in the UN. And then I also argued that they delegate their responsibilities to enforce that sort of pledge, that norm, to the IAEA and through the UN treaty—

CRENSHAW: So, the norms evidence talks about the limited use of the nuclear weapons, does it not.

McGINNIS: It argues—stops the move toward—

CRENSHAW: It's not obtaining the technology; it's talking about the use of.

SECOND AFFIRMATIVE CONSTRUCTIVE
Miguel Delao, Florida State University

Their first overview is on empiricals. (A) subpoint is on balance. I would first argue that this is agencies. The evidence says when you look at the UN as a whole, as they argued in cross-examination, it should be wholistic. Second argument is vague word. It is not something you can vote for, it does not say exactly what is beneficial and certainly you cannot weight exactly what they are talking about. You do not even know what was considered. They consider our arguments.

She says (B) subpoint, no US equals no UN. She is correct. (C) subpoint says agencies would go. That is not true. That evidence only indicates that we actually left the agencies also. We could still fund the agencies by still being in them. We do not necessarily have to cut off funding to the agencies, and I think the Franck evidence at the top of the case indicates that.

Overview two, lofty expectations. First argument is, I don't think its very unreasonable to expect the United Nations to not cause conflict. Certainly we can't expect them to stop every conflict, but you don't want them to create any of them. Second argument is that peacekeeping has worked in the past, but we are claiming that it has changed because of venting as I will argue on case specifically.

Third argument is that we are not dealing with failure. We're not saying that they fail at all peace efforts, but that fact that they create conflicts means we do not need the United Nations because we will argue that it is not unique to the United Nations.

Prolif. First argument is that the IAEA is an agency. Evidence is from Ameri in '82: Although not a specialized agency, the International Atomic Energy Agency (IAEA) is an autonomous intergovernmental agency under the aegis of the United Nations. (26) Second argument is that we must obviously have the bomb out there because the evidence that they read that says that the UN has these norms to stop the use—you only stop the use of nukes after someone has nukes. Which indicates that the UN has not stopped proliferation, otherwise, the norms would not matter.

Third argument is that the debates actually lead to prolif. Becker

The benefit is not a benefit of the UN as defined by the affirmative

Benefit denied

writes in 1985: "Nuclear nonproliferation is not tackled as a security issue but rather as another source of 'discrimination' between 'haves' and 'have nots' . . . . The net result is that the United Nations debates undermine the status of the NPT and become instrumental in legitimizing nuclear weapons proliferation." (175)

Fourth argument is that the NPT spreads nuclear weapons capabilities. Becker in '85: "The NPT will in effect become a treaty for the peaceful uses of nuclear energy, and as such may be instrumental in promoting the very spread of nuclear weapon capability that it was intended to inhibit" (134). Fifth answer is that the IAEA promotes nuclear proliferation. Becker in '85:

> These deficiencies are particularly alarming because of the 'abrogation risk' inherent in the NPT system . . . . In other words, the IAEA system, and particularly its promotional role, allows a state to proceed under the guise of the NPT as far as possible with all its plans for making nuclear weapons and, when ready, merely notify the IAEA and the United Nations Security Council that it is withdrawing from the treaty. (126)

Sixth argument is that the experts agree that the IAEA cannot stop prolif. Becker in '85, quoting Epstine: "Experts agree, and the IAEA itself admits, that there are limits to the extent to which the agency is able to detect diversions and to guarantee an effective international response to an nonproliferation violation, even when it is detected." (126)

Definitions defended

Criteria of our case. She says you need a realistic standard, and they have a funding link but she never indicates that would actually be stopped, i.e. this is the same argument she makes as her overview.

She says number two, Congress equals delegates, and it is the same in the UN. But, if I'm a member of the CIA, I am not a member of Congress. And therefore, the U.S. could still belong to the IAEA, still stop proliferation, and not have to be in the United Nations and stop this venting.

She then extends that, I can't read my own handwriting. Oh, I'm sorry, she says why is Franck correct? And I would argue that this. You can belong in these agencies and this is empirically true. Bennett in '84: "Membership in the specialized agencies affiliated with the UN is independent of UN membership. Several of the specialized agencies have a membership larger than that of the UN." (75) Switzerland belongs to a lot of these specialized agencies and they are not members of the United Nations.

She extends that the League is a poor example because there was no funding link. But she never indicates that there was no funding link between the League of Nations and these agencies, she merely asserts it. And Mr. Franck indicates, that even if we leave the UN, you can still belong to these agencies. And that part of the evidence is granted.

Beneficial. She says, for whose benefit? Should balance. Of course, I would agree. She says, number three, how do you weigh? I would say you give articulate eloquent reasons why your argument outweighs.

(B) subpoint, US national interests. Kennan in '85. She says what are the subdefinitions? I think we provide the subdefinitions on contention one, when we indicate that military security is in our benefit. Number two, I would argue, is that it outweighs everything else, because if we are not militarily secure and our country's involved in a war, or should have a nuclear catastrophe, then surely we cannot have political integrity or well-being.

National security is defended as the reliable criterion for evaluating the resolution

She says number two, why not the others? As I argued above this outweighs. She says number three how do you weigh? Not to be cynical or anything but you use scales and when you weigh me, I'm a bit heavy. (Laughter) Pudgy.

Contention one. (A) subpoint, you need conflict control. She says this does not say UN fosters. Of course not. But it is true that if the UN leads to conflict, this evidence indicates you don't want that, because that would lead to catastrophe.

She says number two, peacekeeping is not the only thing. Fine.

She says (B) sub. On our (B) subpoint we argue small wars are the greatest threat. She says what are the scenarios? I think Mr. Nixon gives you excellent scenarios. He says we'll get sucked in; we'll get dragged in. She says number two, how large do they have to be? Clearly, the evidence indicates when you have these small wars you have this political for escalation and we would ask you to vote for that, at least the evidence at top says you don't want all this conflict out there. That is the Klare evidence.

Extension of analysis related to meeting the reliable criteria for evaluating the resolution

She says number three, does not say UN. You know, so what? We are arguing by links here. And this contention is merely establishing the criteria by which you weight contention number two. And that is where the links are. Contention number two. Tugwell evidence there in '84 says the safety valve theory has been turned on its head. She says Heritage Foundation. First argument is, who the hell, who the heck, is the *Atlantic Monthly*? How come that beats the Heritage Foundation? She doesn't even read a source.

Second argument is that evidence does not say they reach their opinions first. She merely asserts that. Third argument is she should just prove them wrong. If he is so incorrect then just say why they are wrong. She says, number two, that they empirically prevented wars. Obviously not true. It is empirically false because we have wars all the time. And you have all this debate out there and they still go to war. Means at least venting does not lead to peace. Not that it necessarily leads to war, but it does not lead to peace.

She says that they get to vent. But, I want to extend the evidence there in the case that the safety valve has been turned on its head. So that venting is actually bad. Her last argument is no empirics. But the evidence down there that we read later on in the case, that the Arab-Israeli conflict is fueled by the United Nations.

(B) subpoint, venting—sow the seeds of war. She says that they have conflict resolution, but I would argue that they still cause conflicts, and that is not what you want. Kirkpatrick. She says it is better than nothing. '74. She says show empirical example. I would argue that the problem is still around. *World Press Review* in December of '85: "Never before has the UN been so divorced from its functions of preserving peace, settling international disputes, protecting human rights, and creating an atmosphere of dialogue instead of vituperation." (Sethi 39)

Second argument, she says you need empirical standard. I got that above. She says three, no superpowers, do not show snowball. And this is the Nixon evidence that indicates when you have these conflicts, you have this potential for getting sucked in.

(C) subpoint, venting precludes. She says that it is only Israel, and that it is Tugwell. No, the evidence indicates in the whole Middle East, not just Israel. She says MNF equals war and this is all her peacekeeping stuff. Please group. First argument is the UN would not have done better. Nelson in '85: "To assert that the MNF role had been transformed from peacekeeping to enforcement is not to say that it failed per se, not emphatically, that a UN force would have been more successful in the same circumstance...." (82)

Number two, they don't want the UN there. Cuellar in '84: "But the difficulty is that some of these concerned don't want to have the United Nations involved in the Middle East problem. They object to the United Nations presence." (Gauhar 18)

Number three, they will not go to the Middle East. That is the evidence from Tugwell there, indicating only the US can do it.

Number four is, that there will be no more peacekeeping in the future because we've had the non-UN peacekeeping. Cuellar in '84: "On two occasions Multinational forces were set up by the US which is really tantamount to telling the UN that we don't trust you to handle difficult matters. With that background, it seems that the major powers might be unwilling to support UN peacekeeping operations." (Gauhar 17)

Number five, thank you, soldiers are dying and therefore, no one will contribute soldiers to it. Cuellar in '84: "The growing reluctance of members countries to provide troops unless they have some guarantee that the troops will be protected. It is not developing countries who ask for such guarantees, it is the developed countries who insist on it. For instance, the Netherlands and Norway are hesitant to continue providing troops to the United Nation's UNIFL. The Netherlands have told me very frankly that they are prepared to extend their presence in Lebanon for three more months but not beyond." (Gauhar 16) You need the U.S. in there because heck, we're really, you know ready to shoot at them.

(E) subpoint is granted which means you have no reason to. This peacekeeping stuff will come down to uniqueness. If the US can go in there, and at least shoot back and guarantee that people want them to be soldiers, and you can get all this conflict resolution outside the United Nations, that Yeselson card in '74 is granted, that says you go bilateral because you don't want to increase tensions, then the UN is not unique to get the peace.

CROSS-EXAMINATION:
Molly McGinnis questioning Delao

McGINNIS: Are there any peacekeeping forces in operation right now?

DELAO: Yes, there are.

McGINNIS: Yes, there are. How many?

DELAO: Two.

McGINNIS: Two?

DELAO: That's a guess.

McGINNIS: No, I'm asking you a question.

DELAO: Well, you seem to know the answer.

McGINNIS: Oh. Actually, not, that's Paul.

DELAO: Well, we'll take two.

McGINNIS: Any idea where these unnumbered peacekeeping missions might be?

DELAO: UNIFL is one of them.

McGINNIS: UNIFL is one of them. OK. And it's not working? Is conflict there?

DELAO: I don't remember making that argument.

McGINNIS: Now wait a minute.

DELAO: I'd love to make that argument. I probably will.

McGINNIS: You argue they extend the conflict, they institutionalize the conflict, they still cause conflict, all that.

DELAO: Now that's the venting in the General Assembly.

McGINNIS: Now wait a minute, the Kirkpatrick evidence says that UN involvement equals extension of the conflict.

DELAO: In the General Assembly.

McGINNIS: In the General Assembly only, right? So there's no extension of the conflict on the battlefield?

DELAO: Not at. Right, not in that evidence.

McGINNIS: Not in that evidence. Anywhere in 2AC?

DELAO: Nope.

McGINNIS: Nowhere in 2AC?

DELAO: We're not saying peacekeeping is bad, we're just going to, we are going to argue we're going to get it more effectively.

McGINNIS: Oh. OK, sounds good.

McGINNIS: Is there conflict right now?

DELAO: That's a vague question.

McGINNIS: OK, in terms of the definition of conflict used in 1AC, is there conflict now?

DELAO: In the world, yes, there is.

McGINNIS: OK. So, why haven't the super powers been sucked into the horrors of Richard Nixon's scenarios?

DELAO: Luckily, we don't all get sucked into every single conflict.

McGINNIS: Oh, so only a few conflicts do they get sucked into? Any possibility of where that might be?

DELAO: That just shows that it is not in our interest. And it doesn't have to happen every time, but since there is a potential, certainly it is not in our interest. And it doesn't have to happen every time, but since there is a potential, certainly it is not in our interest to want to risk that.

McGINNIS: OK. If it is in our interest to have MNF, or non-U.S. peacekeeping forces, why haven't we sent them everywhere in the world where there is conflict?

DELAO: The last few times peacekeeping forces were used were outside the UN. The last time they were—

McGINNIS: OK. In areas where there are no UN peacekeeping forces or no non-UN peacekeeping forces, why hasn't the US, like, gotten up and done something about it?

DELAO: Peacekeeping forces are not used all of the time. The only time that they have generally been used is when you had a more serious conflict. Its not like everyone uses them—

McGINNIS: A more serious conflict?

DELAO: Not using them is not necessarily a failure. It only means that—

McGINNIS: Excuse me, what's the difference between a more serious conflict where there would be peacekeeping forces and a small conflict which is the greatest risk that Nixon talks about?

DELAO: Oh, OK. The one Nixon is talking about is when you have allies, like superpowers and therefore you have to get involved. I mean when Israel fights somebody, like in the '73 war—

McGINNIS: OK, so now Israel is something that Nixon would talk about, right?

DELAO: Because there is a peacekeeping force there.

McGINNIS: That works?

DELAO: Well when you make that argument, I assure you we will have lots of responses.

McGINNIS: Now wait a minute, your criterion is that we shouldn't get sucked in and you just said that peacekeeping forces—

DELAO: I didn't say it works, I said there is one there.

McGINNIS: But, they aren't sucking us in, right?

DELAO: Not the peacekeeping forces, peacekeeping forces—

McGINNIS: Has the area sucked us in superpower?

DELAO: Obviously, not.

McGINNIS: OK.

SECOND NEGATIVE CONSTRUCTIVE:
Paul Benson, Macalester College

Lofty expectations, it gets big, contention two. Lofty expectations is overview number two. The criteria set up by the 2AC is if you can do it outside the UN better, then you vote affirmative. And what we will argue is, he will have to prove i.e. solvency for this indicating that outside the UN is better. We will contend that UN is the best thing that you've got and it's the only empirical examples of solving for peace.

Please go to his first argument on lofty expectations. He says it's not unreasonable to say that they don't, you know, for them not to cause it. Of course, number one, I will argue they do not cause the wars. I mean the wars happen with or without the United Nations. And nowhere does he indicate that a war would happen because the UN existed.

Second argument is it prevents wars. This is from the *World Press Review* in '85: It would be unjust to consider only the organization's failures. How can we count the number of wars that, thanks to the UN did not break out because of the Security Council.[11] (Balk, 4)

Specifying another benefit of the UN

Next argument is that they decrease tension. Ronald Falkner who's a professor of political science at Tennessee Tech in '83: Its record in view of the tremendous tension reductions in the world has been a good one. The United Nations has served with remarkable effectiveness as a mechanism for reducing friction arising out of the process of change.[12] (490)

Next argument is it controls violence. Indar Rikhye professor of political science at Yale in '74: No one who has carefully studied the performance of these peacekeeping forces in a role closely dictated and controlled by the General Assembly and Security Council lightly dismisses that any of them has made a contribution to the overall control of violence.[13]

I will indicate that these peacekeeping forces are good.

His second argument is that, you know, it has worked, but it has changed now. And I'll indicate below that, you know, even today it's doing some neat stuff.

His third argument is it does not deal with failure. Of course, number one on balance we would indicate that they are beneficial. And you will answer yes to the resolution. And what we are arguing here is, and the evidence above talks about from the *World Press Review*, is that, you know you can't even count the number of wars that have been prevented because of the UN.

Second argument is he drops that the failures are the fault of outside forces. Indicating that the failures are not the fault of the UN, it's because of outside areas.

I want to extend here on lofty expectations. Argument number one is, you should not blame them for no conflict resolution. Raman, who was previously qualified in '83: "There is, consequently, little justification in blaming peacekeeping for a failure to reach a solution in a conflict." (376) It was never their responsibility.

Next argument is if they want to fight, they will. This is from Connor O'Brian who is a UN secretary in 1985: "In cases where both parties are prepared to go to the bitter end—as, for example, in the Falklands—there is no real role for the UN." (19) Indicating, you know, if Iran and Iraq hate each other that much nobody is going to stop them from shooting each other.

Next argument is if the UN wants, you know if they want peace, the UN provides it, indicating beneficiality. Abba Eban the Foreign Minister from Israel in '85: When the belligerents desire to formalize a measure of stability and mutual restraint, the availability of UN symbols and myth helps them to create periods and areas of restraint and then stop the conflict.[14] (45)

Final argument here is you cannot expect them to solve all conflicts. Edward Luck in '85: "The United Nations obviously cannot manage all conflicts and resolve all disputes successfully." (149) Impact of this argument indicates, you know that you can't expect them to do everything great, but man in the stuff they do, it's fantastic.

Past examples of UN benefits to our national security

I want examples here, and I'm going to give you a ton of them. (A) subpoint are past examples. And he's going to say well these are in the past and they don't apply. But I will give you examples where the superpowers have been prevented from getting involved in conflict. And I'll contend that if these things hadn't happened, you may not even have a today.

First example is the Congo. And this is from Indar Rikhye, professor of political science in '84. He argues international peacekeeping not only survived the challenge but established beyond any doubt that, without its involvement, the Congo would have ceased to survive as a unified nation and could easily have become a battleground of super-power warfare.[15] (89)

Next argument is it justifies overall peacekeeping. Rikhye again, this time in '74: The part of the UN in the Congo played deserves its rightful recognition and can clearly be defined as justification for the UN's overall conflict resolution policy.[16] (91)

Indicates justification on a big basis.

Next argument is it prevented superpower confrontation, and I mean that's the evidence that's above.

I'll give you the next empirical example of the Cuban Missile Crisis. Connor O'Brian continues. The Cuban missile crisis suggests that the world might have been more unsafe if it weren't for the UN's repertoire of tricks.[17] (18)

Next argument is essential role by the UN. Brian Urquhart, Social and Political Affairs in '81: The UN played an essential role in the Cuban Missile Crisis in '62, not only providing a forum where both sides could expound their positions publicly but also in suggesting, steps could be taken to deescalate the crisis.[18] (9)

Final argument is Yom Kippur War. Sir Anthony Parson in '83. He's a U.K. Ambassador. "At the end of the Yom Kippur War of October 1973, there was a situation of the most appalling danger to global peace . . . . The world came close to a naked confrontation be-tween the superpowers on a battlefield. Neither side could find a way to climb down. At the last moment, they used the Security Council of the United Nations as a ladder from which to dismount their high horses." (106–7) I'm telling you, in the Yom Kippur War, we might not even have today if it were not for the UN.

Please go now on to the (B) subpoint, which will indicate, you know, current examples. Cyprus is the first one. *UN Chronicle* in '85: "The Secretary General said the continued presence of UNFICYP re-mained indispensable in helping to maintain the calm in the island . . . ." (33).

Current examples of UN benefits to our national security

Next argument is in terms of the Middle East, in UNTSO. This is from Indar Rikhye, professor of political science, previously qualified. "Similarly, UNTSO continues to perform an important role in the Middle East. It keeps the Security Council informed of incidents and other developments that threaten peace." (1983,9)

Next argument is Pakistan. It keeps the peace today. Rikhye again. Uhm, this is, oh excuse me. Selig Harris, [Harrison], Carnegie Endow-ment in '83: The UN effort in Pakistan has come close to successful conclusion, and has been successful in regard to the Soviet withdrawal from Pakistan.[19] (4) Next argument is UNDOF, that's the Golan Heights Force. And this is from Rikhye again. The situation remained unchanged in the Golan Heights, where calm continued to prevail. Thus UNDOF continues to play a useful role between Israel and its remaining, you know, Arab problem.[20] (62)

Next argument is UNIFL. *UN Chronicle* in '85: In spite of the difficult conditions in southern Lebanon, UNIFL's presence continues to be necessary and constitutes an important factor in the stability in the international commitment to upholding Lebanon's independence, sovereignty, and territorial integrity.[21] (7) I think I take all of that out. Man, the empiricals are with the negative.

Please go to contention two. He argues who's the *Atlantic Monthly*? Well, I'll argue the *Atlantic Monthly* is not an unbiased source that reaches its conclusions beforehand. And I mean if you want to call for the evidence at the end of the round, that is what the evidence does indicate. They reach their conclusions, then go off and research it.

I'll argue next argument is, that you know, the Heritage Foundation is basically a mindless organization. William Charles Maynes, Editor of *Foreign Policy* in '85: "[T]he Heritage Foundation . . . has devoted so much of its budget to what seems to outsiders as a mindless assault on the United Nations. (237) Next argument is, remember these guys? These are the guys who said fluoridation of water was a communist plot. (Laughter) I mean empirically, give me a break here.

His second argument is, you know, empirically takes out debate, substitutes for war. Where are the empiricals? He doesn't indicate them. And he drops the Richman evi—I think it's Richman evidence, that indicates, you know debates do substitute.

The third argument he says safety is turned, but all he does is say, you know, extend. I mean our arguments from the Stanley Foundation in '85 beat this.

His next argument, he drops the fourth subpoint that says the Third World gets to vent their aggression, that the Finger evidence and he grants it. He says, you know, we say no empiricals, he says it fuels conflict. No. I mean we argue here that the empiricals rest with the negative. And I think that our evidence pulls through. He does no extension here, all he does is repeat.

Please go now on to where he argues causes conflict. I will argue, no it stops. And I give empiricals. He says they do not keep the peace. That is wrong, he drops the Raman evidence that indicates even if it's prolonged it's better that you have the peacekeeping forces there.

Now on Yeselson and Gaglione. It's '74, the above evidence takes out anyway.

On empirical standards, he says above. I'll say above. He says Nixon takes out superpowers and no snowball. But he drops the answers.

Only Israel is the next argument Molly makes, and he says it's on the whole in the Middle East. Baloney: It's only Middle East and I give other examples.

He then argues that there are these better ways to do it. Of course number one, only Middle East. Number two, drop Vayrynen evidence says we will use it in the future. Number three, drops the MNF evidence that says it wasn't even a peacekeeping force, it was a war.

Next argument is that bypassing the UN is bad. Houghton and Trinka, Center for the Study of Foreign Affairs in '84: The UN has acquired a great deal of expertise in the field. To creat a non-UN organization for the same purpose derogates the prestige of the UN and thus weakens the overall peacekeeping process of the world.[22] (79)

Next argument is it prevents superpower confrontation. Houghton and Trinka again. "[T]he establishment of non-UN peacekeeping force, with US participation . . . is unacceptable to the Soviet Union, even if it is done under the banner of a peacekeeping force. A response by the USSR can be expected, thus creating the risk of a new direct confrontation." (95)

You know, those non-UN forces are nasty stuff.

CROSS-EXAMINATION:
Miguel Delao questioning Benson

DELAO: Can I have the last two cards?

BENSON: Sure.

DELAO: That's a really interesting last card. Paul, I get crucified in cross-ex because I say, you know, why you have conflict and it will escalate and everybody will die. That last card says that when you go outside the UN, the Soviets will nuke us or something to that extent, and we've had two outside the UN, when did they nuke us?

BENSON: Well, no, no, no, see like the MNF and the MFO, I mean, we're not saying it definitely is going to happen—

DELAO: Well, what's the potential for it? (laughter)

BENSON: Well, I mean you argue. If you're going to contend potential, I will contend that there is a greater possibility of this happening here.

DELAO: Why?

BENSON: Because UN forces do not include the superpowers or any members of the Security Council. Non-UN forces—

DELAO: They never do?

BENSON: Huh?

DELAO: They never do?

BENSON: Not currently. I mean, if you want to bring that up I've got the charter.

DELAO: I thought the Cyprus forces had US people there.

BENSON: They did in the past, but they were withdrawn.

Challenging
a position

DELAO: They don't now?

BENSON: No.

DELAO: Can you prove it?

BENSON: Well, I mean the US is continuing to support it via funds, political stuff and that, but our troops aren't over there. And I mean we commit our troops to these non-UN peacekeeping forces. We have to, that's the only way they can function.

DELAO: Can you name me the wars we stopped?

BENSON: The wars we stopped? Yom—

DELAO: You want me to show you the wars we caused?

BENSON: Huh?

DELAO: You want me to show the wars we caused.

BENSON: Well, I'd say this is just a little late—

DELAO: I'm referring to the *World Press Review* card that just says don't just consider the failures—

BENSON: OK. OK. Yom Kippur prevents superpower conflict.

DELAO: So you're going to refer to all the empirics then in 2NC, right.

BENSON: Oh no, I'll contend that all the empiricals that are going on now which I will claim as independent benefits to UN peacekeeping.

DELAO: I think you have a really good argument here that—

BENSON: Well, thank you.

DELAO: Well, let me tell you which one.

BENSON: I think it's a good argument.

DELAO: You may be wrong. Well, I think they are all good.

DELAO: You say it's reasonable that you should not have lofty expectations. Now all the evidence you read says that you should not expect them to stop every war, right.

BENSON: I agree with you.

DELAO: That's an unreasonable expectation. But, is it unreasonable for the affirmative to say that the UN should not contribute? Is that unreasonable?

BENSON: Should not contribute to conflicts?

DELAO: Exactly.

BENSON: Well, I mean that depends like, what your, you know, what empiricals you bring up and whether or not I can turn them (laughter).

DELAO: Whether we win them or not, is that an unreasonable standard?

BENSON: Well, I mean I don't think, you know, I'm not going to grant you that premise at all because I would contend that the wars would with or without the UN and for you to hypothesize that some how the UN caused this to incrementally increase that much, I think that's baloney.

DELAO: That's if you win your argument. If the UN contributes—

BENSON: Even if I don't I think it makes sense.

DELAO: If the UN contributes to it, why is it unreasonable to expect them to not contribute?

BENSON: You just lost me. Why is it unreasonable to expect them to not contribute? They don't—

DELAO: See, you're assuming you win your argument. I am saying—

BENSON: I don't plan on losing it. (laughter)

DELAO: I want to know if, I don't care who wins it, why is it unreasonable to not want them to contribute to it? This is your fourth chance to answer this.

BENSON: Oh, so you mean that the UN would actually like, cause more people to get involved. Is that what you're asking?

DELAO: Why is that unreasonable?

BENSON: You can bring up stuff that says like, it brings in like eight other countries getting involved, well then yeah, I would say that the UN isn't beneficial in that instance.

DELAO: OK.

FIRST NEGATIVE REBUTTAL
Molly McGinnis, Macalester

His first answer on the overview, says that my evidence talks about the UN as a whole, therefore it's obviously not talking about what the affirmative is talking about. First argument, they contradicted this definition. Now that means his definition is different from mine, but I'm arguing that that highlights that there is no definite definition of what is and what is not the UN. Why is my author inappropriate when he says the words UN in his piece of evidence and concludes that on balance, it's beneficial to the United States? And he needs to show that the assumptions my author, why those are different than his. And he has to highlight those dinstinctions before there can be any concrete definitions of UN.

Negative argues that affirmative definitions are inconsistently applied

Second argument is that the money is inextricably tied. And this cross-app's back to the (C) point. Nicholos Platt, from the Bureau of International Affairs, DOS, 1982: "The subsidiary UN bodies and the specialized agencies are another component of the UN, and their activities in fact consume the major portion of UN monies and personnel." (13) UNA Publications, *Financing the UN* says in March of '84: "Also included in the regular budget of the UN are the expenditures of the

Refuting affirmative definition of UN

specialized agencies." (Formuth 2) We get to talk about all of them. OK.

Extending the
benefits of
the UN

Third subpoint is that, on balance the UN is good for us. Frank Church, who as a former congressional delegate to the UN in 1985. "[I]n our world and in these times, such an organization needs to function, and one would hope that it might grow more effective over the course of time. On balance, the UN is far more of a plus for the world than a minus." (Fasulo 114) OK. Which would indicate that no matter what else happens in the round, this author says, you know, vote negative. And there is no same, on balance evidence by the affirmative.

I'm on observation number one on case now. He argues right to define. He argues there is no evidence that money can be cut. I talk about that on the overview. He argues that a member of the CIA is not a member of the Congress. First argument is that it does not indicate that we should not add those folks into our calculus. You know, and that's the same money argument I made on the overview side.

He argues that we belong to the agencies without. First argument is that is arbitrary. And that's a cross-application of the definitional muddle that we talk about on the top of overview number one.

On between World War One and World War Two, the League of Nations. He says I provide no evidence. You know he needs to indicate there is a distinction, because I argue now funding is inextricably linked.

He argues that beneficial is in ones own interest. This is observation number two. I argue, you know, he agrees that we need to argue on balance, which means I win the Church evidence I just read. And I don't know how you weight those sorts of things. He says eloquence. You know.

Extending the
argument that
national
security is
not the most
reliable criteria

On observation number two, (B) point, he says national interest. OK, he says it outweighs anything, and this is only military security. OK, and so he indicates that its our military security which we will win on case. But, he does not indicate that the other things are not as important. And certainly Kennan does not make those distinctions as well, and he's arbitrarily inserted those distinctions.

Underview on this contention. First argument is that we should not contribute to conflict. That is 2AC's question to Paul in cross-ex. Second argument is that there is no affirmative contention that peacekeeping is bad, merely that it doesn't work. And remember we talk about that after 2AC cross-ex. He says that we will not contend that peacekeeping exacerbates the conflict. OK, only that the General Assembly exacerbates conflict. Third argument is only if GA debate spurred conflicts are uncontrolled is there a problem. And there is no indication that any of these are uncontrolled.

Extending the
challenge for
examples

Contention number one, please group. First argument is that there are no empiricals, no indication why we need to fear this at all. Second argument is there is no reason for an increase in fear especially when we win that we use peacekeeping. Final argument is that Nixon has no scenario. I mean we talked about this in cross-ex and he can't indicate when Nixon would indeed be true.

I am on prolif. First argument on Atomic Agency. I win the funding link below. Second argument is equal to UN because I argue the UN deserves the credit for what they sponsored via the IAEA and NPT.

Extending the benefit of non-proliferation

His second argument talks about the norms. Now he does not address the Miller evidence that I read that says that the norms them-selves mean we don't have proliferation of nuclear weapons. That's independent of the specialized agencies and that's the UN in and of itself. Second argument is that there is no harm given to a mere holding of the weapons. OK. They are not used.

Third argument is that norms against harm are increased by the United Nations. This comes from Daniel Poneman from the Center for Science in Harvard, 1983. "As more and more countries become tech-nologically able to produce nuclear weapons, that norm will become the main obstacle to nuclear weapons proliferation." (31)

He argues that Becker, and debate equals prolif. First argument is who is Mr. Becker? All his evidence comes from this man, and we argue from authorities, that I give the qualifications for, that conclude you should vote negative. Second argument is that you can't have a treaty without this discrimination. Joseph Goldblatt from *SIPRI* says in 1985 that "A nonproliferation treaty not containing a distinction be-tween nuclear haves and have nots would have had either to make allowances for a nuclear buildup in nonnuclear weapons states [which he says would contradict the very idea of arms control], or to provide for the elimination of all existing nuclear weapons, [which he says would be infeasible]." (21) This is the best thing we've got.

Third argument is that there are not more nuclear powers. Joseph Goldblatt continues in January of '86: There appears to be no imminent danger of an open expansion of the nuclear club. The incentives to acquire nuclear weapons are still considerably weaker than the disin-centives, which means that the status quo will be maintained for some time.[23] (30)

So when he argues that debate legitimize, that's not enough to outweigh the disincentives. OK.

He argues next that it equals the spread of energy. First argument is that there is no evidence that energy equal the tech for prolif. He argues next that the IAEA is a guide. First argument is that there is no evidence here. Second argument, no empiricals, and I cross-app from above that there are no more proliferation nations. Third argument is that safeguards prevent, and that's evidence from 1NC. He says [unin-telligible] are limited. First argument is limits, but not inability, and all my evidence says we have an effective nonproliferation regime right

now. OK. Scheinman says in '85 that: The IAEA has helped to avoid
the further spread of nuclear weapons and deter the misuse of facilities
and materials intended for civil nuclear purposes.[24] (1) And I think
that's all we need here because we win that there is not enough, and
let there be no new responses on this argument in rebuttals.

FIRST AFFIRMATIVE REBUTTAL:

Carrie Crenshaw, Florida State

Responding to
definitional
challenges Starting with the observations and going straight case. Observation
number one. Please group her extensions. Subpoint one, membership
in the UN is not membership in the agencies. Her definition by her
author is the definition of UN, it is not the definition of membership,
and certainly that is the distinction in 2AC. Subpoint two, Franck
extends that you could pull out and still belong to the agencies and
that the evidence is dropped. Subpoint three, her on balance evidence
is blurby and does not necessarily address the issues that the affirmative team does. And she grants the criteria of military security so it is
her burden to prove that that evidence addresses that.

Extending the
argument that
the UN is not
beneficial   Observation number two on lofty. Please extend Miguel's first
answer not unreasonable, UN causes conflict. Please group his four
answers. Subpoint one, they should not contribute to war or exacerbate conflict and certainly that means that we should indict them for
that. Subpoint two, [unintelligible] drops the case side evidence that
indicates that these countries use the UN for mobilization for war.
Three subpoint we are on the verge of new international anarchy now.
Mr. Ruggie in '85: "With regard to peace and security, the UN Secretary General himself has remarked that the organization's machinery
functions so poorly that the international community finds itself peri-
lously near to a new international anarchy." (343)

Subpoint four, of course, all their extension evidence is in the past.
Extend Miguel's second answer from 2AC, peacekeeping worked in
the past but has changed. Of course, the Tugwell evidence has been
dropped by both negative speakers throughout this round. That means
that you have no more peacekeeping after his examples that he provides. And that evidence is dropped.

Extend Miguel's third answer that it creates conflict and please
group his extensions with that. I would argue first of all venting is not
the same thing as peacekeeping. So if we win that they contribute to
the conflict off of venting, that means that we still win, even if he wins
his peacekeeping stuff. Subpoint two, UN should not contribute to the
conflict, and therefore should be indicted. Subpoint three peacekeeping fails and I will extend those issues on case. Subpoint four, it is not
unique benefit to the UN. It is only peacekeeping, and both countries
agree. In other words, his Cyprus evidence admits that it could be
NATO that could do it. And it's only when these countries agree that

the UN is allowed to insert those forces. So certainly it is not a unique benefit.

Prolif. Please extend Miguel's first answer, the IAEA is an agency. The only thing that she has is all these links above. But first of all, she drops Miguel's specific evidence that says that the IAEA is affirmative. And that evidence is cold. Subpoint two she loses safeguards if she loses agency topicality. And I will,—The others take out the NPT below. And those are the only two links.

Extend Miguel's second answer that they have bomb and the norms do not stop use. Please group her extensions. Subpoint one they do have the bomb, her evidence admits that and her impact evidence assumes an accident scenario. So certainly you could still have the problems from proliferation.

Subpoint two the norms are undermined and the NPT is undermined by the debate. The debates say that you actually legitimized proliferation by undermining the NPT. Extend the third answer, debates undermine proliferation by undermining the NPT. All the — The only answer— The first answer she has here is who is Becker? But she doesn't read all of the qualifications of her sources. Subpoint two Becker is the former Israeli delegate to the UN, and he was one of the drafters of the NPT.

Extend her second and third extensions—those pieces of evidence. Subpoint one that third card is not linked to the UN. Subpoint two, if you actually legitimized prolif by undermining the NPT, then that second answer becomes irrelevant. Extend Miguel's fourth answer NPT spreads weapons capability. The only thing she says is there is no evidence and it says energy—energy is not technology. But if you read that evidence, or call for the evidence after the round, you will find that it says that it spreads the capability for nuclear weapons. And that evidence is dropped. She just misreads it. Now I think that's an independent turn.

As far as all the rest of it goes, the only link she has is the NPT because agencies, the IAEA is out of there and I would ask you to extend the fact that the NPT is undermined by debate.

Observation on criteria, case. The only thing she wants to extend is that, is dollars in terms of what membership is, whether or not it's agencies. Please group her extensions. Subpoint one she drops the evidence on the IAEA is autonomous of dollars. Subpoint two she also drops the Bennett card that's talking membership and not a definition of the UN. Please extend the definition of beneficial and that should certainly address military security on balance.

Extend the (B) subpoint, national interest. Certainly that should address military security. On her overview on case, please group. Subpoint one, venting prevents peacekeeping and that Tugwell evidence has been dropped throughout case. Subpoint two I'll extend venting on case because she did cursory coverage there.

Responding to nonproliferation

Extending the argument that national security is the most reliable criteria

Contention one. The only thing she has here is that there are no empirics and that Nixon gives no scenarios. But I'll ask you to extend the Nixon evidence and indicate that her partner faces the same problem. And certainly you should grant us the risk evidence there because her partner faces the same problem.

Extending the argument that the UN threatens national security

Contention two UN heightens conflict, (A) subpoint. The only thing he wants to extend is the Heritage Foundation indict. But I'd just like to point out, ladies and gentlemen, that we have other sources. Subpoint two, Tugwell is not Pines, you know. If you want to apply this indict, it has to be specific. Subpoint three, he drops Miguel's second answer that they assert it and his third answer is that you should just prove him wrong.

Please extend also specifically on the (A) subpoint the Arab–Israeli conflict is an empirical example. Two subpoint the on balance evidence that says this is true. Three subpoint I'd like to point out that venting is different from peacekeeping. And four subpoint I would extend the evidence that says, it takes out her evidence on case, that says, it indicates the fact that, it indicates the fact that venting would stop peacekeeping. OK? And it also says that venting no longer occurs regardless of what evidence she read.

I would just like to get down to the peacekeeping issues and extend Miguel's 2AC answers which I don't think, you know, have been addressed really by the 2NC or 1NR.

SECOND NEGATIVE REBUTTAL:
Paul Benson, Macalester

Extending the definitional challenges

Far too much is dropped in 1AR. She again indicates membership not equal organizations. Of course drops all of Molly's funding evidence that indicates the funding is tied. Now her second argument is Franck indicates you could pull out. But you know we would argue the real world Congressional analogy, that you know, if you were talking about the real world, whether Congress was beneficial, you would talk about the actions the CIA takes because Congress established the CIA. Indicating, you know, that in the real world we are perfectly reasonable.

Extending the benefit of the UN

Third argument here is she says on balance, card is a blurb. No. She drops out Gardner evidence and also drops the Church evidence which is extended that indicates, on balance is beneficial. And when I talk about Heritage Foundation indicts, the scholars conclude negative.

Please go now on to lofty expectations. She drops off all kinds of things. She says, you know, extend number one. But drops my evidence that indicates it prevents wars, it decreases tensions, and it controls violence. All of that is dropped and I do not want 2AR giving new answers. She says should not contribute to war. I argue that they do not, and she doesn't give any empiricals.

Her second argument is, you know, case evi takes all this out. Of course I argue case, I spend lots of time on case. Third argument here she says we're on the verge of anarchy. Of course number one, he's not talking about peacekeeping. Number two, you know, it does not indicate what the impact of all of this would be. Why this would necessarily be that bad. Third argument is does not indicate that, you know, the entire UN system will fall apart, you know. Fourthly, that this is brand new. I mean this thing should have been cut in. And I will argue the 2AC, because this is an entire position shift. If they're going to argue the UN is going to fall apart, by God they should have that in constructives.

She then argues extend the second answer that he gives. Of course, drops all my answers that indicate, you know, the failures are outside faults, and on balance. She says, you know, venting not equals peacekeeping. Of course, it stops wars and I indicate that that is good in and of itself. And if, you know, their national security criterion is number one, then that would, you know, make it relevent to the round.

She says they should not contribute. I argue that they don't. She argues peacekeeping forces fail. I say no, pull all the empiricals which she punts off. Fourthly, she says not unique to the UN. That would mean that she would have to indicate solvency for non-UN organizations. And she drops all my evidence that I read in the 2NC that indicates you can't do it outside the UN. And I'll talk about that when I get there.

Please go to prolif. On overview number one, she says money is linked directly to the UN. No. Number one, UN deserved credit for the safeguards. Second argument is safeguards take out impact on 2AC UN harm. She says, you know, countries have the bomb. Of course, number one, Goldblatt evidence January '86 says no new members. She drops it. Second argument no evidence about accidents which is what our evidence talks about. Third argument is 1NR Poneman evidence says you won't develop and/or use, and that's dropped.

Extending non-proliferation

On norms. Number one, must have discriminatory treaty. I mean that's dropped as well. Second argument that means the norms are upheld. And third argument is Goldblatt says disincentives outweigh legitimization. She says energy equals development. Of course, no evidence here. My second argument is norms say does not develop. I mean she cannot get that off of this. No prolif equals big time benefit. And I mean that is UN specific.

Please go to overview on criteria. Of course she says only numbers, IAEA autonomous, and Bennett is dropped. Of course she drops why wouldn't we add this to the calculus, and I talk about this above. She says definition of beneficial. Of course Molly argues it's arbitrary, and where's the distinction, and she grants that. She just says extend

Denying national security is the most reliable criteria

(B) point. Drops on balance criteria should be applied here and that our scholars conclude with us.

She argues on the underview venting does not equal peacekeeping. Of course, she applies the Tugwell evidence, again, which is Heritage Foundation, and even if you don't buy the indict, I beat it. She says case takes out, well let's go to case.

On contention one, she says extend Nixon. Drops Molly's third argument that says Nixon gives no scenarios, indicating the Nixon evidence is awful. Drops her first response that says no empiricals are given which beats it at that level.

On contention two. She says we have other sources and Tugwell is not that bad. Of course drops basically our indict which indicates, you know, the Heritage Foundation, you know, reaches conclusions, then does the study. I mean if we did that kind of stuff we'd probably be shot by our coach. (Laughter)

You know, she says we dropped two and three. No. I grouped that together. And I argue that it beats it on that level, and you know, this is brand new. I don't understand how it takes anything out anyway.

She says extend Arab–Israeli. I beat that out with all my empiricals. She then says extend another, you know, conflict. I think I beat that as well on balance.

Extending
examples of
beneficial
UN actions

She says on balance beats. Wrong. I read evidence that indicates on balance it works well and I have all the empiricals in the round. I mean if you're going to decide peacekeeping look at the empirical examples. And she drops when I talk about Yom Kippur, and all that type of stuff. We probably wouldn't even have a today if those conflicts had occurred.

She says venting does not equal peacekeeping. So what. It stops wars which they indicate is the number one priority. And if that is true, you know, that it's irrelevant because it's not peacekeeping, then go down to the very bottom where she argues, you know, these outside the UN peacekeeping forces. They ain't peacekeeping forces. And so if my evidence gets kicked out, her evidence gets kicked out, and where's the only place you have peacekeeping? That is in the UN. OK. And I mean she drops the evidence that I read that indicates it prevents superpower conflict. I mean that evidence is cold.

All I want here is that the peacekeeping forces don't include the superpowers. This is from F. T. Lui, Assistant Secretary General of Political Affairs in '84: Peacekeeping forces presence in areas do not include the superpowers.[25] (25)

I guess I'm supposed to say something nice at the end of this. And all I'd like to say is I've been involved with the activity for about seven years now and I've heard things about the fact that it's starting to die out in certain areas of the country. I don't think that should ever happen and I think that we as members of this type of a community should do our best to keep CEDA, NDT, and other forms of debate alive. Thank you very much. (Applause)

SECOND AFFIRMATIVE REBUTTAL:
Miguel Delao, Florida State

I said exactly what I was going to do in 2AC, and I said what I was going to do in 2AR. I said we're going to go for uniqueness. All right, and that is what I'm going to try to win, because even though he can take out Tugwell, Cuellar evidence indicates that because we went outside the UN, there will be no more peacekeeping in the UN. He can win all his past evidence. The UN was wonderful at it, they will not do it anymore. Of course he raises a good issue, well now we have to show solvency. But last thing Carrie says, you know, in 1AR was (unintelligible) you have to extend all the evidence I read in the 2AC on peacekeeping. And my evidence says, they don't want the United Nations, they won't go there, and it says because they're getting shot at; and that is why I think I made the distinction why the US is good; that evidence says that the Netherlands is sick and tired of getting their people killed. The US fights back. And the evidence I read there said that the UN would not have been any more successful at Lebanon and therefore should not be taken out. That evidence was granted. He had arguments there, but still granted what, everything the evidence indicated. I think that one card that said they are getting shot at and therefore don't want to contribute soldiers, indicates why the US is better. What it comes down to is, you are not going to get the US. The question is, is there a better solution? I mean in any sense is there a slightly more optimal solution? To the extent that we can defend ourselves, we at least guarantee that there is possibility for more peacekeeping. Because you're not going to get it from the UN. That Cuellar evidence is dropped. All he can win is that it used to be great, and you know, I have to agree with him on that.

[margin note: UN no longer involved in peacekeeping]

    Prolif. I'm not going to go for this agency on IAEA, because what I want is the legitimization. Right. He extends that there are no new members. That is true, but the evidence; my second; my third answer in the 2AC—debate would undermine the NPT. That is granted. That is the only evidence that Carrie really goes for in the 1AR. She indicates that this takes out their links, because now the one thing that is bringing about these norms, the one thing that is deterring these people is NPT and it is being undermined. He said they will not develop or use. But the evidence that was read there says they were legitimizing proliferation. Right. That is granted. He says norms are upheld. But they're undermining the NPT, that one card I think is

[margin note: Extending argument on proliferation]

what takes out all these links. Because it indicates that even though this may have been true, what is going on now in these debates is hurting their links.

He says norms mean they will not develop. I simply refer you to the phenomenal evidence that was read in the 2AC. That evidence says that the NPT is instrumental in promoting proliferation. It says the IAEA is also in the same vein. They do the same thing, they lead to proliferation. All he has here, he says, is that the norms mean they won't develop. I want you to weigh that, these norms they won't do it, versus evidence that indicates that it is instrumental. When he runs that, you know; we've always granted, of course, prolif isn't bad; I think that gives us all the military security we need. Because they argue it leads to cataclysmic nuclear war. And if we win that evidence that indicates that it's being legitimized; which now means that people will prolif; and that it is undermining the NPT, which undermines their norms, then I think we certainly outweigh all this peacekeeping stuff which was all in the past. At a minimum, I put a doubt in your mind. At the most, I think I win the turn on peacekeeping because you will not have any in the future. And that was because of the venting.

I'll go to the first observation. Now I granted agencies, so that will not matter. But the third answer, this is 1N overview. All they have is this on balance stuff. You know I think it's the same argument, 2AC's the same argument as 1AR. This is really blurby stuff. Does not say why it is good and you have to weigh this specifically against proliferation. And I think that is a perfect illustration why. Because these authors may be assuming, well, you know, the UN stops prolif. They did not necessarily take into account Mr. Becker's argument that it indeed leads to prolif.

We are giving you specific examples versus, you know, evidence that just says, well you know, the negative would always win every round.

Lofty expectations. He starts off again by saying it prevents war. That is only when you get the peacekeeping and you will not have peacekeeping in the future. That means UN will not, no longer will stop war. The only thing you have to look at is, is there a chance outside the UN and I think we give you that because of the fact that we can shoot back.

My evidence on the verge of peace; of anarchy. He says that it is not peacekeeping. That may be true but it indicates that in general there is going to be war. He says number two, why is that bad? Certainly, I mean it has to be bad, there is no conflict control. We're going to have anarchy and Klare says you want to have conflict control. He says number three, does not mean UN falls apart. That is certainly not the argument we are trying to make. And he says it is new, and the reason he says it is new is because he thinks I'm arguing the UN will fall apart. But he read a lot of evidence in the 2NC

Denying benefits of UN

indicating that right now the UN is good. I don't see why it is illegitimate for Carrie to stand up and read evidence saying no that is not true, right now the UN is bad. That is not new. He thinks we made a different argument about the UN falling apart, which is not what we are claiming.

I think that's all I really want. But I will go to case and take a glance. US national interest. All they extend, on B subpoint of their first observation, must be on balance. I agree, I think the cataclysmic nuclear war on prolif wins it for us, and the fact that only we can get peacekeeping in the future. Contention one. He says scenarios. Certainly we get a scenario off prolif and we get an empirical scenario off peacekeeping. That's the Cuellar evidence I read in 2AC, and it's empirical. It says because we went outside the UN, you will not get peacekeeping in the future. And the evidence says empirically the last two were outside the UN.

Extending national security as the most reliable criteria

I want to thank several people and I'd like to start off with Curtis Austin our coach. At the beginning of this year I was not going to debate. And it is because of the fine human being that he is, that I decided to stay and I'm really glad that I did. I'd like to thank Carrie. Before this tournament she said the one thing she wanted was for us to get here to the final round. And she was going to work her butt off to see that I got here, and she did it for me and I can't thank her enough. And Carolyne, who makes my every day. I enjoyed it fully. Thank you. (Applause) [26]

NOTES

1. Source indicated.
2. "The overwhelming majority of quarrels among allies are settled secretly and bilaterally or within the confines of an alliance setting. Even states basically at odds with each other forego opportunities to utilize the UN when they are unwilling to exacerbate tensions."
3. Grant Killoran, Barb Birr, Peter Richardson, Brenda Smith, Steve Appelget, and Chris Cloutier.
4. "As for wider US withdrawn from the entire UN system, the State Department has pointed out, that the financial loss would constrain UN organizations drastically to cut back programs, including many regarded as especially important; refugee, health, and technical programs, for example."
5. "The primary purposes of these UN missions have been to deter renewed fighting, to gain time for diplomacy, and to discourage external, and especially superpower, intervention that could escalate into larger wars."
6. "One of the most important measures to assure an effective and credible agency enjoying the broad-based confidence so necessary to its effectiveness is a strong and continuing leadership role by the United States both within the agency and among its principal members."

7. "The main norms and practices of this regime are found in the NPT and in regional counterparts such as the Treaty of Tlatelolco, which aims to keep Latin America non-nuclear; in the safeguards, rules and procedures of the International Atomic Energy Agency (IAEA); and in various UN resolutions."

8. "The UN has also contributed to the articulation of norms against the use of nuclear weapons. While the restraint of the superpowers in this area is due more to their perception of self-interest than to UN norms, the reluctance of weaker states to use unclear weapons in local disputes may derive in part from the UN's norm against such an action and from the perception that sanctions (e.g., the cutting off of military assistance by one's allies) will be applied within the UN context against countries that violate the norm."

9. "Despite certain shortcomings, these safeguards can probably detect most illegal uses of these plants and therefore pose a significant deterrent to proliferation."

10. "It is a sign of the times that peacekeeping forces are advocated both within and outside the UN framework. For instance, ASEAN has called for peacekeeping forces for Kampuchea, OAU even sent such forces to Chad—although they later had to be withdrawn—and the Carter Administration proposed the establishment of a UN peacekeeping force to pacify the border areas of Iran and Iraq. Obviously, Wiseman is right in observing that peacekeeping will 'in the next decade, and likely beyond be applied more frequently and with greater variety and complexity than heretofore.'"

11. "Indeed, the prestigious *Le Monde* of Paris, ruminating on the UN four decades after the signing of its charter, observes [June 26], 'it would be unjust to consider only the organization's failures . . . . How can we count the wars that, thanks to the U.N., did not break out? Security Council meetings, however virulent, have the effect of a safety valve.'"

12. "Its record, in view of the tremendous tensions in the world has been a good one. . . . In 1981, [Secretary General Kurt Waldheim] observed that the United Nations had 'served with remarkable effectiveness as a mechanism for reducing friction arising out of the process of change.'"

13. "No one who has carefully studied the performance of these international peacekeeping forces in a role closely dictated and controlled by the mandate that they have been given by the Security Council or General Assembly can lightly dismiss the contribution that any of them has made to the control of violence."

14. "But it remains true when the belligerents desired to formalize a measure of stability and mutual restraint, the availability of suitable UN symbols and myths helps them to create periods and areas of restraints in what would otherwise have been an uncontrolled conflict."

15. "International peacekeeping not only survived the challenge but established beyond any doubt that, without its involvement, the Congo would have ceased to survive as a unified nation and could easily have become a battleground of economic and ideological warfare."

16. "The part that UNCU (United Nation's Congo Operation) played in this

deserves its rightful recognition—and can clearly be regarded as a justification for the United Nation's overall conflict control policy of combining military operations with political and conciliatory efforts."

17. "More than any other episode in the U.N.'s history, the Cuban missile crisis suggests that the world might have been more unsafe if it weren't for the UN's unimpressive repertoire of tricks."

18. "The United Nations played an essential role in the Cuban Missile Crisis in '62, not only providing a forum where both sides could expound their positions publicly, but also in suggesting, through letters from Secretary-General U Thant to Chairman Kruschev and President Kennedy, steps that might be taken simultaneously by both sides to de-escalate the crisis."

19. "Second, critical, interrelated issues remain to be settled, notably, the time frame for Soviet force withdrawals and for the phase out of Pakistani aid to the resistance, as well as, the precise orchestration of these two processes. Much to the surprise of the American officials, however, the UN effort is now moving tantalizingly close to a successful conclusion. Some of the more optimistic Pakistani and Soviet sources say that implementation of the agreement could conceivably begin in early 1984."

20. "The situation remains unchanged along the Golan Heights where calm continues to prevail. Thus UNDOF continues to play a useful role between Israel and its remaining serious Arab antagonists."

21. "In spite of the difficult conditions in southern Lebanon, UNIFL's presence continued to be necessary and constituted an important factor of stability in an international commitment to upholding Lebanon's independence, sovereignty, and territorial integrity."

22. "The UN has acquired a great deal of expertise in the field. To create a non-UN organization for the same purpose derogates from the prestige of the UN and thus weakens an institution which the world looks upon as a major instrument for maintaining peace."

23. "There appears to be no imminent danger of an open expansion of the nuclear club. The balance of nuclear disincentives and incentives is not tipping in the direction of the latter, and the status quo will be maintained for some time."

24. "For more than a quarter-century, an international organization—The International Atomic Energy Agency (IAEA)—has played a leading role in national and international efforts to avoid the further spread, or proliferation, of nuclear weapons and to deter the misuse of facilities and materials intended for civil nuclear purposes."

25. "Secondly, despite their weakenesses, UN peacekeeping forces have one important advantage. Their presence in an area of conflict serves to preclude direct intervention by third-party governments, including Super Powers in that area and thus to insulate the conflict from a potential East-West confrontation."

26. Transcript of the 1986 CEDA Championship from *The 1986 Championship Debates and Speeches,* edited by John K. Boaz and James Brey, pp. 65–99. Copyright © 1986 by the American Forensic Association. Reprinted by permission of the American Forensic Association.

WORKS CITED

Ameri, Houshang. *Politics and Process in the Specialized Agencies of the United Nations*. Aldershot Haunts: Gower Publishing Company Limited, 1982.

Balk, Alfred. "The Editor's Corner." *World Press Review* (August 1985).

Becker, Avi. *Disarmament Without Order*. Westport, CN: Greenwood Press, 1985.

Bennett, A. LeRoy. *On International Organizations: Principals and Issues*. Englewood Cliffs, NJ: Prentice-Hall, 1983.

Cannon, Carroll. *Shaping Our Future Together*. San Diego, CA: United Nations Association, 1984.

Dunn, Lewis. "Controlling Nuclear Arms Includes Curbing Their Spread." *Christian Science Monitor* 11 (October 1984).

Easterbrook, Greg. "Ideas Move Nations." *The Atlantic Monthly* (January 1986).

Eban, Abba. "Multilateral Diplomacy in the Arab-Israeli Conflict." *Multilateral Negotiations and Mediation*, ed. Arthur Lull. New York: Pergamon Press, 1985.

Falkner, Ronnie. "Taking John C. Calhoun to the United Nations." *Polity* (Summer 1983).

Fasulo, Linda. *Representing America: Experiences of US Diplomats at the UN*. New York: Praeger Special Studies, 1984.

Formuth, Peter. *Financing the United Nations*. New York: United Nations Association, 1984.

Franck, Thomas. *Nation Against Nation*. New York: Oxford University Press, 1985.

Gardner, Richard. House Committee on Foreign Affairs. *US Participation in the United Nations*. 97th Congress, 2nd Session. Washington, D.C.: GPO, 1982.

Gauhar, Altaf. "North–South Dialogue: An Interview with Perez de Cuellar." *Third World Quarterly* (1984).

Goldblat, Jozef. *Nuclear Nonproliferation*. London: Taylor and Francis, 1985.

Grenier, Richard. "Yanqui, Si! U.N., No!" *Harpers* (January 1984).

Harrison, Selig. "A Break Through in Afghanistan?" *Foreign Policy* (Summer 1983).

Houghton, Robert, and Frank Trinka. *Multilateral Peacekeeping in the Middle East*. Washington, D.C.: Center for the Study of Foreign Affairs, 1984.

James, Alan. "Painful Peacekeeping: The United Nations in Lebanon 1978–1982." *International Journal* (Autumn 1983).

Keohane, Robert, and Joseph Nye. "Two Cheers for Multilateralism." *Foreign Policy* (Fall 1985).

Kirkpatrick, Jeane J. *The Reagan Phenomenon—And Other Speeches on Foreign Policy*. Washington, D.C.: American Enterprise Institute for Public Policy Research, 1983.

Klare, Michael T. *American Arms Supermarket*. Austin, TX: University of Texas, 1984.

Luck, Edward. "The U.N. at 40: A Supporter's Lament." *Foreign Policy* (Winter 1984).

Lui, F. T. "Comments on the IPA Report." *Peacekeeping and Technology*, ed. Hugh Hanning. Oxford, England: International Peace Academy, 1983.

Maynes, Charles. "A Cause Worth Fighting For." *The Nation* (21 September 1985).

Miller, Debra. "Contributions of the U.N. to International Security Regimes." *The U.S., the U.N., and the Management of Global Change*, ed. Toby Trister Gati. New York: New York University Press, 1983.

Nelson, Richard. "Multinational Peacekeeping in the Middle East and the United Nations Model." *International Affairs* (Winter 1984/85).

Newell, David. "On Morality in Foreign Policy." *Newsweek* (16 December 1985).

Nixon, Richard. *Real Peace*. Boston, MA: Little, Brown and Company, 1984.

Nye, Joseph S. "NPT. The Logic of inequality." *Foreign Policy* (Summer 1985).

O'Brian, Connor. "U.N. Theater." *The New Republic* (4 November 1985).

Parsons, Sir Anthony. "The United Nations and International Security in the 1980s." *Millennium: Journal of International Studies* (Summer 1983).

Platt, Nicholas. House Committee on Foreign Affairs. *U.S. Participation in the United Nations*. 97th Congress, 2nd Session. Washington, D.C.: GPO, 1982.

Poneman, Daniel. House Committee on Foreign Affairs. *Proposed Amendments to the Nuclear Non-Proliferation Act, 1983.*

Puchala, Donald J. "American Interests and the United Nations." *Political Science Quarterly* (Winter 1982–83).

Raman, K. Venkata. "United Nations Peacekeeping and the Future of World Order." *Peacekeeping*, ed. Henry Wiseman. New York: Pergamon Press, 1983.

Rikhye, Indar Jit, Michael Harbottle, and Bjorn Egge. *The Thin Blue Line*. New Haven, CN: Yale University Press, 1974.

Rikhye, Indar Jit. "Peacekeeping and Peacemaking." *Peacekeeping*, ed. Henry Wiseman. New York: Pergamon Press, 1983.

———. *The Theory and Practice of Peacekeeping*. New York: St. Martins Press, 1984.

Ruggie, John. "The United States and the United Nations: Toward a New Realism." *International Organizations* (Spring 1985).

Scheinman, Lawrence. *The Nonproliferation Role of the International Atomic Energy Agency*. Washington, D.C.: Resources for the Future. 1985.

"Security Council Hears Views on Cyprus Efforts, Extends Mandate of Peacekeeping." *U.N. Chronicle*. June 1985.

Sethi, J. D. "Steps Toward Reform." *World Press Review* (December 1985).

Spector, Leonard. "Proliferation: The Silent Spread." *Foreign Policy* (Spring 1985).

Stanley, C. Maxwell. House Committee on Foreign Affairs. *U.S. Participation in the United Nations*. 97th Congress, 2nd Session. Washington, D.C.: GPO, 1982.

Tugwell, Maurice. "The United Nations as the World's Safety Valve." *A World Without A U.N.*, ed. Burton Pines. New York: The Heritage Foundation, 1984.

"UNIFIL Mandate Extended for Six Months." *U.N. Chronicle* (May 1985).

Urquhart, Brian. "International Peace and Security." *Foreign Affairs* (Fall 1981).

Vayrynen, Raimo. "Focus On: Is There a Role for the United Nations in Conflict Resolution?" *Journal of Peace Research* (1985).

Waldheim, Kurt. "The United Nations: The Tarnished Image." *Foreign Affairs* (Fall 1984).

Yeselson, Abraham, and Anthony Gaglione. *A Dangerous Place: The United Nations as a Weapon in World Politics.* New York: Grossman Publishers, 1974.

16

A PUBLIC DEBATE

The following debate considers the resolution "The Historicity of the Resurrection: Did Jesus Rise From the Dead?" The two participants are Anthony G. N. Flew, for many years a professor of philosophy at the University of Reading, England, and Gary R. Habermas, professor of apologetics and philosophy at Liberty University.

The debate was held on May 2, 1985, at Liberty University. The full text of the debate with accompanying commentary appears in the 1987 book *Did Jesus Rise from the Dead? The Resurrection Debate*. We are grateful to Harper and Row for granting us permission to reprint the debate.

The debate was conducted under a modified Lincoln-Douglas format. Each participant gave one constructive and one rebuttal speech. There was a single extended cross-examination period in which the participants took turns asking and answering questions. The one unusual feature of the format is that the advocate for the negative spoke first. Actually, Flew speaking for the negative was speaking against the popular view in our Christian culture. Given this textbook's definition of negative, upholding the position that Jesus did not rise from the dead would be the responsibility of the affirmative.

The debate was evaluated by two panels of experts. One panel consisted of five philosophers, who were instructed to judge the content of the debate and render a winner. The second panel consisted of five professional debate judges, who were asked to judge the argumentation techniques of the debaters. All ten participating judges serve on the faculties of American universities and colleges. The decisions of the judges were as follows. The panel of philosophers cast four votes for Habermas, none for Flew, and one draw. The panel of professional debate judges voted three to two, also in favor of Habermas.

We well understand that the resurrection of Jesus is at once emotional, personal, spiritual, and controversial. Argumentation taken seriously concerns the most important issues in our lives. To refuse to argue is to refuse to engage in the essential activity of human life. It is in this spirit that we offer the "Resurrection Debate" as an example of a dispute over a proposition of fact.

NEGATIVE STATEMENT
Antony G. N. Flew

I will begin by spelling out three fundamentals upon which Dr. Habermas and I are agreed, notwithstanding that many of those still claiming the Christian name will, nowadays, make so bold as to deny one, or two, or all three of these fundamentals.

Clarifying the
terms of the
resolution
First, we both construe *resurrection*, or rising from the dead, in a thoroughly literal and physical way. It is to this understanding that the story of doubting Thomas is so crucially relevant.

Second, we are again agreed that the question whether, in that literal understanding, Jesus did rise from the dead is of supreme theoretical and practical importance. For the knowable fact that he did, if indeed it is a knowable fact, is the best, if not the only, reason for accepting that Jesus is the God of Abraham, Isaac, and Israel.

Third, we are agreed both that that identification is the defining and distinguishing characteristic of the true Christian, and that it is scarcely possible to make it without also accepting that the Resurrection did literally happen. Together these two doctrines constitute what used to be called the scandal of particularity, which would make the discovery of other worlds inhabited by rational moral agents embarrassing to Christianity but not, I think, to any of the other great world religions, and which requires Christians to insist that adherents of all those other religions, and of mine, are, on matters of supreme importance, ruinously wrong.

In these days such fundamentals do need to be reiterated, for sometimes they are denied outright or ignored. Last year, for instance, David Jenkins, a man who has repudiated, and still repudiates, the doctrine of the Resurrection, and that in words too offensive for me to repeat in the presence of genuine believers, was elevated to the senior bishopric of the Church of England. He has since devoted most of his energies—in the name of the very religion he rejects—to denouncing Margaret Thatcher. This successor to the great Bishop Butler is, alas, not alone in thus surreptitiously replacing Christian faith with socialist activism. The World Council of Churches—so aptly described as UNESCO in clerical dress—and your own National Council of Churches too—both preceded on that fashionable primrose path. Being myself an enemy of socialism, I hesitate to say anything that might persuade Dr. Habermas to jettison his faith!

Our agreement on fundamentals, however, goes only so far. I shall therefore devote the rest of my time to disagreements. My argument falls into two parts: first general, and then particular. The first deals with the general difficulty, perhaps impossibility, of establishing the occurrence of a miracle so as to be the foundation of a system of religion. The second turns to the inadequacies of the evidence actually available in the present case.

Everything that I have to say in general derives ultimately from Hume's first *Enquiry*.[1] But, most emphatically, I shall not be representing what is said there, for that has two major and several lesser faults. Critics such as C. S. Lewis have, quite rightly, made much of some of these.[2]

The first major defect is that by previously denying both natural necessity and natural impossibility, Hume disqualifies himself from distinguishing the genuinely miraculous from the highly unusual or merely marvelous. He thus diminishes the force of his own entirely correct contention that the evidence required to establish the occurrence of the former has to be much stronger than that needed to prove the happening of the latter, just as proof of that demands something rather better than everyday evidence.

Presumption is against the resurrection

The second major defect is that Hume, like most of his contemporaries on both sides of this particular great debate, sees little difference between accusing a witness of perjury and conceding that the testimony of that witness constitutes an accurate account of what actually happened. The truth is that the possibilities of honest error are enormous, especially when the depositions are first recorded long after the alleged events, and without cross-examination of the witnesses; when these alleged events have been much discussed both with other witnesses or supposed witnesses; and when all concerned are trying to fit what actually happened into their own several interpretative frameworks.

Attacking the reliability of evidence from testimony

The main general argument concerns what, in a landmark paper stimulated by the work of the nineteenth-century German biblical critics, F. H. Bradley called *The Presuppositions of Critical History* (Oxford, 1874). The heart of the matter is that the criteria by which we must assess historical testimony, and the general presumptions that make it possible for us to construe leftovers from the past as historical evidence, are such that the possibility of establishing, on purely historical grounds, that some genuinely miraculous event has occurred is ruled out.

Challenging the reliable criteria for evaluating the resolution

Hume himself concentrated on testimonial evidence because his conception of historiography—later realized in his own best-selling *History of England*—was of a judge assessing, with judicious impartiality, the testimony. This limitation to testimonial evidence is of no immediate consequence to us, although it is worth mentioning that my general argument will not apply, or will not apply without modification, to the Shroud of Turin. That is something that Hume presumably saw in his visit to Turin, and presumably again, would have dismissed as Roman Catholic superstition, happy that in this dismissal all his Protestant contemporaries would agree.

The argument from the presuppositions of critical history embraces three propositions: first, that surviving relics from the past cannot be interpreted as historical evidence, except insofar us we presume that the same fundamental regularities obtained then as still

Specific reasons why criteria of facticity is unreliable

obtain today; second, that in trying to determine what actually happened, historians must employ as criteria all their knowledge of what is probable or improbable, possible or impossible; and third, that because the word *miracle* must be defined in terms of natural necessity and natural impossibility, the application of these criteria inevitably precludes proof of a miracle.

Hume illustrated the first proposition in his *Treatise*, urging that it is only upon such presumptions of regularity that we can justify the conclusion that ink marks on old pieces of paper constitute testimonial evidence.[3] Earlier in the first *Enquiry* he urged the inescapable importance of the criteria demanded by the second. Without criteria there can be no discrimination, and hence no history worthy of the name. What Hume did not and could not bring out was the crucial importance of the notions of natural necessity and natural impossibility, for a strong idea of a natural order is essential if there is to be room for the notion of a miracle as an overriding of that order by a supernatural power. Apologists suggesting that scientists since Einstein have abandoned the search for laws of nature stating physical necessities and physical impossibilities are, therefore, betraying their own cause, and are also mistaken about where science is going.

The practical upshot of all our three methodological contentions, taken together, comes out sharp and clear in a footnote in which Hume quotes with approval the reasoning of physician De Sylva in the case of Mlle. Thibaut: "It was impossible that she could have been so ill as was 'proved' by witnesses, because it was impossible that she could, in so short a time, have recoverd so perfectly as he found her."

That, with regard to the presuppositions of critical history, is the heart of the matter. Confronted with testimonial evidence for the occurrence of a miracle, the secular historian must recognize that however unlikely it may seem that all the witnesses were in error, the occurrence of a genuine miracle is, by definition, naturally impossible. Yet this should not be the end of the affair. For historians, like everyone else, ought to be ever ready, for sufficient reason, to correct their assumptions about what is probable or improbable, possible or impossible. And this readiness should allow that even the qualification *secular* may, for sufficient reason, have to be abandoned.

In defiance of his own principles, Hume insisted that anything in the Age of Enlightenment he and his colleagues believed to be impossible, was impossible, and that it never could be discovered that any of them had been wrong about impossibilities. So he dismissed stories of two wonders wrought by the Emperor Vespasian, and of several others occurring at the tomb of the Abbe Paris; stories that we now have excellent reason to believe were true. But this, like the appeal to what is supposed to have become the practice of physicists since Einstein is, for the defense of the miraculous, useless. Our reasons for believing that Vespasian did indeed effect two astonishing psychosomatic cures in Egypt are at the same time our reasons for insisting that those cures were not, after all, truly miraculous.

The second point about the need to correct unsound presuppositions is best made by citing Cardinal Newman, who made an unusually strenuous attempt to come to terms with Humean contentions. Newman is prepared to allow the general validity of such principles in the assessment of testimonial evidence. What he challenges is their application to "these particular miracles, ascribed to the particular Peter, James and John . . . ." What has to be asked, Newman continues, is whether they really are "unlikely, supposing that there is a Power, external to the world, who can bring them about; supposing they are the only means by which He can reveal himself to those who need a revelation; supposing that He is likely to reveal himself; that He has a great end in doing so."[4]

Well yes, certainly. If we were in a position to suppose all this, then no doubt the case for the occurrence of these particular miracles, as well as for that of the supreme miracle of the Resurrection, would be open and shut. But those who know all this must already be in possession either of a rich revelation or an unusually abundant natural theology. Given all that, it certainly would be reasonable for them to jettison secular presuppositions, at least in the present context. That, however, is not the situation of those now asked to consider the historical evidence for the Resurrection of Jesus, and this in turn as sufficient reason for identifying Jesus as the God of Mosaic theism.

So much for my general arguments about the presuppositions of critical history. I have tried to show that and explain why purely historical evidence cannot establish the occurrence of any authentic miracle, not, that is, until and unless those presuppositions can be corrected and supplemented, either by a rich and relevant antecedent revelation or by a rich and relevant natural theology. The question now is whether the present case is sufficiently exceptional to require some radical shakeup of secular historiographic presuppositions, either by revising our ideas of what is naturally possible or by admitting that we have a unique and uniquely important case of a supernatural intervention transcending natural impossibilities. To no one's surprise, I am sure, I will argue the negative.

Had I not discredited any such remark in advance by concurring with Hume's contention that we cannot make valid inferences about "the projects and intentions . . . of a Being so different and so much superior," I might have begun my consideration of the evidence in this case by suggesting ways in which a Creator might have been successful in ensuring that everyone received and understood any message that he transmitted. But, of course, any such suggested means might be logically incompatible with the Creator's (naturally) unknown ends. So I have to start with a different employment for Newman's statement.

It serves to remind us of something which, in any examination of

Rejects as unreasonable and unreliable nonhistorical criteria

the New Testament evidence, we must not forget. This is that Jesus lived among, and preached to, a population that was overwhelmingly Jewish. All the twelve disciples were Jews. All the New Testament converts seem to have been converts to Christianity from Judaism: Paul, for instance, is said to have been raised as a Pharisee. Everyone concerned, therefore, believed in and worshiped the God of Abraham, Isaac, and Israel. They all believed also both that God had in the past sent prophets to the people of the Covenant, the authenticity of whose message had been endorsed by the conspicuous working of miracles, and that there was to be at least one more special man sent from God, the Messiah.

Demonstrating bias in the testimony of the witnesses

Given these common assumptions, all concerned were eager to interpret their individual experiences within this shared ideological framework. Most important for us is their restless search, both for passages in the Jewish Bible that might be interpreted as prophecies referring to their own time, and for events in that time that could be identified as the fulfillments of such putative prophecies. That this was a practice prevalent in, although by no means peculiar to, that period is abundantly evidenced both inside and outside the New Testament. In order to indicate how this unfortunate yet entirely honest practice can result in false history, I take as my illustration the shambles of the birth stories.

First, prophecies really did foretell that the Messiah was to be both of the house of David and born in Bethlehem. So if Jesus was indeed the Messiah, he must have been both descended from David and born in Bethlehem. Now, whereas neither Mark nor John suggest any hometown but Nazareth, both Luke and Matthew insist on a birth in Bethlehem. They also provide two totally irreconcilable Davidic genealogies. These disagree even about the name of the grandfather of Jesus. Then, to explain how it was that Mary came to term so far from home, Luke tells the implausible tale of a Roman tax collection census requiring that every householder register not in his or her place of residence, where the taxes were paid, but in his or her birthplace. A Roman census would in any case not have affected Joseph, because in the days of Herod the Great, in which Luke places the birth, neither Galilee nor Bethlehem fell under direct Roman rule.

Inconsistencies in the testimony of the witnesses

Second, Matthew and Luke tell us that Mary was at the birth a virgin, whereas neither Mark nor John nor any of the other New Testament writers make this claim. It seems not to occur to either Matthew or Luke that, if true, it would make their Davidic genealogies not only mutually contradictory but also irrelevant. And whereas Luke has the Angel of the Annunciation appear to Joseph, in Matthew the Angel appears to Mary.

Matthew alone is explicit in relating the whole affair to the prophet Isaiah: "Behold, a virgin shall conceive and bear a son, and his name shall be called Emmanuel." But in the original Hebrew, as opposed to the Greek of the Septuagint, the key word is not *betulah* ("virgin") but *ilmah* ("young woman of marriageable age"). In any case, the context of Isaiah 6:16 makes it clear to the uncommitted reader that the prophecy was intended to refer to a future son of King Ahaz, the later Hezekiah, who lived seven hundred years before Christ. (Perhaps just to tease the prophet, Hezekiah did *not* name the son Emmanuel!)

All this is not the half of it. Yet it should be sufficient to bring out how the search for prophecies and their fulfillments can get in the way of the discovery and the recording of historical truth. The next thing to emphasize is that the earliest written sources still available to us were compiled a long time after the events that they attempt to record. No biblical scholar dates any of the Epistles earlier than the early A.D. 40s, or Mark earlier than the early A.D. 50s, that is to say, roughly ten and roughly twenty years after the Crucifixion, respectively.

By some standards ten or even twenty years is not a long time. Yet it is enough time to permit the forces that corrupt testimony to do irrecoverable damage. Psychic researchers, trying to track down supposed occurrences of what is normally believed to be impossible, would surely regard a case in which there is no hope of finding any contemporary records as unlikely to repay investigation. One does not have to be, though, I myself am, sympathetic to Israeli nationalism, to regret the decisive suppression of the first century Jewish revolt, for in that destruction of Jerusalem we may well have lost some irreplaceable contemporary records, even perhaps something from some non-Jewish witness of some of the Easter events.

Quite apart from the admitted absence of any truly contemporary documentation of the life and death of Jesus, there is also a lamentable lack of evidence about both the authors and the dates of those compositions that we do have. Perhaps this would not matter if we were dealing with narratives telling of ordinary events. But it most certainly does matter when it is claimed that the four Gospels, with all their apparent inconsistencies and prima facie unbelievabilities, constitute the only accounts of the earthly life, death, and Resurrection of God incarnate.

Nor is it only the crucial documents the dates of which are uncertain. The same uncertainty extends to the dating of all events that they purport to record. What actually happened is, of course, immeasurably more important than when it happened. Nevertheless, if the Gospel writers did think of themselves as writing chronicles of not too remotely past events, then it is odd that they apparently felt no call to give a precise date for any of those events. One incongruous consequence is that Christians, who recognize that their religion is peculiarly historical and who affirm that the events of the original Easter constitute the great hinge of human history, remain unable to specify the year in which these events are supposed to have occurred.

With regard not only to the relatively unimportant matter of the lack of precise dates, but also to wider evidential concerns, two things should be said. First, if the Mosaic God really did reveal himself in Palestine in the early A.D. 30s, then he manifestly did not intend the fact and the contents of that revelation to get through to all humanity and to be accepted by everyone. Second, it is only on the assumption that a genuinely revealing revelation was in fact being made that we become entitled to assume that we now possess evidences sufficient to demand the conclusion that that is the case.

In fact, in view of these and many other deficiencies in the materials available, my own conviction is that we have no chance either of developing a modestly acceptable outline account of what actually happened in Jerusalem during that original Easter weekend, or of determining how or when believers first came to believe that on the third day Jesus physically rose from the dead.

The affirmative case cannot uphold the burden of proof and overcome presumption

Be that as it may. For in order to warrant disbelief none of that is necessary. It is only sufficient to show that no evidence has been presented so strong as to call for a radical shakeup of the ordinary presuppositions of critical history.

We have no alternative but to continue in the presumption that anything that is accepted as being naturally impossible did not happen.

Because so many Christians following St. Paul believe that they can see the risen Christ still active in the lives of believers and in his church, it is worth insisting that to the unsanctified eye, all that is visible here are the effects of the believers' beliefs about the risen Christ. What calls for explanation, therefore, is not these effects themselves, striking and impressive though they often are, but how the believers arrived at the beliefs that produce those effects.

More inconsistencies in the testimony

One clue to one possible answer is to be found in what is our earliest testimony about what are alleged to have been post-Resurrection appearances. Most scholars would date this nearer to twenty than to ten years after the Easter events. It is in I Corinthians 15. Before looking at this, I must emphasize how much our picture is distorted by reading the books of the New Testament in their traditional order, rather than in order of composition. We falsely assume that the Christ preached by Paul must have been the Jesus of the Gospels. We thus fail to notice that the Pauline epistles contain no references to Pontius Pilate, or to any birth traditions, or to miracles wrought during the ministry of Jesus. Perhaps most remarkable of all, even when these are most relevant to the controversies in which Paul was engaged, they never quote any of the supposedly dominical sayings later to be recorded in the various Gospels.

Thus the Pauline epistles provide no positive support for the assumption, so strongly suggested by the order of books in the New Testament, that the church in Paul's day was familiar with the biographical materials that we now find there. And when we look at his account of post-Resurrection appearances—an account which, though late, is the earliest we have—we have also to remind ourselves that it also may or may not have been available to and accepted by the Gospel writers.

In four successive verses Paul lists first, Cephas (Peter) and the twelve; second, "above five hundred brethren at once"; third, "James, then . . . all the apostles"; and fourth, "last of all he was seen of me also, as of one born out of due time." Nothing is said to indicate where these events are supposed to have occurred, and all that we can infer about when it occurred is that it was after the third day and before Paul's own reception into the Christian community.

Of the Gospels none, not even Matthew, concedes a first appearance to Peter. They have either not heard or not accepted the story of the appearance to "above five hundred brethren at once"—and this despite the "greater part" being still alive at the time of Paul's writing.

Finally, and this is by far the most significant and damaging fact about this earliest testimony, Paul is clearly taking it that his own visionary experience on the road to Damascus was of exactly the same type as all its perceived predecessors. But this vision, like Macbeth's vision of the dagger, was not even alleged to be "sensible to feeling as to sight." It was not, therefore, at all the sort of thing needed by Dr. Habermas, and supposedly, actually vouchsafed to doubting Thomas.

In the rest of the chapter Paul talked of corruption and incorruption and of the provision of spiritual bodies for the resurrected. Presumably he interpreted his own vision on the road to Damascus as seeing Jesus in a nonphysical body. To the unsanctified eye, however, seeing spiritual bodies is indiscernible from having visions to which no mind-independent realities correspond.

AFFIRMATIVE STATEMENT
Gary R. Habermas

Before turning to the main portion of my presentation, I will begin by noting two limitations. First, Dr. Flew and I have agreed in writing to limit this debate to the historicity of Jesus' Resurrection and not to extend the topic to God's existence, scripture, or other such areas in order to speak directly both on the subject and to each other. Although the Resurrection has implications for these subjects, they are not pursued here. Second, the time element allows me to present only a brief outline of some of the more important evidences for Jesus' Resurrection. Details and additional points will have to await later development, if they can be brought up here at all. Now I will turn directly to my presentation.

The standards of historical scholarship are the reliable criteria for evaluating the resolution

First, a few categorical and critical remarks will be addressed to the contemporary philosophical objections to miracles, such as those just presented by Dr. Flew. Second, after a brief treatment of the critically ascertained historical background, four sets of arguments will provide a contemporary apologetic for Jesus' Resurrection. Yet only an outline can be provided here. The strength of this apologetic is in revealing that even by utilizing contemporary critical principles, the Resurrection can still be shown to be historical. In fact, the major theme of this essay is to point out how this event can be demonstrated even according to such skeptical standards of investigation.

CONTEMPORARY PHILOSOPHICAL OBJECTIONS

Frequently following and updating David Hume's influential essay "Of Miracles,"[5] recent philosophical skepticism often focuses on the relationship between miracle-claims[6] and the laws of nature. Some scholars question whether empirical evidence exists for such claims. Patrick Nowell-Smith, for example, asserts that lawful events are predictable, but nonlawful events are not.[7] Similarly, Antony G. N. Flew[8] and George Chryssides[9] declare that the laws of nature are repeatable, whereas historical claims for miracles are not, and hence the former are more reliable. It is also common to contrast miracle-claims with the laws of nature. Several scholars call for expanding these laws when faced with a strange event.[10] Alasdair McKinnon asserts that all events that occur in nature should be termed natural.[11] Similar views are held by Guy Robinson[12] and Malcolm Diamond.[13] Dr. Flew believes that there is a dilemma between strong laws and real exceptions to these laws.[14]

Because of my time restrictions, I will be able to deal only briefly with these objections, noting five major problems that generally apply to these skeptical doubts. There are numerous individual problems that should be raised with regard to these philosophical questions, which can perhaps be pursued later in our discussion.

Refutation of the negative objections to the reliable criteria

First, most of these philosophical objections are attempts to mount up the data against miracles in an a priori manner (that is, before or in spite of the factual evidence) so that no facts could actually establish their occurrence. For instance, it is an unjustified assumption that whatever occurs in the world must automatically be a natural event having a natural cause. Such an assumption ignores the fact that if a historical miracle occurred it would have to occur in nature. Therefore, to always expand the laws of nature belies a naturalistic prejudice.

Searching for a naturalistic alternative may be an expected skeptical procedure, but the statement that we must always assume a naturalistic explanation is, once again, an a priori assumption against miracles. We can describe a natural process but when we attempt to naturalistically predetermine the case of all events, we beg the very question that we seek to answer, for this is simply another way of assuming that miracles are impossible. As one theistic philosopher remarked concerning Dr. Flew's criticism of miracles, "Flew's argument is an almost classic case of an unfalsifiable position which in the process of justification begs the whole question in favor of naturalism."[15]

Therefore, these naturalistic attempts frequently fail by assuming that which needs to be proven, namely, that all events are indeed natural ones. As C. S. Lewis points out:

> Unfortunately, we know the experience against [miracles] to be uniform only if we know that all reports of them are false. And we can know all the reports to be false only if we know already that miracles have never occurred. In fact, we are arguing in a circle.[16]

We cannot disallow miracles by utilizing faulty definitions, by assuming the evidence needed to prove one's view, or by arguing in a circular fashion. Even while providing a somewhat sympathetic treatment of the naturalistic stance on miracles, another philosopher asserts:

> I believe it is now generally recognized that Hume overstates his case. We cannot a priori rule out the possibility of miracles or of rational belief in miracles. . . . It looks, then, as if Hume's argument against miracles, even as expanded by Flew, fails.[17]

Second, and somewhat conversely, in addition to internal logical problems, these philosophical objections are also mistaken in not allowing for the real possibility of external intervention in nature. But arguing from naturalistic premises inside a system cannot disprove the possibility that a miracle was performed in nature by a stronger power. Therefore, the proper question at this point is not the internal query of the strength of the laws of nature. The more proper question concerns the issue of the supernatural. It should be evident that no matter how strong the natural system is, it is useless to build a case on it if nature is not the supreme reality.[18]

Now it must be noted again that this debate, by agreement, is not about arguments for God's existence and that this is not the issue that I am arguing. Neither am I assuming God's existence or even that a resurrection, by its very nature, is automatically a miracle of God.

Rather, my point is that because the supernatural is at least possible, any claimed evidence for such an event must at least be seriously considered, for if there is even possible evidence for a supernatural act it would make a strong claim to being evidence that is superior to our current evidence regarding the laws of nature.

Third, these philosophical objectives generally treat the laws of nature in an almost Newtonian sense as the final word on what may occur. But these objections too often exhibit little awareness of the current view in physics that the laws of nature are statistical. That is, these laws describe what generally occurs. But laws do not cause or keep anything from happening.[19] As a result, these laws should not be utilized as any sort of barrier to the occurrence of miracles. Richard Swinburne points out that the concept of universal, fixed laws reigned from the eighteenth to the early twentieth centuries, but the statistical concept is more recent and popular today.[20] For reasons such as these, eminent German physicist Werner Schaafs concludes that "even the physicist must officially concede the possibility of intervention by God."[21] Swinburne adds:

> For these latter reasons it seems not unnatural to describe E as a nonrepeatable counter-instance to the law of nature L . . . . To say that a certain such formula is a law is to say that in general its predictions are true and that any exceptions to its operation cannot be accounted for by another formula which could be taken as a law . . . . It is clearly a coherent way of talking . . . . In such a case the conceptually impossible would occur.[22]

Therefore, we may make a general point here. If the laws of nature are represented as inviolable then a question-begging assumption occurs when the evidence for Jesus' Resurrection is ignored, as is often the case. But if these laws are general and statistical, then there is no problem for miracles. There are other options besides these two opposite views, but the treatment of them generally falls into such categories.

Very briefly, a fourth issue concerns the empirical bias of several of the philosophical objections to miracles. Strict empiricism ignores both the empirical (even repeatable) evidence for miracles and the fact that the strict forms of verificational standards are themselves nonverifiable. In other words, to require repeatable, empirical evidence as the only or major epistemological test for truth sets up criteria that are themselves nonempirical and that rule out, a priori, vast ranges of reality. Miracles cannot be ruled out by this method because the methodology rules itself out in the process.[23] Such is the case, for instance, with the claims of Drs. Flew and Chryssides that miracles are questionable because of their nonrepeatable nature. This charge may be dealt with more fully in the rebuttal periods.

Fifth and last, the philosophical approach mentioned here frequently ignores the strong historical evidence for the Resurrection of Jesus. Theists are often requested to provide such evidence; it should not be ignored or ruled out a priori when it is given.

For these and many other reasons, such philosophical objections to miracles cannot rule out the historical evidence for the Resurrection, to which we now turn. This evidence must be answered directly on its own grounds.

THE KNOWN HISTORICAL FACTS

Just before turning to an apologetic for the Resurrection, it should be
mentioned that the critical approach to this topic has changed substantially in recent decades. The naturalistic theories of the nineteenth-
century older liberal theologians are rarely held these days, as will be
mentioned in the next section. Rather, by historical investigation or by
the utilization of form and redaction criticism, contemporary scholars
have approached this event in a different manner. Even by these
critical methodologies, a substantial number of historical facts are
accepted with regard to the death and Resurrection of Jesus.

Application of the standards of historical scholarship to the resurrection

Some events are generally agreed to be facts by practically all
critical scholars who deal with this topic today, whatever their school
of thought or discipline. In other words, criticial historians, philosophers, theologians, and scripture scholars who address this subject
usually accept this factual basis. At least eleven events are considered
to be knowable history by virtually all scholars, and a twelfth event is
considered to be knowable history by many scholars.

(1) Jesus died due to the rigors of crucifixion and (2) was buried.
(3) Jesus' death caused the disciples to despair and lose hope. (4)
Although not as frequently recognized, many scholars hold that Jesus
was buried in a tomb that was discovered to be empty just a few days
later.

Critical scholars even agree that (5) at this time the disciples had
real experiences that they believed were literal appearances of the risen
Jesus. Because of these experiences, (6) the disciples were transformed
from doubters who were afraid to identify themselves with Jesus to
bold proclaimers of his death and Resurrection, even being willing to
die for this belief. (7) This message was central in the early church
preaching and (8) was especially proclaimed in Jerusalem, where Jesus
had died shortly before.

As a result of this message, (9) the church was born and grew, (10)
with Sunday as the primary day of worship. (11) James, the brother of
Jesus and a skeptic, was converted to the faith when he also believed
he saw the resurrected Jesus. (12) A few years later Paul the persecutor
of Christians was also converted by an experience that he, similarly,
believed to be an appearance of the risen Jesus.

These historical facts are crucial to a contemporary investigation
of Jesus' Resurrection. Except for the empty tomb, virtually all critical
scholars who deal with this issue agree that these are the minimum
known historical facts regarding this event. Any conclusion concerning
the historicity of the Resurrection should therefore properly account for
this data. The pivotal fact, recognized as historical by virtually all
scholars, is the original experiences of the disciples. It is nearly always
admitted that the disciples had actual experiences and that something

really happened. Interestingly, varying critical positions that support the literal facticity of Jesus' Resurrection are currently popular.

A CONTEMPORARY APOLOGETIC

Naturalistic Theories

We will now begin our apologetic for Jesus' Resurrection, supported by four major sets of arguments. First, naturalistic theories have failed to explain away this event, chiefly because each theory is disproven by the known historical facts, as are combinations of theories.[24]

One interesting illustration of this failure of the naturalistic theories is that they were disproven by the nineteenth-century older liberals themselves, by whom these theses were popularized. These scholars refuted each other's theories, leaving no viable naturalistic hypotheses. For instance, Albert Schweitzer dismissed Reimarus's fraud theory and listed no proponents of this view since 1768.[25] David Strauss delivered the historical death blow to the swoon theory held by Karl Venturini, Heinrich Paulus, and others.[26] On the other hand, Friedrich Schleiermacher and Paulus pointed out errors in Strauss's hallucination theory. The major decimation of the hallucination theory, however, came at the hands of Theodor Keim.[27] Otto Pfleiderer was critical of the legendary or mythological theory, even admitting that it did not explain Jesus' Resurrection.[28] By these critiques such scholars pointed out that each of these theories was disproven by the historical facts.

Although nineteenth-century liberals decimated each other's views individually, twentieth-century critical scholars have generally rejected naturalistic theories as a whole, judging that they are incapable of explaining the known data. This approach is a usual characteristic of recent schools of thought.

For instance, Karl Barth points out that each of these liberal hypotheses is confronted by many inconsistencies and he concludes that "today we rightly turn up our nose at this."[29] Raymond Brown likewise asserts that twentieth-century critical scholars have rejected these theories, holding that they are no longer respectable. He adds that such contemporary thinkers ignore these alternative views and any popularized renditions of them as well.[30] In addition to Barth and Brown, rejections come from such diverse critical scholars as Paul Tillich,[31] Wolfhart Pannenberg,[32] Gunther Bornkamm,[33] Ulrich Wilckens,[34] John A. T. Robinson,[35] and A. M. Hunter,[36] among others. That even such critical scholars have rejected these naturalistic theories is a significant epitaph for the failure of these views. Perhaps Dr. Flew would like to pursue one or more of these hypotheses later.

Alternative theories of the resurrection cannot meet the standards of historical scholarship

Evidences for the Resurrection

The second set of arguments in our apologetic for Jesus' Resurrection concerns the many positive evidences that corroborate the historical and literal nature of this event. Ten such evidences will be listed here, all of which have been taken from accepted historical facts previously listed. Thus, the factual basis for these evidences is admitted by the vast majority of scholars. Because of the brevity of this essay, these ten will simply be stated with very little elaboration.

The key evidence for Jesus' Resurrection is (1) the disciples' eyewitness experiences, which they believed to be literal appearances of the risen Jesus; these experiences have not been explained by naturalistic theories and additional facts corroborate this eyewitness testimony. Other positive evidences include (2) the early proclamation of the Resurrection by these eyewitnesses, (3) their transformation into bold witnesses who were willing to die for their convictions, (4) the empty tomb, and (5) the fact that the Resurrection of Jesus was the center of the apostolic message, all of which require adequate explanations. It is also found that the disciples proclaimed this message in Jerusalem itself, where it is related that in repeated confrontations with the authorities, (6) the Jewish leaders could not disprove their message even though they had both the power and the motivation to do so.

Additionally, (7) the very existence of the church, founded by monotheistic, law-abiding Jews who nonetheless (8) worshiped on Sunday demand historical causes as well.

Two additionally strong facts arguing for the historicity of the Resurrection are that two skeptics, (9) James and (10) Paul, became Christians after having experiences that they also believed were appearances of the risen Jesus. It is interesting to note here that Reginald Fuller concludes that even if the appearance to James had not been recorded by Paul (I Cor. 15:7), such would still have to be postulated anyway in order to account for both James's conversion and his subsequent promotion to an authoritative position in the early church.[37] The same is even more emphatically true concerning Paul.[38]

When combined with the failure of both the naturalistic theories and the philosophical objections, this minimum of ten evidences provides a strong case for the historicity of Jesus' Resurrection. This is especially so in that each of these evidences was based on a known historical fact.[39] In particular, when the early and eyewitness experiences of the disciples, James, and Paul are considered, along with their corresponding transformations and their central message,[40] the historical Resurrection becomes the best explanation for the facts, especially because the alternative theories have failed. Therefore, it may be concluded that the Resurrection is a probable historical event. An additional two sets of arguments will now be given to further strengthen this case.

The Core Historical Facts

The pivotal point in this discussion is the cause of the disciples' faith. As noted by Fuller:

> The very fact of the church's kerygma therefore requires that the historian postulate some other event, over and above Good Friday, an event which is not itself the "rise of the Easter faith" but the *cause* of the Easter faith. (italics added)[41]

The negative cannot account for a key historical fact

In examining the cause of the disciples' faith, I pointed out earlier that the Resurrection was proclaimed by the earliest eyewitnesses. This is especially based, for instance, on I Cor. 15:3ff., where virtually all scholars agree that Paul recorded an ancient creed concerning Jesus' death and Resurrection. That this material is traditional and pre-Pauline is evident from the technical terms *delivered* and *received*, the parallelism and somewhat stylized content, the proper names of Cephas and James, the non-Pauline words, and the possibility of an Aramaic original.[42]

Refutation of negative description of key historical facts

Concerning the date of this creed, critical scholars almost always agree that it has a very early origin, usually placing it in the A.D. 30s. Paul most likely received this material during his first visit in Jerusalem with Peter and James, who are included in the list of appearances (I Cor. 15:5, 7).[43] In fact, Fuller,[44] Hunter,[45] and Pannenberg[46] are examples of critical scholars who date Paul's receiving of this creed from three to eight years after the Crucifixion itself. And if Paul received it at such an early date, the creed itself would be even earlier because it would have existed before the time he was told. And the facts upon which the creed was originally based would be earlier still. We are, for practical purposes, back to the original events. So we may now realize how this data is much earlier than the ten to twenty years after the Crucifixion as postulated by Dr. Flew. Paul also adds that the other eyewitnesses had likewise been testifying concerning their own appearances of the risen Jesus (I Cor. 15:11, 14, 15).

That these eyewitnesses are said both to have seen the risen Jesus (the creed, I Cor. 15:3ff.) and to have testified concerning these experiences (vv. II, 14–15) is important, for here are two invaluable sources of testimony that link the Resurrection appearances to the earliest eyewitnesses who actually participated in the events.

For the original eyewitnesses, their experiences were literal appearances of the risen Jesus. As explained by Carl Braaten:

> Even the more skeptical historians agree that for primitive Christianity . . . the resurrection of Jesus from the dead was a real event in history, the very foundation of faith, and not a mythical idea arising out of the creative imaginations of believers.[47]

In speaking of the nature of these experiences, it is common to stress the descriptions of Paul's experience on the road to Damascus.[48] Yet even critics also recognize the fact that the Gospels likewise contain some early material concerning the Resurrection appearances of Jesus. For instance, Luke 24:34 is believed to be based on tradition perhaps as early as that of the creed recorded by Paul (I Cor. 15:3ff.). Contrary to Dr. Flew's statement, the appearance to Peter (listed by Paul) is recorded in Luke and is also an early creed, as even Bultmann attests.[49]

After applying form critical techniques to the Gospels, C. H. Dodd shows that the Gospels contain several reports of the resurrected Jesus that rely on early tradition. He cites the appearances recorded in Matthew 28:8–10, 16–20, John 20:19–21, and, to a lesser extent, Luke 24:36–49 as being based on such early tradition. He states, however, that the other Gospel accounts lack the mythical tendencies of much ancient literature and thus also merit careful consideration in a formulation of the appearances of the risen Jesus. At any rate, the Gospel accounts of the Resurrection appearances (and the earliest reports included in them, in particular) should be utilized as records of what the eyewitnesses actually saw.[50] For reasons such as these, many, if not most, critical theologians hold either that the literal event of the Resurrection can be accepted by faith or that some sort of literal appearances (abstract or bodily) may be postulated as historical realities.[51]

Although it is beyond the limits of this essay to attempt to desribe the actual characteristics of Jesus' Resurrection body, it may be stated that the combined testimony of the New Testament is that Jesus rose bodily, but that this body was changed.[52] This is the report of the earliest eyewitnesses.

Twelve events were enumerated earlier, eleven of which are accepted as knowable history by virtually all scholars, and one of which is accepted as knowable history by many scholars. It is the writer's conviction that by utilizing only four of these accepted facts, a brief but sufficient case can be made for the historicity of the Resurrection, which will provide a third major set of arguments for this event. (These core facts are only an example of such an argument. If one feels that they are too brief, one only needs to utilize more of the Known Historical Facts enumerated earlier.) The four facts to be used here are Jesus' death due to crucifixion, the subsequent experiences that the disciples were convinced were literal appearances of the risen Jesus, the corresponding transformation of these men, and Paul's conversion experience, which he also believed was an appearance of the risen Jesus. Few scholars dispute these four facts.[53]

Of these facts, the nature of the disciples' experiences is the most crucial. As eminent historian Michael Grant asserts, historical investigation actually does prove that the earliest eyewitnesses were absolutely convinced they had seen the risen Jesus.[54] Carl Braaten adds that skeptical historians in general agree with this conclusion.[55] One major advantage of these critically accepted historical facts is that they deal directly with the issue of these experiences. These four historical facts are able, on a smaller scale, to both provide a few major refutations of the naturalistic theories and to provide some major positive evidences that relate the historicity of Jesus' literal Resurrection, as claimed by the New Testament authors.[56] A few examples will now illustrate these claims.

First, using these four core historical facts, the naturalistic theories can be disproven. (Of course, nothing near an exhaustive set of critiques can be supplied by these facts alone, yet some of the best criticisms do come from this list.) For instance, the swoon theory is ruled out both by the facts concerning Jesus' death and by Paul's conversion. The disciples' experiences disprove the hallucination and other subjective theories because such phenomena are not collective or contagious, being observed by one person alone and taking place at a wide variety of times and places. The psychological preconditions for hallucinations are also lacking. Paul's experience also rules out these theories because of his psychological frame of mind. That it was the disciples and other early witnesses who had these experiences likewise rules out legend or mythological theories, because the original teaching concerning the Resurrection is therefore based on the testimony of real eyewitnesses (as with the creed in I Cor. 15:3ff.) and not on later legends. Paul's experience likewise cannot be explained by legends, because such could not account for his conversion from skepticism. Last the stolen body and fraud theories are disproven by the disciples' transformation both because this change shows that the disciples really believed that Jesus rose from the dead and because of the probability that a group of such liars would not be willing to become martyrs. Similarly, Paul would not have been convinced by such fraud.[57]

Second, these four core facts also provide the major positive evidences for Jesus' literal Resurrection appearances, such as the disciples' early, eyewitness experiences that have not been explained away naturalistically, their transformation into men who were willing to die specifically for their faith, and Paul's experience and corresponding transformation. Thus these accepted core historical facts provide positive evidences that further verify the disciples' claims concerning Jesus' literal Resurrection, especially in that these arguments have not been accounted for naturally.[58]

But here is the major point of this argument. Because these core historical facts (and the earlier known facts in general) have been established by critical and historical procedures, contemporary scholars should not reject this evidence simply by referring to the "discrepancies" in the New Testament or to its general "unreliability." Not only are such critical claims refuted by evidence not discussed here, but it has been concluded that the Resurrection can be historically demonstrated even when the minimum number of historical facts are utilized. Neither should it be concluded merely that something occurred that is indescribable because of naturalistic premises, or because of the character of history, or because of the "cloudinesss" or "legendary character" of the New Testament. Neither should it be said that Jesus rose spiritually, but not literally. Again, these and other such views are refuted in that the facts admitted by virtually all scholars as knowable history are adequate to historically demonstrate the literal Resurrection of Jesus.

In short, instead of stating what they believe we cannot know concerning the Gospel accounts, skeptics would do well to concentrate on what even they admit can be known about the texts at this point. The factual basis is enough to vindicate the various accounts and show that Jesus' Resurrection is by far the best historical explanation. Although critical doubts may be present with regard to other issues in the New Testament, the known facts (see The Known Historical Facts) are sufficient to show that Jesus rose from the dead.[59]

The Shroud of Turin

The fourth set of arguments for the Resurrection of Jesus concerns the scientific investigation of the Shroud of Turin, the results of which can be treated here in only a sketchy manner. I coauthored a book on the shroud with Kenneth Stevenson, who served as the editor and spokesperson for the scientists who investigated the shroud in 1978. I'll refer the interested person to his work or other good books on the subject.[60]

Archaeological evidence establishes the resurrection as historical fact

The shroud is a piece of linen that bears the image of a crucified man who has all of the wounds associated with Jesus' death, including a pierced scalp, a serious beating, contusions on the knees and shoulders, four nail wounds in the wrists and feet, as well as a postmortem blood flow from a chest wound. The man is in a state of rigor mortis, another evidence of death.

The man has been identified as a Semite, and evidence from coins over the eyes, pollen, and numerous historical references connect the shroud with a likely first-century origin.[61] But not only do the wounds on the cloth parallel those of Jesus, but they do so in more than a half-dozen areas that are unusual for a crucifixion. Several scientific researchers have noted the high probability that the two men are the same person, based largely on these agreements in rare and abnormal aspects.[62] As even an agnostic scientific critic of the shroud asserts concerning these probabilities in *The Skeptical Inquirer*: "I agree . . . . on all of this. If the shroud is authentic, the image is that of Jesus."[63] In other words, this agnostic researcher asserts that if the shroud is not a fake, then it is Jesus' burial cloth.

But perhaps the strongest major conclusion emerging from the investigation is that the shroud is authentic. As one official scientific report states: "No pigments, paints, dyes or stains have been found on the fibrils."[64] Equally intriguing, scientific discoveries concerning the shroud, such as its three-dimensionality, superficiality, and non-directionality are virtually unexplainable in current scientific terms.[65]

Further, there is no bodily decomposition on the shroud, indicating the separation of the body from the cloth. Additionally, the scientific team's chief pathologist has testified that although the body exited, it was probably not unwrapped, as indicated by the condition of the blood stains. Kenneth Stevenson and I, as well as others, have argued that the evidence indicates the probable cause of the image on the cloth to be a light or heat scorch from a dead body.

In fact, the shroud image appears to be a type of photographic negative, caused by heat or light, having the unique empirical and repeatable characteristics previously mentioned, all proceeding from a dead body and possibly even picturing the body leaving the cloth without being unwrapped. But more than an indescribable mystery, when combined with the probable identification of the shroud as Jesus' burial garment, the shroud becomes an additional set of arguments for Jesus' Resurrection. It should be noted that scientific data can change, and nothing in the Christian faith depends on the shroud (unlike the other three sets of arguments). Yet the evidence at present provides some empirically repeatable evidence for the Resurrection.[66]

CONCLUSION

When one assumes a viewpoint or theory in advance of the data in order to arrive at a conclusion and continues to do so in spite of contrary evidence, one is guilty of a priori reasoning. Continued refusals to seriously consider the facticity of such claims in light of extremely strong evidence while generally ignoring the evidence itself is an example of an a priori (and circular) rejection. I therefore encourage Dr. Flew to address himself to the evidence for the Resurrection.

To be more specific, I would respectfully challenge Dr. Flew to answer evidence for the Resurrection, namely, the failure of the naturalistic theories, the positive evidences for this event, the core facts accepted by virtually all scholars, and the Shroud of Turin. The evidence shows that the claims of the earliest eyewitnesses have been vindicated—Jesus' literal Resurrection from the dead in a glorified, spiritual body is the best explanation for the facts. Dr. Flew, please *directly* address the evidence for the Resurrection in your rebuttal.

REBUTTAL
Antony G. N. Flew

Dr. Habermas asked me whether I was an adherent of the swoon theory or any of these other accounts. No, I am not. My argument is that we are simply not in a position to reconstruct an account. I think the whole exercise of who moved the stone and so on is an impossible and misguided exercise because we have not got enough evidence of what actually happened in that undated year of the Easter events.

The negative position is built on a failure of the affirmative to shoulder the burden of proof and overcome presumption. The negative does not defend an alternative historial account.

And the sort of thing that one would like to have, I think, is the sort of thing that might have existed, but if it did, would have been destroyed during the destruction of Jerusalem. One of the reasons, apart from sympathy with Israeli nationalism, for regretting the defeat of the first Jewish rebellion is that the destruction of Jerusalm destroyed any records that the Roman authorities may have had. And the sort of thing I would like to see is the sort of account that a British colonial civil servant would have written of the case. Something such as, "Had an impossible Jewish fanatic to deal with. Do you know the man claimed to be the local god? Good heavens!" That sort of thing, or something from the Jewish authorities about the difficulties they had. All this talk about how we know that the Jewish authorities tried to suppress the evidence and they weren't able to conceal the thing. What we've actually got is statements written down a very long time after those events saying that this is what the Jewish authorities did.

The best objective evidence is unavailable

Let me go on to this thing about my, as I thought, generous statement about ten or, in the other case, twenty years as a minimum estimate. I was not referring to the date of Paul's experience on the road to Damascus but to the presumed earliest date of I Corinthians, when he wrote it down. And I was also taking it, and I wasn't making it 10 or 20 A.D., I meant ten or twenty years after the estimated date of the Easter events, which is roughly 30 A.D., isn't it—this is the agreed date. So I was taking it that the minimum estimate for the date of I Corinthians would be, say, 40 A.D., ten years after the event, which is a long time in the context of psychic research. Anyone who knows anything of the literature in that field would recognize that if your earliest written testimony of some alleged event was ten years later, most people in the field would say, "This is just hopeless. We cannot possibly try to reconstruct what actually happened and who moved the stone and so on on the basis of that, just hopeless, we simply haven't got enough evidence."

Well, so, first thing, why I'm not going to give my account of what happened in the Easter events is that my major point is that we simply have not got enough evidence to reconstruct what happened then. Second thing, there was much I agreed with in what Dr. Habermas said, including some of the things that he was offering as arguments against me, because I certainly wouldn't want to defend what Hume

Insufficient data to meet standards of historical scholarship actually wrote. I was offering something that was a development of that.

Now, neither did I offer a contention about miracles as something unfalsifiable. Oh no, surely I made the point that if we were in a position to start where Cardinal Newman wanted to start, you know, if we knew that there was a God who was wanting to make an acceptable and intelligible and understood revelation, all these things, then indeed we might be able to do it, but if one is not starting form that, then one can't do it.

Strong presumption in favor of natural order

Then, about natural impossibility and laws of nature, well, I think I want to repeat my point that both sides in this debate have a vested interest in insisting on strong notions of natural necessity and natural impossibility, because only if you have a strong idea of a natural order can you suggest that this natural order, if it's overriden, is in this overriding evidence of a supernatural power at work. I'm certainly not dogmatically saying that miracles are inconceivable; on the contrary! I'm explaining that I understand a miracle to be an overriding by a supernatural power of the natural order. I know other physicists say this, but then other physicists say the opposite with equal assurance. They say, "Flew, you've got it all wrong. *All* physicists know . . . ." Then when I repeat what I've been told that all physicists know to the next physicist I meet, "You've got it *all* wrong, Flew, you're simply ignorant of physics. *All* physicists know the opposite." Well, the main point I want you to grasp is that all of us here have a vested interest in the idea of a strong natural order. This ought to be taken as agreed because it's only if there is that strong natural order that there is anything significant about the Resurrection.

Supposing Habermas came up to me and said, "You know, Flew, you're an absolute bigot, resurrections are happening every day of the week in Lynchburg. You ignorant, prejudiced Englishman, you come here saying this can't happen. We do it regularly!" Well, okay, if I came here and found it was happening left, right, and center, I would have to shake up my ideas, but one of the things that it would lead me to think would be, "Wow! Then it probably did happen in Jerusalem in A.D. 30—but so what! Nothing remarkable about Jesus' Resurrection, people in Lynchburg are doing it every day of the week." You really have got to make a miracle naturally impossible if it's going to be something the occurence of which is exciting.

Refutation of specific factual claims offered in support of the resurrection

Then about these Pauline experiences. I think it is significant that Paul offers his own experience on the road to Damascus about which he never claims, you know, that he pressed his fingers in the wounds. He doesn't say this. No, Jesus makes all these appearances, but there's nothing out of the way about a vision when there isn't anything out there that it's a vision of, you know. No one would want to dispute that Bernadette (Marie-Bernarde Soubirous), around whose visions the whole cult of Lourdes arose, no one would want to dispute that she was an honest peasant girl who did indeed have the vision. What the dispute is about, is was this caused by the surviving Mother of God or was there anything there, you know, that the cameras, the television team, the people using instruments, and so on, would have weighed. Well, I take it that Paul is not even claiming that. He's claiming that it was one of these bodies that you put on when corruption puts on incorruption. Now, this is why I made the fuss about all the people concerned being believing Jews, and Paul in particular being a Pharisee believing in the Resurrection and so on. This is why that's significant. He has an experience that is nothing miraculous in itself, and he then interprets it as he's seen not an ordinary flesh and blood body, but a spiritual Resurrection body.

Then, about some of the other things I was talking about. What I think is significant is that what I understood was agreed was that the earliest documents that we have don't have any of the references to the contents of our Gospels that you would expect someone who was preaching the Christian religion as it is now understood to include. Paul never refers to any of the supposedly dominical sayings in the Gospels, never refers to any of the birth stories, never refers to any of these other things. They come in at some later stage. On the road to Damascus (of course I'm not going to deny that Paul had the experience on the road to Damascus that changed his life, certainly this happened), what is in dispute is whether what he was confronted with was what was supposed to have left the tomb, a corruptible body of Jesus of Nazareth. I don't think he's even claiming this.

The point I made about Peter was not that there's not a Gospel record of an appearance to Peter, of course there is, it's the first appearance to Peter that is not even in Matthew. Everyone who knows the Roman church knows Matthew is the favorite Gospel of the church of Rome because of its general emphasis on Peter. Now this is a very odd thing. The writer of the Gospel, later on, who's wanting to build up the position of Peter doesn't say that the first appearance was to Peter, he doesn't seem to have heard about this at all. Isn't it also remarkable that this supposedly enormously sensational collective vision of more than one hundred people is absolutely unmentioned in the Gospels.

Then, about liars. What I hoped I was going to avoid was this sort of eighteenth-century discussion, trial of the witnesses, you've either got to say that these people who died for their convictions were deliberate, conscious liars who cooked the whole story up, you know, in a crafty afternoon. "What stories shall we tell the press?" It is, of course, ridiculous to suggest that, but there's an awful lot of room between recording what actually happened a long time ago and telling deliberate lies about what actually happened a long time ago.

Challenging the reliablity of the witnesses

Why I brought in this stuff about the birth stories was that I thought that this was an example both sufficiently close and sufficiently far away of the way in which the consideration of what was thought to be a prophecy was leading people to adapt their views about what actually happened, arguing, obviously with complete integrity, they thought they knew that in Isaiah this was a prophecy of the birth of the Messiah. They believed also that Jesus was the Messiah. I believe the word *christos* is the translation of the Hebrew for Messiah. So they took it they know that if he was the Messiah and this was a prophecy, which both things were granted, he must have been born in Bethlehem. So the whole thing would seem to them is that we are trying to find what actually happened. We know, don't we, he must have been born in Bethlehem, so how do we account for his being born in Bethlehem? We then scratch around for someone telling a story that might explain the Bethlehem birth. Now, I think this again is significant, how people, utterly honest, utterly dedicated people can over a long time come up with an explanation. You've got people with a specific framework of ideas, specific assumptions, talking with one another, arguing about it, worrying about it, "How do we interpret the visions, you know, we've had these visions, how do we interpret them?" They would come to conclusions very far removed from whatever actually happened.

I want to end by saying I do not believe that anyone is in a position to know what actually happened there, and if ten thousand scholars tell me that they are all agreed that they know that Jesus' tomb was opened on such and such a day, I want to ask them, On what evidence do you know this? You know, when was it recorded and so on. Well, it was, in anyone's view, a long time after, with much going on in between. Well, this wouldn't matter if it wasn't of such ideological importance, because one would just assume that there's no reason for anyone to get this wrong. Again, the point I was making from the beginning is that the sort of evidence that you need for the establishment of a miraculous event is much stronger than the evidence you need for saying that your daughter went out and got a Coke yesterday afternoon. You need much better evidence, so these considerations are a serious matter.

REBUTTAL
Gary R. Habermas

Let me address myself in order to a number of Dr. Flew's claims. I'm going to go back to his original paper and to one of his claims, which, as far as I'm aware, is the only major one on the subject of Jesus' Resurrection that I didn't already say something about in my initial paper. This is his statement that even if the Resurrection of Jesus occurred, there's still the matter of identification. How do we know that it was God who raised Jesus? I will simply outline what I think is a two-fold case for the identification of the Resurrection. How do we know that the Resurrection was an act of God? I will propose two sets of arguments and I will preface them by saying that these are inductive, not deductive.

First of all, what I call a prospective argument proceeds from God's existence forward to the Resurrection. We have agreed not to discuss God's existence or arguments for God's existence, but because Dr. Flew asked me the question, I will tell him the line I would take, without using any single argument. I would say first of all that there are good arguments for God's existence, and second of all that the Resurrection in an event that is consistent with God's attributes. Dr. Flew disagrees with me about God's existence, but I know he agrees that if God's existence could be shown to be true, the general line of my argument from God's existence to the Resurrection follows. For I quote Dr. Flew, "Certainly given some beliefs about God, the occurrence of the resurrection does become enormously more likely."[67] So the Resurrection as an act of God does follow from such a basis.

With the assumption of God's existence the resurrection is a likely historical event

The second argument is one that I call retrospective, and it views Jesus, as we do today, in a post-Easter sense. How can one look back at the claims of Jesus? One does so through the Cross and Resurrection. One cannot see the claims of Jesus unless one looks through his Cross and Resurrection, as did most of the early Jewish believers of the first century. The Resurrection made a difference concerning the claims of Christ. Jesus claimed to have a unique relationship with the God of the universe. This is recognized by virtually all critical scholars today. I'll just mention Rudolf Bultmann as an example of one who admits that Jesus believed this.[68]

There are at least four major indications that Jesus taught that he had a unique relationship with the God of the universe. First of all, this is shown by his self-designations. He claimed that he was the Son of Man and even that he was the Son of God. Let me refer you to Christologies such as those by Oscar Cullmann, Raymond Brown, and Wolfhart Pannenberg[69] for some of the various details. Jesus used terms such as *Abba*, which can be translated as either "Father" or even "Daddy" from the Aramaic, as an evidence of a claim to a unique relationship with God. Let me mention Jeremias on this point.[70]

Jesus was a unique historical figure and not subject to traditional analysis

Second, Jesus claimed authority, unlike any founder of any other major religion in the history of religions. For instance, other religious founders have said, in effect, "I'll show you the way of salvation." Jesus said, "I am the way of salvation." Other religious founders have said, "I'll lead you to the right path." Jesus said, "I am the right path." Again, this is admitted by Fuller, Bultmann,[71] and others. Jesus made unique claims concerning salvation. He also said he could forgive sin (Mark 2:1–12). And when the critics came up to him and said, "Well, you know only God can do that," the implication becomes obvious. Jesus was making a specific claim. Cullmann, for example, has made strong statements about this passage.[72]

Third, his actions showed that he could do more than just make claims. Jesus fulfilled Old Testament prophecy. (Concerning Dr. Flew's mention of the birth narratives in this context, let me just parenthetically add here that I think that they are irrelevant to the subject of the Resurrection. But I would still like to see Dr. Flew respond to A. N. Sherwin-White, an eminent Oxford University Roman historian who defended the Palestinian census that Dr. Flew called a "wildly implausible tale" earlier tonight.[73] And a number of scholars, such as F. F. Bruce, have also defended this account in Luke 2.[74])

But considering Old Testament prophecy, some interesting arguments have been published concerning Isaiah 53, for instance, written by Martin Hengel, Oscar Cullmann,[75] and others, where they argue that Jesus did believe he was fulfilling this prophecy. Now did the Jews believe that the Servant of Isaiah 53 was the Messiah? Well, some early Jewish commentaries do indicate that Jews often understood the Servant of Isaiah 53 to be the Messiah.[76]

Additionally, Jesus said that his miracles were a sign that what he said was true. Edwin Yamauchi, professor of ancient history at Miami University in Ohio, said that Jesus is the only founder of a major world religion for whom there is eyewitness testimony of his miracles.[77] Dr. Flew, Dr. Miethe, and I were in Dallas a few months ago for a number of debates between theists and atheists. On the New Testament panel, two scholars represented the skeptical alternative to the evangelical viewpoint. Even both these critics admitted that the evidence indicated that Jesus performed historical miracles.[78] Jesus said that such were further evidence of his claims.

And last, Jesus said that his Resurrection would be *the* sign that his claims were true. If he did rise, it would be the sign of his unique connection with God. Again, his actions indicate that he was correct.

A fourth indicator of Jesus' claims is the reactions of others toward him. According to Mark 14:61–62, one of the major instigations for Jesus death was that when asked the question, "Are you the Messiah, the Son of God?" he replied, "I am." And Rudolf Bultmann, Reginald Fuller, Raymond Brown and others all say that even his New Testament followers applied the title of God to Jesus.[79]

Now these are some of Jesus' claims. Anybody can make claims, but the facts show that this same Jesus also fulfilled prophecy and performed miracles; in particular he was raised from the dead. And it is reasonable that Jesus would be best able to explain the purpose behind the Resurrection. To repeat, he made unique claims, and he was uniquely raised from the dead. Jesus' testimony is that as the chief miracle, the Resurrection was the major sign that his worldview was verified by an act of God. The only time that a resurrection can be shown to have literally taken place, it occurred to the only person who made such unique claims about his own deity, his special message, and other things concerning his relationship with God. The Resurrection is therefore not a "brute fact" of history that stands alone. Rather, the Resurrection, in conjunction with the claims of Jesus, shows that what Jesus taught is true.[80]

A couple other things that Dr. Flew expressed also need to be mentioned. He said that we need both strong laws of nature and strong exceptions to these laws. I agree, although I don't like the word *violate*. I would say that miracles temporarily supersede the laws of nature. I don't think we can say that we know all about the laws of nature, so I think a miracle supersedes the normally observed and known pattern of nature. This point addresses the concern for strong laws, because it is agreed that an interruption occurs at the level of an empirical observation of these laws. And because I believe that miracles temporarily supersede such an observed pattern, I also hold to strong exceptions brought about by God in order to confirm a message, which is very close to David Hume's definition.[81] I would also respectfully ask Dr. Flew if he could produce a formula that would better account for the evidence for Jesus' Resurrection. In some of his works he suggests that if a miracle were shown to be true, we should expand the laws of nature. He and others make this suggestion. Now what are we going to say about the Resurrection? In order to expand the laws of nature you're going to have something like this: the only time there's an exception to the law of death is with this man called Jesus of Nazareth. I think that's a point in our favor.

Clarifying the definition of miracle

There are several other brief points that Dr. Flew mentioned both in his initial paper and in his rebuttal that I want to refer to quickly. Dr. Flew said that it was odd that God would reveal himself only to the Jews. Wolfhart Pannenberg's popular thesis is that God revealed himself in the Resurrection to everyone through the medium of public history, not just to the Jews.[82] The very fact that an Englishman and an American can stand up here and debate this today shows that it is much more than a Jewish affair.

Dr. Flew questioned some of the data of the Gospels. Let me make three important points here. First, I based my core historical facts argument on the data that the vast majority of scholars accept, thereby making objections to other areas of scripture irrelevant at this point. Second, the Gospels can be shown to be reliable sources anyway. Third, we have a lot more material about the historical Jesus than that in the New Testament alone. Dr. Flew was espousing, I believe, a thesis such as that of G. A. Wells when he questioned the amount of history in the Epistles.[83] Well, first of all, the purpose of the Epistles was not to present history. But second, let me just challenge him to respond to the fact that within 100 to 150 years after the birth of Christ, approximately eighteen non-Christian, extrabiblical sources from secu-

A diversity of types of sources and kinds of data support the claims of the Gospels

lar history, none of them Christian, mention more than one hundred facts, beliefs, and teachings from the life of Christ and early Christendom. These items, I might add, mention almost every major detail of Jesus' life, including miracles, the Resurrection, and his claims to be deity. Now, Dr. Flew might say that these are late sources. But these sources are much closer to the events that they describe than are key portions of historical material recorded by the ancient Roman historians Livy and Tacitus.

But let's handle another "late" claim. Dr. Flew keeps going back to this time of ten to twenty years after the Crucifixion for the earliest Christian writings. He also states that the earliest account is not ten to twenty years later, but that it's I Corinthians, some twenty years after. Now I think he's missed my point, and this is crucial. The pre-Pauline creed may have been written down for the first time in I Corinthians 15, but the creed was an oral confession that dates from a much earlier time. Many New Testament critical scholars today, such as Reginald Fuller, provide details on this creed.[84] It was transmitted orally to Paul, who recorded the creed after he received it, about three to eight years after the Crucifixion. Is this too long a time? No. Rather, it is an amazingly early report. But, as I said, one can get even two stages earlier than that. According to most scholars, Paul received this creed from the apostles, which makes it even earlier, and a creed has to be repeated before it becomes stylized. So now we're right on top of the Crucifixion, and note, it's the eyewitnesses who transmitted this information; it's not hearsay testimony.

According to major New Testament scholars, it was Peter and James who gave this message to the Apostle Paul. So although this confession is recorded in I Corinthians, the eyewitness testimony was noised abroad via witnesses from right after the Crucifixion itself. So far Dr. Flew has not answered this evidence, which has changed the view, as I said, of perhaps most of the critical theologians of the present generation. Wolfhart Pannenberg has said on at least a couple occasions that most critical theologians today are willing to admit that the disciples really saw something that might be called visions of the risen Jesus.[85] The discussions take various forms, such as the nature of Jesus' spiritual body, but most scholars are willing to admit that the disciples saw visions of Jesus. Then Pannenberg goes on to say that hallucinations or other alternate naturalistic theories are not acceptable.[86]

Dr. Flew states that we can't tell what happened back then, that it's too obscure or cloudy. But that's exactly the purpose of my recitation of the core historical facts, exactly the purpose. Probably the reason he says we can't tell is because he doesn't have a naturalistic theory to propose. In other words, all the historical facts we do have, and that scholars agree on, support the literal Resurrection of Jesus.

Now I would like to talk further about the hallucination theory, Refutation of alternative explanation which Dr. Flew hinted at twice. Perhaps in our head-to-head discussion he will tell me about the hallucination theory. He also said, however, that he wouldn't give me a naturalistic theory. I think the reason he says we can't know what happened is because he doesn't have a concrete theory to propose. Again, he's got to come to grips with the case of the early eyewitness testimony given right after the Crucifixion by the men who said they saw the risen Jesus. Now if one doesn't believe they saw him, we're going to have to come up with some other explanation.

Further, Dr. Flew said that this case isn't even good enough for psychic research. Well, as far as I know, the research on the Shroud of Turin was more thorough than any research done on any single event in psychic studies. The shroud may not have warranted a mention in the psychic research annals, but it warranted probably the most intense investigation of any archaeological artifact in modern history.

Dr. Flew agreed in his initial paper that Hume is wrong in his essay on miracles, but he wants to update Hume. That, however, was just my point. I pointed out that Hume, even as updated by Dr. Flew, is mistaken and for practically the same reasons. I don't think he's answered my five objections to this updated Humean position.

One more point about G. A. Wells. Dr. Flew came from the Use of reluctant testimony University of Michigan not too long ago. Dr. Wells was there and he presented his radical thesis that maybe Jesus never existed. Virtually nobody holds this position today. It was reported that Dr. Morton Smith of Columbia University, even though he is a skeptic himself, responded that Dr. Wells's view was "absurd."[87]

Let me say in closing that I've been attempting to get Dr. Flew to deal directly with the evidence for Jesus' Resurrection. I don't think he has done so. All he's said so far is that we can't tell what happened. Please notice, he's not dealt with the four kinds of evidence I've presented. I believe he has generally sidestepped them, yet in one of his essays on miracles, he admits my point when he asserts that "Our only way of determining the capacities and incapacities of nature is to study what does in fact occur."[88] I agree with you, Dr. Flew; we need to look at nature and see what does in fact occur. I've given you four sets of arguments for the Resurrection, and you haven't addressed yourself to the evidence. You say, "We don't need to, we can't get back to the original testimony." But we can.

Even after admitting that we need to study the original event, Dr. Flew further laments in this same essay that "To come closely to grips with the evidence available in particular cases would unfortunately carry us well beyond the limits of both length and subject specified in the present series."[89] In other words, "We need to look at the events, but I'm sorry, I don't have time here. We need to look at the facts that happen in nature, but I can't do it in this essay." But as far as I'm aware (although I may be wrong), he has not dealt with the evidence for the Resurrection in any of his published material on miracles. So my point is that he says we need to look at it, and then I don't think that he ever does.

Use of source proposition imbalance

In one work, however, he does take at least a brief look at the Resurrection. He mentions M. C. Perry's book, *The Easter Enigma*, and his reaction is interesting. I was surprised when Dr. Flew treated this book by M. C. Perry in a positive way, terming some of Perry's ideas "methodologically sound." And later he compliments Perry on his reasonableness.[90] The reason for my surprise at these compliments is that Perry advocates an actual Resurrection of Jesus' glorified body and he supports the notion of life after death. Dr. Flew says that Perry's theory is not actually miraculous, but the prototype for Perry's model, developed in the late nineteenth century by Theodor Keim, was admittedly miraculous.[91] But regardless of the miraculous element, we must note here that Dr. Flew has given some praise to a book that declares that Jesus actually was raised, spiritually and literally, and that life after death is a reality. Although my view differs from Perry's, it would appear that complimenting a theory of Jesus' literal though spiritual Resurrection would be a major point for my thesis tonight.

HEAD-TO-HEAD
Habermas-Flew

HABERMAS: I think we're supposed to fight it out.

FLEW: I'll start then. About the Resurrection and the whole story becoming more probable with the Belief in God, and not just a belief that the universe had a beginning by, was produced by, some sort of power. Surely, to make any account of the supposed Easter events more probable, you've got to have a much richer notion of God than as just a Creator, you've got to have some of the elements that I gave in that quotation from Cardinal Newman. You've got to have some reason for believing he's going to want to produce an intelligible revelation, and presumably Newman was taking for granted the Old Testament story of the chosen people and the Messiah, and therefore thinking that he was in the position, in thinking of this matter, of a Jew contemporary with Jesus who was wondering whether Jesus was the Messiah.

Questioning to establish premises

HABERMAS: I have no problem there, and, as I said, I don't want to pursue evidence for God. But I agree with you. Something more substantial than a mere belief in God's existence has to be there, but I would say that we can argue for coherence with regards to the Resurrection. Let's introduce a hypothetical situation here. A naturalist is arguing with a theist about the Resurrection, and the theist pushes the naturalist and the naturalist comes to admit that, indeed, the Resurrection is a historical event. At that point, would the naturalist have to be at least open to the theist's claims that Jesus is deity and that he speaks authoritatively from God?

FLEW: Yes, that seems to be clear.

HABERMAS: So this is a legitimate argument and the naturalist would have to be open to Jesus' claims?

FLEW: I don't know what he's going to do next. But yes, you've put it rather nicely. You'd have to be open to it. What would happen next, I don't know. But clearly there would have to be some ears opened to some radical new thinking.

HABERMAS: You mean new thinking on the part of the naturalist.

FLEW: Yes, but where the radical new thinking would go, heaven knows.

HABERMAS: Dr. Flew, twice you made quick references to hallucinations.

FLEW: Yes.

HABERMAS: So you might say that the disciples (or Paul) saw something that was not objectively present. The hallucination theory was popular about one hundred years ago, and it was ruled out later. It suffered from a number of shortcomings. In the Miracles class that I teach, which is substantially on the Resurrection, I produce twenty-two refutations of the hallucination theory. Now these are of varying importance and strength. But one point I want to make is that hallucinations are private events observed by one person alone. Two people cannot see the same hallucination, let alone eleven. If eleven people saw Jesus on one occasion, few contemporary scholars would argue that it was a hallucination. That theory has been thoroughly critiqued.

Questioning to set up refutation

Let me say a couple other things concerning the various circumstances of the Resurrection appearances of Jesus. There are too many different times, places, and people involved for the hallucination theory to be valid, and psychological preconditions are lacking. If I can quote from a clinical psychologist here, I'll see if you still want to push the hallucination theory. Let me quote from a well-published psychologist, who says,

> Hallucinations are individual occurrences. By their very nature only one person can see a given hallucination at a time. They certainly are not something which can be seen by a group of people. Neither is it possible that one person could somehow induce an hallucination in somebody else. Since an hallucination exists only in this subjective, personal sense, it is obvious that others cannot witness it.[92]

And this scholar concludes by saying, "For anyone to prove [that the disciples saw hallucinations of the risen Jesus] they would have to go against much of the current psychiatric and psychological data about the nature of hallucinations."[93] Now because you proposed the hallucination theory, let me remind you that you did the same in Dallas when we met three months ago. I replied then that two people couldn't see the same hallucination. You responded that I was correct and that was the end of that discussion. I wonder why you brought it back up again tonight and if you want to pursue it?

Questions and answers of clarification

FLEW: I was only offering this suggestion in the case of Paul, which is the appearance story for which we have the best evidence, which is the statement of the subject himself made not long after the conversion experience in question. It seems to me that Paul is not claiming that he was actually seeing something that would have been visible to anyone else that happened to be there. He was claiming that he had a vision of Jesus with his spiritual body. And I take it that an incorruptible, spiritual body would not normally be visible. He doesn't say it was visible to other people, does he?

HABERMAS: I don't know how you can argue . . .

FLEW: Because if it were visible to other people, there would have been more than one person who saw the appearance on the road to Damascus.

HABERMAS: I don't know how you can ignore the other events surrounding Jesus' appearance to Paul, when the texts provide additional details. And in those instances, although we don't know exactly what his companions saw, we are told that they did see the light and did hear some sounds, although they were not able to comprehend the message. But you also said that Paul's account is early, so he offers the best evidence. But the creed reports the testimony of the disciples before Paul's experience even occurred. So if you're going to grant me early evidence for Paul's appearance, what do we say about the disciples?

FLEW: Of course, of course, the claim, the crucial claim that Jesus was resurrected was part of the doctrine of Christian communities presumably before Paul wrote to one of them in I Corinthians. That's not in dispute. What is in dispute is whether this creed contains stories of the Resurrection appearances. Because modern creeds certainly don't contain more than He rose on the third day, and so on.

HABERMAS: Starting with verse 5 of I Corinthians 15, we have a number of appearances recorded in the creed, and Cephas (Peter) starts the list off. And I think that most New Testament scholars who have pursued the subject have concluded that Paul received this list from Peter and James in Jerusalem on his first visit to the city. By the way, there's an alternative theory, which says he received the creed in Damascus. That would place it even earlier than the Jerusalem date.

FLEW: Yes, but he got this story about the appearances to other people and then he rather oddly discovered that this appearance to him on the road to Damascus was the last one. He got the story, but that isn't the same thing as getting the creed. Now I'm not disputing that there was some sort of creed that all the first members of the Christian churches adhered to, but if it was anything like the Nicene Creed, say, it wouldn't have contained evidence for the Resurrection in the shape of so-and-so and so-and-so saw the resurrected Jesus. If something like this was kicking around, it would have been in something else other than the creed.

HABERMAS: But this early creed *did* report eyewitness appearances to the risen Jesus. Starting with verse 5, it mentions Peter and goes through a half-dozen appearances, ending with Paul. At least some appearances are included in the creed. So let me ask you, do you believe that the original disciples saw hallucinations? You have said you were referring only to Paul.

FLEW: Ah, well, what I don't believe is that there were collective hallucinations where the twelve saw it all at once.

HABERMAS: So you don't believe that the disciples saw collective hallucinations.

FLEW: I don't believe that there was anyone necessarily at the time who claimed that. You know, you keep talking about the whole situation as if the Gospels contained material that the authors were supposed to be telling you now and you were in Jerusalem at the time, you were hearing from these chaps in Jerusalem at the time, and you know it happened down there. And then you say that, oh well, they're saying that Jesus said this, and you take it that Jesus said the things that years afterward they said he said in Jerusalem at the time.

HABERMAS: But I'm not talking about a period of years afterward. I'm only talking about the Resurrection appearances that the disciples reported and handed down to Paul. I also mentioned that Luke 24:34 records an appearance to Peter, a report that is as early as the Pauline creed.[94] Now if Paul got his creed from the eyewitnesses, and the eyewitnesses claim to have seen Jesus, yet you don't believe that the disciples saw hallucinations, then what did happen? What naturalistic theory accounts for the disciples' experiences?

FLEW: Here we have the earliest written document about appearances, and two things in it are inconsistent with what appears in the Gospels. Why didn't the writers of the Gospels report the appearance to the five hundred? Supposing you wanted to tell me about the appearance to five hundred as a thing that couldn't be accounted for by a collective hallucination. Now, wouldn't the Gospel writers, if they were familiar with this story and believed it was true, have brought this into the Gospels?

HABERMAS: The Gospel of Matthew does say that Jesus appeared on a hillside. More may have been there than just the eleven disciples. Besides, I never mentioned the five hundred. I don't think I brought them up once. I still want to base the case on the eleven disciples, who claimed they saw the risen Jesus. Let me paraphrase Rudolf Bultmann who, in his influential 1941 essay "New Testament and Mythology," said that history can prove that the earliest disciples believed that they saw the risen Jesus.[95]

FLEW: Ah.

HABERMAS: Now, what do we do if these were not hallucinations? What were they?

FLEW: They believed they saw him. Now, this is a very different thing from saying that they claimed as a group, "I say, we've all seen the risen Jesus, all of us together." What we've got is the claim that they had all seen him. That's not the claim they'd all seen him on the same occasion.

HABERMAS: But the group appearance to the disciples is recorded in the creed. I Corinthians 15:5 says that Jesus first appeared to Peter, then to the twelve disciples. I repeat Jesus appeared to the twelve. That's the second appearance recorded, and it provides just what you are asking. Now, you have already granted to me that this is an early report and you've already granted that Paul is a good source, but this is even earlier for the other eyewitnesses. And it does say that he appeared to the twelve. This list also includes an appearance "to all of the apostles" (I Cor. 15:7). So we have two separate appearances, to the twelve and to the apostles. So that's in the creed, it's eyewitness testimony, and it dates back to the time of the Crucifixion.

FLEW: Wait a minute, eyewitness testimony. There's a statement in Paul that there was a collective appearance to the twelve apostles, but we haven't got the testimony directly of even one of the twelve. What we have is a statement from Paul that this happened to those twelve other people, and that is very different.

HABERMAS: Let me respond to that in two ways. First of all, Paul received the list from Peter and James, according to the majority of testimony today in New Testament scholarship. He received it from them, so at least Peter is saying that he and the other ten disciples collectively saw the risen Jesus. I additionally made the point in my initial essay that in I Corinthians 15:11, 14, and 15,

Paul states that the message that he was proclaiming was the same as that proclaimed by the apostles. So Paul states that the disciples and he were preaching the same thing about the resurrected Jesus. Paul is not relating circumstantial material; in fact, the creed is not his material at all, as Paul clearly states in verse 3. The creed is an eyewitness report given to Paul, in all likelihood, by persons who saw Jesus.

Second, although many critical scholars today would not grant that the Gospels were written by eyewitnesses such as the disciples, many scholars find a large amount of eyewitness testimony behind the Gospels. For example, Raymond Brown, in writing a major commentary on perhaps the most disputed of the four Gospels, John, concludes that the Apostle John is the chief contributor to the historical tradition behind the Gospel.[96] In the Gospel of John we have two chapters giving evidence concerning the appearances of the risen Jesus. I also mentioned in my opening essay that C. H. Dodd, in an interesting essay on form critical studies, concluded that there are a number of early testimonies in the Gospel accounts of the Resurrection. So when you say we don't have any eyewitness testimony in the Gospels you're going to have to argue with eminent scholars such as Raymond Brown and C. H. Dodd. And concerning the creed, many scholars who are not in my camp say that the earliest eyewitnesses reported the Resurrection appearances of Jesus. In fact, in a famous debate between Bultmann and Barth, Barth said that we ought not to ask for evidence for the Resurrection; we should believe on faith alone. But Bultmann replied that although he agreed with Barth that we don't need evidence for faith (they're both Kierkegaardians), it's clear that Paul was attempting to give evidence for Jesus' Resurrection by citing the list of appearances in I Corinthians 15:5–7. You can check that in volume I of *Theology of the New Testament* by Rudolf Biltmann.[97] Again, I'm citing people who don't always agree with me, but who say that my thesis is sound as far as the original disciples reporting that they saw appearances of the risen Jesus. You've already told me that you don't think that this testimony is accounted for by collective hallucinations, but that we don't have the testimony of the disciples that they saw Jesus collectively. But we do have such testimony. They gave the creed to Paul, and then Paul added that the apostles preached the same Resurrection that he did. And we additionally have eyewitness testimony, including just such group appearances reported in the Gospels.

FLEW: Yes, there's plenty of room in this period, slips on what are fairly small things. The difference between claiming that several people had visions of the risen Jesus and claiming that they all simultaneously had the same one is the sort of difference that we agree is important. It is not clear that the people at the time would have seen this as important, is it?

HABERMAS: It appears to me that I have already clearly answered your question. You said a while ago that we don't have the disciples' testimony about the appearances. I pointed out that we did. You then said that the creed didn't report any collective experiences, and I responded that the creed reports the appearance to the twelve. And you're still saying that we don't know if the visions were simultaneous. Well, the creed states that Jesus appeared to the twelve and to all of the apostles. This is an eyewitness report of appearances of the risen Jesus to the twelve simultaneously.

FLEW: I mean I don't think we have the testimony of the disciples. What we have is Paul saying that two of the disciples told him something about them and the others. This is very different from having an account from the people themselves.

HABERMAS: Well, no, the evidence shows that Paul got it from the eyewitnesses themselves. And I don't think that virtually any scholars doubt that I Corinthians is the work of Paul. Paul took great care to interview the apostles personally in order to ascertain the nature of the Gospel, which includes the Resurrection (Gal. 1:18–20; 2:1–10). It is quite unlikely that Paul was completely wrong in this reported creed, especially since he so carefully checked out its content and indicated that the Resurrection was the central truth of the Christian faith. So even if Paul simply recorded the testimony of eyewitnesses, most likely Peter and James, then we've still got some strong and early eyewitness testimony. But as I said in my initial paper, this creedal material is not Paul's. It is an early eyewitness report, which is what you are requesting.

FLEW: He takes it that they had visions.

HABERMAS: No, they told him that they saw the risen Jesus.

FLEW: They told him that they saw the risen Jesus.

HABERMAS: Yes. "They" are the eyewitnesses. And second, we have some eyewitness testimony from the Gospels

FLEW: But what is to be understood in Paul, presumably, is that they had the same sort of experience as he is claiming to have had. You see, he makes this claim, which doesn't involve physical contact. This is the claim that we'll refer to Shakespeare's Macbeth, "Is this a dagger which I see before me, its handle toward mine hand?" And then there is a test as to whether it's hallucinatory experience or an actual dagger. "Come, let me clutch thee." Now Paul is taking it that it's an important vision in the way it's caused. But that his experience was like that. I think what is significant is that

Paul puts his own experience, which is definitely not the sort of claim that's made about doubting Thomas, in the group of the others. Now you want to construe the others as being in the doubting Thomas category and leave Paul's which he regards as being the same as all the others.

HABERMAS: You'd have to show me that Paul claimed that his appearance was of the same nature as that of the disciples. I don't think Paul said that. Paul said that his appearance came later.

FLEW: Yes, one born out of due time.

HABERMAS: Right, one born out of due time. He said the appearance to him was not at the same time as the appearance to them. He used the Greek word *horao*. It was an old critical habit to say that the word *horao* was utilized for "spiritual vision," and therefore Paul had said that the appearances to the disciples were the same as the appearance to him. Today that argument is not repeated as often, because the word *horao* means not only "bodily appearance" more frequently than it does "spiritual appearance" in the New Testament, but second, *horao* is the same Greek word that Luke uses when in his account Jesus tells the disciples to touch him because he is not a ghost (Luke 24:39). So you have to prove that Paul is saying that Jesus appeared to him in the same manner that he appeared to the disciples. I don't see that anywhere in Paul. I think Paul was arguing that Jesus literally appeared to him, period. I don't think Paul answers the question of whether he could touch Jesus or whether he saw him eat. Paul just ignores those issues.

FLEW: This is all in the context of those puzzling paragraphs about corruption putting on incorruption and how wrong it is to take the Resurrection body as being an ordinary body. Now it doesn't seem to me that someone who is going to say all that would say all that without also saying that what he saw was not like this but something substantially different from this. He's going to say all these things about corruption and incorruption.

HABERMAS: But the Gospel testimony is not that Jesus came back in the same corruptible body with the same limitations. As I mentioned briefly in my initial paper, the Gospels and Paul agree on an important fact: the resurrected Jesus had a new spiritual body. The Gospels never present Jesus walking out of the tomb. The Resurrection, per se, is never recorded in the Gospels, only the Resurrection appearances. When the stone is rolled away, Jesus does not walk out the way he does in the apocryphal literature. He's already gone, so he presumably exited through rock. Later he appears in buildings and then he disappears at will. The Gospels are clearly saying that Jesus was raised in a spiritual body. It was his real body, but it was changed, including new, spiritual qualities. And again, Paul uses the word *horao*, the same Greek word used by Luke. I was referring earlier to a book by A. N. Sherwin-White, published by Oxford University Press, and Dr. Flew told me during the break that he studied under Sherwin-White.

FLEW: My old Ancient History tutor, yes.

HABERMAS: Well, Sherwin-White asserts that the Book of Acts is virtually unquestioned by Roman historians, even in its details. He points out that its historicity has been confirmed.[98] And Acts is the same book that records the Resurrection appearance to Paul. And the appearances to the disciples begin volume two of the Gospel of Luke. But Luke has no problem recording both the bodily appearances of Jesus and the appearance to Paul. Luke, the companion of Paul (as indicated by such signs as the "we" passages from Acts) relates the appearance to the disciples in the Gospel and Acts I as well as Paul's appearance in Acts. But I don't think you're going to be able to report many details about the Resurrection appearance to Paul unless you use the Book of Acts. And the Book of Acts was written by the man who wrote Luke, who had no problem teaching both the seemingly more substantial appearances of Jesus in the Gospels and the appearance to Paul on the road to Damascus. And we have reason to think that Acts is a good historical text.

Use of source-proposition imbalance

FLEW: Yes, but anyone who believes that their visionary experience has been caused in a special way is, of course, going to use the word *see* without quotes around it. But that's not going to mean that the actual experience as described by someone who does not share that person's causal interpretation will be different from the experience of the person seeing it. Think of the Bernadette case, you see where all the dispute within the Catholic church came after, I think, a bad start in which they wrongly questioned the honesty of Bernadette herself. All the dispute was not about the internal nature of the experience, but whether it had been spiritually caused; and I take it that no one was wanting to suggest that if the television cameras had been hiding behind, they would have gotten a picture of anything other than Bernadette.

HABERMAS: Virtually all scholars recognize that the eyewitnesses claimed to have literally seen the risen Jesus—not that they were expressing some spiritual conviction. And you brought up Bernadette again, but I don't think there's any comparison between that case and Jesus' Resurrection. I think the historical evidence for the resurrection is much more substantial, but let me give you an example.

FLEW: But we've got Bernadette! We had the girl going back telling the village that right after the experience, for heaven's sake. We don't have someone some years later saying, "Bernadette told me...."

HABERMAS: Neither was the disciples' report years later. And we do have eyewitness reports of the risen Jesus. But unlike the Bernadette case, the disciples died for their message, and no naturalistic theories have explained away their report. At other points the evidence for Jesus' Resurrection is also stronger, such as the fact that the appearances to the disciples were collective.[99]

NOTES

1.   David Hume, *Enquiries Concerning Human Understanding and Concerning the Principles of Morals*, 3rd ed., ed. L. A. Selby-Bigge (Oxford: Clarendon, 1975), 127.
2.   C. S. Lewis, *Miracles*, (New York: Macmillan, 1947).
3.   See Antony G. N. Flew, "Miracles & Methodology" in *Hume's Philosophy of Belief* (London: Routledge and Kegan Paul, 1961).
4.   John Henry Cardinal Newman, "Essay on the Miracles Recorded in Ecclesiastical History," in *The Ecclesiastical History of M. L'Abbe Fleury* (Oxford: J. H. Parker, 1842), II (viii) 2, 146.
5.   David Hume, *An Enquiry Concerning Human Understanding*, section 10.
6.   I make a distinction here between miracles and miracle-claims because demonstrating the former involves God's actual existence and is hence beyond the agreed scope of this debate. For an apologetic that argues from Jesus' Resurrection to God's existence and theology, see Gary R. Habermas, *The Resurrection of Jesus: An Apologetic* (Grand Rapids, MI: Baker Book House, 1980; Lanham, MD: University Press of America, 1984).
7.   Patrick Nowell-Smith, "Miracles," in *New Essays in Philosophical Theology*, eds. Antony Flew and Alasdair MacIntyre (New York: Macmillan, 1955), 251–253.
8.   *The Encyclopedia of Philosophy*, s.v. "miracles," Antony Flew, 350, 352.
9.   George Chryssides, "Miracles and Agents," *Religious Studies II* (September 1975): 319–327.
10.   For instances, see Antony Flew, *Hume's Philosophy of Belief* (London: Routledge and Kegan Paul, 1961), 193, 201; David Basinger, "Christian Theism and the Concept of Miracle: Some Epistemological Perplexities," *The Southern Journal of Philosophy* 28 (Summer 1980): 137–150.
11.   Alasdair McKinnon, " 'Miracle' and 'Paradox'," *American Philosophical Quarterly* 4 (1967): 309, for instance.
12.   Guy Robinson, "Miracles," *Ratio* 9 (December 1967): 155–166.
13.   Malcolm Diamond, "Miracles," *Religious Studies* 9 (September 1973): 320–321.
14.   *Encyclopedia of Philosophy*, s.v. "miracles," Flew, 347; s.v. Flew, 202.
15.   Norman Geisler, *Christian Apologetics* (Grand Rapids, MI: Baker Book House, 1976), 269.
16.   C. S. Lewis, *Miracles* (New York: Macmillan, 1947), 105.

17. Stephen T. Davis, "Is It Possible to Know That Jesus Was Raised From the Dead?" *Faith and Philosophy* I (April 1984): 148–150.

18. Lewis, *Miracles, 106.*

19. Werner Schaaffs, *Theology, Physics and Miracles,* trans. Richard Renfield (Washington, D.C.: Canon Press, 1974), 55, 65, for instance.

20. Richard Swinburne, *The Concept of Miracles* (New York: Macmillan and St. Martin, 1970), 2–3.

21. Schaaffs, *Theology, Physics and Miracles,* 66.

22. Swinburne, *The Concept of Miracles,* 27–28.

23. For some similar ideas, see David Elton Trueblood, *Philosophy of Religion* (New York: Harper & Brothers, 1957), 195–202.

24. It is impossible in the scope of this essay to deal with each of these naturalistic theories and their refutations. For details, see Gary Habermas, *The Resurrection of Jesus: A Rational Inquiry* (Ann Arbor, MI: University Microfilms, 1976), especially 114–171.

25. Albert Schweitzer, *The Quest of the Historical Jesus,* trans. W. Montgomery (New York: Macmillan, 1968), 21–23.

26. David Strauss, *A New Life of Jesus,* vol. 1 (London: Williams and Norgate, 1879), 412; see also Albert Schweitzer's assertion that Strauss administered the death blow to such rationalistic thought, Schweitzer, *Quest of Jesus,* 56.

27. Friedrich Schleiermacher, *The Christian Faith,* vol. 2, ed. H. R. Mackintoch and J. S. Stewart (New York: Harper & Row, 1963), 420; Schweitzer, *Quest of Jesus,* 54–55; 211–214. James Orr, *The Resurrection of Jesus* (Grand Rapids, MI: Zondervan, 1965), 219.

28. Otto Pfleiderer, *Early Christian Concepts of Christ* (London: Williams and Norgate, 1905), 152–159.

29. Karl Barth, *The Doctrine of Reconciliation,* vol. 4, part 1 of *Church Dogmatics,* eds. G. W. Bromiley and T. F. Torrance (Edinburgh, Scotland: T. and T. Clark, 1956), 340.

30. Raymond Brown, "The Resurrection and Biblical Criticism," *Commonweal* 87 (November 24, 1967): especially 233.

31. Paul Tillich, *Systematic Theology,* vol. 2 (Chicago: University of Chicago Press, 1971), especially 156.

32. Wolfhart Pannenberg, *Jesus—God and Man,* trans. Lewis L. Wilkens and Duane Priebe (Philadelphia: Westminster Press, 1968), 88–97.

33. Gunther Bornkamm, *Jesus of Nazareth,* trans. Irene and Fraser McLuskey with James M. Robinson (New York: Harper & Row, 1960), 181–185.

34. Ulrich Wilckens, *Resurrection,* trans. A. M. Stewart (Edinburgh, Scotland: Saint Andrews Press, 1977), 117–119.

35. John A. T. Robinson, *Can We Trust the New Testament?* (Grand Rapids, MI: Eerdmans, 1977), 123–125.

36. A. M. Hunter, *Bible and Gospel* (Philadelphia: Westminster Press, 1969), 111.

37. Fuller, *The Formation of the Resurrection Narratives* (New York: Macmillan, 1971), 37.

38. *Ibid.,* 37, 46–47.

39. As mentioned earlier, this is, with the exception of the empty tomb, accepted by many recent scholars as historical. See Robert H. Stein, "Was

the Tomb Really Empty?" *Journal of the Evangelical Theological Society* 20:1 (March 1977): 23–29.

40. This does not even include the experience of the more than five hundred people who claimed to have seen the risen Jesus and concerning whom Paul asserted that most were still alive and therefore could be questioned.

41. Fuller, *Resurrection Narratives*, 169; cf. Robinson, "Miracles," 124–125.

42. See especially Joachim Jeremias, *The Eucharistic Words of Jesus*, trans. Norman Perrin (London: SCM Press, 1966), 101–103; Fuller, *Resurrection Narratives*, Chapter Two, among others.

43. Oscar Cullmann, *The Early Church*, ed. A. J. B. Higgins (Philadelphia: Westminster Press, 1966), 65–66; C. H. Dodd, *The Apostolic Preaching and Its Developments* (Grand Rapids, MI: Baker Book House, 1980), 16; Raymond Brown, *The Virginal Conception and Bodily Resurrection of Jesus* (New York: Paulist Press, 1973), 81; George E. Ladd, *I Believe in the Resurrection of Jesus* (Grand Rapids, MI: Eerdmans, 1975), 142, 161; Gerald O'Collins, *What Are They Saying About the Resurrection?* (New York: Paulist Press, 1978), 112.

44. Fuller, *Resurrection Narratives*, 48.

45. A. M. Hunter, *Jesus: Lord and Saviour* (Grand Rapids, MI: Eerdmans, 1976), 100.

46. Pannenberg, *Jesus—God and Man*, 90.

47. Carl Braaten, *History and Hermeneutics*, vol. 2 of *New Directions in Theology Today*, ed. William Hordern (Philadelphia: Westminster Press, 1966), 78.

48. See Acts 9:1–7, 22:5–11, and 26:12–18; I Corinthians 9:1, 15:8.

49. For instance, Jeremias, *The Eucharistic Words of Jesus*, 306; Rudolf Bultmann, *Theology of the New Testament*, vol. 1, trans. Kendrick Grobel (New York: Scribner, 1951, 1955), 45; Brown, *Virginal Conception*, 93.

50. C. H. Dodd, "The Appearances of the Risen Christ: An Essay in Form-Criticism of the Gosepls," in *More New Testament Studies* (Grand Rapids, MI: Eerdmans, 1968).

51. Gary R. Habermas, "Jesus' Resurrection and Contemporary Criticism: An Apologetic" (Paper delivered at the Evangelical Philosophical Society national meeting, Essex Falls, New Jersey, December 16, 1982). Cf. O'Collins, "Models of the Resurrection" in *What Are They Saying?*

52. Brown, "The Resurrection and Biblical Criticism," 235–236.

53. For a sampling of those who accept the historicity of these facts, see Bultmann, *Theology of the New Testament*, 44–45; Paul Tillich, *Systematic Theology*, 153–158; Bornkamm, *Jesus*, 179–186; Wilckens, *Resurrection*, 112–113; Fuller, *Resurrection Narratives*, 27–49; Pannenberg, *Jesus—God and Man*, 88–106; Brown, *The Virginal Conception*, 81–92; Jurgen Motlmann, *Theology of Hope*, trans. James W. Leitch (New York: Harper & Row, 1967), 197–202; Hunter, *Jesus: Lord and Saviour*, 98–103; Norman Perrin, *The Resurrection According to Matthew, Mark and Luke* (Philadelphia: Fortress Press, 1977), 78–84; Paul Van Buren, *The Secular Meaning of the Gospel* (New York: Macmillan, 1963), 126–134.

54. Michael Grant, *Jesus: An Historian's Review of the Gospels* (New York: Scribner, 1977), especially 176.

55. Braaten, *History and Hermeneutics*, 78.

56. See Gary R. Habermas, "Primary Sources: Creeds and Facts" in *Ancient*

Evidence for the Life of Jesus: Historical Records of His Death and Resurrection (Nashville: Nelson, 1984) for this argument in expanded form, including support of these facts.

57. *Ibid.* Expansions of these critiques and many additional ones gathered from the accepted historical facts with regard to these and other such theories cannot be presented here. For a more complete treatment, see Habermas, *The Resurrection of Jesus: A Rational Inquiry*, 114–171.

58. The additional accepted facts enumerated earlier provide other significant arguments for this event, such as the other six evidences previously listed.

59. See Habermas, *Ancient Evidence for the Life of Jesus*, 129–132.

60. For details, see Kenneth E. Stevenson and Gary R. Habermas, *Verdict on the Shroud: Evidence for the Death and Resurrection of Jesus* (Ann Arbor, MI: Servant Books, 1981; Wayne, PA: Dell, 1982); John Heller, *Report on the Shroud of Turin* (Boston: Houghton Mifflin, 1983).

61. See Stevenson and Habermas, "The Shroud and History" in *Verdict on the Shroud*.

62. *Ibid.*, "The Man Buried in the Shroud" and "Is It Jesus?" Cf. Vincent J. Donovan, "The Shroud and the Laws of Probability," *The Catholic Digest* (April 1980): 49–52.

63. Steven D. Schafersman, "Science, The Public, and the Shroud of Turin," *The Skeptical Inquirer* 6 (Spring 1982): 41.

64. Shroud of Turin Research Project (STRP), "Text," New London, CT (October 1981), 1.

65. See Stevenson ad Habermas, "Science and the Shroud" in *Verdict on the Shroud*.

66. *Ibid.*, "The Resurrection of Jesus: New Evidence." Stevenson and I do not presume to speak for others in our conclusions.

67. Antony G. N. Flew, personal correspondence with Terry L. Miethe, April 1, 1985.

68. Rudolf Bultmann, *Theology of the New Testament*, vol. 1, trans. Kendrick Grobel (New York: Scribner, 1951, 1955) especially 7–9.

69. Oscar Cullmann, *The Christology of the New Testament*, trans. Shirley C. Guthrie and Charles A. M. Hall (Philadelphia: Westminster Press, 1963); Raymond Brown, *Jesus—God and Man* (Milwaukee: Bruce, 1967); Wolfhart Pannenberg, *Jesus—God and Man,* trans. Lewis L. Wilkins and Duane A. Priebe (Philadelphia: Westminster Press, 1968).

70. Joachim Jeremias, *The Central Message of the New Testament* (Philadelphia: Fortress Press, 1965), 9–30.

71. Reginald H. Fuller, *The Foundations of the New Testament Christology* (New York: Scribner, 1965), 105–106; Bultmann, *Theology of the New Testament*, vol. 1, 7–9.

72. Cullmann, *Christology of the New Testament*, 282.

73. A. N. Sherwin-White, *Roman Society and Roman Law in the New Testament* (London: Oxford University Press, 1963; Grand Rapids, MI: Baker Book House, 1978), 162–171.

74. F. F. Bruce, *Jesus and Christian Origins Outside the New Testament* (Grand Rapids, MI: Eerdmans, 1974), 192–194.

75. Martin Hengel, *The Atonement*, trans. John Bowden (Philadelphia: Fortress Press, 1981); Cullmann, *Christology of the New Testament*, 282.

76. Frederick Aston, *The Challenge of the Ages*, 16th ed., rev., published by the author in Scarsdale, NY in 1962 and containing a preface by Robert H. Pfeiffer.

77. Edwin Yamauchi, *Jesus, Zoroaster, Socrates, Buddha, Muhammed* (Downers Grove, IL: Inter Varsity Press, 1974), 40.

78. In a debate entitled "The Historical Foundation of Christianity," Howard Kee and Robert M. Price argued for the skeptical position against conservatives Earl Ellis and R. T. France. The dialogue took place at the Dallas Hilton, Dallas, TX on February 9, 1985.

79. Cf. Bultmann, *Theology of the New Testament*, 129; Fuller, *Foundations of New Testament Christology*, 208, 248–249, for instances; Brown, *Jesus—God and Man*, "Does the New Testament Call Jesus God?"

80. See Gary R. Habermas, *The Resurrection of Jesus: An Apologetic* (Grand Rapids, MI: Baker Book House, 1980), "The Existence of God" and "The Person and Teachings of Christ."

81. Hume, *An Enquiry Concerning Human Understanding*, section 10, "Of Miracles," Part I.

82. See especially Wolfhart Pannenberg, ed. *Revelations as History*, trans. David Granskou (New York: Macmillan, 1968).

83. G. A. Wells, *Did Jesus Exist?* (Buffalo: Prometheus Books, 1975).

84. Fuller, *The Foundation of the Resurrection Narratives* (New York: Macmillan, 1971), "The Earliest Easter Traditions."

85. For example, Wolfhart Pannenberg, "A Dialogue on Christ's Resurrection," *Christianity Today* 12 (April 12, 1968): 5–12.

86. Pannenberg, *Jesus—God and Man*, 88–106.

87. Kate DeSmet, "Biblical Accounts of Jesus' Divinity Debated by Scholars," *Detroit News*, 20 April 1985 sec. A, Religion page.

88. Antony Flew, "The Credentials of Revelation: Miracle and History," in his *God and Philosophy* (New York: Dell, 1966), 149.

89. *Ibid.*, 154.

90. *Ibid.*, 155–156.

91. For details of Keim's view, published in 1872, see W. J. Sparrow-Simpson, *The Resurrection and the Christian Faith* (1911; reprint, Grand Rapids, MI: Zondervan, 1968), 110–20. Cf. Albert Schweitzer, *The Quest of the Historical Jesus*, trans. by W. Montgomery (New York: Macmillan), 210–214.

92. Gary R. Collins, personal correspondence with myself, February 21, 1977.

93. *Ibid.* Cf. J. P. Brady, "The veridicality of Hypnotic, Visual Hallucinations," in Wolfram Keup, *Origin and Mechanisms of Hallucinations* (New York: Plenum Press, 1970), 181; Weston La Barre, "Anthropological Perspectives on Hallucination and Hallucinogens," in *Hallucinations: Behavior, Experience and Theory*, ed. R. K. Siegel and L. J. West (New York: John Wiley & Sons, 1975), 9–10.

94. See the reports of Jeremias, Bultmann, and Brown in footnote 45 that follows my debate presentation.

95. Rudolf Bultmann, "New Testament and Mythology," rev. trans. Reginald H. Fuller, in *Kerygma and Myth*, ed. Hans Werner Baitsch (New York: Harper & Row, 1961), 42.

96. Raymond E. Brown, *The Gospel According to John*, vol. 1 (Garden City, NY: Doubleday, 1966), 87–104.

97. Rudolf Bultmann, *Theology of the New Testament,* vol. 1, trans. Kendrick Grobel (New York: Scribner, 1951, 1955), 295.

98. A. N. Sherwin-White, *Roman Society and Roman Law in the New Testament* (London: Oxford University Press, 1963; Grand Rapids, MI: Baker Book House, 1978), 189.

99. Excerpt from *Did Jesus Rise from the Dead* by Gary R. Habermas and Terry L. Mieth. Copyright © 1987 by Gary R. Habermas and Terry L. Mieth. Reprinted by permission of Harper & Row, Publishers, Inc.

GLOSSARY OF TERMS IN ARGUMENTATION

ABSOLUTIST: An ethical absolutist maintains that there are universal standards of good and bad, right and wrong.

ADVOCATE: An advocate is a person supporting one side of an argumentative dispute.

AFFIRMATIVE: The affirmative is one side of the proposition. The affirmative advocate shoulders the burden of proof by providing sufficient reason to overcome presumption.

ARGUMENT$_1$: Argument$_1$ is something one person makes (or gives or presents or utters). It is thus on a par with promises, commands, apologies, warnings, invitations, orders, and the like. Argument$_1$ is defined as a piece of reasoning in which one or more statements are offered as support for some other statement.

ARGUMENT$_2$: Argument$_2$ is something two or more persons have (or engage in). It is classifiable with other species of interactions such as bull sessions, heart-to-heart talks, quarrels, discussions, and so forth.

ARGUMENT FIELDS: A field can roughly be thought of as an area of study. Each area of study is defined by principles that govern the conduct of those operating in the discipline. Each field has different ends and procedures of obtaining those ends. Many fields are not straightforwardly conventional. They include such informal areas of study as restaurant evaluation or vacation determination.

ARGUMENT FROM ANALOGY: Argument from analogy is often referred to by the more familiar name *comparison*. Analogical argument moves from claims about a familiar case to claims about a less familiar instance. Analogical reasoning infers that because two things have some qualities in common they will have an additional quality in common.

ARGUMENT FROM CAUSE: An argument from cause asserts the existence of a relationship between two events or states of affairs such that the first brings about the second.

ARGUMENT FROM EXAMPLE: Argument from example is sometimes termed a generalization. Reasoning from example is often referred to as an *inductive generalization*. Induction is a method of reasoning by which a general law or principle is inferred from observed particular instances.

ARGUMENT FROM SIGN: Arguments from sign are based on the assumption that two or more variables are related in such a way that the presence or absence of one may be taken as an indication of the presence or absence of the other. The key difference between sign and cause is that sign does give an indication that the proposition is true without attempting to explain why it is true. In other words, argument from sign does not explain why the two variables are related.

ARGUMENTATION: Argumentation is the theory and practice of justification based on conceptions of the reasonable. It is distinguished from logic because it deals with those issues that grow out of the context of concrete situations. Argumentation deals with justifying propositions based upon communal conceptions of reasonableness.

ARGUMENTATIVE SITUATION: The argumentative situation is made up of those elements in the argumentative environment that constrain choices and shape the appropriate grounds of justification. The elements of the argumentative situation include audiences, topics, advocates, and occasions.

AUDIENCE: Audiences are made up of those whom advocates wish to influence by their argumentation.

BACKING: Backing is the generalizations that make explicit the body of experience relied on to establish the trustworthiness of the ways of arguing applied in any particular case.

BLAME: Blame is the second stock issue for propositions of policy. The stock issue of blame inquires, "Is there an inherent reason to change?" If the difficulty is inherent, then present arrangements are incapable of alleviating the ill.

BURDENS OF ARGUMENT: These burdens are conceptualized as duties or responsibilities advocates accept when they sincerely argue. When we choose to reason rather than impose our will by force or trickery, these burdens define our obligations to the audience.

BURDEN OF PROOF: Burden of proof is the flip side of presumption. The advocate of change upholds the burden of proof by providing sufficient reason to overcome presumption.

BURDEN OF REBUTTAL: The burden of rebuttal is the responsibility of the arguer to address legitimate opposing arguments.

BURDEN OF VALIDITY: The burden of validity is the arguer's obligation to advance arguments worthy of audience approval.

CASE: A case is the larger structure in which arguments and evidence are placed.

COMPARATIVE ADVANTAGES CASE: The comparative advantages case is an affirmative approach to a proposition of policy. This approach focuses on a comparison between the old and new plan. In this case type the assumption is that the present policy is meeting the intended goal, but not as quickly, effectively, and/or efficiently as it might.

COMPARISON: Comparison is a type of data. Comparison is based on the belief that what is known or believed to be true of one thing will be true of something else as long as it is like the first in all essential characteristics.

COST: Cost is the fourth stock issue for a proposition of policy. The stock issue of cost asks, "Does the policy have more advantages than disadvantages?"

COUNTER-PERSUASION: Counter-persuasion refers to the presentation of a subsequent message that undermines the persuasive impact of an earlier message.

COUNTERPLAN: The counterplan is a negative approach to a proposition of policy. The negative takes on the burden of presenting an alternative proposal that breaks with both the proposition and the present system.

CRITICAL ATTITUDE: The critical attitude is best understood in terms of ideal cultural roles. It is reflected in the habits of mind we expect from the philosopher, scientist, detective, teacher, diplomat, jurist, and journalist. The critical attitude includes commitments to intellectual curiosity, open-mindedness, methodological flexibility, systematic thinking, persistence and decisiveness, and respect for other viewpoints.

CRITICAL THINKING: Critical thinking is the process of evaluating statements, arguments, and experience. An operational definition of critical thinking would consist of all the attitudes and skills used in the evaluating process.

CROSS-EXAMINATION: This type of questioning is used to undermine existing proof.

CROSS-EXAMINATION DEBATE FORMAT: The cross-examination format preserves the standard debate format notion of four constructive and four rebuttal speeches but allows each of the four participants in the debate to both ask and answer questions.

CURE: Cure is the third stock issue for a proposition of policy. The cure issue asks, ''Is there a solution?''

DEBATE: A debate consists of contestants arguing opposite sides of a specific proposition or resolution in order to win the adherence of listeners.

DEFENSE OF THE PRESENT SYSTEM APPROACH: The defense of the present system is a negative approach to a proposition of policy. This approach commits the advocate to defending the present system's approach to the problem.

DIRECT EXAMINATION: This type of questioning is used to enhance or establish proof. On direct examination, the questioner propounds questions for the purpose of eliciting answers that establish the existence of facts favorable to the contentions of the questioner.

DIRECT REFUTATION APPROACH: Direct refutation is a negative approach to a proposition of policy. This approach is characterized by an unwillingness to defend any alternative policy. The stance of the negative employing direct refutation is simply that the affirmative policy is wrongheaded.

DIVERSIFICATION OF SUPPORTING MATERIALS: The persuasive strategy of providing the audience with a variety of supporting materials both in terms of kinds of data and sources of data.

EXAMPLES: Examples establish reality by resort to a particular case. They report or describe real occurrences or observable phenomena in order to establish a claim.

ETHICS: Ethics in argumentation involves making normative judgments about the rightness or wrongness of particular argumentative and persuasive practices.

FIELD-DEPENDENT: A standard is field-dependent when the criteria for its application change from one field to another.

FIELD-INVARIANT: A standard is field-invariant when its meaning remains constant from one field to another.

GOALS-CRITERIA CASE: The goals-criteria case is an affirmative approach to a proposition of policy. The goals-criteria case emphasizes the new proposal's consistency with a set of established principles.

HECKLING DEBATE FORMAT: In this debate format, the audience and/or opponents are allowed to interrupt speakers for the purpose of heckling. This format includes four constructive speeches that may be interrupted a specified number of times.

ILL: Ill is the first stock issue for a proposition of policy. The stock issue of ill asks the question, "Is there a significant reason for change?"

ISSUES: Issues are the vital points that the advocate must establish to justify adoption of the proposition.

LINCOLN-DOUGLAS DEBATE FORMAT: Patterned after the historic debates between Abraham Lincoln and Stephen A. Douglas in 1858, this debate format is designed to allow one individual, rather than a team, to confront another individual. As currently practiced the format provides for two constructive speeches, two cross-examination periods, and three rebuttals.

LOCUS OF REFUTATION: Locus of refutation refers to a rhetorical angle from which refutation may be launched. See REFUTATION.

LOGIC: Logic is the study of the formal principles of reasoning. Logicians do not examine how people do in fact argue, for logic is a theoretical rather than an empirical science.

MINOR REPAIRS APPROACH: Minor repairs is a negative approach to a proposition of policy. The minor repairs approach relates specifically to the blame issue. The advocate adopting this strategy admits that there is something amiss with the present system that prevents it from effectively addressing the ill. However, the defect in the present systm is not an inherent flaw. The defect is fixable without changing the dominant structure or philosophy of the present system.

NEEDS CASE: The needs case is an affirmative approach to a proposition of policy. The needs case emphasizes the problem, the cause of the problem, and recommended solutions to the problem.

NEGATIVE: The negative is one side of the proposition. The negative advocate enjoys presumption.

OCCASION: Occasion is the place and time of advocacy and refutation.

PARLIAMENTARY DEBATE FORMAT: This format is one of the most popular formats for public debates. It is designed for teams, one supporting the affirmative and one supporting the negative, and includes four constructive speeches, one summary speech, and time for audience questions or comments.

PERSUASION: Persuasion is the deliberate human effort to influence the attitudes, beliefs, or behaviors of others.

PLURALISM: Pluralism is the doctrine, in opposition to absolutism and relativism, that ethical decisions concerning the public are subject to reasonable justification.

PRESUMPTION: Presumption is an initial approval of pre-occupied ground.

PRIVILEGED SPHERES OF DECISION MAKING: The notion that certain disagreements are properly decided in the personal, public, or technical arenas.

PROOF: Proof is anything serving or tending to establish the truth of something or to convince one of its truth.

PROPOSITION: A proposition is a statement that specifies the point of discussion. Not only do propositions specify subject matter, but they serve the second function of designating the kind of question under dispute. Third, propositions assign obligations to the participants in the argument. Finally, propositions function to instruct audiences.

PROPOSITION OF FACT: Propositions of fact ask the audience to affirm a particular state of affairs.

PROPOSITION OF POLICY: Propositions of policy ask the audience to take action or to approve of a future action.

PROPOSITION OF VALUE: Propositions of value ask the audience to recommend an evaluation or make a judgment of worth.

REFUTATION: Refutation is the argumentative process that involves the presentation of effective and worthy justifications for decreasing adherence to an opponent's claims.

RELATIVIST: An ethical relativist maintains that there are no universal standards of good and bad, right and wrong.

RHETORICAL DISCOVERY: Rhetorical discovery is the examination of the audience to locate issues and uncover evidentiary requirements.

SOURCE CREDIBILITY: Source credibility is the audience's perception of the advocate that may lead the audience to accept or reject the advocate's message. Traditionally, audience perceptions of the advocate's good sense, moral character, and good will have been deemed important factors in source credibility.

SOURCE-PROPOSITION IMBALANCE: The psychological imbalance caused by divergent evaluation of a source and the position the source advocates.

STANDARD DEBATE FORMAT: Standard debate is the most traditional academic debate format. This method of debating involves two teams with two contestants on each team. The disputants present a series of four constructive and four rebuttal speeches.

STANDARD OF RELEVANCE: The standard of relevance holds that the supporting material used to substantiate a claim should bear a strong and direct relationship to the claim.

STATISTICS: Statistics may be looked at simplistically as numerical expressions of a factual nature about a specific population or sample. In more detailed terms statistics consist of arithmetic and graphic ways for deriving manageable, and useful descriptive summaries from large and heterogeneous collections of data; methods for inferring from the observable to the not observable; procedures for testing a wide variety of hypotheses; and techniques for discovering whether and to what degree one set of events is contingent upon or related to another set of events.

STOCK ISSUES: Stock issues are general points of contention that always adhere to a given propositional type. Stock issues are not the real issues, but rather a formulation of questions that may prove helpful in finding the real issues.

TESTIMONY: Testimony refers to the opinions of experts. Data of this sort usually involve the interpretation and/or evaluation of factual material by an individual who possesses special expertise in the relevant field.

TOPIC: The topic is the subject matter and the form of the question asked about the subject matter in an argumentative situation.

WARRANT: A warrant is a rule that authorizes the move from data to conclusion.

SELECT
BIBLIOGRAPHY

ETHICS AND ARGUMENT

Ayer, A. J. *Language, Truth and Logic*. New York: Dover, 1952.

Brockriede, Wayne. "Arguers as Lovers." *Philosophy and Rhetoric* 5 (1972): 1–11.

Diggs, B. J. "Persuasion and Ethics." *Quarterly Journal of Speech* 50 (1964): 359–73.

Ehninger, Douglas. "Validity as Moral Obligation." *Southern Speech Communication Journal* 33 (1968): 215–22.

Fisher, Walter R. "Toward a Logic of Good Reasons." *Quarterly Journal of Speech* 64 (1978): 376–84.

Haiman, Franklyn S. "Democratic Ethics and the Hidden Persuaders." *Quarterly Journal of Speech* 44 (1958): 385–92.

———. "The Rhetoric of the Streets: Some Legal and Ethical Considerations." *Quarterly Journal of Speech* 53 (1967): 99–114.

Johannesen, Richard L. "An Ethical Assessment of the Reagan Rhetoric: 1981–1982." In *Political Communication Yearbook 1984*, edited by Keith R. Sanders, Lynda Lee Kaid, and Dan Nimmo, 226–41. Carbondale, IL: Southern Illinois University Press, 1985.

———. *Ethics and Persuasion: Selected Readings*. New York: Random House, 1967.

———. "Richard M. Weaver on Standards for Ethical Rhetoric." *Central States Speech Journal* 29 (1978): 127–37.

Legge, Nancy J. "Ethical Standards for Argumentation: An Extension of the Sexual Metaphor." Master's thesis, Indiana University, 1984.

MacIntyre, Alasdair. *After Virtue*. Notre Dame, IN: University of Notre Dame Press, 1981.

Nilsen, Thomas R. *Ethics of Speech Communication*. Indianapolis: Bobbs-Merrill, 1966.

Plato. *Gorgias*. Translated by W. C. Helmbold. Indianapolis: Bobbs-Merrill, 1952.

———. *Phaedrus*. Translated by W. C. Helmbold and W. G. Rabinowitz. Indianapolis: Bobbs-Merrill, 1956.

Stevenson, Charles L. *Ethics and Language*. New Haven: Yale University Press, 1944.

―――. "The Emotive Meaning of Ethical Terms." In *Logical Postivism*, edited by A. J. Ayer, 264–81. New York: Free Press, 1959.

Toulmin, Stephen. *An Examination of the Place of Reason in Ethics*. London: Cambridge University Press, 1970.

Wallace, Karl R. "An Ethical Basis of Communication." *Communication Education* 4 (1955): 1–9.

―――. "The Substance of Rhetoric: Good Reasons." *Quarterly Journal of Speech* 49 (1963): 239–49.

Weaver, Richard M. *Ethics of Rhetoric*. Chicago: Regnery, 1970.

BURDENS OF ARGUMENT

Brown, Robert. "The Burden of Proof." *American Philosophical Quarterly* 7 (1970): 78–82.

Cronkhite, Gary. "The Locus of Presumption." *Central States Speech Journal* 17 (1966): 270–76.

Farrell, Thomas B. "'Validity and Rationality: The Rhetorical Constituent of Argumentative Form." *Journal of the American Forensic Association* 13 (1977): 142–49.

Gronbeck, Bruce E. "Archbishop Richard Whately's Doctrine of 'Presumption' and 'Burden of Proof': An Historical-Critical Analysis." Master's thesis, University of Iowa, 1966.

Johnstone, Henry W., Jr. *Validity and Rhetoric in Philosophical Argument*. University Park, PA: The Dialogue Press of Man and World, 1978.

Leathers, Dale G. "Whately's Logically Derived 'Rhetoric': A Stranger in Its Time." *Western Journal of Speech Communication* 33 (1969): 48–58.

Lee, Ronald, and Karen King Lee. "Reconsidering Whately's Folly: An Emotive Treatment of Presumption." *Central States Speech Journal* 36 (1985): 164–77.

McKerrow, Ray E. "Rationality and Reasonableness in a Theory of Argument." In *Advances in Argumentation Theory and Research*, edited by J. Robert Cox and Charles Arthur Willard, 105–22. Carbondale, IL: Southern Illinois University Press, 1982.

―――. "Rhetorical Validity: An Analysis of Three Perspectives on Justification of Rhetorical Argument." *Journal of the American Forensic Association* 13 (1977): 133–41.

―――. "Whately's Theory of Rhetoric." In *Explorations in Rhetoric*, edited by Ray E. McKerrow, 137–57. Glenview, IL: Scott, Foresman, 1982.

Natanson, Maurice. "The Claims of Immediacy." In *Philosophy, Rhetoric and Argumentation*, edited by Maurice Natanson and Henry W. Johnstone, Jr., 10–19. University Park, PA: Pennsylvania State University Press, 1970.

Sproule, J. Michael. "The Psychological Burden of Proof: On Evolutionary Development of Richard Whately's Theory of Presumption." *Communication Monographs* 43 (1976): 114–29.

Whately, Richard. *Elements of Rhetoric*. Edited by Douglas Ehninger. Carbondale, IL: Southern Illinois University Press, 1963.

FIELDS OF ARGUMENT

Goodnight, G. Thomas. "The Personal, Technical and Public Spheres of Argument: A Speculative Inquiry into the Art of Public Deliberation." *Journal of the American Forensic Association* 18 (1982): 214–27.

Gronbeck, Bruce E. "Sociocultural Notions of Arguments Fields: A Primer." In *Dimensions of Argument*, edited by George Ziegelmueller and Jack Rhodes, 1–21. Annandale, VA: Speech Communication Association, 1981.

Rowland, Robert C. "The Influence of Purpose on Fields of Argument." *Journal of the American Forensic Association* 18 (1982): 228–45.

Toulmin, Stephen. *Human Understanding*. Princeton, NJ: Princeton University Press, 1972.

———. *The Uses of Argument*. London: Cambridge University Press, 1958.

Toulmin, Stephen, Richard Rieke, and Allan Janik. *An Introduction to Reasoning*. New York: Macmillan, 1979.

Wenzel, Joseph W. "On Fields of Argument as Propositional Systems." *Journal of the American Forensic Association* 18 (1982): 204–13.

Willard, Charles Arthur. "Argument Fields." In *Advances in Argumentation Theory and Research*, edited by J. Robert Cox and Charles Arthur Willard, 24–77. Carbondale, IL: Southern Illinois University Press, 1982.

———. *Argumentation and the Social Grounds of Knowledge*. University, AL: Alabama University Press, 1983.

———. "Field Theory: A Cartesian Meditation." In *Dimensions of Argument*, edited by George Ziegelmueller and Jack Rhodes, 21–42. Annandale, VA: Speech Communication Association, 1981.

Zarefsky, David. "Persistent Questions in the Theory of Argument Fields." *Journal of the American Forensic Association* 18 (1982): 191–203.

TESTS OF ARGUMENT AND EVIDENCE

Campbell, Donald T., and Julian C. Stanley. *Experimental and Quasi-Experimental Designs for Research*. Chicago: Rand McNally, 1963.

Cathcart, Robert S. "An Experimental Study of the Relative Effectiveness of Four Methods of Presenting Evidence." *Communication Monographs* 22 (1955): 227–33.

D'Angelo, Edward. *The Teaching of Critical Thinking*. Amsterdam: B. R. Gruner, 1971.

Dresser, William R. "Effects of 'Satisfactory' and 'Unsatisfactory' Evidence in a Speech of Advocacy." *Communication Monographs* 20 (1963): 302–306.

Ehninger, Douglas. "On Inferences of the 'Fourth Class.'" *Central States Speech Journal* 28 (1977): 157–62.

Engel, S. Morris. *With Good Reasons: An Introduction to Informal Fallacies*. New York: St. Martin's Press, 1976.

Gronbeck, Bruce E. "On Classes of Inferences and Force." In *Explorations in Rhetoric*, edited by Ray E. McKerrow, 85–106. Glenview, IL: Scott, Foresman, 1982.

Hamblin, Charles Leonard. *Fallacies*. London: Methuen, 1970.

Haskell, Thomas L, ed. *The Authority of Experts*. Bloomington, IN: Indiana University Press, 1984.

McCroskey, James C. "The Effects of Evidence as an Inhibitor of Counter-Persuasion." *Communication Monographs* 37 (1970): 188–94.

———. "A Summary of Experimental Research on the Effects of Evidence in Persuasive Communication." *Quarterly Journal of Speech* 55 (1969): 169–76.

Spiker, Barry K., Tom D. Daniels, and Lawrence M. Bernabo. "The Quantitative Quandary in Forensics: The Use and Abuse of Statistical Evidence." *Journal of the American Forensic Association* 19 (1982): 87–96.

Sproule, J. Michael. *Argument: Language and Its Influence*. New York: McGraw-Hill, 1980.

Williams, Frederick. *Reasoning with Statistics*. New York: Holt, Rinehart and Winston, 1968.

QUESTIONING

Beard, Raymond S. "A Comparison of Classical Dialectic, Legal Cross-Examination, and Cross-Question Debate." *Journal of the American Forensic Association* 3 (1966): 53–58.

———. "Legal Cross-Examination and Academic Debate." *Journal of the American Forensic Association* 6 (1969): 61–66.

———. "A Survey of the Theories and Trends in Cross-Examination from Ancient Times to Modern." Ph.D. dissertation, Northwestern University, 1954.

Fuge, Lloyd H., and Robert P. Newman. "Cross-Examination in Academic Debating." *Communication Education* 5 (1956): 66–70.

Gallaghar, William. *Technique of Cross-Examination*. New York: Practicing Law Institute, 1955.

Hays, Mortimer. *Tactics in Direct Examination*. New York: Practising Law Institute, 1953.

Henderson, Bill. "A System of Teaching Cross Examination Techniques." *Communication Education* 27 (1978): 112–18.

Iannouzzi, John Nicholas. *Cross-Examination: The Mosaic Art*. Englewood Cliffs, NJ: Prentice-Hall, 1982.

Lake, L. W. *How to Cross-Examine Witnesses Successfully*. Englewood Cliffs, NJ: Prentice-Hall, 1957.

Lee, Ronald. "An Application and Adaptation of Schwartz's Legal Model of Examination for Interscholastic Debate." Master's thesis, Wayne State University, 1976.

Redfield, Roy A. *Cross Examination and the Witness*. Mundelein, IL: Callaghan, 1963.

Schwartz, Louis E. *Proof, Persuasion, and Cross-Examination: A Winning New Approach in the Courtroom*. 2 vols. Englewood Cliffs, NJ: Executive Reports Corp., 1973.

Spellman, Howard Hilton. *Direct Examination of Witnesses*. Englewood Cliffs, NJ: Prentice-Hall, 1968.

Wellman, Francis Lewis. *The Art of Cross-Examination*. 4th ed., rev. and enl. New York: Macmillan Company, 1936.

ARGUMENTATION AND DEBATE

Baird, A. Craig. *Argumentation, Discussion, and Debate*. New York: McGraw-Hill, 1950.

Church, Russell T., and Charles Wilbanks. *Values and Policies in Controversy: An Introduction to Argumentation and Debate*. Scottsdale, AZ: Gorsuch Scarisbrick, 1986.

Ehninger, Douglas, and Wayne Brockreide. *Decision by Debate*. New York: Dodd-Mead, 1963.

Freeley, Austin J. *Argumentation and Debate: Critical Thinking for Reasoned Decision Making*. 6th ed. Belmont, CA: Wadsworth, 1986.

McBurney, James Howard, and Glen E. Mills. *Argumentation and Debate: Techniques of a Free Society*. 2d ed. New York: Macmillan Co., 1951.

Patterson, J.W., and David Zarefsky. *Contemporary Debate*. Boston: Houghton Mifflin, 1983.

Rybacki, Karyn C., and Donald J. Rybacki. *Advocacy and Opposition: An Introduction to Argumentation*. Englewood Cliffs, NJ: Prentice-Hall, 1986.

Ziegelmueller, George W., and Charles A. Dause. *Argumentation: Inquiry and Advocacy*. Englewood Cliffs, NJ: Prentice-Hall, 1975.

GENERAL WORKS ON ARGUMENTATION

Booth, Wayne C. *Modern Dogma and the Rhetoric of Assent*. Notre Dame, IN: University of Notre Dame Press, 1974.

Brockriede, Wayne. "Where Is Argument?" *Journal of the American Forensic Association* 11 (1975): 179–82.

———. "Characteristics of Arguments and Arguing." *Journal of the American Forensic Association* 13 (1977): 129–32.

Burleson, Brant R. "On the Analysis and Criticism of Arguments: Some Theoretical and Methodological Considerations." *Journal of the American Forensic Association* 15 (1979): 137–47.

———. "On the Foundations of Rationality: Toulmin, Habermas and the *a priori* of Reason." *Journal of the American Forensic Association* 16 (1979): 112–27.

Carleton, Walter M. "Theory Transformation in Communication: The Case of Henry Johnstone." *Quarterly Journal of Speech* 6 (1975): 76–88.

Cox, J. Robert. "Deliberation Under Uncertainty: A Game Simulation of Oral Argumentation in Decision-Making." *Journal of the American Forensic Association* 14 (1977): 61–72.

———. "Argument and the 'Definition of the Situation.'" *Central States Speech Journal* 32 (1981): 197–205.

Cox, J. Robert, and Charles A. Willard, eds. *Advances in Argumentation Theory and Research.* Carbondale, IL: Southern Illinois University Press, 1982.

Delia, Jesse G. "The Logic Fallacy, Cognitive Theory, and the Enthymeme: A Search for the Foundations of Reasoned Discourse." *Quarterly Journal of Speech* 56 (1970): 140–48.

Ehninger, Douglas. "Argument as Method: Its Nature, Its Limitations and Its Uses." *Communication Monographs* 37 (1970): 101–10.

Hample, Dale. "Predicting Immediate Belief Change and Adherence to Argument Claims." *Communication Monographs* 45 (1978): 219–28.

———. "Predicting Belief and Belief Change Using a Cognitive Theory of Argument and Evidence." *Communication Monographs* 46 (1979): 142–46.

———. "The Cognitive View of Argument." *Journal of the American Forensic Association* 16 (1980): 151–58.

———. "The Cognitive Context of Argument." *Western Journal of Speech Communication* 45 (1981): 148–58.

Jackson, Sally, and Scott Jacobs. "Structure of Conversational Argument: Pragmatic Bases for the Enthymeme." *Quarterly Journal of Speech* 66 (1980): 251–65.

Jacobs, Scott, and Sally Jackson. "Argument as a Natural Category: The Routine Grounds for Arguing in Conversation." *Western Journal of Speech Communication* 45 (1981): 118–32.

Johnstone, Henry W., Jr. *Philosophy and Argument.* University Park, PA: The Pennsylvania State University Press, 1959.

———. *The Problem of the Self.* University Park, PA: The Pennsylvania State University Press, 1970.

Johnstone, Henry W., Jr., and Maurice Natanson, eds. *Philosophy, Rhetoric, and Argumentation.* University Park, PA: The Pennsylvania State University Press, 1965.

Kneupper, Charles W. "Rhetoric, Argument, and Social Reality: A Social Constructivist View." *Journal of the American Forensic Association* 16 (1980): 173–81.

Miller, Gerald R., and Thomas R. Nilsen, eds. *Perspectives on Argumentation.* Glenview, IL: Scott, Foresman, 1966.

Natanson, Maurice. "Rhetoric and Philosophical Argumentation." *Quarterly Journal of Speech* 48 (1962): 24–30.

O'Keefe, Daniel J. "Two Concepts of Argument." *Journal of the American Forensic Association* 13 (1977): 121–28.

Perelman, Chaim. *The Idea of Justice and the Problem of Argument.* New York: Humanities Press, 1963.

———. *Justice.* New York: Random House, 1967.

———. *The Realm of Rhetoric.* Translated by William Kluback. Notre Dame, IN: University of Notre Dame Press, 1982.

Perelman, Chaim, and L. Olbrechts-Tyteca. *The New Rhetoric: A Treatise on Argumentation*. Trans. by John Wilkinson and Purcell Weaver. Notre Dame, IN: University of Notre Dame Press, 1969.

Rieke, Richard D., and Malcolm O. Sillars. *Argumentation and the Decision Making Process*. 2d ed. Glenview, IL: Scott, Foresman, 1984.

Rowland, Robert C. "On Defining Argument." *Philosophy and Rhetoric* 20 (1987): 140–59.

Wenzel, Joseph W. "Toward a Rationale for Value-Centered Argument." *Journal of the American Forensic Association* 13 (1977): 150–58.

GENERAL WORKS ON PERSUASION

Applebaum, R. F. "The Factor Structure of Source Credibility as a Function of the Speaking Situation." *Communication Monographs* 39 (1972): 216–22.

Aristotle. *Rhetoric*. Trans. by Lane Cooper. New York: Appleton-Century-Crofts, 1960.

Bandura, A. *Principles of Behavior Modification*. New York: Holt, Rinehart and Winston, 1969.

———. *Social Learning Theory*. Englewood Cliffs, NJ: Prentice-Hall, 1977.

Beighley, K. C. "An Experimental Study of the Effect of Four Speech Variables on Listener Comprehension." *Communication Monographs* 19 (1952): 249–58.

———. "A Summary of Experimental Studies Dealing with the Effect of Organization and of Skill of Speaker on Comprehension." *Communication Journal* 2 (1952): 58–65.

Berlo, D. K., J. B. Lemert, and R. J. Mertz. "Dimensions for Evaluating the Acceptability of Message Sources." *Public Opinion Quarterly* 33 (1969–70): 563–76.

Bettinghaus, E. "The Operation of Congruity in an Oral Communication Situation." *Communication Monographs* 28 (1961): 131–42.

Bettinghaus, E., G. Miller, and T. Steinfatt. "Source Evaluation, Syllogistic Content, and Judgments of Logical Validity by High and Low Dogmatic Persons." *Journal of Personality and Social Psychology* 16 (1970): 238–44.

Bowers, John Waite. "Some Correlates of Language Intensity." *Quarterly Journal of Speech* 50 (1964): 415–20.

Burgoon, Michael. "Empirical Investigations of Language Intensity: III. The Effect of Source Credibility and Language Intensity on Attitude Change and Person Perception." *Human Communication Research* 1 (1975): 251–54.

Burgoon, Michael, and L. B. King. "The Mediation of Resistance to Persuasion Strategies by Language Variables and Active-Passive Participation." *Human Communication Research* 1 (1974): 30–41.

Burgoon, Michael, M. Cohen, M. Miller, and C. L. Montgomery. "An Empirical Test of a Model of Resistance to Persuasion." *Human Communication Research* 5 (1978): 27–39.

Cronkhite, Gary. *Persuasion: Speech and Behavioral Change*. New York: Bobbs-Merrill, 1969.

Delia, Jesse G. "A Constructivist Analysis of the Concept of Credibility." *Quarterly Journal of Speech* 62 (1976): 361–75.

Eagley, A. H., and S. Chaiken. "An Attribution Analysis of the Effect of Communicator Characteristics on Opinion Change: The Case for Communicator Attractiveness." *Journal of Personality and Social Psychology* 32 (1975): 136–44.

Festinger, Leon. *A Theory of Cognitive Dissonance*. Stanford, CA: Stanford University Press, 1957.

Fishbein, M. *Readings in Attitude Theory and Measurement*. New York: Wiley, 1967.

Fishbein, M., and I. Ajzen. *Beliefs, Attitudes, Intentions and Behavior: An Introduction to Theory and Research*. Reading, MA: Addison-Wesley, 1975.

Heider, Fritz. "Attitudes and Cognitive Organization." *Journal of Psychology* 21 (1946): 107–12.

Holtzman, P. D. *The Psychology of Speaker's Audiences*. Glenview, IL: Scott, Foresman, 1970.

Hovland, C. I., I. L. Janis, and H. H. Kelley. *Communication and Persuasion*. New Haven: Yale University Press, 1953.

Hovland, C. I., and M. J. Rosenberg, eds. *Attitude Organization and Change*. New Haven: Yale University Press, 1960.

Infante, Dominic A. "The Function of Perceptions of Consequences on Attitude Formation and Communicator Image Formation." *Central States Speech Journal* 23 (1972): 174–80.

———. "Forewarnings in Persuasion: Effects of Opinionated Language and Forewarner and Speaker Authoritativeness." *Western Journal of Speech Communication* 37 (1973): 185–95.

———. "Differential Functions of Desirable and Undesirable Consequences in Predicting Attitude and Attitude Change Toward Proposals." *Communication Monographs* 42 (1975): 115–34.

Insko, C. *Theories of Attitude Change*. New York: Appleton-Century-Crofts, 1967.

Karlins, M., and H. I. Abelson. *Persuasion: How Opinions and Attitudes Are Changed*. 2d ed. New York: Springer, 1970.

Katz, E., and P. F. Lazarsfeld. *Personal Influence*. New York: Free Press, 1964.

Klapper, J. T. *The Effects of Mass Communication*. Glencoe, IL: Free Press, 1960.

Littlejohn, Stephen W. *Theories of Human Communication*. Columbus, OH: Charles E. Merrill, 1978.

McGuire, W. J. "Persistance of the Resistance to Persuasion Induced by Various Types of Prior Belief Defenses." *Journal of Abnormal and Social Psychology* 64 (1962): 241–48.

Miller, Gerald. "Studies in the Use of Fear Appeals: A Summary and Analysis." *Central States Speech Journal* 14 (1963): 117–25.

Nelson, C. E. "Anchoring to Accepted Values as a Technique for Immunizing Beliefs against Persuasion." *Journal of Personality and Social Psychology* 9 (1968): 329–34.

Norton, R. W., and L. S. Pettigrew. "Communicator Style as an Effective Determinant of Attraction." *Communication Research* 4 (1977): 257–82.

Osgood, C. E., and P. H. Tannenbaum. "The Principles of Congruity in the Production of Attitude Change." *Psychological Review* 62 (1955): 42–55.

Rokeach, M. *The Open and Closed Mind.* New York: Basic Books, 1960.

———. *Beliefs, Attitudes, and Values: A Theory of Organization and Change.* San Francisco: Jossey-Bass, 1969.

———. *The Nature of Human Values.* New York: Free Press, 1973.

———. *Understanding Human Values.* New York: Free Press, 1979.

Roloff, Michael E., and Gerald R. Miller. *Persuasion: New Directions in Theory and Research.* Beverly Hills, CA: Sage, 1980.

Rosnow, R., and E. Robinson, eds. *Experiments in Persuasion.* New York: Academic Press, 1967.

Sherif, C., and M. Sherif. *Attitude, Ego-Involvement and Change.* New York: Wiley, 1967.

Spillman, B. "The Impact of Value and Self-Esteem Messages in Persuasion." *Central States Speech Journal* 30 (1979): 67–74.

Steinfatt, T., and D. Infante. "Attitude-Behavior Relationships in Communication Research." *Quarterly Journal of Speech* 62 (1976): 267–78.

Tedeschi, J., ed. *The Social Influence Process.* Chicago: Aldine, 1972.

Triandis, H. C. *Attitude and Attitude Change.* New York: Wiley, 1971.

Vohs, J. L. "An Empirical Approach to the Concept of Attention." *Communication Monographs* 31 (1964): 355–60.

Vohs, J. L., and R. L. Garrett. "Resistance to Persuasion: An Integrative Framework." *Public Opinion Quarterly* 32 (1968): 445–52.

Zajonc, R. "Attitudinal Effects of Mere Exposure." *Journal of Personality and Social Psychology* 9 (1968): 1–27.

Zimbardo, P. G. "Involvement and Communication Discrepancy in Determinants of Opinion Conformity." *Journal of Abnormal and Social Psychology* 60 (1960): 86–94.

INDEX

Absolutism, 16, 17, 21, 25
Academic debate. *See* Interscholastic debate
Advocates
  and consistency, 204–205, 210
  control by, 219–221
  credentials of, 205–206, 210
  credibility of, 202–203, 210
  and data, 72, 73, 87
  as elements of the argumentative situation, 10–13
  and issues, 69
  judgments of, 206, 210
  knowledge/experience of, 206, 210, 219–220
  as loci of refutation, 202–206, 210
  motives of, 203–204, 210
  and proof, 71
  and standards of reasonableness, 124–125
Affirmative case
  and the burden of proof, 150, 168, 175, 282, 295
  construction of the, 150–168, 226–227, 228–229, 230–231, 235–238, 247–251
  and definitions, 152, 158, 163, 169, 235–236, 247–248, 262
  designating the, 150
  and duties of speakers, 232–233
  and evidence, 293
  and field, 168
  and formats of debate, 226–227
  and interscholastic debate, 230–231, 235–238, 247–251
  and meeting the criteria, 153, 158–159, 236, 249
  and presentational strategies, 153–155, 159–161, 164–169
  and presentation of argument, 149–169
  and presumption, 150, 168, 282, 295
  and propositions of fact, 150–155
  and propositions of policy, 161–168, 169
  and propositions of value, 155–161, 235
  in public debate, 232–233, 283–294
  rebuttals for the, 226–227, 230, 231–232, 262–264, 267–269, 298–304
  and reliable criteria, 152–153, 158, 160–161, 235, 236, 249, 263–264, 269, 283, 284
  requirements for the, 152–153, 158–159, 163–164, 168–169
  and stock issues, 163–164, 165–167, 169, 175
  summary of the, 228–229

Analogy, 96–97, 104, 114
Andrews, James, 7
Approval, 35, 43, 52–53
Argumentation
  concerns of, 7
  definition/function of, 6, 12, 13, 35, 153
  and justification, 59, 71
  and logic, 12, 124
  rules of, 56
Argumentative situation
  and basic terms, 3–6, 12–13
  elements of the, 6–13
  and expectations, 7–8, 10, 12, 13
  and questioning, 9, 10
Argument fields. *See* Field
Argument$_1$ and argument$_2$, 90–91, 103–104
Arguments. *See also name of specific topic*
  and case, 168
  definition of, 89–91, 128–129, 143
  ethics of, 24–25
  forms of, 89–104
  legitimizing a variety of, 125–128
  nontraditional, 126–128
Aristotle, 12, 58, 70n1
Attitudes, 10–12, 84, 85, 86, 101–102, 129, 130–133, 143.
  See also Beliefs
Audiences. *See also* Expectations; Presentational strategies
  and backing, 92
  and burdens of argument, 29, 42
  and case, 149
  and credibility, 11
  and data/evidence, 45, 72, 83–87, 109
  and discovery of issues, 58–60
  as elements of the argumentative situation, 7–8, 12–13
  and the format of debates, 228–229, 233
  initial perception of, 86
  and justification, 72
  knowledge of topic of, 84, 86
  as loci of refutation, 196–199, 210
  and nontraditional arguments, 126
  as objects, 21
  perceived role of, 86
  and premise, 198–199, 210
  and presentational strategies, 149, 153–155, 176

and presumption, 32
and proof, 71, 120, 123, 214–218
and propositions, 48, 53–54, 56, 65–66, 121, 176
and public debate, 227–229, 233
and questioning, 214–218
and rhetorical discovery of issues, 69
and standards of reasonableness, 124–125
and stock issues, 65–66
types of, 121–122
and validity, 35, 36, 92
values of, 84
Authority, 92, 101–102, 120–121, 122, 125, 127

Backing, 91–104
Badgering, 220
Behavior, and beliefs/consistency, 102–103, 104
Beliefs, 101–103, 104
Bettinghaus, Erwin P., 85
Bibliographic notations, 81–82, 87
Blame, 66–69, 70, 163, 165–167, 169, 184–185,
    187–188, 230
Body of experience, 93–94
Brockriede, Wayne, 23
Burden of proof
    and the affirmative case, 150, 168, 175, 282, 295
    definition of, 43
    and field, 31–32, 43
    and presumption, 29–32, 31, 43, 282, 295
    and propositions, 48
Burden of rebuttal, 33–34, 43
Burdens, 28, 29, 42, 56, 92. See also Burden of
    proof; Burden of rebuttal; Burden of valid-
    ity; Presumption
Burden of validity, 34–42, 43

Card catalogues, 76
Case. See also affirmative case; Negative case;
    Presentational strategies
    and audiences, 149
    comparative, 165–167, 169
    definition/characteristics of, 149, 168
    and evidence, 168
    goals-criteria, 167–168, 169
    needs, 164–165, 169
    and propositions, 149, 168
Cathcart, Robert S., 85
Causality, 49–52, 62–64, 97–100, 104, 150
Censorship, 139–140, 143
Challenge
    and cross-examination, 257–258
    and the negative case, 241–245, 257–258, 260–
        261, 264, 297
    and questioning, 216, 218, 221
    and rebuttals, 260–261, 262, 264
Clarification of a position, 215–216, 218, 221, 238–
    239, 246, 276, 301, 306
Classification, 49–52, 62–64, 150
Cliches, 138–139
Coercion, 23–24, 25, 26, 133–143
Collins, Barry, 86
Comparative case, 165–167, 169

Comparison
    and argument from analogy, 96–97
    direct/indirect, 114
    as evidence/proof, 84, 114–116, 120, 122, 123
    tests of, 114–116, 120
    as a type of data, 73, 74, 75, 87, 112
Competence, 203, 220–221
Computerized databanks, 80–81
Concerted audiences, 121–122
Conclusion, 23, 36–37, 38, 42, 90–92, 93, 100, 104
Consequence, arguments from, 161
Consistency
    and advocates, 204–205, 210
    and authority, 101–102, 120–121
    and behavior, 102–103, 104
    and beliefs, 102, 104
    and censorship/disinformation, 140, 143
    and critical thinking, 143
    and the negative case, 280, 282
    and propositions of policy, 167–168
    and psychological backing, 101–103, 104
    and refutation, 204–205, 210
    and statistics, 118–120
    and testimonies, 116–117, 280, 282
Construction
    of the affirmative case, 150–168, 226–233, 235–
        238, 247–251
    and duties of speakers, 230–231
    and formats of debate, 226–227
    of the negative case, 171–189, 226–233, 240–
        245, 253–257
Control
    by advocates, 219–221
    of information, 139–140, 143
Cost, 66–69, 70, 164, 165–167, 169, 185–186, 187
Counter-persuasion, 86–87
Counterplan, 186, 188–189, 190
Credentials of advocates, 205–206, 210
Credibility
    of advocates, 202–203, 210
    as an element of the argumentative situation,
        10–12
    and attitude change, 86
    and audiences, 11
    and evidence/supporting material, 84, 85, 86,
        101, 120, 123
    and questioning/cross-examination, 216–217,
        218, 221, 240
    and refutation, 202–203, 210
Critical attitude, 129–133, 143
Critical thinking, 129–144
Cross-examination
    and challenge, 257–258
    and clarifying a position, 238–239, 246
    and credibility, 240
    and format of debate, 226–227
    function of, 221
    and head-to-head, 229, 304–313
    and interscholastic debate, 238–240, 245–247,
        251–253, 257–259
    and premises, 239

Cross-examination (*cont.*)
　and proof, 221
　as a strategy of questioning, 212–222
　and supporting material, 239–240, 245–247
Cross-Examination Debate Association, 226
Cross-examination debate format, 226, 229, 230–
　232
Cure, 66–69, 70, 163–164, 165–167, 169, 185, 187
Curiosity, 130, 143

D'Angelo, Edward, 129
Data. *See* Evidence/supporting material
Debate. *See also specific type of debate*
　formats of, 225–229
　function of, 223, 225
　speakers' duties in, 229–233
Deception, 20–21, 24–25, 26, 133–143, 220
Decision making, 140–143, 144, 164–168
Deduction, 103, 104
Definitional backing, 93–94, 103, 104
Definitional disputes, 55–56
Definitions
　and the affirmative case, 152, 158, 163, 169,
　　235–236, 247–248, 262
　and duties of speakers, 232
　and format of the debate, 230, 232
　and jurisdiction, 201–202
　and the negative case, 180, 184, 190, 242–243,
　　259–260, 264, 276, 301
　and propositions, 55–56, 173–174, 180, 190
　questions of, 201–202
　and rebuttals, 259–260, 262, 264
　and refutation, 201–202
　and speakers' duties, 230
　and topics, 201–202
Descartes, Rene, 130, 131
Design, 97–98, 118–120
Direct comparison, 114
Direct examination, 214–218, 219, 221
Direct refutation, 186, 187, 190
Direct relationship, 122–123
Discovery. *See* Evidence/supporting material;
　Rhetorical discovery of issues
Disinformation, 139–140, 143
Division of the House or Vote, 228
Duties
　and burdens, 28, 42
　of speakers, 229–233

Edelman, Murray, 136–137
Effectiveness. *See* Ethics; Justification
Ehninger, Douglas, 129
Elements of Rhetoric [Whately], 30
Ethical standards of discourse, 19–26, 31. *See also*
　Field-dependency
Ethics. *See also* Field-invariancy
　of argument, 24–25
　and coercion, 23–24, 25, 26
　and deception, 20–21, 24–25, 26
　and evidence, 87
　and fields, 17–19, 31

　and form of arguments, 23
　and manipulation, 21–22, 24–25, 26
　and methodological flexibility, 131–132
　of persuasion, 24–25
　and power, 23
　sample cases about, 19–26
　and standards of practice, 19–26
Ethos. *See* Credibility
Evaluation. *See also* Evaluation of argument
　standard of moral, 127–128
　of supporting material, 107–123
　and testimonies, 74–75, 116
Evaluation of argument. *See also* Critical think-
　ing; Ethical standards of discourse; Meet-
　ing the criteria; Reliable criteria; Proposi-
　tions of value
　and curiosity, 130, 143
　and evidence, 38, 41–42
　and field, 128, 143
　and legitimizing a wider variety of argument,
　　125–128, 143
　and logic, 122, 143
　and open-mindedness, 130–131, 143
　and persistence, 132–133
　and premise-conclusion relationship, 38, 42
　and questioning, 130
　and reasonability, 128–143
　and relevancy, 38, 41
　and respect for other viewpoints, 133, 143
　and systematic reasoning, 132, 143
　and tests of argument, 124–144
　and validity, 37–42
Evidence/supporting material. See also Burden
　of proof; Reliable criteria; Meeting the
　criteria
　and advocates, 71, 72, 73, 87
　analysis of, 87
　and attitude change, 85
　and audiences, 45, 71, 72, 83–87, 109, 120, 123,
　　214–218
　and case, 168
　comparisons as, 84, 114–116, 122, 123
　computerized, 80–81
　and credibility, 84, 85, 86, 101, 120, 123
　and cross-examination, 221, 239–240, 245–247
　definition/function of, 71, 72, 87, 109
　and direct examination, 214–218, 221
　and direct relationship, 122–123
　discovery of, 71–87
　diversity/variety of, 85, 87, 121–122, 123, 301
　effectiveness/worthiness of, 109
　and ethics, 87
　evaluation of, 38, 41–42, 87, 109–123
　and example, 84, 113–114, 122, 123
　and expectations, 87
　and facts, 9
　and field, 18, 110–112, 123
　and general tests of proof, 109–112, 122–123
　and interpretation, 87
　kinds/types of, 73–75, 87, 112, 120, 123
　locating, 73–75, 75–81, 87

and occasions, 45, 71, 72, 87, 214–218
organizing of, 83, 87
and presentation/delivery, 85–86
and propositions, 120–121, 123
psychological impact of, 84–87
and questioning, 72, 216, 218, 221
recording of, 81–82, 87
and reliability, 120
rhetorically effective use of, 120–122
selection of, 45, 83–87
and specific tests of proof, 112–120, 123
statistics as, 84, 118–120, 122, 123
synthesis of, 87
testimonies as, 84, 116–117, 122, 123
and tests of argument, 107–123
and topics, 10, 71, 72, 87, 214–218
and validity, 38, 41–42
Example
  argument from, 94–95, 96–97, 104
  and diversity of evidence, 122
  as a kind of evidence/proof, 73–74, 84, 87, 112, 113–114, 123
  and material backing, 94–95, 96–97, 104
  and the negative case, 187–188
  and observation, 113
  and proposition of policy, 187–188
  tests of, 113–114, 120
Existence, 49–52, 62–64, 150
Expectations, 7–8, 10, 12, 13, 36, 72, 83–87
Experience/experimentation, 93, 95–96, 104
Experts, 59, 74–75, 116–117, 208

Facts, 8–10, 50–52, 74–75, 116, 137–138, 183. See also Propositions of fact
Fair play, 33
Fair-time provisions, 33
Field. See also Field-dependency; Field-invariancy
  and the affirmative case, 168
  and critical thinking, 131–132
  definition of, 17, 110
  and definition of terms, 136–137
  and ethical standards of discourse, 19–26
  and ethics, 17–19
  and evaluation of argument, 128, 143
  and evidence/supporting material, 18, 111–112, 123
  informal, 18–19
  law as a model, 17–19
  and legitimacy, 34
  and methodological flexibility, 131–132
  and pluralism, 25–26
  and presumption, 168
  and refutation, 195, 209–210, 210
  and relationship, 18–19
  and setting, 18–19
  and subject matter, 18–19
Field-dependency
  and backing, 92, 104
  and ethical standards, 31
  and evidence/proof, 31–32, 43, 110–112, 123

and language, 136–137
and legitimacy, 33–34
and presumption, 31–32, 43
and propositions, 62–63, 65–66
and rebuttal, 43
and relevance, 110
and reliable criteria, 152
and standard of evaluation, 128
and stock issues, 62–63
and validity, 35–42, 43, 92
Field-invariancy
  and burden of proof, 31, 43
  and burden of rebuttal, 43
  and ethics, 31
  and presumption, 31, 43
  and propositions of fact, 63
  and relevance, 110
  and stock issues, 63
  and validity, 34–35, 43
Field research, 75, 81, 87
First Amendment, 33
Flexibility, 131–132, 143
Focus, 127, 219
Form of argument, 23, 92, 131. See also Conclusion; Premise
Format of debate. See also name of specific format
  and the affirmative case, 226–227
  and audiences, 228–229
  and cross-examination, 226–227
  and definitions, 230, 232
  function of, 225
  and interscholastic debate, 225–227
  and meeting the criteria, 230, 232
  and the negative case, 226–227
  and rebuttal, 226–227
  and reliable criteria, 230, 232
  and speakers' duties, 225, 229–233
  and stock issues, 230, 232
  and time limits, 226–227, 228, 229
Forms of argument, 89–104
Future action, 52–53

Gallup, George, 20–21
General tests of proof, 109–112, 122–123
Goals-criteria case, 167–168, 169
Goodnight, G. Thomas, 140–141
Government documents, 78–80
Gronbeck, Bruce, 18

Halo effect, 84
Head-to-head, 229, 304–313
Heckling debate format, 228–229

Ideal cultural roles, 129–130
Ill, 66–69, 70, 163, 165–167, 168, 169, 184, 187–188, 189, 230
Indexes/abstracts, 76–77
Indirect comparison, 114
Individual format. See Format of debate; name of specific format
Induction, 93, 97, 100, 103, 104
Inference, 90–92, 96, 104

Influence. *See* Psychological backing
Informal discussions, 73
Inherency, 67–69, 70, 184
Insight, 84
Intellectual curiosity, 130, 143
Intent in employing terms, 137–138
Interpretation, 55–56, 74–75, 87, 116, 118–120, 122
Interrogation. *See* Questioning
Interscholastic debate
   and the affirmative case, 230–231, 235–238, 247–251
   construction in, 230–231
   and cross-examination, 238–240, 245–247, 251–253, 257–259
   and data, 73
   and definitions, 232
   and duties of speakers, 229–233
   example of, 234–275
   formats of, 225–227
   and the negative case, 230–231, 240–245, 253–257, 264–267
   and propositions, 230, 230–232
   and questioning, 213
   and rebuttals, 230, 231–232, 259–269
   and refutation, 194
   and reliable criteria, 263–264
   rules of, 73
Interviews, 75, 81
Issues, 60–61, 69, 70. *See also* Stock issues

Johnstone, Henry, 130
Judgment, 206, 210
Jurisdiction, 199–202, 210
Justice, 18
Justification
   and argumentation, 5–6, 12, 13, 59–60, 71
   and audiences, 72
   and coercion, 23
   definition/function of, 5–6, 71
   and ethical standards, 20–21
   expectations about, 7–8
   and inference, 91
   and justice, 18
   and pluralism, 16
   and refutations, 210

Knowledge/experience, 206, 210, 219–220

Language, 134–139, 143, 166–167
Law, 17–19, 93
Legge, Nancy, 7
Legitimacy
   and the burden of rebuttal, 33–34, 43
   and field, 33–34
   and a variety of arguments, 125–128
Library research, 75, 76–81, 87
Lincoln-Douglas debate format, 227, 229, 232, 233
Loci, 195–196. *See also name of specific loci*
Logic, 3–6, 12, 35–37, 122, 124, 143
Lying. *See* Deception

McBurney, James, 99
McCroskey, James C., 85–86
Manipulation, 21–22, 24–25, 26, 133–143
Material backing, 93, 94–96, 103, 104
Meeting the criteria
   and the affirmative case, 153, 158–159, 236, 249
   and format of debate, 230, 232
   and the negative case, 174–175, 181, 190, 243
   and propositions of fact, 174–175, 190
   and propositions of value, 158–159, 181, 190
   and speakers' duties, 230
Message as the locus of refutation, 209–210
Methodological flexibility, 131–132, 143
Mill, John Stuart, 33, 130
Mills, Glen, 99
Minor repairs, 186, 187–188, 190
Misuse of language, 134–139, 143
Moral evaluation, standard of, 127–128
Motives, 140, 203–204, 210

National Debate Tournament, 226
National Forensic League, 226
Needs case, 164–165, 169
Negative block, 231
Negative case
   and blame, 184–185
   and challenge, 241–245, 257–258, 260–261, 264, 297
   and clarification, 276, 301
   and consistency, 280, 282
   construction of the, 171–178, 178–189, 226–231, 240–245, 253–257
   and cost, 185–186, 187
   and counterplan, 186, 188–189, 190
   and cross-examination, 226–227
   and cure, 185, 187
   and definitions, 180, 184, 190, 242–243, 259–260, 264, 276, 301
   designating the, 170–171
   and direct refutation, 186, 187, 190
   and duties of speakers, 232–233
   and evidence, 295, 301
   and example, 187–188
   and format of debate, 226–229
   and ill, 184, 187–188
   importance of, 170, 190
   and interscholastic debate, 240–245, 253–257, 264–267
   and meeting the criteria, 174–175, 181, 190, 243
   and minor repairs, 186, 187–188, 190
   and presentational strategies, 175–178, 181–183, 186–189
   and presentation of argument, 170–190
   and presumption, 170–171, 189–190, 277, 282, 295, 296
   and propositions of fact, 171–178, 190
   and propositions of policy, 183–189, 190
   and propositions of value, 178–183, 190
   and public debate, 232–233, 275–283
   and rebuttals, 230, 231–232, 259–262, 264–267, 295–298

and refutation, 296–297, 303
and reliability, 277–279, 297
and reliable criteria, 174, 175–178, 180–182, 190, 243, 260, 264–265, 277–279, 297
requirements of the, 173–175, 180–181, 184–186
and stock issues, 183, 187
summary of the, 229
and testimonies, 280, 282, 303
Nonreciprocal signs, 99–100
Nontraditional arguments, 126–128
Norms for good argument, 128–143

Obligations, and propositions, 48, 56
Observation, 93, 94–95, 104, 113
Occasions, 10–13, 45, 69, 71, 72, 87, 124–125, 207–209, 210, 214–218
Occurrence, 49–52, 62–64, 150
Off-case issues, 231, 232, 233
O'Keefe, Daniel, 90
Open-mindedness, 130–131, 143
Oregon-style debate format, 226, 228

Parliamentary style debate format, 228
Passive audiences, 121–122
Pedestrian audiences, 121–122
Perelman, Chaim, 153
Persistence and evaluation of argument, 132–133, 143
Personal decision making, 140–143, 144
Personal hobby perspective of rhetorical discovery, 59
Person, arguments to the, 126, 127–128
Persuasion, 5–6, 24–25, 100, 218. See also Logic
Philosophical statement, 230, 284–286
Plan meet advantage argument, 231
Plan meet need arguments, 231
Plato, 212–213
Pluralism, 15–16, 25–26, 202. See also Field
Policy, 8–10, 168. See also Propositions of policy
Popular sentiment, 127
Premise, 23, 37, 38, 42, 198–199, 210, 217–218, 221, 239, 304–305
Presentational freedom, 153
Presentational strategies
    for the affirmative case, 153–155, 159–161, 164–168, 168–169
    and audiences, 149, 153–155, 176
    and case, 149
    definition of, 175
    freedom of, 168
    importance of, 168
    and the negative case, 175–178, 181–183, 186–189
    and propositions of fact, 153–155, 175–178
    and propositions of policy, 164–168, 169, 186–189
    and propositions of value, 159–161
    and reliable criteria, 175–178
    and stock issues, 155
Presentation of argument. See also Presentational strategies
    and the affirmative case, 149–169

and the negative case, 170–190
    quality of, 85–86
    and questioning, 212–222
    and refutation strategies, 191–210
Presidential debates. See Public debate
Presumption
    advantages of, 171, 189–190
    and the affirmative case, 150, 168, 282, 295
    and audiences, 32
    and the burden of proof, 29–32, 31, 43, 282, 295
    definition of, 30, 32, 43, 168, 170
    and field, 31–32, 43, 168
    and the negative case, 170–171, 189–190, 277, 282, 295, 296
    and propositions, 48
Principle and policy relationship, 168
Private occasions, 207–208
Professional occasions, 208–209
Proof. See Burden of proof; Evidence/supporting material; Reliable criteria; Meeting the criteria
Propositions. See also Propositions of fact; Propositions of policy; Propositions of value
    and audiences, 48, 53–54, 56, 121
    and backing, 103
    and burdens, 48, 56
    and case, 149, 168
    confusion about, 55–56
    and counterplan, 189
    and deduction/induction, 103
    definition of, 47
    and definitions, 55–56, 103
    and duties of speakers, 229–233
    form of, 47
    functions of, 45, 47–48, 53, 55, 56
    and interpretation, 55–56, 56
    and issues, 53–54, 56, 60–61, 69, 168
    kinds/types of, 47–56
    and obligations, 48, 56
    and presumption, 48
    and proof, 120–121, 123
    and public debate, 232–233
    and questions, 56
    and sign, 99
    and topics, 47–48, 56
    and warrant, 91
Propositions of fact
    and the affirmative case, 150–155
    and audiences, 56, 176
    case requirements for, 152–153, 173–175
    and causality, 62–64, 150
    and classification, 62–64, 150
    definition of, 150
    and definitions, 173–174, 190
    and existence, 49–50, 62–64, 150
    and field, 62–63
    function of, 48, 49–50
    and meeting the criteria, 174–175, 190
    and the negative case, 171–178, 190
    and occurrence, 62–64, 150
    and presentational strategies, 153–155, 175–178

Propositions of fact (*cont.*)
  and public debate, 233
  and reliable criteria, 174, 190
  and stock issues, 61, 62–64, 70, 155
  and subject matter, 63
Propositions of policy
  and action, 52–53, 164–168
  and the affirmative case, 161–168, 169
  and audiences, 56
  and blame, 163, 165–167, 169, 184–185
  case requirements for, 163–164
  and consistency, 167–168
  and cost, 164, 165–167, 169, 185–186, 187
  and counterplan, 186, 188–189, 190
  and cure, 163–164, 165–167, 169, 185, 187
  and decision making, 164–168
  and direct refutation, 186, 187, 190
  and example, 187–188
  functions of, 48–49, 52–53
  and ill, 163, 165–167, 168, 169, 184, 187–188
  and interscholastic debate, 230, 230–232
  and issues, 70
  and language, 166–167
  and minor repairs, 186, 187–188, 190
  and the negative case, 183–189, 190
  and presentational strategies, 164–168, 169,
    186–189
  and public debate, 232–233
  and refutation, 190
  and stock issues, 61, 66–69, 165–167, 187
Propositions of value
  and the affirmative case, 155–161, 235
  and audiences, 56, 65–66
  case requirements for, 158–159
  and definitions, 180, 190
  and field-dependency, 65–66
  function of, 48–49, 50–52
  and interscholastic debate, 230, 230–232
  and meeting the criteria, 158–159, 181, 190
  and the negative case, 178–183, 190
  and presentational strategies, 159–161
  and public debate, 232–233
  and reliable criteria, 158, 160–161, 180–181, 190
  and stock issues, 61, 64–66, 70, 183
Psycho-logic, 100–103, 104
Psychological backing, 93–94, 100–103, 104
Psychological factors of questioning, 219–220,
  222
Public debate
  and the affirmative case, 232–233, 283–294
  and audiences, 227–229, 233
  and duties of speakers, 229–233
  example of, 275–318
  formats of, 227–229
  head-to-head in, 304–313
  and the negative case, 232–233, 275–283
  and propositions, 232–233
  rebuttals in, 232–233, 295–304
  and topics, 232
Public decision making, 140–143
Public occasions, 207–208

Public opinion, 7
Public sphere of decision making, 144

Questioning. *See also* Cross-examination; Direct
  examination
  and academic debate, 213
  and argumentative situations, 9, 10
  and audiences, 214–218
  and challenge, 216, 218, 221
  and clarification, 215–216, 218, 221, 306
  and credibility, 216–217, 218, 221
  cross-examination as a strategy of, 212–222
  and deception, 220
  of definition, 201–202
  and the evaluation of an argument, 130
  and expectations, 10
  and focus, 219
  forms of, 9, 10, 72
  functions of, 213–218, 221
  importance of, 213, 213–214
  issues as, 60–61
  and knowledge/experience, 219–220
  and occasions, 214–218
  and persuasion, 218
  and premises, 217–218, 218, 221, 304–305
  preparation for, 218–219, 220, 221–222
  and presentation of argument, 212–222
  and propositions, 56
  psychological factors of, 219–220, 222
  and refutation, 305
  and relevance, 201
  strategies of, 212–222
  and subject matter, 201, 214–218
  substantive factors of, 220–221, 222
  and supporting material, 72, 216, 218, 221
  of tradition, 202

Reasonability and norms for good argument, 87,
  128–143, 210, 284
Rebuttals
  and the affirmative case, 226–227, 230, 231–232,
    262–264, 267–269, 298–304
  burden of, 33–34, 43
  and challenge, 260–261, 262, 264
  and definitions, 259–260, 262, 264
  and duties of speakers, 230, 231–232
  and formats of debate, 226–227
  and interscholastic debate, 230, 231–232, 259–
    262, 262–264, 264–267, 267–269
  and the negative case, 226–227, 230, 231–233,
    259–262, 264–267, 295–298
  and public debate, 232–233, 295–304
  and reliable criteria, 260, 264–265, 269
Reciprocal signs, 99–100
Reference books, specialized, 77–78
Refutation
  advocates as loci of, 202–206, 210
  and the affirmative case, 284
  approaches to, 195–209
  audiences as loci of, 196–199, 210
  and character, 203
  and competence, 203

and consistency, 204–205, 210
and credentials, 205–206, 210
and credibility, 202–203, 210
and definition, 201–202
definition of, 193–194
direct, 186, 187, 190
and field, 195, 209–210, 210
and interscholastic debates, 194
and judgment, 206, 210
and jurisdiction, 199–202, 210
justifications, 210
and knowledge/experience, 206, 210
message as the locus of, 209–210
and motive, 203–204
and motives, 210
nature of, 192–195
and the negative case, 190, 296–297, 303
occasions as locus of, 207–209, 210
and premise, 198–199
and presentation of argument, 191–210
and propositions of policy, 186, 187, 190
purpose of, 210
and questioning, 305
and reasonableness, 210
strategies of, 191–210
topics as loci of, 199–202, 210
and tradition, 202
Relationships, 10–12, 18–19
Relativism, 16, 17, 25
Relevance, 38, 41, 110, 122–123, 201
Reliability, 118–120, 277–279, 297
Reliable criteria
and the affirmative case, 152–153, 158, 160–161,
235, 236, 249, 263–264, 269, 283, 284
and field-dependency, 152
and format of debate, 230, 232
and the negative case, 174, 175–178, 180–182,
190, 243, 260, 264–265, 277–279
and presentation strategies, 175–178
and propositions, 158, 160–161, 174, 180–181,
190
and rebuttals, 260, 264–265, 269
and speakers' duties, 230
Requirements of case. See Affirmative case; Negative case
Respect for other viewpoints, 133, 143
Responsibilities, 28, 29, 42
Responsible advocacy. See Ethics
Rhetorical discovery of issues. See also Stock issues; name of specific stock issue
approach to, 58–60
and audiences, 58–60, 69
definition/function of, 58–59, 60, 69
personal hobby perspective of, 59
and the self-proclaimed expert, 59
and stock issues, 61–69
Time magazine philosophy of, 59
Rhetorical effects, 58
Rhetorical event, 58
Rhetorical theory, 58

Selected audiences, 121–122
Self-proclaimed expert, 59
Setting, 18–19
Sign, argument from, 98–100, 104
Socrates, 130, 212–213
Speakers, duties of, 225, 229–233
Specialized references, 77–78
Specific tests of proof, 112–120, 123
Spheres of decision making, 140–143, 144
Standard of reasonableness. See Evaluation of ar-
gument
Standpoint, critical, 130–133
Statement of philosophy, 230, 284–286
Statistics, 73, 75, 84, 87, 112, 118–120, 122, 123
Stevenson, Charles, 35, 203–204
Stock issues. See also name of specific stock issue
and the affirmative case, 163–164, 165–167, 169,
175
and audiences, 65–66
as components of contention, 60
definition of, 60, 61–62, 69
and duties of speakers, 230, 232
and field, 62–63
and format of debate, 230, 232
functions of, 60
importance of, 155
and the negative case, 183, 187
and presentational strategies, 155
and propositions, 61, 62–69, 70, 155, 165–167,
168, 183, 187
Subject matter. See Topics
Subsidiary issues and propositions, 53–54, 56
Substantive factors of questioning, 220–221, 222
Summary
of the affirmative case, 228–229
of the negative case, 229
Supporting material. See Evidence/supporting
material
Surveys, 75, 81
Synthesis, data, 87
Systematic reasoning, 132, 143

Team format. See Format of debate; name of specific format
Technical decision making, 140–143, 144
Testimonies
and consistency, 280, 282
and evaluation of argument, 116
as evidence, 84
and experts, 116–117
and facts, 116
and interpretation, 116, 122
as a kind of data, 73, 74–75, 87
and the negative case, 280, 282, 303
and proof, 116–117, 122, 123
tests of, 116–117, 120
as a type of data, 112
Tests
of comparison, 114–116, 120
of examples, 113–114, 120
of experience, 93, 94–96

Tests (*cont.*)
  of statistics, 118–120, 120
  of testimonies, 116–117, 120
Tests of argument
  and evaluation of argument, 124–144
  and evaluation of supporting material, 107–123
Threats. *See* Coercion
Time limits
  and format of debate, 226–227
  and format of debates, 228–229
Time magazine philosophy of rhetorical discovery, 59
Tolerance, 133
Topics
  audience knowledge of, 84, 86
  and data/proof, 10, 71, 72, 87, 214–218
  and decision making, 140–141
  and definition, 201–202
  as elements of the argumentative situation, 8–10, 12–13
  and expectations, 10
  and field, 18–19
  and issues, 69

and library research, 75–81
as loci of refutation, 199–202, 210
and propositions, 47–48, 56, 63
and public debate, 232
and questioning, 201, 214–218
and standards of reasonableness, 124–125
and tradition, 202
Toulmin, Stephen, 19, 26n5, 28, 91, 92, 104
Tradition, 25–126, 127, 202, 299

Validity, 34–42, 43, 92, 118–120
Values, 8–10, 16, 84, 101–102, 137–138, 183. *See also* Beliefs; Ethics; Propositions of value

Warrant and backing, 91–93, 103, 104
Whately, Richard, 30
Willard, Charles, 31
Workability arguments, 231
Worthiness. *See also* Ethics; Justification; Propositions of value; Value

Zarefsky, David, 129, 143
Zenon of Elea, 212–213